Women and Minorities in Science, Technology, Engineering and Mathematics

Women and Minorities in Science, Technology, Engineering and Mathematics

Upping the Numbers

Edited by

Ronald J. Burke

Professor of Organizational Behavior, Schulich School of Business, York University, Canada

Mary C. Mattis

Program Officer, The Wallace Foundation, New York, USA

Edward Elgar

Cheltenham, UK • Northampton, MA, USA

Published by
Edward Elgar Publishing Limited
Glensanda House
Montpellier Parade
Cheltenham
Glos GL50 1UA
UK

Edward Elgar Publishing, Inc.
William Pratt House
9 Dewey Court
Northampton
Massachusetts 01060
USA

A catalogue record for this book
is available from the British Library

Library of Congress Cataloging in Publication Data
Women and minorities in science, technology, engineering and mathematics: upping the numbers / edited by: Ronald J. Burke, Mary C. Mattis.
    p. cm.
Includes bibliographical references and index.
1. Women in science. 2. Women in technology. 3. Minorities in science. 4. Minorities in technology. 5. Women in mathematics 6. Minorities in mathematics. 7. Women in engineering. 8. Minorities in engineering.
I. Burke, Ronald J. II. Mattis, Mary C.

Q130.W652 2007
305.43′5—dc22
                                                                    2007016049

ISBN 978 1 84542 888 4

Printed and bound in Great Britain by MPG Books Ltd, Bodmin, Cornwall

Contents

Contributors

Margaret-Ann Armour, Faculty of Science, University of Alberta, Edmonton, AB, Canada

Barbara Bagilhole, Department of Social Sciences, Loughborough University, UK

Diana Bilimoria, Department of Organizational Behavior, Weatherhead School of Management, Case Western Reserve University, Cleveland, OH, USA

Ronald J. Burke, Schulich School of Business, York University, Toronto, Canada

Ilene J. Busch-Vishniac, School of Engineering, Johns Hopkins University, Baltimore, MD, USA

Rachel G. Campbell, Department of Sociology, University of Alberta, Edmonton, AB, Canada

Tina T. Chen, Sempra Energy Utilities, San Diego, CA, USA

Daryl E. Chubin, Director, Center for Advancing Science and Engineering Capacity, American Association for the Advancement of Science, Washington, DC, USA

Anna-Lisa Ciccocioppo, Counselling Centre, University of Calgary, Calgary, AB, Canada

Wendy L. Coffin, Career and Placement Services, University of Alberta, Edmonton, AB, Canada

Dallas M. Cullen, Women's Studies Program, University of Alberta, Edmonton, AB, Canada

Andrew Dainty, Department of Civil and Building Engineering, Loughborough, University, UK

Donald D. Davis, Department of Psychology, Old Dominion University, Norforlk, VA, USA

Donna J. Dean, President, Association for Women in Science, and Senior Science Advisor, Lewis-Burke Associates, Washington, DC, USA

Heather J. Downey, Department of Psychology, Old Dominion University, Norfolk, VA, USA

Albert A. Einsiedel, Faculty of Extension, University Extension Centre, University of Alberta, Edmonton, AB, Canada

James L. Farr, Department of Psychology, The Pennsylvania State University, University Park, PA, USA

Anne Fleckenstein, Association for Women in Science Post Doctoral Fellow, Washington, DC, USA

Lisa M. Germano, Department of Psychology, Old Dominion University, Norfolk, VA, USA

Jeffrey P. Jarosz, School of Engineering, Johns Hopkins University, Baltimore MD, USA

Ronit Kark, Departments of Psychology and Sociology, Bar-Ilan University, Ramat Gan, Israel

Kerry Kawakami, Department of Psychology, York University, Toronto, Canada

Xiangfen Liang, Academic Careers in Engineering and Science Program, Case Western Reserve University, Cleveland, OH, USA

Helen M. Madill, Centre for Health Promotion Studies, School of Public Health, University of Alberta, Edmonton, AB, Canada

Debra A. Major, Department of Psychology, Old Dominion University, Norfolk, VA, USA

Mary C. Mattis, The Wallace Foundation, New York, USA

Susan Staffin Metz, School of Engineering, Stevens Institute of Technology, New York, USA

T. Craig Montgomerie, Department of Educational Psychology, University of Alberta, Edmonton, AB, Canada

Abigail Powell, Department of Civil and Building Engineering, Loughborough University, UK

Leah Reisz, Department of Psychology, York University, Toronto, Canada

Cynthia J. Rothwell, School of Resources and Environmental Management, Chemical Technology, Northern Alberta Institute of Technology, Edmonton, AB, Canada

Janis Sanchez-Hucles, Department of Psychology, Old Dominion University, Norfolk, VA, USA

Jody Sherman, Department of Educational Psychology, University of Alberta, Edmonton, AB, Canada

Jennifer R. Steele, Department of Psychology, York University, Toronto, Canada

Leonard L. Stewin, Department of Educational Psychology, University of Alberta, Edmonton, AB, Canada

Stanley Varnhagen, Department of Educational Psychology, University of Alberta, Edmonton, AB, Canada

Bevlee A. Watford, National Science Foundation, Washington, DC, USA

Amanda Williams, Department of Psychology, York University, Toronto, Canada

Preface

Ronald J. Burke and Mary C. Mattis

Advances in science, technology, engineering and mathematics (STEM) have been key factors in contributing to past and future economic performance and success of both developed and developing countries. This success has then been translated into higher living standards and improved quality of life for their citizens. Such advances were the products of educated and skilled STEM workforces.

However, these countries are facing a likely skill shortage of workers knowledgeable and skilled in STEM. The STEM workforce, comprised mainly of white males, is aging, with many on the verge of retirement. Immigrants from developing countries such as China, India, Russia and Singapore made up a significant percentage of the STEM workforce in North America and Europe in the past, but as their home countries become increasingly developed, fewer choose to leave. In addition, women, minorities and the disabled, though talented, have historically been underrepresented in STEM education and occupations. It has been shown that these groups face unique challenges at all stages of the STEM pipeline. They are less likely to choose careers in STEM, more likely to drop out of STEM educational programs and STEM occupations, and less likely to advance in STEM careers, in both academic and business settings. These outcomes reflect the failure to create the conditions in which talented women and minorities can fully and fairly participate in STEM should they choose to do so. This may have negative effects on the quality of STEM education and contribution in the short term, with potential adverse effects on economic performance and quality of life in the long term.

It is necessary to encourage more women and minorities to participate in STEM in order to meet the needs for skilled employees. Fortunately, research and writing over the past 20 years has provided considerable understanding of the issues women and minorities face in contemplating and preparing for STEM careers. In addition, some initiatives have proven to be successful in supporting women and minorities in the pursuit of these STEM options and reducing obstacles to success.

The reasons for the underrepresentation of women and minorities in STEM are complex and exist at several levels (individual, family, the educational system, the workplace, and in society at large); action strategies and solutions must also address each of these levels.

This collection provides an overview and integration of what is currently known about the status of women and minorities in STEM. It includes contributions from researchers with an ongoing interest in women and minorities in STEM, contributions from researchers interested in women and minorities in management and the professions more generally, and contributions from both academics and STEM program administrators. Our hope is that readers will be motivated to take individual action to address the challenges identified in the chapters that follow.

OVERVIEW OF THE CONTENTS

This volume is divided into five parts. Part I, Women and Minorities in STEM: The Big Picture, includes two chapters that provide an overview of the importance of including women and minorities in the STEM workforce, the challenges that lie ahead, and action strategies that have proven to be effective.

Ronald Burke sets the stage for the chapters that follow. His review considers the importance of STEM for continued economic success, why a skilled STEM workforce is critical, the looming shortage of STEM workers, the underrepresentation of women and minorities in STEM and why this represents a waste of educated and skilled talent, the benefits of including more women and minorities in STEM, barriers women and minorities face in the STEM journey, and action strategies that address these barriers. While these issues are not new, there is an urgent need to address them today.

Donna Dean and Anne Fleckenstein, following a review of statistical evidence indicating that women drop out of the STEM pipeline at higher rates and at earlier stages than men, and make slower career progress, examine barriers to women's full participation in science. These obstacles, while perhaps more subtle today, are not new. Young girls and women choose not to pursue careers in STEM, often the result of a lack of self-confidence. Girls and women receive less encouragement, lack female role models, face discrimination in the workplace, endure the male culture of science, and express concerns about successfully integrating work and family. Fortunately, some solutions have proven to be successful. The authors review initiatives, mostly in academic settings, targeting recruitment and hiring decisions, supporting the visibility of women scientists in the larger community, and system change permitting more workplace flexibility around maternity and the tenure clock. In addition, they summarize efforts at various levels of the educational system to recruit more girls and women to STEM careers. The important role of professional societies is also addressed. They end on a hopeful note, concluding that although girls and women face obstacles, they can still succeed in STEM if they have a love of science itself.

Part II, Experiences of Women and Minorities in STEM, includes five chapters that consider women in engineering programs in the UK, women's experiences in IT, the experiences of African Americans in PhD STEM programs, women's experiences in the Israeli high-tech sector and career experiences and progress of Asian-American scientists in the USA.

Abigail Powell and her colleagues explore how women experience engineering in higher education in the UK. While increases in the numbers of women in engineering education remain small, these increased numbers in education have not been translated into increases in female engineering professionals. The authors provide a deep analysis of the engineering culture in both employing organizations and higher education. Based on interviews and focus groups with women engineering students, they illustrate experiences ranging from 'good' to 'bad' to 'ugly'. Women engineering students were positive about their courses, lecturers and programs of study. They were critical of the teaching and learning methods, however. And they experienced negative attitudes from male peers and teachers that made commitment to engineering difficult. They conclude with suggestions for change that build on the 'good', and address the 'bad' and the 'ugly'.

Debra Major and her colleagues examine the extent to which common myths or beliefs about women and men in the IT workforce are true or not. Women are underrepresented at all stages of the IT pipeline. Gender myths can have powerful effects in organizations subordinating women and minorities in IT. Some myths include: women are too emotional and irrational to be good leaders; IT work is best done in isolation; and IT work is unsuitable for women because it is boring and solitary. They report findings from a longitudinal study of gender and workplace climate in 11 IT organizations in the USA. Some myths were supported (e.g. the IT work environment is fairer for men, women have a harder time developing work relationships) and some were not (e.g. women were effective leaders). If perception is reality, women in IT have made some progress, but there is still a long road ahead.

Daryl Chubin focuses specifically on the experiences of African Americans in STEM. He reports the results of focus group discussions with 40 black graduate students in STEM supported as Packard Scholars. The Packard Program supports a significant number of African-American students pursuing PhDs in STEM. What did these students voice? They felt pressure to reach out to other minority students. It was also difficult being a trailblazer. They faced difficulties associated with racial and gender bias. Chubin also distills strategies and practices that helped these students. New PhDs underestimated their skills. Successful students felt accountable to fulfill the 'performance contract' between themselves and their faculty supervisors. In addition, some university departments were outstanding at supporting minorities. The Packard Scholars Program emerged as an important and unique opportunity to diversify the STEM workforce, and warrants replicating.

Ronit Kark considers women in the high-technology sector in Israel, a country that has made dramatic strides in this sector (patents, start-ups) in the past 20 years. The findings of her study of women in STEM in Israel seem strikingly similar to those carried out in North America and Europe. Women are underrepresented in STEM here as well. She discusses four barriers to women in STEM in Israel: the educational system; mandatory military service; family and motherhood; and the use of the Hebrew language. The Israeli government, aware of the need more fully to utilize women in STEM, is undertaking projects targeting the educational system, military service and the family. It is too soon to assess whether these efforts will bear fruit.

Tina Chen and James Farr report the results of an empirical study of the glass ceiling for Asian Americans in STEM. Asian Americans are overrepresented in STEM fields and are often seen as a 'model minority'. Would a 'model minority' face a glass ceiling? They considered both gender and racial aspects by comparing men with women and Asian Americans with African Americans. They used four waves of data collected by the National Science Foundation on scientists and engineers. White males fared better than all other groups, with larger differences found in the managerial sample. There was evidence for a glass ceiling effect for Asian Americans over a seven-year period for respondents at all stages of their careers. So much for the benefits of being a 'model minority'!

Part III, Building Interest and Commitment to STEM, includes three chapters. These address the role of stereotype threat in reducing young women's interest in STEM, factors that influence young women's interest and commitment to STEM education, and ideas for increasing women's enrollment in university engineering programs.

Jennifer Steele and her colleagues focus specifically on the barriers that gender stereotypes can impose on women in STEM. Girls at an early age begin to differentially associate male and female with particular academic content. The research evidence suggests that having awareness of self-relevant stereotypes, termed stereotype threat, might reduce performance and lessen interest in stereotyped areas for some women. Stereotype threat occurs when members of a negatively stereotyped group (e.g. women in

STEM) face the prospect of confirming the stereotype of their group. Unfortunately several context factors appear to reduce women's performance in STEM. Steele and her colleagues review possible interventions to reduce the negative effects of stereotype threat, including changing educational environments so that girls and women feel less concern they will be viewed stereotypically, self-affirmation, and changing one's susceptibility and responses to stereotype threat.

Susan Metz, building on data showing that engineering-ready women choose engineering at lower rates than other professions, tackles the question of attracting more women to engineering. The good news is that women are prepared to study the subject. But how can we interest and engage women and minority students in engineering? She focuses on two aspects of engagement in her chapter – *emotional* – a positive reaction to the academic setting, and seeing engineering as both fun and intellectually rewarding, and *vocational* – seeing engineering as meeting their aspirations and leading to valued long-term rewards. This involves challenging common stereotypes of engineering, improving the portrayal of engineering in the media, and broadening the descriptions of engineering to open up more career possibilities. The reality is that engineers can be found in most professions.

Helen Madill and her colleagues review what is known about developing career commitment to STEM-related fields. Girls and women (and some men) have problems identifying a career focus prior to university, being a success in their first jobs following graduation, and advancing in their careers. They report findings from three studies to better understand women's career decision making in STEM. They found specific initiatives (science career workshops, paid research assistant jobs) increased STEM interest and commitment. In addition, other people (family/friends) influenced people's STEM choices, as did hands-on work experiences. The authors identify seven myths (e.g. recruitment is the real issue; once I get a degree everything will fall into line) and consider research evidence addressing each, debunking all as wrong or incomplete. They conclude with practical suggestions to develop career commitment to STEM – a process than can be unpredictable, with a wide variety of possible options. The pipeline in STEM is not a linear progression but instead has multiple entry points and options.

Part IV, Enriching the Educational Experience, in two chapters, suggests ways for making the university educational experience more relevant to women and minorities. These include efforts to make the pedagogy and content more meaningful, ways to make the transition from high school to university smoother, and how mentoring via the Internet can provide information, advice and support to women and minorities.

Ilene Busch-Vishniac and Jeffrey Jarosz focus on the STEM courses in the undergraduate experience of science and engineering students. They come at this from the perspective of how students are taught (pedagogy) and what is taught (curriculum). Progress is being made on both fronts. More attempts are being made to link learning and pedagogy, there is less of a 'boot camp' atmosphere intending to 'weed out' students, more use of writing and experience and less use of memorizing, more student feedback, greater efforts to generate more student involvement; and more use is being made of team projects and efforts to create a more supportive learning environment. There has been less effort to address course content, however. Interesting efforts here have involved creating links between various courses, more use of applications, more emphasis on social relevance, including diversity and multiculturalism in the curriculum, reducing prerequisites and streamlining the curriculum. The authors offer specific suggestions on how topics can be linked with applications. They believe strongly and argue convincingly that the educational experience would be significantly richer if contributions of women and minority STEM contributors were more widely represented in the engineering curriculum as well.

Bevlee Watford describes three different types of student programs within the College of Engineering at Virginia Tech. These initiatives aim to help women and underrepresented minority populations make the transition from high school to college so they can become successful students. These programs target three areas of student development: academic, professional and personal. She discusses these three programs in some detail: pre-college bridge or transition programs, mentoring programs and residential communities, providing enough detail (e.g. advertising, operations, forms, bibliographies) so that other institutions interested in one or more of them can undertake initial planning and implementation strategies.

In the last part, Part V, Improving the Professional Experience, efforts to support women and minorities in academia and the engineering profession are outlined.

Xiangfen Liang and Diana Bilimoria considered the respresentation and experiences of women faculty in STEM. There are relatively few of these, reflecting the small numbers of women STEM graduates. Women faculty are less likely to achieve career advancement; they feel isolated, lacking in role models and mentors; they have to work harder to earn reputation and credibility. In sum, women faculty face a 'chilly climate'. The authors present data from focus groups of women at their university supportive of the existence of a 'chilly climate', driven in part by the attitudes of male colleagues and administrators. The findings are remarkably consistent with the experiences of women faculty in STEM at other US universities. The authors conclude their chapter with a description of their university's efforts supported by an NSF Advance award, to transform the STEM cultures of various departments. Initiatives were undertaken at university, department/school and individual faculty member levels. As this effort is relatively young, it was too soon for the authors to determine its effects.

Finally, Mary Mattis, using the metaphor of a pipeline, explores conditions upstream and downstream that impact the attraction/recruitment, retention and advancement of women in the engineering workforce, drawing on findings from national datasets, surveys and focus groups with girls and young women, benchmark studies, and the efforts of engineering firms and corporations to increase the gender diversity of their technical workforce. The discrete environments upstream (factors impacting attraction and recruitment of girls and young women to academic engineering programs) and downstream (the culture and work environment of engineering companies/firms that impact recruitment, retention and advancement of women engineers) are discussed, along with possible feedback loops from each end of the pipeline to the other that impact women's representation in the engineering workforce. Best practices that address negative conditions upstream and downstream are explored, along with recommendations to influencers of young women's career aspirations and to corporate decision makers.

Acknowledgements

I have been interested in understanding factors that support women's career advancement for several years and for a variety of reasons. My mother had a series of jobs – but not a career – for almost all of her life. When I started teaching at the Schulich School of Business in 1968, there were no women in my MBA classes. A few years later there was one, but she quit. Next year there was also one, and she stayed. Now women represent about one-third of our MBA students. In 1968, there were no women faculty teaching Organizational Behavior at Schulich; today more than half my OB colleagues are women.

I have previously collaborated in editing projects in the general area of women in management with Marilyn Davidson, Mary Mattis and Debra Nelson. Mary's move to the National Engineering Association for a period of time shifted our focus to the experiences of women in science, technology, engineering and mathematics. Working with her has always been a joy.

This initiative was supported in part by the Schulich School of Business. Louise Coutu managed the flow of correspondence and manuscripts at my end. I also thank our international contributors for their fine work.

Finally, for Sharon, Rachel and Liane – the future is yours.

Ronald J. Burke

I would like to acknowledge my co-editor, Ronald J. Burke. Our felicitous collaboration writing and speaking about gender diversity, which dates back to the late 1980s, has provided continuity and reassurance to me through periods of occupational and geographic dislocation. Thanks Ron. This volume also brings together the voices of many colleagues with whom I worked at the National Academy of Engineering. I would like to acknowledge their commitment and contributions to increasing opportunities for underrepresented groups in science, engineering and technology.

Mary C. Mattis

PART I

Women and minorities in STEM: the big picture

1. Women and minorities in STEM: a primer

Ronald J. Burke

If the cure for cancer is in the mind of a girl, we might never find it.

Myra Sadker

INTRODUCTION

This chapter provides a partial review of literature highlighting the situation of women and minorities in science, technology, engineering and mathematics (STEM), the challenges they face at various stages in the STEM journey, and action strategies that address these challenges. It lays the foundation for chapters that follow which address these issues and solutions in greater depth. It includes the following content:

- The contribution of STEM to economic success and performance
- The key role of the STEM workforce
- The looming shortage of STEM workers
- The underrepresentation of women and minorities in STEM
- Benefits of including more women and minorities in STEM
- Barriers faced by women and minorities in STEM at all stages of the pipeline
- Action strategies for increasing the number of women and minorities in STEM.

ECONOMIC EFFECTS OF STEM

There is convincing evidence that scientific excellence and technological innovation were (are) important both for past and future economic performance. STEM is critical for national security, economic success and scientific leadership. STEM contributes directly to the standard of living

3

and quality of life of a country's citizens. Thus a country's prosperity, security and health depend on the contributions of STEM.

There are several challenges now present for STEM occupations in all countries (Bybee and Fuchs, 2006). There are a greater number of economic competitors both in the developed world (USA, Canada, France, Germany, Japan) and the developing world (China, Hong Kong, India, Israel, Singapore). The development of a skilled workforce in STEM is both complex and ambiguous in a global environment characterized by uncertainty, change and heightened competition. Such development is obviously a long-term project taking anywhere from ten to 50 years. But it is a potential win–win for various countries since STEM knowledge and innovations can spread worldwide. Therefore there is a need for a workforce with heightened scientific and technological skill and interest in STEM careers (Morella, 2002). Failure to invest in STEM, and to reform STEM education, becomes a threat to a country's economic health and future security (Clewell et al., 1992).

A SKILLED STEM WORKFORCE IS KEY

Breakthroughs and innovation in STEM are the product of a skilled and motivated STEM workforce. STEM human resources are central. Society needs people to innovate and develop new products, and improve current products and services. As a consequence, countries need to use all their human resources (Catalyst, 1999).

Education is the most important investment a country makes in generating future prospects. As countries continue to move to knowledge-based economies, education becomes more important. This is reflected in the fact that an increasing number of jobs now require STEM knowledge. In addition, STEM workers are well paid, allowing them to contribute to the economic well-being of their country. A country needs a strong STEM workforce to prosper.

THE LOOMING SHORTAGE OF SKILLED STEM WORKERS

Scientists are made, not born.

Many developed countries are facing a potential shortage of skilled STEM workers (Atkinson, 1990; Pearson and Fechter, 1992, 1994; Georgi, 2000). There are several reasons for this. First, the STEM workforce is aging; with advancing age, more STEM workers are nearing retirement. Second, a decreasing number of students are acquiring STEM skills, and there is a suggestion that students in some developed countries are not performing as well as students in developing countries. Third, there is a corresponding shortage of qualified STEM teachers. Fourth, some developed countries relied on immigrants with STEM skills to meet their needs (Bouvier and Martin, 1995; North, 1995). The immigration of STEM workers has slowed as their home countries become more advanced (no need to go elsewhere to use their skills) and the events of 9/11 make it more difficult to move to particular countries.

Finally, women and minorities are underrepresented in STEM educational programs and in the STEM workforce (Margolis and Fisher, 2002; Preston, 1994). Although women have steadily increased their participation in the workforce, their participation in STEM occupations has changed little, even dropping in some (e.g. IT).

THE UNDERREPRESENTATION OF WOMEN AND MINORITIES IN STEM

> Who can look at these numbers and not say that we as a faculty have failed – failed our students, our institution, and most of all, failed our nation?
>
> Professor Nancy Hopkins, MIT

Most of the remaining chapters in this volume will present facts documenting the underrepresentation of women and minorities in various STEM disciplines (e.g. engineering, IT). Thus only an overview will be provided here.

- Many girls opt out of math and science courses in grades 6–8.
- While girls are equally capable as boys to develop STEM skills (math, science), they are generally not encouraged to do so.
- More men than women in their last year of high school expect to be a STEM major in university.
- Men, more than women, persist on the STEM path from high school to bachelor's degree.
- More women than men switch out of STEM programs in university (Seymour and Aikenhead, 1995; Seymour and Hewitt, 1997).
- Following a STEM bachelor's degree, more women move into biological sciences than STEM fields such as engineering and the physical sciences.
- Women in computer science declined from 30 percent of undergraduate degrees in 1984 to 20 percent in 1999.

- Women earned 53 percent of master's degrees in biological science, and 12 percent in engineering in 1996.
- Women are less likely to work in STEM occupations.
- Women are more than twice as likely as men to leave computer science careers (Margolis and Fisher, 2002; Wright, 1997; Robinson and McIlwee, 1991).
- Only 9 percent of American engineers are women, and only 20 percent of engineering degrees are earned by women.
- Women are less than 10 percent of engineering faculty.
- Considering university first-year-student preferences, there was declining interest in STEM, particularly engineering and computer sciences over the past decade (Astin et al., 1997).
- In 2005, women's participation among full-time first-year engineering students was 16.4 percent, down from 19.6 percent in 1998.
- Women's representation among practicing engineers increased by only 1 percent between 1994 and 2005, from 10 percent to 11 percent.
- Married women, particularly those with children, are more likely to leave school and work than are men and women in other status (Xie and Shauman, 2003).
- Married women with STEM bachelor's degrees, particularly those with children, are less likely than men to continue in STEM careers (Xie and Shauman, 2003).
- Among masters STEM graduates, married women are more likely to withdraw from further education and the labor force than male peers, particularly if they have children.
- Female STEM workers are more likely to be single or divorced.
- Married female STEM workers are less likely to have children than married male STEM workers.
- Male STEM workers are likely to be employed full time; female STEM workers to be unemployed, employed part time or working in fields outside their degrees (National Science Foundation, 2002).
- Women engineers earn less money than do male engineers.
- China and India show an increase in the production of engineers while engineering programs in North America struggle for students. China produces three times as many engineers as the USA.
- By 2000, more than 90 percent of all scientists and engineers will live in Asia.
- South Korea, with one-sixth the US population, graduates as many engineers as the USA.

BENEFITS OF HAVING MORE WOMEN AND MINORITIES IN STEM

The more women and minorities who enter STEM, the latter being significant contributors to national productivity, the larger will be the pool of scientists and engineers, the greater the quality of this pool and the greater the productivity of a country's labor force (Davis et al., 1996). In addition, this diversity is likely to improve the level of creativity, innovation and quality of STEM products and services. Diversity also makes the university educational and learning experience richer and more valuable for all students.

Excluding women and minorities from STEM education and the STEM workforce wastes a lot of talent and does not fill the needs of organizations for skilled STEM employees (Etzkowitz et al., 2000). Women and minorities in STEM are able to successfully use their skills, earn income and contribute to society as a whole (Spelke, 2005).

In order to remain competitive, women and minorities represent an untapped resource. Although efforts have been made to attract and retain these groups in STEM over the past 25 years, little progress has been made to date.

WHY ARE THERE SO FEW WOMEN IN STEM?

A gender-biased society teaches girls to have gender stereotyped interests.

Makrakis (1992, p. 285)

The Experiences of Young Girls

Young girls and young women face a number of obstacles in their pursuit of education and careers in STEM at all stages of their STEM journey (Sadker and Sadker, 1994). By the age of 12, children have already formed firm beliefs about the subjects at which they excel and those at which they fail. Twice as many boys as girls took advanced placement tests in physics in 2004, for example (Weinburgh, 1995).

School curricula, teachers' expectations and the computer culture fit male notions about competing and assume male competence and female disinterest (Bodzin and Gehringer, 2001). The computing culture, inhabited by boys and men with a passion for computing, places a premium on technical skills and supports male competence (Margolis et al., 2000). The link of male traits with competence in computing leads to male-biased beliefs about who fits the more technical STEM roles. The resulting low expectations of female interest and competence likely create a barrier to women's opportunities in STEM. Seymour and Hewitt (1997) found that math anxiety and instructors' lowered expectations have reduced women's participation in STEM.

Science textbooks and curricula rarely represent females equally in photos, illustrations and text content (Ford and Varney, 1989). Science content in schools, particularly in the physical sciences, does not seem as relevant to the real-life experiences of girls as it does to boys (cars, sports, guns), and in the classroom, girls have fewer opportunities to use tools and equipment (Jones et al., 2000). Farrell (2002) believes that STEM education has not made its content relevant or of social value. There is a large gap between the subject matter and applications to students' life and life experiences. This has been found to be particularly true for the attraction of women to STEM (Kahle, 2004; Lederman, 2003). Outside of school, girls engage in fewer science and technology-related activities than boys (Catsambis, 1995; Lottero-Perdue and Brickhouse, 2002).

Some minority groups have values at odds with the individualism and competition associated with science. Women may have difficulty with competition, and problems with majoring in STEM coupled with low self-ratings of their STEM abilities.

The Experiences of Women in University and College

Powell et al. (2000) examined whether the masculine culture of the engineering profession permeated the culture and curriculum in engineering education and, if it did, what impact it had on women engineering students. They conducted semi-structured interviews with 46 second-year female students from a range of engineering disciplines and courses. Though these women had chosen engineering as a career, the authors conclude that the structure and culture of the engineering education system, being designed for males, benefits male students more than female students. They argue that university engineering education must examine its structure, culture, practices and curriculum if it is to retain future graduates in the profession and attract more women students.

Engineering is seen as a male-oriented and male-dominated profession (Dryburgh, 1999). Given the shortage of technical and engineering skills, efforts have been made to encourage women to pursue engineering education. Though these efforts have had some success, there has not been a similar increase in the numbers of women in the profession, suggesting that engineering education may discourage women from pursuing these careers.

Engineering is seen as dull, uncreative, tough, heavy, dirty, and using machinery. It is a masculine profession; most of the workforce and the culture of engineering is male. Engineering is therefore unsuitable for women, creating a self-fulfilling cycle (Wyer, 2003).

When young women enter university, they often do not have enough mathematics and science background to major in STEM. This results from insufficient educational resources in high schools to foster girls' interest and skill in math and science, social pressure from negative image of scientists and engineers (Parsons, 1997), a lack of encouragement plus active discouragement from peers and teachers, limited out-of-school STEM experiences for girls, and the lack of female role models in the STEM professions (McCormick and McCormick, 1991).

What makes the university environment chilly for women? This results from the lack of women faculty and assistants to serve as role models, projects designed for male interests, diminishing women's contributions to STEM sometimes attributing them to men, hostility from a few male students, instructors' expectations of poor performance from women, and the use of male language (Curtan et al., 1997). Women students can cope with the engineering work, but not with the engineering culture.

The Experiences of Women Faculty in STEM

Etzkowitz et al. (1994) examined the experiences of women PhD students and faculty members in four science and engineering departments. Data were collected from departmental records on advisors and advisees, and interviews with male and female faculty, female graduate students and administrators. In addition they had data on students that had dropped out of these programs.

They found that females encountered barriers to entry and advancement at all stages of the academic career. These included differential socialization of men and women, and marriage and family, the routine practice of academic science such as advising patterns, and the male model of doing science.

The first differential socialization stems from the different gender experiences of boys and girls. Girls are socialized to be help seekers and help givers rather than being self-reliant. Women often enter graduate programs in science with low self-confidence, which drops during graduate school. This results in reduced aspirations. Women graduate students also expect to be penalized when they have children. Women are frequently less mobile in the pursuit of their careers. Female students also tended to have greater difficulties in their relationships with male supervisors. Finally, there was the male model of academic success – a total time commitment to scientific work, and aggressive, competitive relations with peers (Loder, 2000; Schneider, 2000).

Women and minority faculty in STEM have fewer interactions with faculty peers; some believe they were hired because of equity concerns, not STEM capability (Kemelgor and Etzkowitz, 2001). They report the lack of an influential mentor or sponsor, and difficulty getting research grants even with a record of high-quality research (Etzkowitz et al., 2000).

Due to unconscious assumptions we all have, women and the work performed by women receive lower evaluations than men and the work performed by men (Valian, 1999), even when the evaluators are women. Women STEM faculty need more output to be rated as competent as men; women get shorter and gendered letters of reference, and more 'doubt raisers'.

Occupational Experiences of Women in STEM

McIlwee and Robinson (1992) found that the transition from engineering schools, where academic work is valued (and women do well), to the workplace, which emphasizes masculine strengths such as interest in technology and an aggressive style (where women fare poorer) is a difficult one for women. To succeed in the workplace, women have to be competent in their knowledge and skills, but also behave consistent with masculine norms.

The experiences of women in engineering has received the most research attention of any of the STEM occupations. The culture of engineering is a culture of industry, not universities. The workplace experiences of women in engineering influence decisions young women make to enter and continue in engineering programs.

Downstream experiences of women engineers include:

- isolation and exclusion from informal communication and networks critical for advancement;
- technical credibility issues;
- stereotyping and downplaying of women's abilities and suitability for engineering;
- lack of role models and mentors;
- fieldwork environment and culture;
- work–family balance issues;
- sexual and other forms of harassment;
- relocation difficulties;
- lack of development plans for their growth and advancement;
- companies more focused on recruiting women than on developing and retaining them.

Why Such Slow Progress?

Valian (1999) builds on social psychological research findings in under-standing the slow advancement of women. Why are women evaluated less favorably than men in achievement-related contexts? Why is an argument made by a man received differently than the same argument made by a woman? Why is a resumé with a male name at the top evaluated more favor-ably than the same resumé with a female name at the top? More generally, why are women evaluated negatively relative to men in the work context?

The term glass ceiling implies that invisible (subtle) barriers exist, that these barriers will not disappear on their own, and objective performance differences do not explain sex difference in salary, rank, and rates of pro-motion (Sonnert and Holton, 1995a, 1995b, 1999).

Valian uses the term 'gender schemas' to refer to 'a set of implicit or unconscious hypotheses about sex differences' that affect our expectations of men and women, our evaluations of their work, and their performance as professionals' (Valian, 1999, p. 2).

Both women and men hold the same gender schemas and develop them in early childhood. Men are overvalued, women underrated; men are advantaged, women are disadvantaged. Gender schemas are hypotheses about women and men. Though typically unstated, they affect our reaction to women and men. Unfortunately – for women – schemas contain errors.

Accumulation of Advantage

The accumulation of social differences in the evaluation and treatment of women and men results in the glass ceiling. Very small differences in treat-ment can lead to large disparities over time. For example, Martell et al. (1996) developed a computer simulation model of promotion in a hypo-thetical corporation having eight levels of hierarchy staffed by equal numbers of women and men at the lowest level. The model assumed a certain percentage of promotion over time and a small bias in favor of pro-moting men. After many series of promotions, the highest level was 65 percent male. Their findings likely underestimate the problem women face since they only addressed promotion; there are countless other opportuni-ties for advantages and disadvantages to occur.

When women first join an organization they are at a small disadvantage. They have lower status, are less likely to be taken seriously, they talk less than men do, and have to meet higher standards than men do.

Individuals attribute different traits and behaviors to women and then respond to women and men consistent with their expectations, creating a self-fulfilling prophecy. Men and women become what we expect, supporting our hypotheses about the differences between women and men. Women and men develop expectations of their own behavior based on characteristics we think we have. Men are assertive, independent, agentic; women are nurturers, emotional and communal. But nearly everyone has both sides of characteristics to some degree; the sexes are more alike than different.

ACTION STRATEGIES

No person in the United States shall, on the basis of sex, be excluded from participation in, be denied the benefits of, or be subjected to discrimination under any educational program or activity receiving Federal financial assistance.
                                                    Title IX of the Education Act

This section highlights a number of initiatives that have been proposed, and in some cases have been shown to have positive effects on the experiences of women and minorities in STEM. These efforts focus on educational programs in the early years, educational programs in high school and university, the climate of women faculty in STEM and women working in STEM occupations.

Early and High School Education Programs

Q: What do you call a 'Nerd' ten years after high school graduation?
A: Boss.

Eccles (1994) developed a theory proposing that advancement-related choices are 'made within a context linking educational, vocational, and other advancement-related choices most directly to two sets of beliefs: the individual's expectations for success and the importance or value the individual attaches to the various options perceived by the individual as available' (p. 587). This leads to two potential emphases for STEM education. First, make STEM courses and careers more attractive to girls, and second, increase girls' perceptions that they can be/are now successful in STEM activities. This involves increasing their knowledge of the available STEM options, presenting accurate information about these options, reducing negative stereotypes of STEM, and enhancing girls' self-concepts and abilities in math and science (Storobin and Laanan, 2005).

Girls have little knowledge of what scientists and engineers do in their jobs on a day-to-day basis, and the ways in which they integrate their work and personal lives. Most girls do not know a male or female scientist. Most girls have few female role models available to them. Most girls had little work experience in fields related to STEM.

Efforts have been made both in the traditional educational setting as well as outside of the educational system to interest more girls and young women in pursuing STEM education and STEM careers (Wood, 2002; Mason and Kahle, 1988). These include:

- more information about STEM-related career opportunities and their prerequisites;
- the need for high school career counselors to encourage math and science courses for girls;
- fewer sex-stereotyped views of science and scientists in textbooks;
- more hands-on courses such as science activities and equipment, shop and mechanical drawing classes;
- the need to have well-equipped, organized and perceptually stimulating classrooms;
- use of non-sexist languages and examples;
- information on women scientists;
- provision of career information;
- stress creativity and basic STEM skills;
- use of field trips and guest speakers;
- encouragement of parental involvement;
- asking girls to assist with classroom demonstrations;
- use of laboratories, discussions and weekly quizzes;
- concentration on applications and usefulness in the greater society rather than 'new gadgets';
- highlighting the need for more women in STEM;
- A website, e.g. 'Girls go tech'.

Innovative programs have been developed to teach math to children in grades 3 to 6 in new exciting ways. JUMP (Junior Undiscovered Math Prodigies), developed in Toronto in 1998, has volunteer math tutors work with young boys and girls.

Informal science education often carried out by museums and science centers can provide opportunities for mentoring, improving science and job skills, countering negative stereotypes of science, increasing understanding and value of science, developing new skills, providing a chance to use tools and science equipment, and resultant increased feelings of success and achievement (Eccleston, 1999; Storobin and Laanan, 2005). The goal of these efforts was to provide the information, encouragement and confidence that girls need to consider careers in STEM areas. Important elements of successful programs included:

- summer and academic year classes;
- STEM information learned;

- field trips;
- chance to travel and attend other programs;
- careers and scientists;
- friends made in the program;
- college information acquired;
- job skills and paid positions;
- volunteering;
- the museum as a fun and safe place;
- having staff to talk with.

What makes a good out-of-school program for girls?

- It is not like school.
- It is fun.
- It includes a lot of hands-on activities, projects and opportunities (Strand and Mayfield, 2002).
- It places less emphasis on knowledge than on doing new things.
- The environment is not competitive.
- It offers an opportunity to women (and men) to learn about math and science careers.
- It offers a chance to ask questions of people who want to answer them fully.

How can we get more girls to take math and science?

- Intervene in seventh or ninth grade when students decide whether to take STEM courses (algebra) in the ninth grade.
- Intervene in tenth grade when students decide whether to take more math (or STEM courses).
- Have the courses offer more fun, a more relaxed atmosphere, more small-group work and more hands-on projects (Springer et al., 1999).

How can we open up more math and science career options?

- Get beyond the 'nerd' stereotype of people good in math and science.
- Expose girls to various careers in math and science. Have scientists talk about their work, and how they integrate their work with their life in general.
- Encourage girls in hands-on science and engineering activities.
- Provide opportunities to girls to just talk with each other.

How can we get girls to come to summer science programs?

- Combine these programs with other activities such as sports.
- Link these programs with other organizations that provide activities for girls.
- Organize a one-day launch on Saturday for parents and girls.

How can we get more high school girls to come to science programs?

- Organize intensive summer residential programs; these seem to work well.
- Give girls extra credit for participating in programs conducted during the school year.
- Ask high school maths and science teachers to nominate/recruit girls.

In the classroom:

- Pay equal attention to girls and boys.
- Have equal numbers of girls lead study groups.
- Have all students do hands-on activities.
- Make sure girls and boys are made aware of the importance of math and science for future careers.
- Make sure girls are comfortable asking questions and that they receive supportive answers.
- Make sure girls don't defer to boys and boys don't expect them to.

Girls see mathematicians and scientists as 'nerds', loners, and social misfits. Math and science are seen as male dominated, as a man's job. Girls need to get to know women working in science and engineering, and see that they are not 'nerds', to spend time with other girls who are good at math and science and are facing the same challenges as they are, and to see that science and a social life are both achievable.

What can parents do? Parents need to know that math and science are important. Both are critical factors in jobs, getting into colleges, and building successful careers in the future. Parents can provide encouragement, do STEM things with their children such as going to science museums, doing puzzles together, and taking things apart. Parents can also challenge a teacher's decision to suggest 'average level math' for a daughter instead of 'advanced math' if she likes math and is good at it.

Gilbride et al. (1999) describe an effort to attract more women into engineering. This program, the Discover Engineering Summer Camp, initiated in 1991, was developed to educate young women about the challenges and rewards of engineering, to show that engineering was a viable profession for women to enter and to motivate women to choose engineering. They report that 83 percent of the 1996 camp participants said they found the camp experience to be beneficial, and 76 percent indicated that it had made a large difference in their awareness of what engineering was all about. Follow-up surveys of earlier camp sessions showed that about 60 percent of young women who attended the Discover Engineering Camp went on to pursue engineering, citing camp attendance as a key factor.

Targeting the Leaning Ivory Tower – Universities

How can we reduce the 'chilly climate' young women report in their university STEM programs? Considerable progress has been made in identifying a classroom environment more supportive of women and minorities. In addition, there are specific suggestions available to university teachers on how to achieve this (Blum, 2001).

Throughout the curriculum:

- Create a classroom environment that makes it easy to ask questions.
- Use group projects that foster cooperative learning.
- Show how STEM knowledge is used in industry.
- Communicate the use of STEM to broader life and social issues.
- Choose projects that make applications clear and that build on the student's previous experiences.
- Offer women and minorities remedial classes.
- Offer women and minorities extra help.
- Use inclusive language and examples.
- Address teachers' sexist beliefs and stereotypes.
- Grade assignments blind to the identity of the students.
- Use information such as web documents to encourage students to take STEM courses (Single et al., 2005).
- Use various teaching methods to appeal to different learning styles.
- Offer summer school courses to help talented pre-college students overcome deficiencies in their backgrounds and build confidence in their skills in STEM.

For graduate education:

- Use contacts at other universities to identify and recruit qualified female and minority undergraduates.
- Write supporting letters for female and minority students listing their qualifications and accomplishments similar to those written for male students.

- Build your department's reputation for attracting students with respect, fairness and support, and talented women and minorities will apply.

Clewell et al. (2006) conducted an evaluation of the Louis Stokes Alliances of Minority Participation (LSAMP) designed to increase the quality and quantity of minority students who successfully complete undergraduate education in STEM and go on to graduate education in their fields. This program was established in 1991 by the National Science Foundation to increase minority participation in STEM. LSAMP relies on alliances among colleges, universities, national research laboratories, business, industry and various government departments to reach its goals. In addition, hands-on research experiences and mentoring to build student interest in STEM are the central building blocks of their efforts. The following factors were found to have made a difference.

- A supportive institutional environment that provided adequate resources and support from faculty and administrators.
- Collaborative activities among partner institutions.

Successful institutions followed a two-pronged approach: (1) student retention by integrating students into their universities, and (2) a disciplinary socialization by immersing students into science as a profession. Key elements cited for success by the students themselves were: student research projects (82 percent); 'summer bridge' opportunities (67 percent); mentoring (60 percent); financial stipends (48 percent); and tutoring (32 percent).

Professional Associations

The National Association of Engineers has created a workforce diversity talent task force with the express purpose of developing a strong domestic talent pool. The Association convened a summit on Women in Engineering in May 1999, developed the Celebration of Women in Engineering website and the Engineering Girl website, and held a workshop to develop the business case for diversity. There are also dozens of professional societies in North America and in other countries working to increase numbers of women and minorities in STEM.

The IEEE (Institute of Electrical and Electronics Engineers) Women in Engineering Association recognizes women's outstanding achievements in electrical and electronics engineering through IEEE Announcements, organizes receptions at major technical conferences to enhance networking, advocates women in leadership roles for women in the profession, and facilitates the development of programs and activities that promote women's entry into and retention in engineering programs. They have also developed a number of programs and website-based initiatives targeted specifically for girls. These include:

- IEEE for girls
- Discover engineering
- Engineer Girl
- Future Scientists and Engineers of America
- MentorNet
- Women of NASA Projects
- Nerd Girl

Advancing Women Faculty in STEM

Since the education of young women and men at the university and college level is critical to their developing skills required for successful careers in STEM, considerable effort has been made to support the advancing of women and minority faculty in STEM disciplines. The ADVANCE programs initially funded by the National Science Foundation were the earliest of these efforts.

LaVaque-Manty and Stewart (2007) examined the University of Michigan's ADVANCE program and highlighted the critical roles played by *collective* organizational catalysts (a faculty committee) as well as *individual* organizational catalysts.

In 2001, the National Science Foundation (NSF) began a program called ADVANCE to support an intervention in education settings to encourage the success of women faculty in science and engineering. These interventions were designed to improve their institutional climates and their recruitment and retention.

The University of Michigan undertook the following initiatives, among others:

- grants to departments interested in improving their climate, recruitment or retention;
- grants to individual women scientists and engineers to support their projects and career;
- a university-wide network that offered women in faculty in science and engineering opportunities to meet and socialize, attend potentially helpful workshops (e.g. on leadership, negotiation) and mentor one another;

- a theater troupe that supported and cultivated discussion of difficult, often contentious, climate issues.

The leadership committee has been a key factor in increasing hiring of women faculty in science and engineering at Michigan, fostering greater understanding of gender among community members, and adding depth to the discussion of gender across university faculty.

The Michigan experiment proved so successful that senior university administrators decided to both continue the program for several more years and extend it to other faculties (besides science and engineering).

The steering committee comprised eight distinguished full professors in science and engineering nominated by the deans of their colleges who believed they had credibility with their colleagues and cared about diversity issues in science. It was also important to have sufficient staff support for committee activities, to have regular communication with deans, to have several committee members meet with search committees, including both men and women in every meeting, if possible, and to have data available to discuss demographics in each field. They also reported findings from a survey of all female tenure-track science and engineering faculty at or above the rank of assistant professor ($n = 259$), male tenure-track faculty in engineering and science ($n = 339$), and female tenure-track social science faculty at or above the rank of assistant professor ($n = 156$). Scientists and engineers appreciate data!

The committee used social science research findings to appeal to the research orientation of faculty. Two areas were central to their work:

- *Gender schemas* – hypotheses about what men and women are like.
- *Evaluation bias* – tendency of both men and women to overvalue men and undervalue women.

They also organized presentations to search committees, created a recruitment handbook, and advocated that staff be hired for science (merit), not gender.

After two years, the committee added more colleagues who might later join the steering committee. They developed a chair program – two half-days to share past efforts and learnings to work on wider culture change. They also offered sessions to non-science and non-engineering units. Six topics were addressed:

1. What is the problem?
2. Why diversity matters
3. Unconscious bias in evaluation

4.   Recruitment strategies
5.   Dual career and family policies
6.   How family matters for evaluation bias.

There has been a strong increase in the hiring of women in science and engineering since this program began. Ten women were hired in the two years before the committee was launched (14 percent) and 46 in the next three years (34 percent) in the science and engineering schools.

Georgia Tech's ADVANCE program focused on family-friendly policies such as stopping the tenure clock during maternity leave, developing a formal tenure and promotion process to remove potential barriers, a mentoring network established by senior women faculty, and two retreats that give tenure-track women access to senior administrators.

Rosser (2004) provides some suggestions on how STEM departments can get more women on faculty. These include: on-site daycare, mentorships, reducing the demands on both women and men, and providing large rewards to faculty that do an outstanding job in the classroom and in their research laboratories. In addition, universities should be held accountable for the career development and advancement of women and minorities.

Bailyn (2003) distills some lessons learned from MIT's efforts to address gender issues in their science faculty. Gender issues have been seen as problematic at universities for over 20 years, with little real progress taking place. Gender equity was based on equality, fairness and integration, with MIT making progress on the first two but not the third. In Bailyn's view, faculties of science need to have the numbers of women in their faculties equal the number of female students, and to stop the leaky pipeline, insure that women faculty have an equally positive experience as men, and to have no faculty member – male or female – disadvantaged by family responsibilities.

Valian (1999) offers several suggestions for countering the negative consequences of gender schemas and equalizing women's and men's ability to obtain and accumulate advantage. These include:

● More accurate evaluations of women's performance
● Learning about gender schemas
● Become aware of our own biases
● Switch the sexes in considering particular behaviors
● Educating children about gender schemas
● Make less use of gender schemas through devoting more time to the task at hand
● Making people accountable for their evaluations and judgements
● Increasing the number of women in the candidate pool (or work group)
● Improving reasoning

- Awareness training about gender schemas for managers and executives
- Organizational policies that support women's and minority advancement
- Leaders committed to fairness
- Making greater use of objective criteria.

Equalizing the accumulation of advantage

- Women can learn about the ways they are disadvantaged by gender schemas.
- Actually be competent
- Be seen as competent
- Work in fields and organizations where women are well represented
- Be impersonal, friendly and respectful
- Build power
- Seek information
- Become an expert
- Get endorsed by legitimate authority in the system
- Negotiate, bargain and seek advancement
- Overcome one's internal barriers to effectiveness (attributions for success) and not seeing very small advantages as useful
- Men need to undertake more of the home and family responsibilities
- Develop an egalitarian relationship.

There were two learnings that emerged form the early efforts of the Michigan ADVANCE initiatives (Stewart et al., 2006). The first was that the problem of women's underrepresentation in STEM faculty was complex and the action strategies similarly complex. The second was that it was important to set realistic and achievable targets.

Interventions that seemed to make sense to support the goals of the program included:

- Mentoring for women and minority faculty
- Family-friendly policies
- Enlightening the chairperson on their critical role in hiring and development
- Help place male partners
- Encourage women faculty to come and stay
- Offering grants for women faculty
- Offering grants to departments to develop their own approach to recruiting, retaining and promoting women faculty

- Implementing university-wide policy changes addressing family-friendly policies, recruitment and the tenure clock
- Encouraging the use of data – this appeals to scientists – for example: gender schemas, evaluation bias, accumulation of disadvantage.

Government Initiatives

In the UK, the government has begun a program to encourage female engineers to return to work after taking time off to have children. Their research indicated that about 50 000 women engineers, scientists and technology graduates were not currently working. They developed a range of possible initiatives. These included: allocating funds to the Women in Science and Engineering (WISE) campaign, funding a similar program for women engineers returning to work after a career break, launching the Franklin medal to boost women's profile in science by awarding it annually to a female researcher for scientific innovation, and creating a strategy group, with a female research scientist (Baroness Greenfield) advising it on how to get more women into the sciences.

The these initiatives have two objectives: to encourage female scientists to return to science and to have more women pursue successful scientific careers. Women in the UK are underrepresented in science, engineering and technology (SET). Only one-sixth of SET graduates are women, 50 000 female SET graduates are not working at any one time, only about 8000 of these return to a job that uses their qualifications and training, and only about 1 in 20 SET and math professors in higher education are women. The aim is to get more women and minorities starting, staying and succeeding in sciences.

The UK government will develop a science resource center that will: recognize and reward good employers; raise the profiles of women in science; make a database of successful women in STEM; provide mentoring and networking possibilities for women in STEM; and disseminate organizational best-practice efforts.

The European Union has introduced a number of initiatives to promote a healthier gender balance in their member countries, beginning in 1999 with an action plan calling for research by, for, and about women. These include the Helsinki Group on Women and Science created in 1999, a 2001 Science and Society Action Plan, the hosting of several conferences in this area, undertaking research and the collection of statistics on the situation of women scientists in member countries.

These measures have addressed the number of women in science, the fields in which they are located in STEM, their levels within their field, whether women were treated fairly in comparison with men, and the status and experiences of women scientists in new member states, most of which were formerly communist countries now undergoing a difficult transition to free market economies.

WHERE DO WE GO FROM HERE?

It is predicted that several developed countries will experience a shortage of skilled STEM workers (Prestoj, 2004). This 'war for talent' must be confronted 'head on' if innovation and scientific advancements, the engines of economic growth, are to be sustained. We cannot continue to waste the talents of many of our educated women and minorities (Layne and Chin, 1998).

Although there are still questions about the barriers these groups face at all stages of the STEM pipeline and the nature of interventions likely to have benefits, much is known (Clewell and Campbell, 2002). Barriers include:

- male nature of organizations
- male nature of science
- stereotyping of scientists and engineers as male
- few female role models for girls
- few female mentors for girls
- young girls/women lack confidence in STEM
- career counselors ill prepared to encourage STEM for girls
- teachers of science do not make it interesting for either boys or girls
- burdens of children/family responsibilities
- career breaks and part-time work put women at a disadvantage in terms of working with the latest concepts, theories and technologies (Zuckerman et al., 1991).

But progress is being made in the education system from kindergarten through high school and in colleges and universities; universities are creating a more level playing field, as witnessed by the success of the ADVANCE initiatives, and organizations are becoming more women- and family-friendly places in order to attract and retain more women and minorities (Clewell and Campbell, 2002).

- *Interventions* – national programs have had some positive effects for young girls. Mentoring, role modeling, summer camps, extra-curricular activities, professional development for teachers, and activities for parents have all played a role here.

- *National policies* – the governments of various countries, aware of the looming shortage of STEM workers and the importance of STEM activities in contributing to economic success and citizen well-being, have undertaken both research and policy efforts to address this concern. This has involved reforms to the educational system, the setting of national standards for teaching STEM and support for women with STEM education to re-enter the workforce.

While these challenges are not new, there is a heightened sense of the nature of the problem coupled with a more focused commitment to do something about it. Only time will tell how successful we will be. Talented and educated women and minorities deserve no less (Selby, 1999).

ACKNOWLEDGEMENT

Preparation of this chapter was supported in part by the Schulich School of Business. It has benefited from discussions with Mary Mattis; Mary also interested me in the challenges faced by women in STEM. Louise Coutu prepared the manuscript.

REFERENCES

Astin, A.W., Parrott, S.A., Korn, W.S. and Sax, L.J. (1997), *The American Freshman: Thirty-year Trends*, Los Angeles: Higher Education Research Institute.
Atkinson, R.C. (1990), 'Supply and demand for scientists and engineers: a national crisis in the making', *Science*, **248**, 425–32.
Bailyn, L. (2003), 'Academic careers and gender equity: lessons learned from MIT', *Gender Work and Organization*, **10**, 137–53.
Blum, L. (2001), 'Transforming the culture of computing at Carnegie Mellon', *Computing Research News*, **13**, 2–9.
Bodzin, A. and Gehringer, M. (2001), 'Breaking science stereotypes', *Science and Children*, **38**, 36–41.
Bouvier, L.F. and Martin, J.L. (1995), *Foreign-Born Scientists, Engineers and Mathematicians in the United States*, Washington, DC: Center for Immigration Studies.
Bybee, R.W. and Fuchs, B. (2006), 'Preparing the 21st century workforce: a new reform in science and technology education', *Journal of Research in Science Teaching*, **43**, 349–52.
Catalyst (1999), *Women Scientists in Industry: A Winning Formula for Companies*, New York: Catalyst.
Catsambis, S. (1995), 'Gender, race, ethnicity, and science education in the middle grades', *Journal of Research in Science Teaching*, **32**, 243–57.

Clewell, B.C. and Campbell, P.B. (2002), 'Taking stock: where we've been, where we are, where we're going', *Journal of Women and Minorities in Science and Engineering*, **8**, 255–84.

Clewell, B.C., Anderson, B. and Thorpe, M. (1992), *Breaking the barriers: Helping Female and Minority Students Succeed in Mathematics and Science*, San Francisco, CA: Jossey-Bass.

Clewell, B.C., Decohen, C.C., Tsui, L. and Deterding, N. (2006), *Revitalizing the Nation's Talent Pool in STEM*, Washington, DC: The Urban Institute.

Curtan, J.M., Blake, G. and Cassaynan, C. (1997), 'The climate for women graduate students in physics', *Journal of Women and Minorities in Science and Engineering*, **3**, 95–117.

Davis, C., Ginorio, A.B., Hollenshead, L.S., Lazarus, B.B. and Raynmab, P.M. (1996), *The Equity Equation: Fostering the Advancement of Women in the Sciences, Mathematics and Engineering*, San Francisco, CA: Jossey-Bass.

Dryburgh, H. (1999), 'Work hard, play hard: women and professionalization in engineering – adapting to the culture', *Gender and Society*, **13**, 664–82.

Eccles, J.S. (1994), 'Understanding women's educational and occupational choices: applying the Eccles et al. model of achievement recalled choices', *Psychology of Women Quarterly*, **18**, 585–609.

Eccleston, J. (1999), 'Girls only, please: an after-school science club for girls promotes understanding and involvement', *Science and Children*, **37**, 21–5.

Etzkowitz, H., Kemelgor, C. and Uzzi, B. (2000), *Athena Unbound: The Advancement of Women in Science and Technology*, London: Cambridge University Press.

Etzkowitz, H., Kemelgor, C., Neuschatz, M., Uzzi, B. and Alonzo, J. (1994), 'The paradox of critical mass for women in science', *Science*, **266**, 51–3.

Farrell, E.F. (2002), 'Engineering a warmer welcome for female students', *Chronicles of Higher Education*, **48**, 14–31.

Ford, D.C. and Varney, H.L. (1989), 'How students see scientists: mostly male, mostly white and mostly benevolent', *Science and Children*, **26**, 8–13.

Georgi, H. (2000), *Who Will Do the Science in the Future?*, Washington, DC: National Academy Press.

Gilbride, K.A., Kennedy, D.C., Waslen, J.K. and Kyvano, M. (1999), 'A proactive strategy for attracting women into engineering', *Canadian Journal of Counseling*, **33**, 55–65.

Jones, G.M., Brader-Araje, L., Carboni, L.W., Carter, G., Rua, M.J., Banilower, E. and Hatch, H.J. (2000), 'Tool time: gender and students' use of tools, control and authority', *Journal of Research in Science Teaching*, **37**, 760–82.

Kahle, J.B. (2004), 'Will girls be left behind? Gender differences and accountability', *Journal of Research in Science Teaching*, **41**, 961–9.

Kemelgor, C. and Etzkowitz, H. (2001), 'Overcoming isolation: women's dilemmas in American academic service', *Minerva*, **39**, 153–74.

LaVaque-Manty, D. and Stewart, A.J. (2007), 'A very scholarly intervention: recruiting women faculty in science and engineering', in L. Schiebinger (ed.), *Gendered Innovations in Science and Engineering*, Palo Alto, CA: Stanford University Press, pp. 142–75.

Layne, P. and Chin, K. (1998), 'Women in engineering: how far have they come? Although women are finally breaking through the glass ceiling, they still have a long way to go to reach parity with men', *Chemical Engineering*, **165**, 84–90.

Lederman, M. (2003), 'Gender/inequity in science education: a response', *Journal of Research in Science Teaching*, **40**, 604–6.

Loder, N. (2000), 'The imbalance of men and women in the School of Science at Massachusetts Institute of Technology', *Nature*, **405**, 713–14.

Lottero-Perdue, P.S. and Brickhouse, N. (2002), 'Learning on the job: the acquisition of scientific competence', *Science Education*, **86**, 756–82.

Makrakis, V. (1992), 'Cross-cultural comparison of gender differences toward computers in Japan and Sweden', *Scandinavian Journal of Educational Research*, **36**, 275–87.

Margolis, J., Fisher, A. and Miller, F. (2000), 'Caring about connections: gender and computing', *Technology and Society*, **18**, 13–20.

Margolis, J. and Fisher, A. (2002), *Unlocking the Clubhouse*, Cambridge, MA: MIT Press.

Martell, R.F., Lane, D.M. and Emrich, C. (1996), 'Male–female differences: a computer simulation', *American Psychologist*, **51**, 157–8.

Mason, C.L. and Kahle, J.B. (1988), 'Student attitudes toward science, and science-related careers. A program designed to promote a stimulating gender-free learning environment', *Journal of Research in Science Teaching*, **26**, 25–39.

McCormick, N. and McCormick, J. (1991), ' "Nor for men only." Why so few women major in computer science', *College Student Journal*, **25**, 345–50.

McIlwee, J. and Robinson, J. (1992), *Women in Engineering: Gender, Power and Workplace Culture*, London: Policy Studies Institute.

Morella, C. (2002), 'Recognizing a threat to America's economy', *Journal of Women and Minorities in Science and Engineering*, **8**, 377–80.

National Science Foundation (2002), *Science and Engineering Indicators 2002*, Washington, DC: National Science Foundation.

North, David S. (1995), *Soothing the Establishment: The Impact of Foreign-Born Scientists and Engineers on America*, New York: University Press of America.

Parsons, E.E. (1997), 'Black high school females' images of the scientist: expression of culture', *Journal of Research in Science Teaching*, **34**, 745–68.

Pearson, W. and Fechter, A. (1992), *Who Will Do Science?*, Baltimore, MD: Johns Hopkins University Press.

Pearson, W. and Fechter, A. (1994), *Human Resources for Science*, Baltimore, MD: Johns Hopkins University Press.

Powell, A., Bagilhole, B., Dainty, A. and Neale, R. (2000), 'Does the engineering culture in UK higher education advance women's careers?', *Equal Opportunity International*, **23**, 21–38.

Prestoj, A. (2004), 'Plugging the leaks in the scientific workforce – much more needs to be done to reverse the high rate of attrition of both men and women early in their scientific careers', *Issues in Science and Technology*, **20**, 69–73.

Preston, A.E. (1994), 'Why have all the women gone? A study of exit of women from the science and engineering professions', *American Economic Review*, **84**, 1446–59.

Robinson, J.G. and McIlwee, J.S. (1991), 'Men, women, and the culture of engineering', *Sociological Quarterly*, **32**, 463–72.

Rosser, S.V. (2004), *The Science Glass Ceiling*, London: Routledge.

Sadker, M. and Sadker, D. (1994), *Failing at Fairness: How America's Schools Cheat Girls*, New York: Charles Scribner's & Sons.

Schneider, A. (2000), 'Female scientists turn their backs on jobs at research universities', *The Chronicle of Higher Education*, **46**, A12–14.

Selby, Cecily, C. (1999), *Women in Science and Engineering: Choices for Success*, New York: New York Academy of Sciences.

Seymour, E. and Aikenhead, G.S. (1995), 'The loss of women from science, mathematics, and engineering undergraduate majors', *Science Education*, **79**, 437–73.

Seymour, E. and Hewitt, N.M. (1997), *Talking about Leaving: Why Undergraduates Leave the Sciences*, Boulder, CO: Westview.

Single, P.B., Muller, C.B., Cunningham, C.M., Single, R.M. and Carlsen, W.S. (2005), 'Mentornet: e-mentoring for women students in engineering and science', *Journal of Women and Minorities in Science and Engineering*, **11**, 295–310.

Sonnert, G. and Holton, G. (1995a), *Gender Difference in Science Careers: The Project Access Study*, New Brunswick, NJ: Rutgers University Press.

Sonnert, G. and Holton, G. (1995b), *Who Succeeds in Science? The Gender Dimension*, New Brunswick, NJ: Rutgers University Press.

Sonnert, G. and Holton, G. (1999), 'Women in science and engineering. Advances, challenges and solutions', in C.C. Selby (ed.), *Women in Science and Engineering: Choices for Success*, New York: New York Academy of Sciences, pp. 34–57.

Spelke, E.S. (2005), 'Sex differences in intrinsic aptitude for mathematics and sciences?', *American Psychologist*, **60**, 950–58.

Springer, L., Stanne, M.E.E. and Donovan, S.S. (1999), 'Effects of small-group learning on undergraduates in science, mathematics engineering, and technology: a meta-analysis', *Review of Educational Research*, **69**, 121–51.

Stewart, A.J., Malley, J.E. and LaVaque-Manty, D. (2006), *Advancing Women in Science and Engineering*, Ann Arbor, MI: University of Michigan Press.

Storobin, S.S. and Laanan, F. (2005), 'Influence of precollege experience on self-concept among community college students in science, mathematics, and engineering', *Journal of Women and Minorities in Science and Engineering*, **11**, 209–30.

Strand, K.J. and Mayfield, E. (2002), 'Pedagogical reform and college women's persistence in mathematics', *Journal of Women and Minorities in Science and Engineering*, **8**, 62–83.

Valian, V. (1999), *Why so Slow? The Advancement of Women*, Cambridge, MA: The MIT Press.

Weinburgh, M. (1995), 'Gender differences in student attitudes towards science: a meta-analysis of the literature from 1970–1991', *Journal of Research in Science Teaching*, **32**, 387–98.

Wood, S.L. (2002), 'Perspectives of best practices for learning gender-inclusive science: influence of extracurricular science for gifted girls and electrical engineering for women', *Journal of Women and Minorities in Science and Engineering*, **8**, 25–40.

Wright, R. (1997), *Women Computer Professionals: Progress and Resistance*, Lewiston, NY: Edward Mellon Press.

Wyer, M. (2003), 'Intending to stay: images of scientists, attitudes toward women, and gender as influences on persistence among science and engineering majors', *Journal of Women and Minorities in Science and Engineering*, **9**, 1–6.

Xie, Y. and Shauman, K.H. (2003), *Women in Science: Career Processes and Outcomes*, Cambridge, MA: Harvard University Press.

Zuckerman, H., Cole, J. and Bruer, J. (1991), *The Outer Circle: Women in the Scientific Community*, New York: Norton.

2. Keys to success for women in science

Donna J. Dean and Anne Fleckenstein

INTRODUCTORY OVERVIEW

Today, more women are entering scientific fields than ever before, energized by challenges and intellectual inquiry at the boundaries of the unknown. They follow pathways forged by female scientists before them or blaze new trails of their own. The employment picture for those women and men trained in scientific disciplines has been, largely, a good one over the past two decades. While subfields may experience declines and resurgences as economic realities intercede, scientists in general encounter a job market that welcomes their skills. Moreover, survey after survey of the American public has documented that the profession of scientist is one of the most respected. In a world that has become increasingly driven by scientific and technological breakthroughs that affect every facet of day-to-day life, the need for a well-trained workforce in these areas can only increase. The analytical skills and content knowledge obtained in pursuing a scientific degree can position individuals for employment in a broad array of occupations and an unlimited number of settings. However, faculty at academic institutions and members of professional societies fail to articulate the diversity of opportunities that are available for young people with strong interests in science; these more senior colleagues often revert to narrow perspectives of what constitutes 'success'. The challenge is to present the bright young female who has a strong interest in science, technology, engineering, and/or mathematics (the STEM disciplines) with welcoming environments, challenging research problems, and a framework for success that will successfully see her through the many stages of her career and life.

A CHANGING DEMOGRAPHIC PROFILE

In 2001, women earned 53 percent of science and engineering bachelor's degrees and, in 2003, were awarded 37.5 percent of all science and engineering doctorates in the USA (NSF, 2006). This distribution exemplifies a trend that has been growing for the past 30 years: between 1970 and 1995, the number of science doctorates awarded to women increased six-fold. There are many factors which likely account for this increase, ranging from less stereotypical societal expectations for females to the unlimited opportunities presented by late twentieth- and early twenty-first-century science and technology.

The strong showing of women's achievements in acquiring bachelor's degrees in science and engineering has not automatically translated into more women in senior positions, however. There is a well-documented trend of women dropping out of science and engineering at all levels of academia. In college, more women than men leave science majors and those who receive bachelor's degrees are less likely to continue on to graduate school. While women earn almost 40 percent of the doctorates, they comprise only 25 percent of the total science and engineering workforce. In 1999, 43 percent of all postdoctoral fellows were women, but in 2003, women comprised only 29.1 percent of faculty members and they are more likely to be junior faculty instead of full professors or administrators. Similar numbers are seen in industry. The number of women faculty and researchers does not represent the number of women who are earning science and engineering degrees, and remains far below that of men both in absolute numbers and as a percentage.

More disturbingly, the proportion of women in science is not equal across disciplines. They are overrepresented (when compared to men) in fields such as psychology, where women comprise 78 percent of degree holders, but are almost missing in engineering and computer sciences, where only 21 percent and 27 percent of bachelor's degrees, respectively, are awarded to women. The numbers become even lower when data are analyzed for advanced degrees awarded and faculty positions held. Even today, women faculty in engineering, computer science and the physical sciences are likely to be the sole women in their departments.

Much has been written about career pipelines and the declining numbers of women at all stages of post-baccalaureate training and disciplinary career ladders. However, the pipeline analogy is inadequate for conveying the scope, magnitude and potential causes of the lack of parity and equity for women across their careers. Indeed, most references to the 'leaky pipeline' are predicated on the view that the pipeline is linear, with one entry point (educational environment), and with one exit point (definition of a certain kind of career success). What has been missing from these simplistic views is the concept that pipelines have many entry points and many branch points, all of which provide value and integrity to the system as a whole. To carry the analogy a bit further, the effective and functioning pipeline must have been designed to meet a specified need, constructed to meet that need, and maintained for robustness over time by constant monitoring. For women in science, could it be that the pipeline has been designed and maintained in a manner that filters out their participation? One must consider that women are diverted from the pipeline at higher rates and earlier stages than men, and that the pipeline is porous in a selective way that forces out more women than men.

WHAT IS THE PROBLEM?

Why are women not progressing? They comprise approximately one-half of the undergraduate science and engineering population, but only 37.5 percent of the doctorate degrees and less than 13 percent of full professors in academic departments if averaged across all the STEM disciplines. Women who do enter the workforce are less likely to advance than men. Research has shown that women who received their doctorates in mathematics are more likely than men to obtain their first job in departments that do not have graduate students (Ruskai, 1996). These women are then less able to move on to higher-ranked research institutions and their careers stall. A study that followed those who earned mathematics doctorates between 1970 and 1974 (Billiard, 1991) found that, 20 years later, only 45 percent of the women compared with 70 percent of the men had been promoted to full or associate professor. This trend is observed in other disciplines as well. Across the board, women progress slower and are underrepresented at all levels of tenured faculty. In addition to the lack of career progress, women earn on average 24 percent less than men of the same rank in academic departments (Ruskai, 1996).

What are some of the barriers to women's full participation in science? Girls are still not pursuing careers in science and mathematics, even with the greater educational opportunities that are open to them. While outright discrimination and harassment are becoming things of the past, obstacles remain and have become more subtle. Unfortunately, these issues are not new. In 1987, the federal government convened the Task Force on Women, Minorities, and the Handicapped in Science and Technology in response to a law passed by the US Congress. The 49-member Task Force, composed of leaders from 15 federal agencies and from the private sector and higher education, was mandated to develop a long-range plan that would broaden participation in science and engineering. At that time, women comprised 45 percent of the US workforce, but only 11 percent of all employed scientists and engineers. In the mid-1980s, women earned 30 percent of all bachelor's degrees in science and engineering, 34 percent of the doctorates in the life sciences, but only 16 percent of the doctorates in physical sciences and 7 percent in engineering. Faculty surveys for 1985 had shown that women were only 13 percent of all college and university science faculty and 2 percent of engineering faculty. Women were also twice as likely to be found in non-tenure-track positions. The Task Force's findings with regard to female scientists remain compelling 20 years later (US Congress, 1988, p. 36):

> Women scientists and engineers also face two special problems. Even when women score higher academically than men, because of their work situation they are more likely to lose self-confidence and feel less satisfied. During their 20s and 30s – just when their career demands the most time – women need to make decisions about childbearing.

The report further noted,

> In graduate school, a far smaller portion of women than men complete the doctorate. This may be because women are more likely than men to be self-supporting during this period. They are also more likely to be assigned teaching assistantships, where they deal with students, rather than research assistantships, where they work with mentors and peers.

After conducting seven public hearings across the country, the Task Force explicitly stated the cause of the problem: 'The factors – racism, sexism, and prejudice against people with disabilities – that have limited opportunities for many in America are also narrowing access to science and engineering careers.' Over 90 concrete action steps were directed toward specific sectors and organizations: federal government agencies, the President and US Congress, governors and state legislators, school boards, industry, universities and colleges, educators, media and professional societies (US Congress, 1989). Unfortunately, almost two decades later, little action has been taken in response to the report.

As noted above and in many other studies, one of the main reasons that girls and women may choose not to pursue science at all is a lack of self-confidence. Girls receive less encouragement in mathematics and science courses, even when women teach these courses. Those girls who excel in mathematics and science courses, and whom others view as capable, report lower self-confidence than their male counterparts. Lower self-confidence can cause girls to rule out careers in science, because they become convinced that they are not good enough to succeed. In college, female undergraduates lose confidence in their abilities more often than do men (Huang, 2003), mostly out of a fear of failure. Women tend to internalize failure, which causes them to blame themselves and feel as though their personal worth has decreased, while men tend to have an easier time depersonalizing failure. Once women are juniors or seniors in college, or even in graduate school, they are not encouraged to pursue science as a career as often as men, and the lack of female role models in many departments can further reinforce the stereotype that these fields are not appropriate for women. Because of this dearth of female scientists, women who do graduate with advanced degrees often lack the mentors and role models who can demonstrate that being both a woman and a scientist are not mutually exclusive.

This lack of self-confidence can have far-reaching consequences. Women scientists tend to perfectionism, which can manifest itself in setting unreasonable expectations, more than men. While striving for excellence is an admirable trait, perfectionism can cause a researcher to hold on to experiments too long, to keep hammering away for the next piece of data that will tell the complete story, and to delay publishing. In these days, when tenure and promotion decisions can hinge on the number of publications, waiting until everything is known about a topic before publishing can be disastrous.

Is this lack of self-confidence the reason that women who received their doctorates in mathematics in 1994 and 1995 were more likely than men to obtain their first positions in departments that only award bachelor's degrees? Or does date of first hire suggest that most of the women who received science, technology, engineering or mathematics degrees in the 1980s did not enter jobs conducive to development of a robust academic research career? The early jobs out of graduate school are extremely important to careers in academia. If a scientist cannot conduct top-level research in a respected institution, the likelihood of progressing to a higher-level research institution or university decreases considerably. Women may take themselves out of consideration for challenging positions because they feel that they are not competitive enough to obtain them. Even those who work in highly regarded research institutions tend to find a niche research area and not enter the fray of a hot topic.

Of course, some of these circumstances are not entirely due to women's internalization of society's values. In 1971, a study demonstrated that female job candidates were evaluated differently than male candidates (Lewin and Duchan, 1971). In this study, the *curriculum vitae* of an average man and woman and of a superior woman were sent to departmental chairs at research institutions. Of the average candidates, the man was consistently ranked higher than the female candidate. While the superior woman was ranked higher than the average man, the departmental chairs were concerned more about how she would fit in the department and where her husband would work. Unfortunately, similar problems persist today. In 2003, two researchers published a report that examined over 300 letters of recommendation written for medical faculty at large American medical schools in the mid-1990s (Trix and Psenka, 2003). They found that letters written for female candidates were shorter than those for men, lacked basic features of the candidate's *curriculum vitae*, had a higher percentage of clauses that raised doubt, and reinforced gender stereotypes of women as teachers and men as researchers. These statements and opinions all served to weaken the overall recommendation and make female candidates appear less desirable than equally qualified male candidates.

Other areas of importance to a successful scientific career also show patterns of gender difference. In 2006, it was reported that women faculty members obtain patents at about 40 percent of the rate of men (Ding et al., 2006). In examining data over a 30-year period, the researchers showed that women in the life sciences are publishing and patenting at a much higher rate than three decades ago, but still at rates considerably less than their male colleagues. 'Limited commercial networks' and 'traditional views of academic careers' were cited as barriers to achieving parity with men on patenting rates. However, in a more encouraging vein, they found that younger women scientists exhibited more proactive approaches to patent seeking despite a remaining gender gap.

THE CULTURE OF SCIENCE AND THE STEREOTYPICAL SCIENTIST

Further hampering women in scientific careers is the basic culture of science itself. Until recently, science has been an exclusively male enterprise and it is resisting the incorporation of women. These cultural barriers and rigid stereotypes of what constitutes a successful person and personality in science also must be of concern for the full inclusion of underrepresented minority groups in scientific careers. Traditionally, scientific research in all disciplines has demanded single-mindedness, exclusive devotion, and aggressive self-promotion that are not appealing to many women and to many ethnic or cultural groups historically underrepresented in the STEM disciplines. The image of the scientist in the laboratory at all hours of the night and weekend is not far from the reality sometimes demanded. Scientific research does not easily allow for other pursuits such as care of a family, especially during the early years of a career. It is much easier for men to conform to this obsessive standard than women. Often, a woman's biological clock and tenure clock are out of synchrony, and women feel they have to choose between having children when they are young, thereby risking their ability to obtain tenure, or to focus on their scientific careers when young and delay having children until they are older, when it may be more difficult. Having young children early in their careers is negatively related to women's chances of earning tenure (NSF, 2003), but at the same time, women with no children still progress more slowly than men (Zandonella, 2004).

While women in American society have made great strides in gender equality, they are still the main caretakers of the young and, increasingly, of the elderly. Unfortunately, many institutions do not allow for flexible work schedules. Even when academic departments do offer maternity leave and flexible schedules, many women are hesitant to take them for fear of being penalized later. When up for tenure, woman are afraid they may be deemed not productive enough, especially when compared with a man who did not change his schedule when his baby was born. Time not spent in the laboratory can not only change a department's perception of the woman scientist, but also a gap in productivity could mean getting scooped by a competitor in an experiment, being excluded from departmental decisions, and/or a loss of grant funding.

In 1971, women were subjected to blatant discrimination, unequal pay, and fewer opportunities for advancement. In response to that dismal picture, the Association for Women in Science (AWIS) was founded in 1971 to counteract the traditional all-male network by acting as a female one. For example, at that time, 75 percent of all women employed by the federal government's National Institutes of Health, the largest biomedical research agency in the world, were employed in ranks of GS 9 or below, and there were no women in the top GS 16 and GS 17 ranks (Edisen, 1971). While there were many qualified women available to fill these positions, most jobs at the time were not advertised and candidates learned of them only through networking. As well, female scientists were not an integral part of the grants peer review system of the National Institutes of Health, nor were they significant recipients of the research grants issued by the agency. The professional networks at the time comprised solely men and therefore women were often unaware of opportunities. In a multifaceted approach to the serious problems facing women scientists' advancement at that time, AWIS began activities to facilitate interactions between women engaged in all scientific disciplines, established a national registry of women scientists that could be used as a source of job candidates, appointments and awards, and initiated lawsuits to enhance the professional environment for women in science. Today the National Institutes of Health must include women on peer review panels and the government must enforce affirmative action principles and equal opportunity laws because of the legal actions brought by AWIS and other professional organizations. These organizations have also petitioned Congress to strengthen the application of Title IX to science, technology, engineering and mathematics departments in academia. Such actions have helped to open more widely academia's door to women; there are more women faculty, the wage gap has narrowed and women have been able to become administrators and presidents. However, ongoing vigilance and monitoring is essential to ensure that federal agencies and academic institutions do not renege on their commitments.

FINDING SOLUTIONS THAT WORK

The problems articulated above are faced by women in virtually every sector of science and technology, and demand sweeping institutional change. Some research institutions have made progress by stopping the tenure clock for women who take time out to have children; time spent on maternity leave extends the time until tenure review, giving the mother the same amount of research time as others. However, this does not answer other systemic problems such as funding and the lack of integration of women scientists that form barriers to successful career progression and advancement. In 2005, AWIS organized the National Conference for Women in Science, Technology, Engineering, and Mathematics (STEM) Disciplines at Smith College to address some of these institutional problems as part of its work to address the academic climate under an ADVANCE leadership award from the National Science Foundation.

The conference focused mainly on the needs of women in academia and identified several practices that could not only help recruit woman scientists, but also allow them to remain in academia and thrive. Recruitment should not be limited to placing advertisements and waiting for replies, but should use personal contacts to scout for qualified female scientists. Departments must institute flexible hiring practices that allow shared or part-time tenure positions and create part-time research positions, offer childcare and make it available in the evenings. These policies should be available to both women and men equally in the department; the best departments have almost no measures targeted solely at women, but rather have a culture that encourages a healthy work–life balance for all employees. Departments must establish diverse search committees that not only include women and minorities, but also faculty from other departments. These search committees must be trained to read evaluation letters because often women applicants have letters of recommendation that may have a different tone or be less enthusiastic than those of male applicants. This difference in recommendations reflects an unseen gender bias in science because, often without being conscious of it, people use different language to describe equally qualified men and women. When committees have to make decisions based on these letters of recommendation, the lukewarm language used to recommend women can be a liability. More important than flexible schedules, diverse search committees and recruitment, departments must ensure that female faculty members are made visible to the larger community. They should be encouraged to present their research at other institutions and should be nominated for awards. The importance of exposure for junior faculty members is paramount and cannot be overstated. Only visible and esteemed scientists will be asked to serve on scientific advisory and peer review panels and have the opportunities to progress up the academic ladder.

The Smith College report (Sztein, 2005) deals mainly with changes that academic institutions can make to improve the environment for woman scientists. However, universities are not the only institutions that hire scientists. The entire scientific community needs to adapt to the needs of woman scientists. Recently, the InterAcademy Council, a multinational organization of science academies, established an Advisory Panel on Women for Science with a mandate to propose what scientific academies around the world can do to encourage the development of more woman scientists (InterAcademy Council, 2006).

The InterAcademy Council is focused on increasing the participation of women worldwide in science and technology careers until their numbers in these professions reflect their numbers in the general population. Women make up one-half of the human population, and in many Western countries over one-half of the working population, yet remain conspicuously absent from the fields of mathematics, physical sciences and engineering. Even in those fields such as psychology and biology where the number of women is reaching higher levels and parity with that of men, women scientists drop out at the early career stage at a much higher rate than men. Given that fewer women enter these fields and then more drop out than men, it is amazing that there are any women who have been able to attain leadership roles in science and technology fields. The lack of female scientists worldwide is further affected by the fact that in many parts of the world, women who might otherwise become brilliant scientists are never given access to quality education that would allow them to fulfill their promise. The underrepresentation of women in science and technology remains a worldwide phenomenon and the InterAcademy Council believes that action must be taken immediately to remedy this problem. Including women's talents, perspectives and skills will enrich the scientific community and ultimately the global community.

The Advisory Panel on Women for Science of the InterAcademy Council identified some common problems that contribute to the low representation of women in scientific careers. Some of these, such as girls' limited access to education and the role of women as mothers and caregivers, are manifested differently around the world. In some developing countries, science education for all is minimal and not conducive to the development of future scientists of either sex. In other countries, girls are not allowed access to mathematics and science education. Moreover, in other places the discrimination against girls in mathematics and science is more insidious: society convinces them that they are not capable or that their only meaningful role in life is as a wife and mother. Hence education for females is not deemed important. This view, combined with a lack of female role models, prevents many from pursuing careers in these fields. The Advisory Panel recommends that to engage women in the developing world in technology, access to quality education must be ensured, women scientists and engineers should be educated at specialized research centers that are better able to support them, and these women must then go out into society to be role models and teachers.

Not all of the Panel's recommendations focus exclusively on women in developing countries. Worldwide, the Panel emphasizes actions that national scientific academies must take. Women and girls must be attracted to science and technology, and supported throughout their education and careers. To this end, academies should establish panels to take responsibility for gender issues. Such panels would review all policies and procedures for their impact on women and monitor the progress of women in science. The academies should also make an effort to recruit existing woman scientists to become members and fully include them in senior and leadership positions. Tailoring some scientific events to the general public and holding these events in venues other than universities can improve interactions with the public sector. Increasing public awareness and appreciation of science will help attract more people, both women and men, to these fields.

Not only do institutions need to change in order to encourage women to pursue scientific careers; all levels of education and society need to change as well. In September 2000, the report *Land of Plenty: Diversity as America's competitive edge in science, engineering and technology* (US Congress, 2000), issued by the Congressional Commission on the Advancement of Women and Minorities in Science, Engineering and Technology, looked at what could be done systemically to help recruit girls and women to science and technology careers. Reflecting 18 months of hearings, testimony and individual efforts, the report from the 11-member Commission contains practical steps for action for federal agencies and for the private sector framed within six recommendations. To address pre-college education, the Commission recommended that (1) mathematics and science curricula and mathematics and science teacher qualifications become more robust, with state-level implementation of comprehensive high-quality education standards. To address entry into the college level, (2) aggressive, focused intervention efforts at the high school level, at the transition into postsecondary education and at the community college transition into four-year colleges are needed; and (3) financial investment by the federal and state governments must be significantly expanded in support of underrepresented groups. In professional life, recommendation (4) stated that both public and private employers in the science and technology sector should be held accountable for the career development and advancement of women and underrepresented minorities. The final recommendations concerned (5) targeted efforts to transform the image of the science and technology professions so that the image is positive and inclusive, and (6) a collaborative body with power to oversee and implement strong and feasible action plans. Again, there has been relatively little forward movement on a national level in implementing the report's resounding message that in order for the USA to retain its pre-eminence in science and technology, it needs to tap the scientific imagination of all of its citizens, not just the male portion.

WHAT PROFESSIONAL SOCIETIES CAN DO

Over the past 30 years, we must acknowledge that the environment for women in science has improved considerably, though not in all fields and not at equitable rates. As noted earlier, the Association for Women in Science has been strongly engaged in working toward the full participation of women across all fields of science since 1971. AWIS was founded with the goal of promoting equal opportunities for women to enter the scientific professions and then progress to leadership positions. Recognizing the ongoing need for an organization to be a network, a resource and a voice for women across the entire spectrum of the sciences, AWIS seeks common patterns, common issues and transportable strategies that work in most, if not all, fields of science. While disciplinary-based professional societies, such as the American Society for Cell Biology and the American Society for Engineering Education, have undertaken aggressive efforts among their membership to transform the culture of research and education within their specific fields, a strong need remains for addressing issues across the entire spectrum of science and technology. Such efforts as the series of workshops and activities entitled 'Achieving XXcellence in Science (AXXS)', sponsored by the Office of Research on Women's Health at the National Institutes of Health, have spotlighted the role that professional societies can and should play in helping to advance the careers of women in science. Recognizing that there were concrete action steps that professional societies could implement and/or facilitate, the AXXS report articulated 14 specific initiatives with specific details and action plans (Office of Research on Women's Health, 2000). Because of the significance of this work and its pragmatic articulation of clear action steps that professional societies can undertake immediately, these initiatives merit repeating here in their entirety. With regard to leadership, visibility and recognition, professional societies can

1. develop forums to highlight successes of women scientists,
2. formalize mechanisms for opportunities, awareness and development for women in science,
3. increase the number of women in society leadership roles,
4. find and implement new strategies for leadership development programs within societies, and
5. provide training and facilitate understanding regarding the 'rules of the game' as they pertain to networking, promotion and tenure, etc.

With regard to mentoring and networking, professional organizations can

6. establish a national mentorship system for women,
7. establish mentoring as a core activity of professional societies,
8. develop effective mentoring programs, and
9. create a networking website for scientists.

To foster approaches that are effective,

10. best practices can be designed for the advancement of women and
11. shared through a best practices clearinghouse.

Because history has shown that oversight, tracking and accountability are essential to ensure that change occurs, it would be essential to

12. create an umbrella organization of professional societies to facilitate networking and exchange of information and ideas,
13. develop a database of women scientists, and
14. establish a report card on the status of women in science and engineering.

Subsequent AXXS efforts translated those recommendations into targeted approaches applicable to women in clinical research careers (Shaywitz and Hahm, 2002).

MENTORING AS A TOOL THAT WORKS

One of the most important things institutions and professional groups can do to support women in science and slow the attrition rate of young woman scientists is to establish mentoring groups. This is especially important considering that women are less likely than their male counterparts to receive encouragement and positive reinforcement from their professors. In addition to helping to recruit and retain woman scientists, mentoring has been associated with higher income, greater self-esteem and creativity, and higher levels of job satisfaction (Project ENHANCE, 2004). To increase the number of women pursuing advanced careers in science, AWIS established a mentoring project that designed activities to foster supportive relationships among women scientists. The project, started in 1990, linked undergraduate and graduate students in the sciences with women at more senior career levels. Local AWIS chapters worked both independently and in collaboration with other national scientific organizations (such as Sigma Xi, The Scientific Research Society, or the American Chemical Society) to implement the program. This combination of community-based programs within national organizations ensures that the program can respond to local needs while at the same time encouraging institutionalization and replication within a larger framework.

The majority of the students (80 percent) who participated in the mentoring program recognized that they faced barriers as female scientists (AWIS, 1993). After three years of mentoring, 62 percent felt that the mentoring they had received helped them to handle these barriers. Additionally, many of those who, on beginning the program, described their commitment to science as tentative were more likely to remain in science at the end of the program. In the words of one of the participants, 'the program provided constant commitment and involvement in science, thus . . . I didn't just give up. The best aspect of the program is that it doesn't allow you to just fade out of science.'

Because of its work with this mentoring project, AWIS was awarded a Presidential Mentoring Award for 'Creating Tomorrow's Scientists: Models of Community Mentoring'. This project also led to AWIS's most successful and in-demand publication to date – the 500-page mentoring handbook, *A Hand Up: Women mentoring women in science*, originally published in 1993 and extensively updated in 2005 (Fort, 2005). Combining pragmatic advice, interviews with scientists at all career stages and with students, and resources for mentors and aspiring young scientists, the book's wealth of strategies gives today's female scientists the tools with which to take charge of their own careers.

Mentoring not only can help students with the academic aspects of science, but also can help to reconcile the woman/scientist dilemma. Often women cannot see themselves pursuing science because they think the roles of woman and of scientist conflict. Having mentors and role models who have both families and successful scientific careers shows younger women that these two roles are not mutually exclusive. In a manner less formal than a structured mentoring program, attending local AWIS chapter meetings can provide some of the same support. Meeting other women who have faced similar problems allows an exchange of ideas to learn what works and what does not. Often female scientists are the only women in their respective departments, and interacting with other women who are experiencing the same problems alleviates the sense of isolation they feel in their professional lives. The balancing of careers and families, along with other personal life matters, is especially important to many women. Most believe that, with careful planning, women can be scientists, mothers, wives and active participants in the communities in which they live. Interaction with other women helps reinforce that, while it may not be easy and certain choices must be made, it is not impossible.

In addition to offering mentoring opportunities, professional organizations such as AWIS present other professional opportunities. The diverse members can yield information about and provide perspectives on many types of scientific careers that might not be available otherwise. Graduate departments and research laboratories are often poorly equipped to educate students about careers outside the academic environment because most professors and principal investigators have spent their entire careers in academia. With no experience of other routes, it is therefore difficult for them to articulate the rewarding and productive career paths that scientists can take in other arenas. Professional organizations can help fill in the gaps.

For women working in the same career fields, professional organizations are an invaluable networking resource that can counteract the 'old boys' networks' still prevalent in industry and academia today. Women need their own networks in addition to breaking into existing ones in order to succeed. This network can help members find new jobs, opportunities to present research, or service on professional panels. To gain power for themselves, women must focus on self-empowerment: they must celebrate and support women as well as share experiences and educate each other. Professional organizations are also good at educating members and disseminating information. Many have monthly or bi-weekly publications and electronic media that can keep members up to date on issues that affect them. These publications can include information about employment, research and the achievements of members.

Many of the changes that have been made institutionally are recent and even today are not widely applied. Women continue to struggle more than men to create a scientific career, and many continue to opt out at all career stages. What are the keys to success for current female scientists? Through interviews and associations with successful woman scientists, AWIS has been able to identify several characteristics that are essential for women to thrive in science, engineering and technology careers. Many of these women entered science before the cultural and institutional changes that have opened the doors for future scientists, although much of what they encountered will not seem alien to young women today.

Successful woman scientists must have a level of self-confidence that allows them to brush aside and ignore the discouragement and outright discrimination that women can face. The road to success in science is crowded with obstacles and hindrances. Confidence and stubbornness are required to overcome these (Gary, 2004). Because they are less likely to be encouraged by professors, women must seek out their own support networks and form relationships with peers and colleagues. At the most basic level, self-confidence can allow a young scientist to persevere in the laboratory, an area where being assertive and fighting for your ideas are required. If a young scientist cannot defend her beliefs and scientific findings, she will not be able to convince anyone that she is correct. In the laboratory, the loudest, most insistent voice is the one that triumphs and, all too often, that voice is not female. Other aspects of the laboratory culture work against timid women. Research personnel being bullied and treated badly by principal investigators and laboratory directors is so widespread that it is no longer surprising anymore (AAAS Career Forum, 2006); it is often considered just part of paying the dues necessary for a career in science. This problem affects postdoctoral fellows more than anyone else because they tend to be exclusively dependent on the senior scientists for funding and have little available recourse for action. Women are more likely to suffer at the hands of abusive principal investigators because they start with lower levels of confidence than men and are often less likely to fight back.

Confidence in one's abilities and ideas is also required for the self-promotion that is necessary to succeed. Self-promotion is part of the business of science and, to progress, a woman needs to make sure that her department chair and dean or division director and senior executives know about her work and her successes. Being an excellent scientist will not automatically result in recognition and promotion on its own. In addition, scientists must be ambitious and not undervalue their contributions; women who are quiet and self-effacing will not be perceived as great scientists and will therefore not be treated as such (Swiss, 1996).

Life in science also requires resilience. In the day-to-day workings of a laboratory, scientists are more likely to experience disappointments and setbacks than true successes. Successful scientists learn how to adapt to new developments, cope with disaster, and regroup. Often, the mistakes and oversights can be more illuminating and informative than achievements, but researchers have to be able to take advantage of these opportunities.

True success does not rely on any one person, but rather on the support network the scientist can employ. While professional organizations are an important network, family and friends are crucial as well. Most of the prominent woman scientists never would have entered science at all if it had not been for the encouragement of close family members. Most attribute their love of science to their parents, especially their fathers, and know that they never would have persevered through the many years of schooling without the support of families. If parents are instrumental in supporting the early years of school, spouses or partners play an important role in how a woman progresses through her scientific career. A scientist married to a man who does not support her scientific career will have a tough decision ahead of her: she may have to choose either work or her husband. Woman scientists need to deal with the personal issues of their lives more than their male colleagues because they are still the main caretakers of the family. Until society sees big changes at home, all women who work will be at a disadvantage. In the words of Rita Colwell, a former director of the National Science Foundation, 'You have to marry the right person!' (Sztein, 2005, p. 15).

The most important quality required to succeed is a love of science itself. First and foremost, every scientist must love her field of research. Often, things in the laboratory go awry (contamination, equipment malfunction, favorite hypothesis being disproved), and the scientist who cannot get back in there and try again and is not genuinely excited about the opportunity to conduct research will not be able to persevere. A sense of wonder, the need to be challenged and to solve puzzles is what draws people into scientific research in the first place, and those who succeed never lose this drive. Being incurious and content with the status quo will never lead to a successful career in science.

Each of us should never fail to encourage our young colleagues and our peers with the simple words 'you can do it'. Over and over, these words can instill confidence and provide a boost to female scientists and other aspiring scientists when they most need to hear it.

REFERENCES

AAAS Career Forum (2006), from www.sciencecareers.sciencemag.org/career_ development/ tools_resources/forum/home, retrieved 12 July.

AWIS (Association for Women in Science) (1993), *Mentoring Means Future Scientists: A Guide to Developing Mentoring Programs Based on the AWIS Mentoring Project*, Washington, DC.

Billiard, L. (1991), 'The past, present and future of women in the mathematical sciences', *Notices*, **38**, 707–14.

Ding, W.W., Murray, F. and Stuart, T.E. (2006), 'Gender differences in patenting in the academic life sciences', *Science*, **313**, 665–7.

Edisen, A. (1971), *AWIS Newsletter*, **1** (Summer), 1.

Fort, D.C. (ed.) (2005), *A Hand Up: Women Mentoring Women in Science*, Washington, DC: AWIS.

Gary, S. (2004), 'On Mentoring', *AWIS Magazine*, **33** (Autumn), 7.

Huang, A. (2003), 'Confidence or arrogance?', *AWIS Magazine*, **32** (4), 6–9.

InterAcademy Council (2006), *Women for Science Advisory Panel 2006*, Amsterdam, The Netherlands: InterAcademy Council.

Lewin, A.Y. and Duchan, L. (1971), 'Women in academia', *Science*, **173**, 892–4.

National Science Foundation, Division of Science Resources Statistics (2003), *Gender Differences in the Career of Academic Scientists and Engineers: A Literature Review*, Arlington, VA: NSF.

National Science Foundation, Division of Science Resources Statistics (2006), *Science and Engineering Indicators 2006*, Arlington, VA: NSF.

Office of Research on Women's Health (2000), *Achieving XXcellence in Science: Advancing Women's Contributions to Science through Professional Societies*, NIH Publication No. 00-4777, Bethesda, MD: National Institutes of Health.

Project ENHANCE (2004), from http://enhance.technopsychology.com, retrieved 19 June 2006.

Ruskai, M. (1996), 'Thoughts on affirmative action', *AWM Newsletter*, **26** (March–April).

Shaywitz, S. and Hahm, J. (eds) (2002), *Achieving XXcellence in Science: Role of Professional Societies in Advancing Women in Science: Proceedings of a Workshop AXXS 2002*, Washington, DC: National Academy of Sciences.

Swiss, D. (1996), *Women Breaking Through: Overcoming the Final Ten Obstacles at Work*, Princeton, NJ: Pacesetter Books.

Sztein, A.E. (2005), *Women in Science: Assessing Progress, Promoting Action. Conference Report*, Washington, DC: AWIS.

Trix, F. and Psenka, C. (2003), 'Exploring the color of glass: letters of recommendation for female and male medical faculty', *Discourse and Society*, **14**(2), 191–220.

United States Congress, Task Force on Women, Minorities, and the Handicapped in Science and Technology (1988), *Changing America: The New Face of Science and Engineering*, Washington, DC.

United States Congress, Congressional Commission on the Advancement of Women and Minorities in Science, Engineering, and Technology (2000), *Land of Plenty: Diversity as America's Competitive Edge in Science, Engineering, and Technology*, Washington, DC.

Zandonella, C. (2004), 'Turning choices into success: women in science', *New York Academy of Sciences*, from www.nyas.org/ebriefreps/main.asp?intSubsectionID=1305, retrieved 7 July 2006.

PART II

Experiences of women and minorities in STEM

3. The good, the bad and the ugly: women engineering students' experiences of UK higher education

Abigail Powell, Barbara Bagilhole and Andrew Dainty

INTRODUCTION

The UK engineering industry is quantitatively and hierarchically male-dominated. This is significant given the societal importance and impact of engineering on people's lives. Engineering has a popular image of being tough, heavy and dirty, and from a student's point of view, hard sums and greasy metal. These powerful cultural images have helped to reproduce occupational segregation whereby engineering has been perceived as unsuitable for women. Despite these widely held views, some women do decide to study engineering with the possibility of pursuing a career in the sector.

This chapter explores how some of these women experience engineering in higher education (HE) in the UK. The first part examines the issue of women in engineering and engineering education, highlighting the importance of increasing the number of professional women engineers. The second part investigates the cultures that persist in engineering and higher education generally which act as barriers to women's progression, before addressing specific cultural factors in engineering education that may hinder women's advancement to the engineering professions. The final part of the chapter sets out the findings of an Economic and Social Research Council project into these issues. It begins by describing the methodology used and proceeds to analyse women's experiences of UK engineering education in terms of the good, the bad and the ugly. These terms are explained using examples from the research findings later in the chapter.

WOMEN IN ENGINEERING

Nancy Lane, co-author of 'The Rising Tide' report on women in science, engineering and technology (SET), has commented that 'Engineering . . . is a subject where women are currently catastrophically underrepresented' (1997, p. 41). That women remain a minority in engineering has been explained in various ways, including poor or inadequate career guidance before starting university; early differential socialization of males and females; lack of support from family, friends and professional engineers; and cultural and occupational barriers (Dryburgh, 1999). Sagebiel (2003), for example, argues that studies in Europe and elsewhere have shown that women are driven away from technology not by inability in abstract thinking but by the prevailing content and climate, which construct an atmosphere of dominant masculinity.

Bagilhole (1997) has maintained that there is a business case for the increase of women in male-dominated work spheres. This essentially rests on two premises: that the industry is under-utilizing the full range of skills and talents in the population because of continuing unequal opportunities for some groups in society; and that it should be possible for organizations to increase their efficiency and effectiveness by projecting a more pluralistic self-image, thereby widening their pool of potential customers. The beneficial effects of identifying and removing discriminatory practices are direct and quantifiable, and include the reduction of costs related to staff turnover, reduced litigation fees, and accessing largely untapped reserves of skill and talent through a wider pool of applicants. Indirect benefits include improved customer service and enhanced staff morale (Dainty et al., 2004).

Over the past two decades, a number of government initiatives have been established to increase the numbers of women entering engineering education and employment. In 1984 the Women into Science and Engineering (WISE) campaign was established, promoted by the Equal Opportunities Commission and Engineering Council. The Engineering Training Authority (EnTra) has taken positive action to recruit girls and runs an Insight programme (a week-long residential course) designed to facilitate this. Approximately 40 per cent of those attending the Insight course subsequently choose to attend engineering courses at university (Opportunity 2000, 1996). The Construction Careers Service, a part of the CITB (Construction Industry Training Board), also has a number of initiatives to heighten awareness in the construction sector. These include work shadowing, provision of speakers at careers events, free brochures, videos and literature, careers seminars for teachers and careers advisers, school/industry links, and curriculum centres (Gale, 1994).

While these initiatives are commendable, and have been effective in attracting women to the industry (Dainty, 1998), such measures are a response to skill shortages in technological expertise, rather than a determined drive to tackle the gendered culture of the industry (Walker, 2001), which will be discussed in more detail below. In this case it may be appropriate to question whether more women should be encouraged to become engineers, given the problems they are likely to face in the industry (Carter and Kirkup, 1990). Furthermore, Etzkowitz et al. (2000) have indicated that policies to increase numbers of women in engineering are not sufficient, as it does not automatically mean a change in culture (for further discussion of the 'critical mass' debate see Powell et al., 2006).

WOMEN IN ENGINEERING EDUCATION

Initiatives such as those described above have had some success in increasing the proportion of women studying engineering. Glover (2000) reported that in 1973 only 3 per cent of engineering and technology undergraduates were women. This is compared to 15 per cent in 2004/05 (HESA, 2006). However, figures vary widely by subject, with highs of 68 per cent and 60 per cent in polymers and textiles and ceramics and glasses, respectively, and lows of 8 per cent and 10 per cent in mechanical and electrical engineering respectively (HESA, 2006). The proportion of women studying engineering not only remains low in comparison to other subjects (only 1.6 per cent of all female students in HE are based in engineering, HESA, 2006), but the increase in women engineering students has failed to translate into an equivalent increase in female engineering professionals, with suggestions that less than 10 per cent of professional engineers are women (Fielding and Glover, 1997). More recent estimates suggest that women only account for 6 per cent of engineers and technologists in professional or associate professional and technical occupations (ONS, 2000). This is also despite recent research funded by the Scottish HE Funding Council indicating that although numbers may be low, female engineers are generally perceived to be better qualified and more highly motivated than their male counterparts, and at graduation women often receive numerous job offers (SHEFC, 1997).

CULTURE

Much of the above analysis indicates that the difficulties women have penetrating the engineering industry may be a result of the deep-seated culture ingrained within engineering organizations. Evetts (1997), for example, considers that cultural aspects and gendered images have been important in explaining statistical differences between men and women's career achievements. This section will, therefore, further investigate organizational culture and the relationship between organizations and gender, as well as looking specifically at the engineering culture.

How we choose to define culture has important consequences for how we attempt to examine it. Brown (1995) writes that there are many different definitions of organizational culture, although most commentators have chosen to think of culture as an objective entity. Agreement on this, however, still leaves room for a broad spectrum of opinion on other details. According to Pacanowsky and O'Donnell-Trujillo (1982), an organization *is* a culture, and all features of an organization, including its systems, policies, procedures and processes, are elements of its cultural life. While this is an intellectually coherent position, many theorists have resisted it, because if everything is culture, it is impossible for the concept to frame causal explanations of other aspects of organizational activity. In contrast, other authors, such as Schein (1985), have suggested that culture is best thought of as a set of psychological predispositions that members of an organization possess, and which leads them to think and act in certain ways. While the view that culture is essentially a cognitive phenomenon residing in the psychology of organizational participants is widespread, many theorists, such as Eldridge and Crombie (1974), acknowledge that patterns of behaviour are equally important. Brown (1995, p. 9) chooses to define organizational culture as 'the pattern of beliefs, values and learned ways of coping with experience that have developed during the course of an organisation's history, and which tend to be manifested in its material arrangements and in the behaviour of its members'.

Gender is fundamental to the culture of organizations, as has been shown in studies in other sectors (for example, Ledwith and Colgan, 1996). Itzin (1995) described organizational culture as hierarchical, patriarchal, sex-segregated, sexually divided, sexist, misogynist, resistant to change, and to contain gendered power structures. Hofstede (1984) contends that masculinity forms a key element of corporate culture. West and Zimmerman (1987), for example, suggest that men and women 'do' gender in social interaction, despite perceiving that they act in gender-free or gender-neutral ways. Since people bring their beliefs about gender into social relations with little thought, gendered performance is pervasive and taken for granted (Ridgeway, 1997). While participants in organizational culture may believe they express personal taste and inclinations, Gherardi (1994) maintains that knowledge of what fits with the organizational style is an acquired skill. Gherardi therefore argues that the way we 'do' gender in work can help diminish or increase inequality between the sexes.

Engineering Culture

The central role of engineering in society and the economy is not evident to the public at large, nor to the media in particular. The engineering profession is, according to Malpas (2000), considered by many as a somewhat dull, uncreative activity, associated with the so-called 'old economy'. Historically the image of engineering has been tough, heavy and dirty, and to do with machinery. In terms of cultural image, engineering is perceived as a masculine profession. This is not only because the workforce is male, but because the prevailing culture and ethos of the industry appears to be extremely male (Gale, 1994). These cultural images have remained powerful and have helped to reproduce the perception that engineering is unsuitable for women (Evetts, 1998). This is a somewhat cyclical process, reinforcing the masculinity of the industry. It has been argued that this is a result of the polarized characteristics supposedly attached to gender in the process of socialization. Sagebiel (2003) states that engineering can be considered gendered in three ways. First, gendered structures are visible in gender difference in the division of labour and in the work styles of women and men. Second, the symbols and images of engineering knowledge and practice are gendered through cultural associations between masculinity and technology. And third, individual engineers have gendered personal and professional identities and experiences.

It is also the case that women suffer if they go against such cultural dictates (Evetts, 1998). This is supported by Glover et al. (1996), who indicated that women actively choose not to enter SET careers in the knowledge that they are likely to feel discomfort. This is because when women undertake 'male work', they upset a widely accepted sense of order and meaning (Cockburn, 1985). Although women can cope with the actual engineering work, they are likely to find it much more difficult to cope with the engineering culture (Evetts, 1998). Some women therefore pay both personal and social costs when they cross the threshold into a male domain. Opportunity 2000 (1996) suggests that this is because young women in science and engineering, for example, find themselves working with the values, systems and performance criteria that have been set up by men for men, and not for women.

By contrast, Bennett et al. (1999) claim that women who seek a career in the construction industry are socialized into its culture through the education system and appear actively to seek that culture. Gale (1994) described gender values as a continuum ranging from male to female and suggests that women holding similar values are attracted to similar occupations. Bennett et al. (1999) do, however, concede that the reverse is also true: many women reject the construction culture as acceptable, as do many men.

HE Culture

The Hansard Society Commission Report (1990) described British universities as male bastions of privilege and power, and claimed that women's
chances of entry, promotion and retention are generally lower than
women's. Morley (2000) argues that academia maintains its gendered
power relations through everyday practices such as bullying, stalling, sab-
otage, manipulation and spite. Such occurrences appear trivial, subtle and
difficult to capture, but at the same time they reveal the ways in which competition and domination are played out. According to Morley, the study of
micropolitics in HE can illuminate ways in which organizational power
accrues. Even in countries that are considered to be at the forefront of promoting gender equality, such as Finland, women still encounter subtle
forms of discrimination (Husu, 2001).

Bebbington (2002) suggests that the pattern of vertical segregation (the
further one goes up the hierarchy, the fewer the women) persists in all disciplines, including business, social studies and language-based studies.
There are nevertheless disciplinary differences, with women best represented in language-based studies at almost every grade and worst represented in engineering and technology.

Bagilhole and Woodward (1995) have shown that sexual harassment is
an underrecognized and underestimated phenomenon in the UK academic
profession and a strong indicator that the problem lies with the academic
culture. Morley (1999) argues that employment issues are highly linked
to epistemology, with discrimination against women perpetuating and
upholding the male perspective in academia.

Davies and Holloway (1995, p. 13) found that in the HE sector, 'equal
opportunities . . . is seen very much as an employment issue, and not as an
issue which relates to the delivery of educational courses and research'.
This is a serious omission because, as Weiner explains, the curriculum is 'of
crucial interest because it highlights and problematises taken for granted
assumptions about knowledge, gender and culture . . . it is socially constructed and as such, is both a reflection of dominant ideas and a place
where these ideas are played out or resisted through practice' (1994,
pp. 3–4). However, there are some exceptions. Thomas (1990), for example,
looked at the relationship between the 'culture' of certain subjects and how
women and men students related to them, exploring gender relations in the
context of specific curriculum discourses and practices. She found that
female science students saw themselves as a homogeneous group that was
different and uncomfortably visible in 'a masculine preserve'. Evans (1995,
p. 73) argues that because 'control, rather than consumption [of the
curriculum], is in the hands of men . . . the very assumptions of

the academy – its claims to universal and generally applicable knowledge – have to be challenged'. Bagilhole and Goode (1998) suggest that male academics have defined not only what is taught in universities, but also how it is taught, in a way that marginalizes women.

Despite some re-evaluation of curricula, Bagilhole and Goode (1998) have found that changes in the actual practice of curriculum design, staff–student interaction and assessment are slower and more patchy in traditional institutions of learning, such as 'old' universities, where questions of epistemology and pedagogy have gone largely unexamined. They suggest that the innovation now taking place in universities seems to have come from three directions. First, equal opportunity (EO) specialists are now beginning to undertake EO audits of the curriculum. Second, where women scholars are themselves represented, *completely new curricula* have appeared as a result of feminist endeavours. Third, in the traditionally male-dominated science and engineering disciplines, concerns have centred around *access to subjects* where female representation is poor. Bagilhole and Goode (1998) also found that individuals could operate either a 'narrow' or 'broad' definition of the curriculum, whereby the curriculum might be taken as simply referring to the topics to be covered in a particular course/module or the whole process of teaching and learning and all the activities in their various contexts which take place during that process.

HE Engineering Culture

Mills and Ayre (2003) suggest that there have been a number of findings that many women experience a 'chilly climate' in SET courses, and it is likely that other minority groups share similar experiences. Unhappy or uncomfortable students are unlikely to achieve their full potential and may even leave the course. Some of the features of the 'chilly climate' identified by Mills and Ayre (2003) include:

- false assumptions by lecturers that all students have prior 'tinkering' experience (practical familiarity with technology, equipment and appliances) (Lewis, 1995);
- lack of excitement in the content or presentation of the course (Nair and Majetich, 1995);
- apparent lack of relevance in the curriculum content (Lewis, 1995; Lintern, 1995);
- teaching methods that are appropriate for only a very limited range of learning styles (Lewis, 1995; Jolly, 1996);
- disruptive behaviour of majority groups (e.g. white male students throwing paper planes) (Lintern, 1995; Jolly, 1996), and

- classroom atmosphere uncomfortable for some students because of racism, sexism, or similar attitudes (Lewis, 1995; Lintern, 1995; Jolly, 1996; McLean et al., 1997).

On the other hand, McIlwee and Robinson (1992, p. 50) argue that engineering HE culture values academic work at which women excel, and that it is engineering workplace cultures that value such masculine strengths as 'a fascination with technology, expertise as a tinkerer, and an aggressive style of self-presentation'. They argue that knowing how to conform to the masculine engineering culture and doing it well are critical to women's success in the workplace. However, they consider that this only becomes an issue when women make the transition from education to work. They believe that in the workplace women engineers not only have to show competence in their knowledge and skills, but also have to learn to perform and enact masculine norms of attitude and interaction. While this is not disputed, McIlwee and Robinson fail to recognize that the very knowledge and skills women learn in engineering education, or at least the ways in which these skills are taught and learnt, also encompass masculine norms and attitudes.

Sagebiel (2003) argued that an improved curriculum could make both the climate and content of teaching appropriate to attract and retain both men and women. Brainard et al. (n.d.) suggest that improved teaching is particularly relevant to women and that men are less affected by poor teaching, poor organization of course material and by dull course content. The US National Council for Research on Women report (Thorn, 2000) has shown the importance of the first year for women having entered engineering in HE. Since women tend to evolve an interest in technology over time, the typical first-year 'killer' exams designed to weed out students rather than invite their participation may be counterproductive for retaining female students. Copeland (1995, p. 18), however, indicates that 'recognising the different skills, perspectives and learning styles that women bring to engineering and incorporating these into the teaching and learning environment' means challenging the assumptions and practices within engineering itself.

Part of the problem may be that once the decision to study engineering has been made, commitment to the field does not automatically follow. Etzkowitz et al. (2000, p. 133) show that educational experiences have a cascade effect on commitment: 'A cascade of affirming experiences serves to amplify a string of positive effects, until there is a short-circuit and the process is reversed . . . what had the potential for a cumulative positive cascade of experience becomes short-circuited by negative experiences.'

Lewis (1995, p. 270) found engineering teaching to be strongly male biased: 'The research questions, methods, criteria of success, and styles of teaching are male defined, and consequently, the knowledge itself reflects a bias towards a male cognitive style in its practices, theories, and ways of teaching.' This is a worrying trend given that Mills and Ayre (2003) emphasize the desirability of structuring an engineering curriculum around a general recognition that students from diverse backgrounds bring different perspectives, attitudes and values to the engineering classroom, without making distinctions between the specific cultural groups represented in the class. This is supported by Sagebiel (2003), who suggested that an improved curriculum would make both the climate and content of teaching appropriate to attract and retain both men and women. Improved teaching is particularly relevant to women, as the WEPAN (Women in Engineering: Programmes and Advocates Network) policy climate survey, exploring the environment for undergraduate engineering students, found that men are less affected by poor teaching, poor organization of course material and by dull course content (see Sagebiel, 2003).

Thomas (1990) showed that disillusionment among students has arisen through excessive maths and quantitative content, narrowness and the abstraction of the curriculum, lack of relevance to the 'outside' world, too early specialization and the need to conform to rigid rules, without the opportunity to challenge them. This has led to passive learning, acceptance of facts on trust, and frustration. In terms of the learning context and curriculum, both Greed (1991) and Thomas (1990) describe the impersonal and indifferent atmosphere of science and technology departments. This is manifested, for example, in formal teaching methods and the interpretation of professionalism in masculine terms. As Byrne (1987) points out, teaching styles in science and technology are instrumental and non-negotiable. As a result of these methods of teaching there is little debate, interaction or concern for the aesthetic.

Madhill et al. (2003) write that career decision making is affected by a number of factors, of which hands-on experience is particularly influential. Without the opportunity for hands-on learning, students report that they do not automatically appreciate the application of what they are studying to their personal aspirations and the things they care about. Many students in Srivastava's (1996) study also pointed to the lack of opportunity for practical work. They felt that the emphasis on broad, theoretical, historical and textbook contexts was irrelevant, limited in usefulness and remote from industry.

Mills and Ayre (2003) suggest that the typical engineering curriculum has been blamed for the difficulties in recruiting and retaining female engineering students. Beder (1989) describes it as showing an 'obsession with the technical, the mathematical, and the scientific, and an almost complete neglect of the social, political and environmental issues' which discourages 'students with broader interests, a different range of talents . . . ; those who want to work with people rather than machines and numbers, those who care about social relations. Too often it is the female students who are put off' (Beder, 1989, p. 173). Thomas (1990) also suggests that HE curriculum is male-centred. She shows that subjects are not neutral but gendered in that they are socially and culturally constructed.

Using construction as a specific example of a SET subject or discipline, Srivastava (1996) recommended a number of changes be made to the HE curriculum. These included presenting construction disciplines in a social context; considering practical applications; integrating modules from social sciences and humanities; questioning assumptions, traditions and the culture of construction education and practice; relating topics to a range of student experiences; addressing the social and environmental impact and benefits of construction; incorporating interactive, qualitative, critical and ethical considerations in projects; and mentoring of students and staff who are in a minority. She also suggested that feminist perceptions of science and technology should be incorporated into the construction curriculum, to facilitate questioning of assumptions, and challenge conservatism and traditionalism in the construction curriculum industry. There should be further easing of professional bodies' influence on construction course design and content, and more autonomy given to construction tutors to make space in the curriculum for new and more relevant areas, and also for independent study, reflection, discussion and debate.

Bagilhole and Goode's (1998) research found that in science and engineering faculties a narrow definition of the term curriculum was predominantly in use, seen as referring to a well-defined body of knowledge which was to be transferred to students largely by lecturing. This is in line with Thomas's (1990) study, which showed science departments characterized by a formality of pedagogy which involved the definitive authority of lecturers and the passivity and dependency of the students, the predominant use of the lecture, the abstract nature of the subject content, and the heavy amount of prescribed and controlled laboratory work. Bagilhole and Goode found that although concerns in science and engineering departments centred around access, in practice this referred to access to courses, in terms of recruitment of undergraduates, and did not encompass access to the curriculum itself, or considerations of how far there are differential curricula and therefore differential access to and engagement with particular aspects of the curriculum.

Bagilhole and Goode's study showed that awareness of issues in curriculum innovation was highest in the social sciences and humanities where a gender dimension had been introduced into the curriculum. However, departments with few women students or staff failed to recognize the issues.

Bagilhole and Goode identified that the main problem in these departments was with the common view that any 'problem' lies 'out there' rather than 'in here', alongside a view that women undergraduates were going to have to operate in the 'real world'. The university was seen therefore to serve them best by equipping them, while they were there, to cope with rather than to challenge discrimination when they leave.

Bagilhole and Goode consider that the educators in the engineering world are stuck in an increasingly outdated mould. It is perceived that women need to change to accommodate industry, not the other way around – women must learn to adjust to industry, cope with it, become fitted to it. Women engineering undergraduates at the university in their study were apparently learning to be discriminated against. The role of the university was seen simply to prepare them for 'real life' and anything else was seen as unfair. Both the formal and informal curricula remain gender-blind in their operation – and in the name of equality are treating all students 'the same'.

METHODOLOGY

The research presented in this chapter is based on an Economic and Social Research Council funded project aimed at developing an understanding of women engineers' earliest encounters with engineering workplaces on their future career intentions. Workplace experiences were examined in the form of the year-long industrial placement taken in HE, as this usually represents women's first main contact with the engineering industry. A major part of this research also included an investigation of women students' experiences of engineering education across a range of engineering and related disciplines, including construction/civil, aeronautical, mechanical, design and technology, and materials. The research adopted a longitudinal, mixed methods approach, combining interviews, focus groups, documentary analysis and a questionnaire.

The initial stage of the research used a qualitative approach to explore the experiences and reflections of women engineering students. Two semi-structured interviews were conducted with 26 industrial placement students at a pre- and post-1992 university. Access to students was facilitated through university databases and industrial placement coordinators in each of the engineering, or related, departments at the two universities. The use of a semi-structured interview schedule for both sets of interviews meant that key issues identified by the researchers (e.g. influences and reasons for undertaking their particular degree, experiences of their learning environment, the transition to work, placement experiences, future career intentions, and so on) could be explored, while at the same time interviewees could define issues according to their own experiences and understandings. Following this stage, two focus groups of the same women were conducted. The purpose of the focus groups was to explore how women's attitudes and career intentions had changed as a result of the placement process, and to allow the women to compare and contrast their experiences. Only 13 of the original cohort participated in the focus groups, as a number of women dropped out of the research due to other commitments having to take priority.

The pre-placement interview stage of the research was complemented by including an additional 26 interviews with women students at the pre- and post-1992 universities who had chosen not to go on industrial placement. These interviews explored similar issues to those described above, as well as investigating women's decisions not to go on placement. Access to these students was facilitated through university databases and programme coordinators.

The interviews were tape-recorded and the focus groups video-recorded, then transcribed verbatim and anonymized, before being analysed with the computer software NVivo. NVivo was used to employ an approach informed by grounded theory, searching for meaning in the data and generating theory from rich, detailed descriptions in the interview transcripts. The initial analysis began with open coding, breaking down, examining, comparing, conceptualizing and categorizing the data (Strauss and Corbin, 1990); axial coding then ensured relationships between categories were systematically developed and that all similarities and differences were captured in the final analysis (Langdridge, 2004). The cumulative analysis of findings led to the eventual development of theories and explanations grounded in the data, reflecting the complex nature of the social phenomena investigated.

FINDINGS AND DISCUSSION

The research revealed a number of findings relating to women students' experiences of engineering in HE, which range from 'good' to 'bad' to 'ugly'. The findings under each of these headings are elaborated below, although it is important to note that findings are not exclusive but intertwined and mutually reinforcing. Interestingly, a number of the findings concerning women's attitudes are also contradictory, indicating that the themes discussed below are operating on a subconscious level for the women involved in the research and as a result of negotiating complex discourses concerning their relationship with gender and engineering (French, 2005).

The Good

The majority of women engineering students interviewed were positive about their career choice and their courses. The 'good' aspects of studying engineering at university were described as peer camaraderie and relationships with other students, the support of lecturers and personal tutors, and the opportunity to undertake an industrial placement between years two and three of the degree programme.

One particularly favourable aspect about engineering programmes was deemed to be the student relationships and camaraderie, a view often expressed with comparison to other courses:

> All my course mates, they're really friendly and helpful, not like some other courses. Some other courses they don't know who are on the course and they don't communicate. (Victoria, Chemical Engineering student)

> The best thing is the people you meet. They're all kind of like minded . . . because it's such a difficult degree everybody helps each other, like when we've got a really tough piece of coursework . . . the people who've done it will come over and help the people who haven't. It's a really nice spirit amongst everyone. (Jenny, Aeronautical Engineering student)

This is possibly a result of the levels of group work and the volume and intensity of the work involved in engineering programmes (although, as will be shown later, these women students were more critical of these issues in themselves).

Women students were found to praise lecturers, with most students finding them approachable, supportive and motivating:

> Some of the lecturers are quite good and it makes you think, I want to go into the industry, because they've been in the industry before . . . he'll tell you what sort of things have happened, and how it can be fun and exciting and it can sound very interesting. (Frances, Air Transport Management student)

> There's always the support there and the lecturers are really good. If you've got a problem you can always go and find them and get help. (Sophie, Mechanical Engineering student)

The same praise was afforded to personal tutors too, although less frequently, possibly as a result of the under-utilization of the personal tutor system. However, students' positive regard of personal tutors suggests that it is an area that should be encouraged and promoted within the university system.

> I really feel like [personal tutor] really looks out for me. And I see him more as a final student or big brother figure. (Katie, Industrial Design and Technology student)

Women students also favoured the diversity of engineering courses, often citing this as a reason for having chosen to study engineering over other courses:

> I think there's always something different you know, there's never two days the same. (Diana, Mechanical Engineering student)

> With aeronautical . . . I liked it because it was so broad, you learnt everything from, you know, electrical to mechanical to, you know, say systems and programming. (Emily, Aeronautical Engineering student)

However, this also created something of a dilemma for students, who, while valuing the diversity of their courses, often found it difficult to recognize the relevance of aspects of the course and criticized the volume and intensity of their work load, as will be demonstrated later.

The opportunity and experience of taking an industrial placement was also perceived as advantageous. The placement was perceived as an opportunity to experience a side of engineering that cannot be taught or replicated in the classroom. It also had the potential to ease students' transition to engineering employment by familiarizing them with the engineering workplace.

> [The placement] shows that you have got some idea [that you are] grounded in industry rather than saying I know all this theory like everyone else does. You can apply it, know what's needed for what. (Hayley, Mechanical Engineering student)

> [The placement will] be learning about the whole different way of how it all works and meeting different people, earning some money, and being one step closer to actually being independent. (Lisa, Materials Engineering student)

Generally, university support for finding placements was viewed well, although provision for this varied between departments. For further discussion of women's experiences of the engineering placement see Powell et al. (2005).

Although some students chose not to go on placement, this was usually for personal reasons such as having had industrial experience before starting university, being restricted to a particular geographical location, or not wanting to lose friends from courses who didn't go on placement, rather than viewing the placement as worthless.

The Bad

Women students were, however, found to be more critical of structural issues, such as the teaching and learning methods on their engineering programmes. Criticism was particularly directed at curriculum content and the relevance of particular modules:

> Some of the work we do, you're like why? Why do I need to know this? Or, why are we learning it now? I think we could have spent more time on other stuff. (Hannah, Civil Engineering student)

> Sometimes . . . you think what the hell is going on here? When you're doing this crazy maths you think 'what does this apply to?' But you've just got to ask, 'what's this in real life?' and then they'll tell you. (Tracey, Aeronautical Engineering student)

Negative perceptions of the volume and intensity of work involved in engineering were particularly forthcoming on the Industrial Design and Technology course:

> It's been a lot more hours than I thought it'd be, it's like 24-7, just working. I've got lectures most of the day, and then I'm working at night to do the stuff that they've set us in our lectures. (Jessica, Industrial Design and Technology student)

> The worst things are the amount of work . . . we have a lot of deadlines in at the same time. You don't get much sleep at all. A lot of the work is very time consuming . . . there's always an on-going project. But then, I suppose that's something I like anyway. (Elizabeth, Industrial Design and Technology student)

The women students also complained about the lack of practical work. While most students realized that theory was an essential part of the learning process, they also believed that practical hands-on work could play a greater role in the course:

> I expected it to be a bit more practical. The theory isn't too bad, but there's so much to take in and to understand . . . I think for me, I'd personally like a bit more of the practical. (Chloe, Mechanical Engineering student)

Students also had a tendency to prefer coursework to exams, although it accounted for very little of the assessment:

> I think the worst thing is definitely the exams, because they were so hard, and I worked really hard for them . . . I think the people that are more practical are probably the people who don't do so well in these exams. They are so theoretical. (Samantha, Civil Engineering student)

These experiences are not entirely surprising given that Lewis (1995) described the teaching and learning methods that make up the structure of engineering HE as 'strongly male biased'. While students' opinions in the research are not as strong as those described in the literature, it is evident that the women students did not always approve of, of feel comfortable with, curriculum content, assessment methods, the volume of work and the emphasis on theory, rather than practice.

Possible solutions to the traditional teaching and learning methods in engineering and related courses involve, among other things, introducing greater choice for students, such as the option to choose management or social science modules, or 'softer' engineering modules that address the social and environmental impact of engineering, as suggested by Srivastava (1996). The difficulties with this are that core modules may have to be dropped to make way for change; the volume of work the students had was considered overwhelming, so to introduce additional modules would be unrealistic. However, on many courses the modules and topics covered are dictated by the professional bodies that accredit courses (students also need to cover certain areas to get Chartered Engineer status), which are unlikely to favour the introduction of optional modules. The ethos and rigidity of the system in engineering therefore implies that if individuals want to achieve in the sector they must conform to existing masculine norms and attitudes (McIlwee and Robinson, 1992). Furthermore, with regard to the lack of practical engineering, Short et al. (2003) have written that where students are able to see the reality of engineering and the application of their knowledge to real engineering problems, their enthusiasm can more easily be generated, suggesting that such an improvement to engineering programmes would benefit all students regardless of gender.

The Ugly

The findings described as 'ugly' relate less to the structure of engineering education and more to non-structural aspects of the engineering culture, such as people's attitudes towards women in engineering. It is felt that these aspects are particularly detrimental to women students and their commitment to engineering. These everyday occurrences build up to the point where some students decide engineering is not for them.

In contradiction to the favourable remarks concerning camaraderie among engineering students, women students were also found to have difficulties communicating with male students and staff, and being taken seriously when it came to work:

> Trying to get the boys to listen to anything you're saying is difficult . . . the boys just wouldn't listen to a word that Rachel was saying . . . I had to persuade them to listen to what she was saying, and I found that really frustrating that they just wouldn't listen. (Emma, Mechanical Engineering student)

Communication was non-existent and I was left out in one way or another. They wouldn't tell me there was a group meeting . . . It was peer assessed . . . they marked me right down, which I felt was completely unfair because within the boundaries they'd placed on me, I'd done the best I could. (Andrea, Civil Engineering student)

While students generally thought that group work was beneficial, poor communication appeared inherent. This is somewhat paradoxical given that group work at university is presumably intended to improve communication skills for the workplace. There are two possible explanations here. First, students are not taught how to do or manage group work, but it is expected that they will learn through practice. Second, it may be that collaboration and teamwork is ineffective in HE because of the individualistic nature of the university system, where students achieve, and are awarded degrees, on the basis of individual merit.

Relationships between staff and female students and staff and male students were often perceived as unequal. This was particularly apparent with regard to tutorial and laboratory work, where some members of staff, often technicians rather than lecturers, were found to give more help to female students:

It's nice [tutors] go all out to help you, but it can feel sometimes that it's because you're a girl that they go all out to help you and it can be a little bit sleazy. One guy . . . he's just really unbelievable. He'll take you from the back of the queue, bring you right in front of all these lads and help you – pretty much do it for you, which you're not going to complain if someone's offering to help, but then you get grief off the lads . . . they put you at a disadvantage. (Fiona, Industrial Design and Technology student)

However, one student legitimized this, suggesting that female students attract more help because they appear less confident with their work than male students:

I think some of the male lecturers are more helpful to the girls than to the guys . . . but then I think it might be because the girls come across as less confident that the teachers want to help them more. (Elizabeth, Industrial Design and Technology student)

While some students described the extra help they unwittingly received as a result of the gender as patronizing, many women perceived this as positive. Nevertheless, this poses a particular problem because it indicates that women in engineering are seen as less capable than their male counterparts, which may be counterproductive in the long term. For example, while it may seem useful to get extra help, in the future it may result in women being overlooked when promotion decisions are being made, if they are perceived by employers as requiring extra help and support to succeed in the work-place. In the more immediate term it may instil resentment in male col-leagues and works to reinforce the idea that women are less capable in engineering among male engineering students:

> There's this one assistant in our department and he is known for helping girls out more than boys . . . the boys get a bit angry. (Maria, Industrial Design and Technology student)

The differential treatment of male and female students by staff went beyond the women students receiving more help, to sexist attitudes and humour, although this was generally accepted as 'joking' by women.

> One of our lecturers just makes women jokes, which are alright, they're not offensive, but you just get bored with them every lesson. (Paula, Mechanical Engineering student)

> Now and then they'll make obviously female jokes but I wouldn't say they nec-essarily treat you differently on purpose. (Amanda, Industrial Design and Technology student)

There was also a feeling among students that male lecturers felt uncom-fortable with female students:

> Well some of [the male lecturers] struggle . . . they're quite happy to sit and chat to the guys but then find it very hard . . . they don't really know what to say [to the women students] it's almost as if you're not somebody who's normal. I mean there are extreme sides of it, there's one lecturer who completely could not hold down a conversation with a girl if he tried. (Eve, Civil Engineering student)

In addition, one student felt she was made particularly visible because of her gender and singled out when a lecturer complained to her personal tutor that she had missed a lecture. The student felt victimized because the lecturer failed to notice if male students were absent from class. Another student felt that when she complained that the male students she was working with were treating her unfairly, her female personal tutor failed to take her seriously:

> I told [my personal tutor] there were boys who were harassing me . . . they'd end up giving me the work . . . I told her about it and she was like, 'well, it'll pass' . . . she didn't even call them to talk to them. (Anna, Commercial Management and Quantity Surveying student)

A final factor described by women engineering students was the idea that universities may be 'playing a numbers game' by trying to increase the number of women on engineering courses to improve their image. There are two key problems with this. While a drive to recruit more women is a positive step, alone this is unlikely to challenge or transform the masculine cultures and structures in engineering education and industry. Furthermore, as demonstrated in this research, it has the effect of making women doubt their own capability to do the work required:

> They were desperate to get me on the course because they needed to balance out their numbers. I've always felt like I don't know if I would have got on this course if I'd been a bloke . . . They didn't even look at my work, so they couldn't have known, and every bloke I've spoken to has a really vigorous interview. (Rebecca, Industrial Design and Technology student)

> One guy . . . said you are bound to get [a bursary] because at the end of the day they really need girls in engineering. And it really, really upset me. (Sophie, Mechanical Engineering student)

CONCLUSIONS AND RECOMMENDATIONS

To summarize, this chapter has explored women engineering students' experiences of UK higher education. It has investigated the pervading culture of engineering education and shown that women's experiences of this range from good to bad to ugly. Women's 'good' experiences included peer camaraderie, staff support and the industrial placement, while 'bad' experiences have been focused on structural aspects of HE, such as teaching and learning methods, and the 'ugly' (judged to be the most harmful to women students' commitment and career aspirations) has been associated with what others have called a masculine engineering culture, largely consisting of people's negative attitudes towards women in engineering.

It is clear from these interpretations that women's experiences of engineering education are contrasting and at times in conflict with one another, highlighting the fact that the 'good', the 'bad' and the 'ugly' experiences are in many ways mutually reinforcing. While the ugly experiences are the only area where women have faced obvious discrimination, the gendered culture of engineering and more subtle forms of discrimination are evident throughout. Peer camaraderie, for example, may demonstrate women's socialization into the masculine engineering culture, as this issue was often framed competitively, with students comparing their experiences to those of students on other courses. This is supported by Bennett et al. (1999), who maintained that women who seek a career in a male-dominated industry are socialized into its culture through the education system, and appear to actively seek that culture. This also corroborates West and Zimmerman's (1987) argument that both men and women 'do' gender, despite believing that their behaviour is gender-neutral. The apparent criticism of staff and student relationships also makes it difficult to comprehend women's praise for staff support and peer camaraderie. However, it is important to note that women's experiences were categorized by the authors rather than the women themselves. In fact, women engineering students generally viewed the whole experience of engineering education positively in spite of admitting to the various structural and cultural problems identified above. This is further evidence of women's assimilation to the engineering culture and their, probably subconscious, knowledge that they are likely to suffer if they go against the unspoken cultural norms (Evetts, 1998). In this way, women engineers may help maintain gender inequality through their knowledge of what fits with the accepted organizational style (Gherardi, 1994).

In addition, the bad and ugly experiences, or the structural and cultural problems which women engineers experience in HE, are closely intertwined, with both impacting heavily on women's learning experiences. While the structural aspects of engineering education, namely the teaching and learning methods, or the formal curriculum, could be readily changed if desired (and possibly to the benefit of many male students), previous research has shown that re-evaluation of the curricula is slow to happen (Bagilhole and Goode, 1998). This is probably because the control of the curriculum is in the hands of men (Evans, 1995), who often believe that women need to change to accommodate industry, or learn to be discriminated against (Bagilhole and Goode, 1998). In other words, the structure or curriculum in engineering education is socially constructed, as Weiner (1994) has argued, and highlights assumptions about gender and knowledge. Bagilhole and Goode (1998) have also shown that the culture and dominant attitudes, or what they call the informal curriculum, is learnt by both male and female students, resulting in maintenance of the masculine ethos of engineering.

These arguments point to some of the difficulties of transforming the engineering culture to ensure the engineering professions are a place where women can not only survive, but also thrive. Even change in areas that could be achieved, such as in teaching and learning methods, may be difficult due to resistance from those who uphold the masculine culture of engineering. However, it might also be argued that improved teaching and learning methods could stimulate cultural change.

In conclusion, this chapter has supported and elaborated the extant knowledge on women in engineering education. However, it has also offered a new classification of the structural and cultural influences impacting upon women's experiences (the 'good', the 'bad' and the 'ugly'). At the same time, it is evident from the findings that any progress towards change requires a multi-institutional approach aimed at enhancing the 'good', addressing the 'bad', and precluding the 'ugly'. While such an approach should build on the positive aspects identified by women, such as personal tutor support and the industrial placement, responsibility for implementing structural change should be taken by professional engineering bodies, such as the UK Engineering Council, and cultural change by HE employers, trade unions and student unions, among others. As Sagebiel (2003) has argued, the success of such important and much-needed changes are also likely to be dependent on promoting the benefits they could have for *all* students, not just women.

REFERENCES

Bagilhole, B. (1997), *Equal Opportunities and Social Policy: Issues of Gender, Race and Disability*, London: Longman.

Bagilhole, B. and Goode, J. (1998), 'The "gender dimension" of both the "narrow" and "broad" curriculum in UK higher education: do women lose out in both?', *Gender and Education*, **10**(4), 445–58.

Bagilhole, B. and Woodward, H. (1995), 'An occupational hazard warning: academic life can seriously damage your health. An investigation of sexual harassment of women academics in a UK university', *British Journal of Sociology of Education*, **16**(1), 37–51.

Bebbington, D. (2002), 'Women in science, engineering and technology: a review of the issues', *Higher Education Quarterly*, **56**(4), 360–75.

Beder, S. (1989), 'Towards a more representative engineering education', *International Journal of Applied Engineering Education*, **5**(2), 173–82.

Bennett, J.F., Davidson, M.J. and Gale, A.W. (1999), 'Women in construction: a comparative investigation into the expectations and experiences of female and male construction undergraduates and employees', *Women in Management Review*, **14**(7), 273–91.

Brainard, S.G., Staffin Metz, S. and Gillmore, G.M. (n.d.), *WEPAN Pilot Climate Survey: Exploring the Environment for Undergraduate Engineering Students*. Available at: www.wepan.org/associations/5413/files/Climate%20Survey.pdf (accessed June 2006).

Brown, A. (1995), *Organisational Culture*, London: Pitman Publishing.

Byrne, E.M. (1987), 'Education for equality', in M. Arnot and G. Weiner (eds), *Gender and the Politics of Schooling*, London: Unwin Hyman, pp. 23–34.

Carter, R. and Kirkup, G. (1990), *Women in Engineering: A Good Place to Be?*, Basingstoke: Macmillan.

Cockburn, C. (1985), *Machinery of Dominance*, London: Pluto Press.

Copeland, J. (1995), *Not Stirring Up Trouble: Women Engineering Students' Talk*, Melbourne, Australia: Second Australian Women in Engineering Forum, pp. 13–18.

Dainty, A.R.J. (1998), *A Grounded Theory, of the Determinants of Women's Underachievement in large Construction Companies*, PhD thesis, Loughborough University.

Dainty, A.R.J., Bagilhole, B.M., Ansari, K.H. and Jackson, J. (2004), 'Creating, equality in the construction industry: an agenda for change for women and ethnic minorities', *Journal of Construction Research*, **5**(1), 75–86.

Davies, C. and Holloway, P. (1995), 'Troubling transformations: gender regimes and organisational culture in the academy', in L. Morley and V. Walsh (eds), *Feminist Academics: Creative Agents for Change*, London: Taylor & Francis, pp. 7–21.

Dryburgh, H. (1999), 'Work hard, play hard: women and professionalisation in engineering – adapting to the culture', *Gender and Society*, **13**(5), 664–82.

Eldridge, J.E.T. and Crombie, A.D. (1974), *A Sociology of Organisations*, London: Allen and Unwin.

Etzkowitz, H., Kemelgor, C. and Uzzi, B. (2000), *Athena Unbound: The Advancement of Women in Science and Technology*, Cambridge: Cambridge University Press.

Evans, M. (1995), 'Ivory towers: life in the mind', in L. Morley and V. Walsh (eds), *Feminist Academics: Creative Agents for Change*, London: Taylor & Francis, pp. 73–85.

Evetts, J. (1997), 'Women and careers in engineering: management changes in the work organization', *Women in Management Review*, **12**(6), 228–33.

Evetts, J. (1998), 'Managing the technology but not the organization: women and careers in engineering', *Women in Management Review*, **13**(8), 283–90.

Fielding, J. and Glover, J. (1997), *Gender and Science, Engineering and Technology*, Research Summary, Roehampton Institute, University of Surrey.

Fielding, J. and Glover, J. (1999), 'Women science graduates in Britain: the value of secondary analysis of large scale data sets', *Work, Employment and Society*, **13**(2), 353–67.

French, S. (2005), 'Double trouble in the academy: taking "positions" in the discipline of computing', presented at the Gender, Work and Organisation Fourth International Interdisciplinary Conference, 22–24 June, Keele University, UK.

Gale, A.W. (1994), 'Women in non-traditional occupations: the construction industry', *Women in Management Review*, **9**(2), 3–14.

Gherardi, S. (1994), 'The gender we think, the gender we do in our everyday lives', *Human Relations*, **47**(6), 591–610.

Glover, J. (2000), *Women and Scientific Employment*, Basingstoke: Macmillan.

Glover, J., Fielding, J. and Smeaton, D. (1996), 'What happens to women and men with SET degrees?', *Labour Market Trends*, **104**(2), 63–7.

Greed, C. (1991), *Surveying Sisters: Women in a Traditional Male Profession*, London: Routledge.

Hansard Society Commission Report (1990), *Women at the Top*, London: Hansard Society for Parliamentary Government.

HESA (Higher Education Statistics Agency) (2006), *All HE Students by Subject of Study, Domicile and Gender*, available at www.hesa.ac.uk (accessed March 2006).

Hofstede, G. (1984), *Culture's Consequences*, London: Sage.

Husu, L. (2001), *Sexism, Support and Survival in Academia: Academic Women and Hidden Discrimination in Finland*, Helsinki: University of Helsinki.

Itzin, C. (1995), 'The gender culture in organisations', in C. Itzin and J. Newman (eds), *Gender, Culture and Organisational Change: Putting Theory into Practice*, London: Routledge, pp. 30–53.

Jolly, L. (1996), 'The first year engineering ethnographic project: An overview', Department of Anthropology and Sociology, University of Queensland, Australia.

Lane, N. (1997), 'Women in science, engineering and technology: the rising tide report and beyond', in M. Maynard (ed.), *Science and the Construction of Women*, London: UCL Press.

Langdridge, D. (2004), *Introduction to Research Methods and Data Analysis in Psychology*, Harlow: Prentice-Hall.

Ledwith, S. and Colgan, F. (1996), *Women in Organisations: Challenging Gender Politics*, London: Macmillan.

Lewis, S. (1995), 'Chilly courses for women? Some engineering and science experiences', paper presented at Women, Culture and Universities: A Chilly Climate?, University of Technology, Sydney, Australia, 19–20 April.

Lintern, S. (1995), 'Oh look . . . a girl!', University of South Australia, Mawson Lakes, Australia.

Madhill, H.M. et al. (2003), 'Making choices and making transitions – creating a web resource, proceedings of the GASAT 11 International Conference, Mauritius, 6–11 July 2003.

Malpas, R. (2000), 'The universe of engineering: a UK perspective', available at: www.engc.org.uk/publications/pdf/Malpas_report.pdf (accessed 29 April 2004).

McIlwee, J.S. and Robinson, J.G. (1992), 'Implementing an inclusive curriculum for women in engineering education', *Journal of Professional Issues in Engineering Education and Practice*, **129**(4), 203–10.

McLean, C., Lewis, S., Copeland, J., Lintern, S. and O'Neill, B. (1997), 'Masculinity and the culture of engineering', *Australasian Journal of Engineering Education*, **7**(2), 143–56.

Mills, J. and Ayre, M. (2003), 'Implementing an inclusive curriculum for women in engineering education', *Journal of Professional Issues in Engineering Education and Practice*, **129**(4), 203–10.

Morley, L. (1999), *Organising Feminisms: The Micropolitics of the Academy*, London: Macmillan.

Morley, L. (2000), 'The micropolitics of gender in the learning society', *Higher Education in Europe*, **25**(2), 229–35.

Nair, I. and Majetich, S. (1995), 'Physics and engineering in the classroom', in S. Rosser (ed.), *Teaching the Majority: Breaking the Gender Barrier in Science, Mathematics and Engineering*, New York: Teachers College Press, pp. 25–42.

ONS (Office for National Statistics) (2000), *Labour Force Survey Spring 2000*, London: HMSO.

Opportunity 2000 (1996), 'Tapping the talent', available at: www.lboro.ac.uk/orgs/opp2000/tapping.html (accessed 7 May 2004).

Pacanowsky, M.E. and O'Donnell-Trujillo, N. (1982), 'Communication and organisational culture', *The Western Journal of Speech Communication*, **46**(Spring), 115–30.

Powell, A., Bagilhole, B. and Dainty, A. (2006), 'The problem of women's assimilation into UK engineering cultures: can critical mass work?', *Equal Opportunities International*, **25**(8), 688–99.

Powell, A., Bagilhole, B., Dainty, A. and Neale, R. (2005), *Coping in Construction: Female Students' Perspectives*, Conference Proceedings, ARCOM 21st Annual Conference, 7–9 September, School of Oriental and African Studies, London, UK.

Ridgeway, C.L. (1997), 'Interaction and the conservation of gender inequality: considering employment', *American Sociological Review*, **62**, 218–35.

Sagebiel, F. (2003), 'New initiatives in science and technology and mathematics education at the formal level: masculinity cultures in engineering departments in institutions of higher education and perspectives for social change, *GASAT 11 Gender, Science, Technology and Economic Paradigm Shift*, 6–11 July 2003.

Schein, E.H. (1985), *Career Dynamics: Matching Individual and Organisational Needs*, Reading, MA: Addison-Wesley.

Scottish Higher Education Funding Council (1997), *Winning Women: Access Guide*, Edinburgh: SHEFC.

Short, T.D., Garside, J.A. and Appleton, E. (2003), 'Industry and the engineering student: a marriage made in heaven?', *Global Journal of Engineering Education*, **7**(1), 77–85.

Srivastava, A.K. (1996), *Widening Access: Women in Construction Higher Education*, PhD thesis, Leeds Metropolitan University.

Strauss, A. and Corbin, J. (1990), *Basics of Qualitative Research*, Newbury Park, CA: Sage.

Thomas, K. (1990), *Gender and Subject in Higher Education*, Buckingham: Open University Press.

Thorn, M. (ed.) (2000), *Balancing the Equation: Where are the Women and Girls in Science, Engineering and Technology?*, New York: National Council for Research on Women.

Walker, M. (2001), 'Engineering identities', *British Journal of Sociology of Education*, **22**(1), 75–89.

Weiner, G. (1994), *Feminisms in Education: An Introduction*, Buckingham: Open University Press.

West, C. and Zimmerman, D. (1987), 'Doing gender', *Gender and Society*, **1**(2), 125–51.

4. Myths and realities in the IT workplace: gender differences and similarities in climate perceptions

Debra A. Major, Donald D. Davis, Janis Sanchez-Hucles, Heather J. Downey and Lisa M. Germano

It's commonly said that perception is reality. This is certainly true in the workplace. Perceptions about the workplace represent a synthesis of one's experiences with the work environment and with those who work in it. These perceptions guide one's beliefs about and reactions to the workplace. We explore in this chapter the extent to which common beliefs about men and women in the IT workplace are true or not. We use the idea of myth to represent the truth of these beliefs. Myth (taken from the Greek *mythos*) can refer to stories describing supernatural, divine or heroic beings. Although not intended to be taken literally, this type of myth often reveals universal truths about the human condition. Myth can also be used to describe stories that claim to be based on fact but upon further and deeper examination are shown to be fictional. Pickford (1985) has noted that myths are integral to societies and tend to originate from psychological drives, which serve to arrange or obscure facts in order to protect individuals from realities that they do not wish to face.

Gender myths can have a great deal of power in shaping work organizations. Acker (1998) has described gender as a group of patterned, socially constructed differences between males and females that typically subordinate women. This subordination is achieved through creation of gender divisions, use of symbols and images, reinforcement of gender-appropriate attitudes and behaviors, and maintenance of systems of interaction that emphasize subordination of women and dominance of men. Myths may subordinate women and members of minority groups in IT. Common myths in the IT workplace include: women are too emotional and irrational to be successful leaders; technical competence is sufficient for effectiveness; IT work is best done in isolation.

The result of this growing association between white males and the power of the IT revolution has served to block access to those who are different due to gender and race. These barriers are perpetuated by those in power, often unintentionally, and are deeply ingrained in women and minorities. The white male culture in IT can cause women and minorities to fear entering this field and doubt the possibility of success and advancement. The idea that IT work is inherently unsuitable for women because it is boring and solitary serves to reinforce myths about women and IT (Myers et al., 2006).

Research has increasingly focused on examining gender as an ongoing social construction that depends on individual differences, power differentials and the demands of different contexts (Wharton, 1992). Gender is a system of power relations that is embedded in other power relations that are themselves gendered (Stewart and McDermott, 2004). It has also become apparent that gender intersects with other aspects of identity such as personality traits, age, race, culture, sexual orientation and ability level. All individuals have multiple identities that interact with their job responsibilities and functions as well as the identities of others in work groups. Identity is not only multidimensional. It is also interactive in that it involves a process of integrating what we think of ourselves with how others perceive and think about us.

Simply increasing exposure to others in and of itself does not necessarily increase harmony and minimize potential conflict due to differences (Tolbert et al., 1996). Where identity issues become salient in IT work groups, psychological and behavioral differences can be exaggerated, leading to more polarized and stereotyped understandings of sex role differences (Turner, 1982). It is important to recognize that these perceived differences are based on social constructions of gender differences and not due to measurable innate abilities (Wilson, 2004). In other words, perceptions of others may not be connected to reality.

A reality in the IT workforce is that women are vastly underrepresented. Whereas females in the USA represent 50 percent of the professional workforce, they account for only 29 percent of IT professionals and only 11 percent of corporate officers in Fortune 500 companies (National Center for Women and Information Technology, 2006). Furthermore, the situation is not improving as the number of women in this area has dropped 18 percent during the period 1997–2005 (Chabrow, 2005) and 40 percent since 1986 (Tapia and Kvasny, 2004).

The underrepresentation of women in IT begins in the university and continues upon graduation. Much research has been done to identify the factors that predict the attraction and retention of women in IT education, that is, the IT 'pipeline'. Attraction and retention of women in the IT workplace, the end of the pipeline, continue to be challenging after graduation from university or technical school (Major, Davis et al., 2006). We discuss in this chapter myths about the IT workplace climate that influence retention of women in the IT workplace.

Retention of women in the IT workplace is a function of two broad classes of factors: (1) characteristics of the person, that is, individual differences (Trauth, 2002) and (2) characteristics of the work environment (Major, Davis et al., 2006). This fact reflects one of the oldest truths in psychology; human behavior is a function of both the person and the environment (Lewin, 1951). Characteristics of the person include aspects of personal history and experience such as knowledge, skills, abilities, personality traits, and previous life and work experiences. Characteristics of the work environment include factors such as organization culture and climate, policies, procedures and working conditions. We focus in this chapter on how women and men differentially experience characteristics of the workplace. We first discuss workplace climate and its relevance to IT. We next describe how gender may influence perceptions of workplace climate. We then describe a longitudinal research study we conducted that examined the relationship between gender and workplace climate in 11 IT organizations throughout the USA. We organize the presentation of our results around four common myths about the IT workplace and use our results to show the extent to which these myths are true or not. Finally, we provide a model of workplace inclusion that helps to understand the impact of workplace climate on men and women.

IT WORKPLACE CLIMATE

Organizational climate represents one of the most important aspects of the workplace because it influences a wide variety of highly sought individual and organizational outcomes, such as satisfaction, commitment, performance and retention (Ostroff et al., 2003). Organizational climate represents what people see and report happening to them and others in the organization. Climate is a summary perception abstracted from interaction with the surrounding work environment. This perception is real and measurable. Because perceptions of the environment shape and influence behavior, perceptions of the workplace influence how one reacts to it. Organizational climate consists of shared and agreed-upon perceptions of organizational policies, practices and procedures (Reichers and Schneider, 1990). These perceptions are typically targeted to specific features and levels of the organization, thus yielding multiple climates in every organization. Common examples include climate for safety (Zohar, 1980), climate for service (Schneider, 1990), and climate for opportunity (Hayes et al., 2002).

Organizational climate has been studied for decades, although it has only recently been the focus of research in IT. Hundreds of studies have shown that climate is related to important individual outcomes such as job satisfaction, organization commitment and performance (Kozlowski and Hults, 1987), helping behaviors (Naumann and Bennett, 2000), tolerance of sexual harassment (Hulin et al., 1996), and absenteeism and turnover intentions (Jackofsky and Slocum, 1988; Ostroff, 1993). Organizational outcomes related to climate include improved customer service and satisfaction (Schneider and Bowen, 1985; Schneider et al., 1980; Schneider et al., 1998), financial performance (Borucki and Burke, 1999), safety (Zohar, 2000), and overall organizational effectiveness (Lindell and Brandt, 2000).

OUR RESEARCH ON GENDER MYTHS IN THE IT WORKPLACE

We examined in a three-phase research project the myths and realities of how men and women experience IT work climate. During Phase 1, 916 IT employees from 11 organizations completed a web-based survey. In order to broadly represent the diversity of IT work experiences and workplace climates, organizations were selected to vary in terms of industry, size and geographic location. Participating organizations represented the following industries: healthcare, education, local government, consumer and industrial products, publishing, business and IT consulting, chemical manufacturing, and waste management. Participating organizations ranged in size from seven employees to more than 68 000 employees. Organizations were located nationwide, including small single-site organizations and large multinational firms with many locations. Of the survey participants in Phase 1, 58 percent were male, 33 percent were ethnic minorities, 70 percent were married, and 69 percent had at least a bachelor's degree. See Major and Germano (2006) for a description of survey measures and Major, Davis et al. (2006) for a discussion of gender differences in the sample.

Phase 2 of the project consisted of a survey feedback intervention. Survey data collected during the first phase were fed back to each participating organization. Data from the entire sample were used to benchmark performance for each organization and to identify climate strengths as well as areas that could serve as a focus for climate change.

After the reports were disseminated to the leadership at each company, feedback meetings with company executives were conducted and feedback presentations were given to IT employees. In addition, we invited IT employees to participate in focus groups. The aim of the focus group discussions was to obtain qualitative data to aid in interpretation of the survey results, clarify ambiguities, and to uncover issues that were not addressed in the web-based survey. Hence the survey data were used to drive the focus group discussions. Interviews were also conducted with high-performing supervisors as identified by survey results and focus group findings. Then, based on the survey findings, focus group feedback and supervisor interviews, we worked with management to develop action plans that capitalized on particular climate strengths (e.g. strong supervisor–employee relationships) and addressed climate weaknesses (e.g. low percentage of employees reporting having a mentor). Use of survey feedback in this manner has been shown to facilitate organization change (Waclawski and Church, 2002). Phase 3, the final phase of the project, involved surveying employees in participating organizations a second time to assess effectiveness of the interventions implemented during Phase 2 of the project.

The findings reported here are based on the interview, focus group, and survey data collected during Phases 1 and 2. Our focus in this chapter is using our research findings to distinguish myth from reality in terms of how men and women experience IT workplace climate. We examined ethnic differences within gender as well in our research, but the small sample size for some ethnic groups did not allow us to form reliable judgments about the interaction of gender and ethnicity.

Myth 1: IT Organizations are more Fair for Men than for Women

A common belief about IT organizations is that, because they are typically created by white men, these work environments represent their values and preferences. As a result, these work environments are more supportive and hospitable to white men and may even be hostile to women and minorities (Hoonakker et al., 2006; Roldan et al., 2004; Tapia, 2004, 2006). Common examples of bias in IT work environments include emphasis on traits commonly associated with males, for example, willingness to work alone and sacrifice family and personal life to work long hours, positive stigma associated with being a 'geek', reduced opportunities for promotion and lower earnings for women performing similar jobs (Rosenblum et al., 2006; Todd et al., 2005).

To consider the notion of fairness broadly, we examined three aspects of the work environment and gender differences related to them: pay, access to opportunities, and workplace fairness. These factors represent attributes of organizational justice. Organizational justice has four dimensions: distributive, procedural, interpersonal and informational

(Colquitt, 2001). Distributive justice represents the extent to which allocation of pay and rewards and other outcomes is viewed as fair. Procedural justice refers to fairness of policies and procedures as well as fairness in their implementation and application. Fair procedures are ethical and moral, lack bias, and are applied consistently. Moreover, they provide opportunity for participation in decision making and opportunity to appeal decisions perceived to be unfair. Interpersonal justice refers to fairness in social interactions with superiors and others in authority, such as being treated with dignity, politeness and respect. Informational justice reflects communication from authority figures concerning organizational policies and procedures that is candid, clear, reasonable and timely. These features of organizational justice are related individually and collectively to many important organizational outcomes, for example, job satisfaction, organizational commitment, evaluation of authority, organizational citizenship behavior, performance, and withdrawal from the organization (Colquitt et al., 2001). Increased organizational justice is related to positive organizational outcomes.

We examined gender differences in pay, a type of distributive justice. After controlling for several possible alternative explanations for differences in pay (experience in IT and the organization, education, marital status and number of children), gender was significantly related to salary with women earning lower salaries than men. The impact of gender, however, was small.

To better understand gender differences in pay, we examined gender differences within nine different salary groups. Women were more likely than men to earn less than $30000 and between $50000 and $59000 per year. Men were more likely to earn $100000 or more per year. Salary differences were unrelated to type of IT position. In sum, our data show that women earn lower salaries than men and are overrepresented in the lowest pay group and underrepresented in the highest pay group. These results indicate that distributive justice is lower for women due to lower pay.

We further explored the relationship between pay, fairness and gender by examining the link between gender and perceptions of organizational fairness after controlling for differences in pay. We expected that gender differences in perceptions of organizational fairness would be partly explained by pay differences. Men reported greater fairness than women, but this relationship was substantially reduced when salary was taken into consideration. Thus women's perceptions regarding organizational fairness are explained in part by the fact that women are paid less than men. In sum, Myth 1 is correct: the work environment in IT is fairer for men.

Myth 2: Women Are Not Effective Leaders in the IT Workplace

Women's underrepresentation in the IT workforce is particularly notable in upper management and senior leadership positions. For instance, women hold fewer than 5 percent of IT executive positions, such as chief information officer (Gingras, 1999). Historically, women have faced challenges because leadership effectiveness has been defined in terms of behavior and characteristics that are stereotypically masculine (Kanter, 1977). Women who attempt to lead by demonstrating masculine work styles, however, also face challenges when they are perceived to be violating feminine gender norms (Sumner and Werner, 2001). Females encounter a 'feminine competency bind', because acting feminine is perceived negatively and acting competently is associated with masculinity and in violation of feminine gender norms. Women often conclude that their only path to positions of leadership is to act in ways that are masculine despite the potential negative consequences for doing this (Jamieson, 1995).

Members of ethic minorities encounter a similar competency bind in that they must act like middle-class white males to be perceived as strong leaders. Achieving positions of leadership can be even more daunting for minority women due to the 'double outsider' status imposed by race and gender. Promotion opportunities are more challenging for these women as their perceived lack of fit imposes 'concrete ceilings' and 'sticky floors' that they must shatter before they even encounter the sexism of glass ceilings (Catalyst, 2001).

Recently, management theorists and researchers have begun to consider the ways in which women may possess a leadership advantage (Eagly and Carli, 2003). Traditionally feminine characteristics and behaviors, such as negotiating, listening and collaborating, may make women especially effective leaders (Helgesen, 1990). A recent meta-analysis revealed that women exhibit more transformational leadership behaviors, which have a strong relationship emphasis, than men (Eagly et al., 2003). However, Haynes (2006) argues that in the male-dominated IT work environment women's relational leadership skills are likely to be undervalued. Moreover, given the feminine competency bind described above, transformational leadership behaviors might be devalued in IT when demonstrated by women due to their strong relationship emphasis.

Leader–member exchange (LMX) theory describes leadership effectiveness in terms of the quality of supervisor–subordinate relationships (see Graen and Uhl-Bien, 1995 for a review). A high-quality relationship (high LMX) between a leader and a subordinate is characterized by mutual trust, respect, liking and reciprocal influence (Liden et al., 1993). In general, high LMX develops when leaders perceive subordinates to be competent, trustworthy and willing to take on responsibility (Dansereau et al., 1975). In contrast, subordinates who have low LMX with leaders have little negotiating latitude, are more closely supervised, and experience more strictly defined role relationships (Duchon et al., 1986). Research over the past 25 years has shown that LMX is positively related to job satisfaction, organizational commitment and performance, and negatively linked to turnover intentions, turnover and stress (Bernas and Major, 2000; Gerstner and Day, 1997; Graen and Uhl-Bien, 1995). Gender differences in LMX have not been reported in reviews of the LMX literature (Gerstner and Day, 1997; Graen and Uhl-Bien, 1995).

In our research, there were no mean differences in the levels of LMX reported by male and female IT professionals. That is, men and women reported having equally high-quality relationships with their supervisors. However, when we examined the gender composition of leader–subordinate pairs, differences in the level of LMX emerged. Specifically, men reported having the highest-quality relationships with their supervisors when the supervisor was a woman. Women, on the other hand, reported equally high-quality relationships with male and female supervisors.

While our findings do not necessarily contradict the notion that women in IT may have more difficulty making their way into leadership positions than men, our findings do debunk the myth that women will be ineffective leaders in male-dominated IT workplaces. In fact, our findings suggest that women are particularly good leaders in such environments because they are better able than male supervisors to develop high-quality working relationships with male subordinates. Our findings also speak to the relationship-building skills of women in IT. Women IT professionals were able to develop high-quality relationships with both male and female supervisors, whereas men tended to enjoy higher-quality relationships with female rather than male supervisors. It may be that women, and perhaps minority women especially, have been able to develop such effective leadership skills in IT as a result of having to observe and learn about their organizations from the margins rather than from the mainstream. This possibility has been referred to as 'positive marginality' (Mayo, 1982).

Our focus group findings reinforced this interpretation of the empirical survey results. In our discussions of quality of supervision, technical competence was seldom cited as a shortcoming. Instead, IT professionals bemoaned their supervisors' lack of interpersonal skills and inattention to the quality of working relationships. Although our focus groups revealed many examples of both men and women with excellent leadership skills, men were more likely to be deficient in the relational side of leadership. Participants described supervisors who had been promoted on the basis of their technical expertise, but who lacked the skills necessary for effectively managing people. Such supervisors failed to connect emotionally with their employees and had difficulty acknowledging them as individuals. In the IT department of a municipal government office, for example, participants described a supervisor who would walk by employees in the mornings without acknowledging or greeting anyone, and who would then proceed to go into his office, shut the door, and send email to employees sitting steps away. In a large technology organization, participants expressed a preference for supervisors who could connect with them as individuals. Supervisors who asked about family, special events and non-work activities were preferred over supervisors who knew little and cared less about employees as individuals.

Classic leadership theory and decades of leadership research suggest that both task-oriented skills and relationship-oriented skills are essential for leadership effectiveness (Fleishman and Harris, 1962; Judge et al., 2004). Effective supervision in the IT workplace is likewise defined by the same essential sets of behavior (Major, Davis et al., in press). Furthermore, effective leadership is an essential component in recruiting and retaining IT professionals (Agarwal and Ferratt, 2002). Our findings demonstrate that, contrary to myths regarding their leadership ineffectiveness, once women make their way into IT supervisory positions they are very effective in these male-dominated work environments and can be tremendous leadership assets to the organization because of their relationship skills. Thus Myth 2 is not correct; women are effective leaders in IT.

Myth 3: IT is a Man's World, Making it More Difficult for Women to Develop Effective Work Relationships

> It is in the context of relationships with others that people may experience themselves as anchored in organizational contexts and situations that are, like high seas, turbulent and frightening. Work relationships have the potential to help people feel connected rather than disconnected, held fast rather than floundering, soothed rather than disquieted. (Kahn, 1996, p. 163)

In addition to supervisory relationships described above, an individual's broader social network contributes substantially to well-being and career progress (Podolny and Baron, 1997; Seibert et al., 2001). Supportive relationships with co-workers, for instance, are beneficial in a variety of ways. Co-worker support increases job satisfaction and organization commitment, and reduces stress and intention to leave the organization (Baruch-Feldman et al., 2002; Ducharme and Martin, 2000; Lee, 2004).

When women, especially women of color, do not feel included in the work environment, it may be difficult for them to determine the cause. Does it relate to sexism, racism, tokenism, stereotyping, or the old boys' network?

Women with multiple identities often are forced to examine subtle as well as obvious cues to determine which dimensions of their identity are fostering a sense of isolation or exclusion. They can feel more marginalized if others view their concerns as trivial or as an indication that they are being too sensitive (Sanchez-Hucles and Sanchez, 2007).

Mentors play a vital part in employees' social networks. A mentor is typically defined as a senior individual with advanced expertise and knowledge who provides upward support and mobility to his or her protégés' careers (Ragins and Cotton, 1999; Wanberg et al., 2003). Mentors typically offer both career development (e.g. making protégés aware of opportunities for development) and psychosocial support (e.g. acting as a sounding-board, listening). Mentoring is associated with numerous positive outcomes for protégés. Compared to those without mentors, individuals with mentors have higher job performance ratings, are promoted more frequently, have higher satisfaction with their jobs, and have higher incomes (Allen et al., 2004; Ragins and Cotton, 1999).

As in other career fields, social networks are important to career progress in IT (Morgan and Trauth, 2006). Research suggests, for instance, that social networks may be more important than human capital in predicting job offers and pay for those entering the IT field (Koput et al., 2005). Experienced IT professionals likewise rely on their social networks in making career transitions, although men report being better able to employ them to facilitate lateral career moves than women (Sumner and Werner, 2001). Although social networks provide a key form of coping for women in IT (Pegher et al., 2006), the inadequacy of women's social networks and lack of mentoring have been discussed extensively as a major career barrier for women in IT (Ahuja, 1995; ITAA, 2000; Kaplan and Niederman, 2006; Todd et al., 2005).

We assessed gender differences in co-worker support and mentoring. We examined two types of co-worker support: affective and instrumental. Affective co-worker support is a form of psychosocial support that co-workers offer by being sympathetic, listening to problems, and expressing care and concern. Co-workers demonstrate instrumental support by offering more tangible forms of help, such as willingness to trade work schedules and helping others with their work. Men and women reported equal satisfaction with the social environment in the workplace. Women and men also reported receiving similar levels of affective support from co-workers. Women, however, reported receiving significantly more instrumental support from co-workers than men.

Although men and women in our study reported comparable satisfaction with the mentoring they received, results showed that women were actually more likely than men to report having at least one mentor. Overall,

47 percent of men reported receiving mentoring compared to 61 percent of women. Taken together, the results for co-worker support and mentoring may suggest that, in terms of these aspects of social networking, women in IT do at least as well as men and that barriers to mentoring may be overstated.

Focus group discussions, however, suggested other possible explanations for these findings. First, men may be less willing than women to acknowledge receipt of help or assistance from others. In focus group discussions both men and women were able to provide numerous examples of receiving co-worker instrumental support. Men, however, were less likely to use terms such as 'help' and 'support'. Instead, they described support and assistance from co-workers as a regular part of getting work done. Likewise with regard to 'mentoring', it seemed that women had a broader interpretation of the term than men. Although the survey provided all participants with a common definition of mentoring, women were more likely than men to label helping behaviors from senior colleagues as mentoring. Once again, men described such instances of assistance as just a regular part of working together. Thus, although our results suggest that women IT professionals are finding the co-worker support and mentoring that they need in the IT workplace, potential differences in definition and interpretation of the concept of mentor create the possibility that women are not necessarily receiving more support than men.

Myth 4: Women Feel Less Included in the IT Workplace

An inhospitable workplace atmosphere is among the explanations most frequently offered for the underrepresentation of women in IT (CAWMSET, 2000; Hoonakker et al., 2006; ITAA, 2000). IT culture is considered male-dominated, antisocial, individualistic, competitive, and all-encompassing (Tapia and Kvasny, 2004). Moreover, the IT workplace climate is perceived to be more negative by women than by men (Hoonakker et al., 2006). In a study of IT employees in six organizations in the USA, for example, the work environment was perceived by women to be more rejecting, frustrating, cold, unfriendly and hostile than it was perceived by men. Moreover, minorities were more likely to perceive it to be frustrating, cold and unfair. These negative perceptions were linked to lower job satisfaction, weaker commitment to the organization, and increased stress (Hoonakker et al., 2006). These characteristics illustrate the 'chilly climate' that women and minorities can face in IT work environments.

In short, it appears that women are less likely than men to feel included in the IT workplace. This can be particularly true for minority women, who may feel marginalized and invisible, or equally excluded by being made excessively visible to others. They may feel pressure to obscure any aspect of their cultural identities that they believe may not meet white male standards.

Building an inclusive workplace climate has been hailed as the critical difference between merely managing diversity and capitalizing on diversity as a strategic human resource advantage that benefits all employees and organizations (Miller, 1998; Miller and Katz, 2002; Mor Barak, 2000, 2005). Although definitions vary (cf. Miller, 1998; Mor Barak and Cherin, 1998; Pelled et al., 1999), most agree that an inclusive workplace climate is one in which everyone in the organization feels a sense of belonging, is invited to participate in important decisions, and feels that their input matters. Inclusive workplace climates offer a recruitment advantage because prospective employees are more attracted to organizations in which they feel valued (Powell and Graves, 2003). Exclusion is associated with reduced organizational commitment, decreased job satisfaction and increased turnover (Greenhaus et al., 1990) and reduced retention of IT professionals (Agarwal and Ferratt, 2002).

Workplace climates can vary in strength across organization levels and units, and be perceived differently by employees (Ostroff et al., 2003). Climate for inclusiveness is no exception. In our research, we compared the experiences of men and women in relation to three aspects of inclusive climate: belonging, participation and influence. Results showed that men and women felt an equal sense of belonging in the IT workplace. In addition, women and men reported comparable levels of participation. Thus, at least in our research, men and women felt equally welcome in the IT work environment and were able to take part equally in decision making. However, in terms of feeling that one's contributions actually have an impact in the IT work environment (i.e. the influence aspect of inclusion), women reported having less influence than men.

Our findings suggest that there is some myth and some reality regarding the lack of inclusive climate for women in IT. Notably, women do feel equally included in terms of the more relational aspects of inclusive climate. Women are able to develop a sense of belonging and are able to participate in decision making. This may be attributable, at least in part, to the strength of women's skills in building relationships. Research suggests that women's relationship skills help them develop effective and satisfying relationships with others at work (Fletcher, 1999). Recall that our findings showed that women were particularly good at developing relationships with others when they served as leaders. Nonetheless, the unfortunate reality is that women report having significantly less influence than men in the IT workplace. This suggests that women's social networking successes have not necessarily translated into power and influence in the IT work environment.

This lack of influence reported by women may be related to gender differences in socialization. Women are taught and rewarded for showing patience, cooperation, non-competitiveness and lack of aggression, which may poorly prepare them to be seen as decisive, authoritative and influential, male traits often associated with influence. Moreover, Turkle (1988) argues that males are reinforced for positions of influence that are congruent with the IT culture via skill in decomposition, analysis, decisiveness and imposition of will. Applewhite (2002) concurs, and asserts that masculine styles of extroversion and self-promotion of one's accomplishments are viewed as signs of intelligence, whereas women's style of being low key and self-effacing are not. Carli and Eagly (1999) have noted that women are more limited than men in the kinds of behavior they can demonstrate and still be considered influential. This reflects the competency bind we discussed above.

A final factor that may help us understand gender differences in influence may be linked to perceptions of power. In a recent study of powerful men and women in work organizations, both men and women were viewed as able to get results and to make things happen, but they did it differently (Merill-Sands et al., 2005). Men were more likely to assert control over others, whereas women were more likely to work with others, make collaborative decisions, communicate in compelling ways, and develop others. Hence women may be seen as powerful but not influential because of their different style of assertion.

Our research findings demonstrate the importance of the work context in fostering important organizational outcomes such as job satisfaction, organization commitment and retention. Gender differences in our findings demonstrate that men and women perceive the IT work environment differently. These perceptions guide their work behavior and influence their work outcomes. In other words, different work experiences lead to different perceptions which, in turn, lead to different realities for men and women in the IT workplace. Although our data were insufficient to draw firm conclusions, we believe that ethnic differences exist as well within gender differences; that is, women of color have different work experiences in the IT workplace than white women. Our data show that being a token (i.e. the only representative of one's ethnicity in a work group) influences perceptions and experiences in IT (Major et al., 2004). We believe that inclusiveness in the workplace provides a useful means for understanding ethnic and gender differences in work experience as well as a powerful means for managing these differences. Key characteristics of individuals' identity, such as gender and ethnicity, serve as lenses through which the workplace is perceived and enacted. Understanding the manner in which these lenses operate will help us to understand the myths and realities of the IT workplace.

THE LENS OF GENDER IN THE IT WORKPLACE

Perception is reality in the work context. Everyone perceives the work context differently. Although they are exposed to the same aspects of the work environment, for example organizational climate, justice, leadership practices, workplace relationships and inclusion, people perceive and experience these characteristics differently. Individual characteristics, such as gender, influence these differences in perception. Gender acts like the lenses in a pair of eyeglasses through which people view their work environment. People wearing different lenses perceive the work environment differently and, as a result, react differently toward it. They report different levels of job satisfaction, organization commitment and so forth as a result of these different perceptions (see Figure 4.1).

The lenses each individual wears influence what is perceived in the IT work environment. Much like eyeglasses, these lenses are particular to the wearer, the specific prescription determined by key aspects of identity such as gender and ethnicity, and change over time based on experiences and interactions with the work environment. The same work environment characteristics are split into different perceptions depending on our own

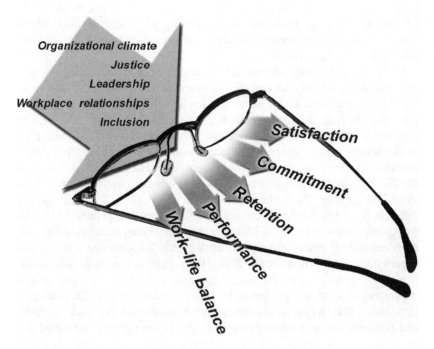

Figure 4.1   The lenses of perception

particular lenses which, in turn, influence subsequent interactions with these work environment characteristics. Over time, this cycle of interaction shapes our beliefs about the IT work environment and influences how we respond to it. Thus, although men and women may share the same work environment, their perceptions and experiences of it may be different. Perception is reality and, because gender shapes perception, it also shapes the myths and realities of the IT workplace.

ACKNOWLEDGEMENT

This material is based upon work supported by the National Science Foundation under Grant No. 0204430. We thank Robert Jones for graphic design and creation of Figure 4.1.

REFERENCES

Acker, J. (1998), 'Hierarchies, jobs, and bodies: a theory of gendered organizations', in K.A. Myers, C.D. Anderson and J. Risman (eds), *Feminist Foundations: Towards Transforming Sociology*, Thousand Oaks, CA: Sage, pp. 299–317.

Agarwal, R. and Ferratt, T.W. (2002), 'Enduring practices for managing IT professionals', *Communications of the ACM*, **45**(9), 73–9.

Ahuja, M.K. (1995), 'Information technology and the gender factor', *Proceedings of the 1995 ACM SIGCPR Conference*, New York, pp. 156–66.

Allen T.D., Eby, L.T., Poteet, M.L., Lentz, E. and Lima, L. (2004), 'Career benefits associated with mentoring for protégés: a meta-analytic review', *Journal of Applied Psychology*, **89**, 127–36.

Applewhite, A. (2002), 'Why so few women?', *IEEE Spectrum Online*, **39**(5), 65–6.

Baruch-Feldman, C., Brondolo, E., Ben-Dayan, D. and Schwartz, J. (2002), 'Sources of social support and burnout, job satisfaction, and productivity', *Journal of Occupational Health Psychology*, **7**, 84–93.

Bernas, K.H. and Major, D.A. (2000), 'Contributors to stress resistance: testing a model of women's work–family conflict', *Psychology of Women Quarterly*, **24**, 170–78.

Borucki, C.C. and Burke, M.J. (1999), 'An examination of service related antecedents to retail store performance', *Journal of Organizational Behavior*, **20**, 943–62.

Carli, L.L. and Eagly, A.H. (1999), 'Gender, interpersonal power, and social influence', *Journal of Social Issues*, **55**, 81–99.

Catalyst (2001), *Women of Color Executives: Their Voices, Their Journeys* (Publication Code D48), New York: Catalyst.

CAWMSET (2000), *Land of Plenty: Diversity as America's Competitive Edge in Science, Engineering, and Technology*, Washington, DC: Congressional Commission on the Advancement of Women and Minorities in Science, Engineering, and Technology Development.

Chabrow, E. (2005), 'Little progress made in diversifying tech workforce', *Information Week*, **37**, 61.

Colquitt, J.A. (2001), 'On the dimensionality of organizational justice: a construct validation and measure', *Journal of Applied Psychology*, **86**, 386–400.

Colquitt, J.A., Conlon, D.E., Wesson, M.J., Porter, O.L.H. and Ng, K.Y. (2001), 'Justice at the millennium: a meta-analytic review of 25 years of organizational justice research', *Journal of Applied Psychology*, **83**, 425–45.

Dansereau, F., Graen, G. and Haga, W.J. (1975), 'A vertical dyadic linkage approach to leadership within formal organizations: a longitudinal investigation of the role making process', *Organizational Behavior and Human Performance*, **13**, 46–78.

Ducharme, L.J. and Martin, J.K. (2000), 'Unrewarding work, coworker support, and job satisfaction: a test of the buffering hypothesis', *Work Occupations*, **27**, 223–43.

Duchon, D., Green, S.G. and Taber, T.D. (1986), 'Vertical dyad linkage: a longitudinal assessment of antecedents, measures, and consequences', *Journal of Applied Psychology*, **71**, 56–60.

Eagly, A.H. and Carli, L.L. (2003), 'The female leadership advantage: an evaluation of the evidence', *Leadership Quarterly*, **14**, 807–34.

Eagly, A.H., Johannesen-Schmidt, M.C. and van Engen, M. (2003), 'Transformational, transactional, and laissez-faire leadership styles: a meta-analysis comparing women and men', *Psychological Bulletin*, **95**, 569–91.

Fleishman, E.A. and Harris, E.F. (1962), 'Patterns of leadership behavior related to employee grievances and turnover', *Personnel Psychology*, **15**, 43–56.

Fletcher, J.K. (1999), *Disappearing Acts: Gender, Power, and Relational Practice at Work*, Cambridge, MA: MIT Press.

Gerstner, C.R. and Day, D.V. (1997), 'Meta-analytic review of leader–member exchange theory: correlates and construct issues', *Journal of Applied Psychology*, **82**, 827–44.

Gingras, A. (1999), 'Cherchez la femme', *Computerworld*, **49**, 18 January.

Graen, G.B. and Uhl-Bien, M. (1995), 'Relationship-based approach to leadership: development of leader–member exchange (LMX) theory of leadership over 25 years: applying a multi-level multi-domain perspective', *Leadership Quarterly*, **6**, 219–47.

Greenhaus, J.H., Parasuraman, S. and Wormley, W.M. (1990), 'Effects of race on organizational experiences, job performance evaluations, and career outcomes', *Academy of Management Journal*, **33**, 64–86.

Hayes, B.C., Bartle, S.A. and Major, D.A. (2002), 'Climate for opportunity: a conceptual model', *Human Resource Management Review*, **12**, 445–68.

Haynes, A. (2006), 'The glass ceiling in IT', in E.M. Trauth (ed.), *Encyclopedia of Gender and Information Technology*, Vol. 1, Hershey, PA: Idea Group Reference, pp. 733–8.

Helgesen, S. (1990), *The Female Advantage*, New York: Doubleday.

Hoonakker, P., Carayon, P. and Schoepke, J. (2006), 'Discrimination and hostility toward women and minorities in the IT work force', in E.M. Trauth (ed.), *Encyclopedia of Gender and Information Technology*, Vol. 1, Hershey, PA: Idea Group Reference, pp. 207–15.

Hulin, C.L., Fitzgerald, L.F. and Drasgow, F. (1996), 'Organizational influences on sexual harassment', in M.S. Stockdale (ed.), *Sexual Harassment in the Workplace*, Thousand Oaks, CA: Sage, pp. 127–50.

ITAA (2000), *Building the 21st Century Information Technology Workforce: Underrepresented Groups in the Information Technology Workforce*, Arlington, VA: Information Technology Association of America.

Jackofsky, E.E. and Slocum, J.W. Jr (1988), 'A longitudinal study of climates', *Journal of Organizational Behavior*, **8**, 319–34.

Jamieson, K.H. (1995), *Beyond the Double Bind: Women and Leadership*, New York: Oxford University Press.

Judge, T.A., Piccolo, R.F. and Ilies, R. (2004), 'The forgotten ones? The validity of consideration and initiating structure in leadership research', *Journal of Applied Psychology*, **89**, 36–51.

Kahn, W.A. (1996), 'Secure base relationships at work', in D.T. Hall (ed.), *The Career is Dead – Long Live the Career*, San Francisco, CA: Jossey-Bass, pp. 158–79.

Kanter, R. (1977), *Men and Women of the Corporation*, New York: Basic Books.

Kaplan, D.M. and Niederman, F. (2006), 'Career management concerns for women in IT', in E.M. Trauth (ed.), *Encyclopedia of Gender and Information Technology*, Vol. 1, Hershey, PA: Idea Group Reference, pp. 84–9.

Koput, K.W., Douma, B., Paddock, E.L. and Gutek, B.A. (2005), 'Ties that blind: why are women under-represented in Information Technology?', paper presented at the Academy of Management Annual Meeting, Honolulu, HI, August.

Kozlowski, S.W.J. and Hults, B.M. (1987), 'An exploration of climates for technical updating and performance', *Personnel Psychology*, **40**, 539–63.

Lee, P.C.B. (2004), 'Social support and leaving intention among computer professionals', *Information & Management*, **41**, 323–34.

Lewin, K. (1951), *Field Theory in Social Science*, New York: Harper and Row.

Liden, R.C., Wayne, S.J. and Stilwell, D. (1993), 'A longitudinal study on the early development of leader–member exchanges', *Journal of Applied Psychology*, **78**, 662–74.

Lindell, M.K. and Brandt, C.J. (2000), 'Climate quality and climate consensus as mediators of the relationship between organizational antecedents and outcomes', *Journal of Applied Psychology*, **85**, 331–48.

Major, D.A. and Germano, L.M. (2006), 'Survey feedback interventions in IT workplaces', in E.M. Trauth (ed.), *Encyclopedia of Gender and Information Technology*, Vol. 2, Hershey, PA: Idea Group Reference, pp. 1134–41.

Major, D.A., Fletcher, T.D. and Sanchez-Hucles, J. (2004), 'The experience of tokenism in the information technology workforce', paper presented at the 112th Convention of the American Psychological Association, Honolulu, HI, August.

Major, D.A., Davis, D.D., Sanchez-Hucles, J., Germano, L.M. and Mann, J. (2006), 'IT workplace climate for opportunity and inclusion', in E.M. Trauth (ed.), *Encyclopedia of Gender and Information Technology*, Vol. 2, Hershey, PA: Idea Group Reference, pp. 856–62.

Major, D.A., Davis, D.D., Germano, L.M., Fletcher, T.D., Sanchez-Hucles, J. and Mann, J. (in press), 'Managing human resources in information technology: best practices of high performing supervisors', *Human Resource Management*.

Mayo, C. (1982), 'Training for positive marginality', in C.L. Bickman (ed.), *Applied Social Psychology Annual*, Vol. 3, Beverly Hills, CA: Sage, pp. 57–73.

Merrill-Sands, D., Kickul, J. and Ingols, C. (2005), 'Women pursuing leadership and power: challenging the myth of the "opt out revolution"', *Insights*, **20**, 1–4.

Miller, F.A. (1998), 'Strategic culture change: the door to achieving high performance and inclusion', *Public Personnel Management*, **27**, 151–60.

Miller, F.A. and Katz, J.H. (2002), *The Inclusion Breakthrough: Unleashing the Real Power of Diversity*, San Francisco, CA: Berret-Koehler.

Mor Barak, M.E. (2000), 'The inclusive workplace: an ecosystems approach to diversity management', *Social Work*, **45**, 339–52.

Mor Barak, M.E. (2005), *Managing Diversity: Toward a Globally Inclusive Workplace*, Thousand Oaks, CA: Sage.

Mor Barak, M.E. and Cherin, D.A. (1998), 'A tool to expand organizational understanding of workforce diversity: exploring a measure of inclusion–exclusion', *Administration in Social Work*, **22**, 47–64.

Morgan, A.J. and Trauth, E.M. (2006), 'Women and social capital networks in the IT workforce', in E.M. Trauth (ed.), *Encyclopedia of Gender and Information Technology*, Vol. 2, Hershey, PA: Idea Group Reference, pp. 1245–51.

Myers, M., Moody, J., Beise, C. and Woszczynski, A. (2006), 'The pipeline and beyond', in E.M. Trauth (ed.), *Encyclopedia of Gender and Information Technology*, Vol. 2, Hershey, PA: Idea Group Reference, pp. 1005–11.

National Center for Women and Information Technology (2006), *Women and Information Technology by the numbers*, from www.ncwit.org (retrieved 27 July).

Naumann, S.E. and Bennett, N. (2000), 'A case for procedural justice climate: development and test of a multi-level model', *Academy of Management Journal*, **43**, 881–9.

Ostroff, C. (1993), 'The effects of climate and personal influences on individual behavior and attitudes in organizations', *Organizational Behavior and Human Decision Processes*, **56**, 56–90.

Ostroff, C., Kinicki, A.J. and Tamkins, M.M. (2003), 'Organizational culture and climate', in W.C. Borman, D.R. Ilgen and R.J. Klimoski (eds), *Handbook of Psychology: Industrial and Organizational Psychology*, Vol. 12, Hoboken, NJ: John Wiley & Sons, pp. 565–93.

Pegher, V., Quesenberry, J.L. and Trauth, E.M. (2006), 'A reflexive analysis of questions for women entering the IT workforce', in E.M. Trauth (ed.), *Encyclopedia of Gender and Information Technology*, Vol. 2, Hershey, PA: Idea Group Reference, pp. 1075–80.

Pelled, L.H., Ledford, G.E., Jr and Mohrman, S.A. (1999), 'Demographic dissimilarity and workplace inclusion', *Journal of Management Studies*, **36**, 1013–31.

Pickford, L.J. (1985), 'The superstructure of myths supporting the subordination of women', in B.A. Stead (ed.), *Women in Management*, Englewood Cliffs, NJ: Prentice Hall, pp. 165–74.

Podolny, J. and Baron, J. (1997), 'Resources and relationships: social networks and mobility in the workplace', *American Sociological Review*, **62**, 673–93.

Powell, G.N. and Graves, L.M. (2003), *Women and Men in Management*, 3rd edn, Thousand Oaks, CA: Sage.

Ragins, B.R. and Cotton, J.L. (1999), 'Mentor functions and outcomes: a comparison of men and women in formal and informal mentoring relationships', *Journal of Applied Psychology*, **84**, 529–50.

Reichers, A.E. and Schneider, B. (1990), 'Climate and culture: an evolution of constructs', in B. Schneider (ed.), *Organizational Climate and Culture*, San Francisco, CA: Jossey-Bass, pp. 5–39.

Roldan, M., Soe, L. and Yakura, E.K. (2004), 'Perceptions of chilly IT organizational contexts and their effect on the retention and promotion of women in IT', *Proceedings of 2004 SIGMIS Conference*, San Diego, CA, pp. 108–13.

Rosenblum, J.L., Ash, R.A., Coder, L. and Dupont, B. (2006), 'IT workforce composition and characteristics', in E. Trauth (ed.), *Encyclopedia of Gender and Information Technology*, Vol. 2, Hershey, PA: Idea Group Reference, pp. 850–55.

Sanchez-Hucles, J. and Sanchez, P. (2007), 'From margin to center: the voices of diverse feminist leaders', in J.L. Chin, B. Lott, J. Rice and J. Sanchez-Hucles (eds), *Women and Leadership: Transforming Visions and Diverse Voices*, Malden, MA: Blackwell Publishing, pp. 209–27.

Schneider, B. (1990), 'The climate for service: an application of the climate construct', in B. Schneider (ed.), *Organizational Climate and Culture*, San Francisco, CA: Jossey-Bass, pp. 383–412.

Schneider, B. and Bowen, D.E. (1985), 'Employee and customer perceptions of service in banks: replication and extension', *Journal of Applied Psychology*, **70**, 423–33.

Schneider, B., Parkington, J.J. and Buxton, V.M. (1980), 'Employee and customer perception of service in banks', *Administrative Science Quarterly*, **25**, 252–67.

Schneider, B., White, S.S. and Paul, M.C. (1998), 'Linking service climate and customer perceptions of service quality: test of a causal model', *Journal of Applied Psychology*, **83**, 150–63.

Seibert, S., Kraimer, M. and Liden, R. (2001), 'A social capital theory of career success', *Academy of Management Journal*, **44**, 219–37.

Stewart, A.J. and Mc Dermott, C. (2004), 'Gender in psychology', *Annual Review of Psychology*, **55**, 519–44.

Sumner, M. and Werner, K. (2001), 'The impact of gender differences on the career experiences of information systems professionals', *Proceedings of the 2001 ACM SIGCPR Conference*, San Diego, CA, pp. 125–31.

Tapia, A.H. (2004), 'The power of myth in the IT workplace: creating a 24-hour workday during the dot-com bubble', *Information Technology & People*, **17**(3), 303–26.

Tapia, A.H. (2006), 'Making of a homogenous IT work environment', in E. Trauth (ed.), *Encyclopedia of Gender and Information Technology*, Vol. 2, Hershey, PA: Idea Group Reference, pp. 870–75.

Tapia, A.H. and Kvasny, L. (2004), 'Recruitment is never enough: retention of women and minorities in the IT workplace', *Proceedings of 2004 SIGMIS Conference*, Tucson, AZ, pp. 84–91.

Todd, K., Mardis, L. and Wyatt, P. (2005), 'We've come a long way, baby! But where women and technology are concerned, have we really?', *Proceedings of the 2005 SICUCCS Conference*, pp. 380–87.

Tolbert, P.S., Andrews, A.O. and Simons, T. (1996), 'The effects of group proportions on group dynamics', in S.E. Jackson and M.N. Ruderman (eds), *Diversity in Work Teams: Research Paradigms for a Changing Workplace*, Washington, DC: American Psychological Association, pp. 131–59.

Trauth, E.M. (2002), 'Odd girl out: an individual differences perspective on women in the IT profession', *Technology & People*, **15**(2), 98–118.

Turkle, S. (1988), 'Computational reticence: why women fear the intimate machine', in C. Kramarae (ed.), *Technology and Women's Voices*, New York: Routledge & Kegan Paul, pp. 41–61.

Turner, J.C. (1982), 'Towards a cognitive redefinition of the social group', in H. Tajfel (ed.), *Social Identity and Intergroup Relations*, Cambridge: Cambridge University Press, pp. 15–40.

Waclawski, J. and Church, A.H. (eds) (2002), *Organization Development: A Data-driven Approach to Organizational Change*, San Francisco, CA: Jossey-Bass.

Wanberg, C.R., Welsh, E.T. and Hezlett, S.A. (2003), 'Mentoring research: a review and dynamic process model', in G.R. Ferris and J.J. Martocchio (eds), *Research in Personnel and Human Resources Management*, Vol. 22, Greenwich, CT: Elsevier Science/JAI Press, pp. 39–124.

Wharton, A.S. (1992), 'The social construction of gender and race in organizations: a social identity and group mobilization perspective', in P.S. Tolbert and S. Bacharach (eds), *Research in the Sociology of Organizations*, Vol. 10, Greenwich, CT: JAI Press, pp. 55–84.

Wilson, M. (2004), 'Conceptual framework for studying gender in IS research', *Journal of Information Technology*, **19**, 81–92.

Zohar, D. (1980), 'Safety climate in industrial organizations: theoretical and applied implications', *Journal of Applied Psychology*, **65**, 96–102.

Zohar, D. (2000), 'A group-level model of safety climate: testing the effect of group climate on microaccidents in manufacturing jobs', *Journal of Applied Psychology*, **85**, 587–96.

5. Voices of the future: African-American PhD candidates in the sciences

Daryl E. Chubin

A CHRONIC PROBLEM FOR US SCIENCE

America's science and engineering (S&E) workforce barely resembles the rest of America. The gender and ethnic composition of the general US population and workforce is far more diverse. Why is the increasingly diverse student population not opting for S&E careers? Students select careers based on a combination of interests, aptitude, role models, market influences, (mis)information and luck. Graduate and professional schools select students based on a set of indicators (mainly standardized test scores and college performance), perceptions and expectations that are similarly flawed. (For more on this, see www.bestworkforce.org/PDFdocs/BEST_BridgeforAll_HighEdDesignPrincipals.pdf.)

We don't measure 'potential' well. This is especially injurious to those who have not historically participated in these professions, notably minority students, who are a growing segment of the student population. Stereotyping and self-fulfilling prophecies crush aspirations and undermine development of America's diverse talent pool of African-American, Latino, American-Indian students, and those with disabilities (see www.aaas.org/standingourground).

The pattern for African Americans, observed for over half a century among US students, is bleak. The workforces of medicine, law, business and S&E remain overwhelmingly non-minority (www.cpst.org). According to *Doctorate Recipients from United States Universities: Summary Report 2004* (www.norc.uchicago.edu/issues/docdata.htm),

> Fewer than 2000 African American citizens and permanent residents earned PhDs in science and engineering fields. That represents 7 percent of the total awarded in S&E, with African American women earning almost twice as many as men. By broad field, African Americans represented 1.6 percent of the PhDs granted in engineering in 2004 to US citizens and permanent residents

(over 60 percent of the engineering PhDs went to noncitizens and temporary visa holders). Three percent of the life sciences doctorates were earned by African Americans. The numbers in some disciplines are so tiny as to defy sensibility: 17 in computer and information science, 13 in physics, 10 in mathematics, *zero* in astronomy!

INVESTMENT AS SOLUTION

The picture is all too clear, which makes the Graduate Scholars Program of the David and Lucile Packard Foundation (www.packardscholars.org/about.html) that much more vital. Established in 1992 and managed by the American Association for the Advancement of Science (www.aaas.org/news/releases/2005/0725gsp.shtml), since 2002, the Packard Graduate Scholars Program supports a significant fraction of African-American students pursuing a PhD in a science or engineering discipline. Students are nominated by the historically black colleges and universities (HBCUs) from which they are graduating and compete for a $20 000 annual stipend that is paid to the graduate institution and renewable for up to five years. Selections are made by a distinguished advisory panel. Their selection recognizes achievement and potential, defining them as an atypical sample buoyed by strong support from family, peers, mentors and role models.

Such support can be decisive. In the USA, one in two graduate S&E students fails to complete the PhD. And in nearly every US graduate science or engineering program, an African-American student will be visibly different, representing a small minority, and carrying a burden beyond the pressure to demonstrate academic excellence and attract investment of time and energy by faculty researchers.

These burdens are too seldom detailed. We don't ask graduate students what they think of the road to completing degree requirements and preparing for a career in science or engineering. We go to administrators, faculty and sponsors, but we don't ask the main educational client what they make of what is happening to them.

VOICES OF PACKARD SCHOLARS, 2005

In July 2005, 40 black graduates of HBCUs, all graduate students in science and engineering supported as Packard Scholars, sat clustered around tables in a meeting room at the Monterey Bay Aquarium. They reflected on their experiences two to five years after entering graduate school, having heard earlier that morning from five recently minted PhDs – alumni of the Packard program. Those still taking courses and learning the secrets of survival and teamwork were asked to discuss strategies, nagging concerns, what has changed and what hasn't during their journey through a rigorous doctoral program. What follows is a synopsis, largely in their voices, of their experiences.

The ruminations by this captive audience of doctoral students express some universal themes:

1. Pressure on Minority Students to Participate in Outreach to other Minority Students

I don't normally see outreach as a burden. I actually feel a great benefit from mentoring others, talking to others. I realize I spend a lot of my time on it, but I'm finishing my 5th year and going to the 6th. I realize I get something extra out of it, so I don't take it as an extra burden. When my advisor says, 'I need to be selfish with my time,' I just feel I can choose certain areas to be selfish with my time. However, I feel I can be the person to help another just starting grad school. Or I can be the professor who mentors a student, who goes to the high schools and be a science fair judge. That's just a personal thing: you have to figure out if you want to be a trailblazer.

The program I selected had four African American graduates in the last 10 years. Two more are there now and another came in with me. We're all happy. And that makes a huge difference. So create a pipeline. Establish a great relationship with one student; make one happy and others will hear their story. That is the easiest way to recruit because if they went to a black school, there are other students in their department who are looking for a good graduate program.

I can't honestly encourage anyone to come to my school. Why? Because all the meetings about diversity and minority participation – and I'm starting my 5th year – are the exact same meetings that were going on my 1st year. So it's like, what about the people that come after me? If in these past four years nothing has been done, I find myself sitting on the fence because I can't encourage, but I can't discourage either.

2. The Personal Conflicts of Students who Must Assign Competing Priorities to Outreach and their Research Agendas

At my institution, they are constantly doing surveys and holding meetings on how can we keep black people here, how can we help with retention, tell us what we could do. Most of us go to top tier universities, our professors are writing their own books, doing original research, testing all kinds of theories, and this and that. And you're going to tell me you can't come up with a way to keep me here? *No*, you're too smart for that and besides, I'm telling you what you should do. Diversity will not be an issue until you start diving into their pockets, their budgets, because they'll do anything and everything they have to do to get and keep their grants. But, if a university is #1 in the nation and they have all the money they need and new buildings, but they have never graduated an African American person, that's not their concern. Until it is urgent to them, they are not going to care. It's too easy to say, 'Oh, we don't know what to do, or we don't have the resources.' That's bull, because if you want the resources you can get them.

The problem that I and a lot of my colleagues have is that we are called upon to do a lot of diversity issues for the university. To sit on panels every time a black student is invited to the school, to take them out to attend meetings, to attend conferences, to take pictures for publications that show the diversity of the university. While we are doing these things, our counterparts are in the lab doing research and producing publications. It's just the torn feeling that I have and that I'm sure many people here share: how do I keep myself connected to community? When a first-year student comes in, I want them to see another black face, and to know that the BGSA [Black Government Student Association] is there. But how do I maintain that research direction and focus? I have an extra burden not carried by my majority colleagues. My time is torn between two places.

3. Students' Conflicting Ambivalence about their Need to be 'Trailblazers' in the Field

It's not fun being a trailblazer in 2005, because there are certain things we should not have to deal with. When you already have the responsibility and expectation of class work, nobody wants to carry the burden of the entire race and deal with issues that should have been resolved a long time ago. So my suggestions are for programs to implement diversity sensitivity training, and the school I'm at now, they have done that for the faculty. That stops a lot of the comments and issues in the labs and in the classroom. There is much better integration of the different cultures where I am now. Among the faculty, students, and staff it's a much friendlier environment.

For graduate school, I'm still at the same university I attended as an undergraduate, but I'm in a different department. There are only two of us, two black females. And when I was admitted they said, 'We're glad you're coming. We also have somebody else for you.' And I'm like what are you talking about? There was another new student who arrived later from [University X] and they just assumed since we are both black we are going to work together gung ho and do all of that good stuff. We were brought into director of minority affairs' office; it was like sitting in the principal's office when you're a little kid. He said, 'You guys have got to work together because the competition is going to be there. Keep in mind that there has never been an African American woman or man who has graduated from this department.' I'm all about trailblazing. That's why I went there. But, when he sat down and told us, 'They are going to look at you two and they are going to pick the better one and then probably nurture that one.' From that conversation on, this other student and I were *at it*. It was not a good situation at all. Long story short, she dropped out before I did and I went as far as my masters, because my thing is you want to be a trailblazer, you want to do certain things, but in my old age of *25*, I'm picking my battles and you know there are certain things you can and cannot do.

Yeah, I wanted to be a trailblazer, but I also want the Nobel Prize in physics. I don't want to trailblaze in race relations at the university. I want to focus on my research and come up with a new laser treatment for cancer, that's my focus. I don't want to have to deal with the other stuff. Let me be me, let me shine, get your foot off of my neck, let me do my work.

4. Frustrations with Mentoring during their PhD Studies

Competition is very healthy because it forces you to look at what the next person is doing and where they are. You form relationships and you start working with them. My mentor emphasizes collaboration. Because no matter where you go or what you do, you're going to have to work with someone. I've seen some faculty members who do not press collaboration and their students suffer because they get out in the world and they don't know how to communicate with anyone. And that is a big, big disadvantage. I think competition is good because it can be healthy and lead to collaboration.

When I started graduate school, the faculty taught us to work together, yet teach each other how to be competitive. In our first semester we collaborated a lot, and everybody else told us now it's your turn to break away. You need to stop being so dependent on one another. And we learned how to compete with one another, but in a healthy way. If I asked her how to do something she would guide me, but she wouldn't tell me. Our advisor treats the four of us differently. He told us, 'You are different people, and I'm going to approach you at your level, so I may not ask you to do something that I asked your cohort to do because you are at a different place. But the results should be the same, because you are all here to get the PhD. So don't compare yourself based on what I'm doing with him, because you are not at the same place.'

Just think about how far the world has come in ten years. Most of these cats [faculty] we're working for got their PhD in the 1980s, 70s. The technology is moving way too fast and with the stuff that we know we'll take their jobs. Some of them do everything they can to keep you from completing these programs, making it that much more difficult. The last thing they want to do is lose a job to you.

5. The Special Challenges Associated with Racial and Gender Bias (specifically African-American Women in PhD Programs)

Coming from an HBCU where the learning environment was more constructive and symbiotic to [University X], to be frank about it, I was overlooked several times because I was the only black in the class. I came up with strategies to cope. My best friend and I would intentionally split up in groups, so that if we weren't in the same group and would pair up with an Indian person or some other person. We were able to survive because he would bring the information back to me and vice versa. I have colleagues whose frame of reference is they know two or three Nobel Prize winners. They grew up in that environment. And I haphazardly chose to get a PhD!

When I came into my program, there were 72 students and there were 2 black people out of the whole group, me and another guy. And, it was pretty discouraging for me, at the beginning, and I sort of reached the point where there was this conflict. I felt the need to run and tell the world. You know, y'all are not doing enough. But at the same time, I didn't want to ruffle feathers and make it harder for me in the program. When do you decide you are going to be the activist? You can say, 'Oh I'm going to wait until I become a professor'. But you've got to get tenure, and how long is that going to take? You might be 65 by the time you're speaking out. So, that's my personal conflict. One thing I do is work with the dean of diversity in our college. I went to talk to her, and asked 'What are you doing about retention?' and she said, 'To be honest with you, we're doing a horrible job.' And I was like, 'Do you even know why people are leaving?'

I'm in medical school now [as an MD/PhD student], and there are institutionalized mechanisms that are designed with the philosophy that if we bring you to the school, it looks bad if we can't bring you to completion. Some of these or similar mechanisms, like 'big sib, little sib' mentoring situations can be implemented early. If you start to intervene after the first warning signs, these are still very much preventable problems. I think we would see a much improved attrition rate if we didn't wait until the problem is full blown – a classic ounce of prevention is worth a pound of cure.

REFLECTIONS LEAVENED BY RESEARCH AND FIELDWORK

The Packard Scholars' observations allow some generalizations beyond race, ethnicity or gender. They apply to all S&E advanced graduate students, as the AAAS Center for Advancing Science and Engineering Capacity (www.aaascapacity.org) has discovered. The Capacity Center was created to provide technical assistance to universities and colleges committed to improving the success of all students and faculty, especially those of color. The Packard Scholars confront the barriers that we often see in our site visits, focus groups, and data reviews (for the Center's approach, see www.awis.org/voice/magazine/34-1/chubin.pdf). We try to distill from our work with academic clients those strategies and practices that make a difference in a particular institutional and/or disciplinary context, as illustrated below.

- *New PhDs underestimate the skill sets that they possess* They don't realize how much they know and can do. Their orientation is to a single sector or career pathway that represents immediate job opportunity but little demand for versatility. It also reflects the biases of their major professors who have had a particular kind of career. Oddly, the doctoral training process reproduces the past, the traditions that fit an earlier time. Consequently, the PhD experiences *minimize* belief and understanding about skills. The Capacity Center illuminates the skills that twenty-first-century organizations, academic and non-academic alike, crave: teamwork, problem solving, communication, cultural competence.

- *It is the student's responsibility to establish the terms of fulfillment of the doctorate* This form of accountability is a 'performance contract' between student and major professor (if not one's dissertation committee). It reveals to the student the delicate balance of his/her endeavor: to earn a PhD you are supposed to be an independent researcher and yet, during the process leading to the completion of the degree you have to accommodate what your major professor and committee want. The Center counsels negotiating with faculty and team leaders the terms of declaring independence while building trust and becoming valued as a member of the team.

- *Interpersonal relations in a department or program are shaped in part by larger institutional and cultural realities* Different kinds of institutions can be 'minority serving': the largest producers among baccalaureate institutions of PhDs in S&E, disaggregated by group, show that HBCUs dominate the undergraduate origins of African-American doctoral production, and HSIs for Latinos who go on to earn the PhD. But Cal-Berkeley, MIT, Michigan and Stanford, among others, have distinguished records as the baccalaureate origins of minorities who go on to earn a doctorate in science or engineering. In addition, relative newcomers such as University of Maryland-Baltimore County (Meyerhoff Scholarship Program, www.umbc.edu/meyerhoff/) and Louisiana State University (Louisiana Science, Technology, Engineering and Mathematics [LA-STEM] Research Scholars Program, www.lsu.edu/lastem/index.htm (and a Capacity Center client) are undergraduate models of student preparation for science-based PhDs.

- *There are seemingly timeless, trans-generational elements to the graduate experience* For all the praise of mentors and role models, there will always be successful professional women and persons of color who will say, 'Hey, look it was tough for me and it's going to be tough for those who come behind me.' These folks will not reach out. This has nothing to do with when or where they earned their degree or their field. That's just the way they are. They make assumptions, suppress memories of the help they received, and approach students *their* way. But this has a very large public policy dimension. It's also why we have programs like the Packard Scholars and the NSF suite of programs offered at every level of education. We know there are more capable students out there than we are producing. And if they need a little more support at some time, then these programs are designed to provide it. They offer opportunities and change lives.

- *This is about leadership – the need to grow leaders*   Change comes as new professionals ascend to positions that control resources and decisions. If it means climbing up the academic ladder, fine. If it means going non-academic, fine. Both routes demonstrate that it's who you know plus what you know that matters. Not one or the other exclusively. Who's in your network? Who talks to whom? First, you must get your foot in the door. Then you perform.

ANOTHER DATA POINT – THE 2006 ANNUAL PACKARD SCHOLARS CONFERENCE

In July 2006, 30 Packard Scholars journeyed to Washington, DC, to reunite with friends and update their research progress in poster sessions and reflect again on their experiences. (In the previous 12 months, another eight Scholars had either been conferred the PhD or were scheduled before the end of the summer of 2006 to defend their dissertation.) An 'open discussion' session, moderated by two recent Packard alumni and this author, tapped into new lodes of information about the transition into the workforce and the professoriate – not only what did or did not help them to get there, but also how it feels and what could be different for the cohorts that follow.

Three themes emerged from the free-flowing 90-minute discussion: faculty induction; undergraduate preparation for graduate study in the sciences and engineering; and how confidence is self-renewing and -sustaining. The Scholars report that roughly two of three have accompanied faculty to a professional meeting. A similar majority has presented a research talk at such a meeting. And one of three collaborates with someone at another institution.

The benefits of these experiences are both obvious and subtle. Peers outside one's home department/institution enrich research programs. They also compensate for indifferent faculty back home who are not inclined to mentor or even socialize their students into life as a professor. Such 'tormentors' come in all ethnicities and both sexes. In contrast, there is a caring, nurturing faculty style that imparts both the professional preparation and political skills needed to flourish in the academic culture (www.aaas.org/news/releases/2006/0802packard.shtml). Indeed, most Scholars point to political struggles – and strategies that help in coping in the lab or with a recalcitrant professor – as more daunting than the coursework.

Sometimes organizations such as the National Society of Black Physicists and the National Organization for the Professional Advancement of Black Chemists and Chemical Engineers afford networking and presentation opportunities with those whose academic origins and trials most resemble the Packard Scholar's own. This is where fellowship support is vital. It provides an independent source of funds that can cover travel and meeting registration expenses. It is the link to the professional community, job advice, and the collegiality of other recent PhDs. Above all, it is an incomparable vehicle for building confidence.

Confidence is an elusive characteristic to gauge, its expression both personal and idiosyncratic. The common denominator with the Packard Scholars is an educational foundation in an HBCU. When they arrive at their doctoral institutions, they exude confidence. Then coursework begins. The competition has never been tougher. But they realize, over time and through interaction with their peers, that they are no less prepared than those with an Ivy League or Big Ten baccalaureate. Focus on the doctorate and due diligence in progressing toward it are huge confidence boosters. Perseverance in the face of adversity – intellectual, emotional, financial – spells the difference between completion of the degree requirements and termination with the master's.

Most Packard Scholars earn the PhD (Completion data for the population are being assembled, but the estimate over the life of the program is about 70 percent, which would far exceed the national average for all students in science and engineering.) Even for the survivors, however, the graduate experience takes a toll. Most face more years in a postdoctoral position. Some decide that after 'getting beat up' as the only African American, or one of a very few minorities in their doctoral institution, to return to an HBCU as an assistant professor. Most know the value of having faculty who look like the students. Role models matter.

Nevertheless, career trade-offs are difficult. Research universities have better infrastructure for developing a research program. But at what cost – isolation, hostility from some in one's department, indifference from the campus community? For a few, non-academic prospects further confound decision making. Industry beckons – less flexibility in the focus of research, but more welcoming work environment and often near a city rich in ethnic diversity. Welcome to 'career launch' in science in the new millennium!

Where to commit to a first job is a very personal decision. It is not unlike the student's decision to study at a majority institution rather than an HBCU. No one can prescribe the most appropriate path. We each must travel independently – find a path or make our own.

CLOSING THOUGHTS

As a response to a national policy issue, the Packard Scholars Program provides a unique opportunity to diversify the science and engineering workforce. At the same time, it affords glimpses at a population in the throes of professional career development. The nation has invested in science and engineering since Sputnik – a half-century – in a very serious, sustained way. This investment is intended to advance the national interest.

The National Academies' Board on Life Sciences has established a Committee on Encouraging Underrepresented Minorities to Pursue Biomedical Research Careers, which builds on a 2005 National Research Council report, Assessment of NIH Minority Research Training Programs: Phase 3 (www.nap.edu/catalog/11329.html). The Committee seeks to identify intervention programs that 'enhance the participation of underrepresented minorities in conducting mentored scientific research at the undergraduate and graduate levels'. As a member of that Committee, I plan to cite the Packard Graduate Scholars Program as 'exhibit A' of an intervention that works (though no new awards have been made after 2003).

If students are not being recruited and nurtured to degree completion, we are wasting talent and material resources. It's to the detriment of the nation and in defiance of student demographics. That's the value – and promise – of the Packard Scholars. This is the future of US science and technology.

ACKNOWLEDGEMENTS

Daryl E. Chubin, PhD, is grateful to his AAAS colleagues Linda Akli, Yolanda George and Shirley Malcom for proposing the 2005 'talk-back' session and the 2006 'open discussion' on which this chapter is partially based; to Jason Carmichael for transcribing the audiotapes of the 2005 session; to the research support of Sabira Mohamed; and to the sage team at Laufer Green Isaac for assisting in myriad ways. Some material in this chapter elaborates on 'Minding the student client', InsideHigherEd.com, 13 February 2006, www.insidehighered.com/views/2006/02/13/chubin.

6. Women in the land of milk, honey and high technology: the Israeli case

Ronit Kark

In the 1990s, Israel emerged as a leading center for technology start-ups and innovation. In the year 2000, near the peak of the high-tech boom, Israel had about 4000 high-tech firms and new ones were forming at the rate of about 500 start-ups per year (de Fontenay and Carmel, 2004). At this stage Israel had the highest number of engineers per capita in the world and the high-tech sector comprised 15 percent of Israel's overall economy (Adams et al., 2003). The centrality of high technology to the Israeli economy can be seen in the fact that its exports in 2000 accounted for approximately one-third of the country's total industrial exports (Israel Central Bureau of Statistics, 2002). Israel has the third (after the USA and Canada) highest number of companies listed in NASDAQ (Breznitz, 2005; Eidelman and Hazzan, 2005). As early as the 1960s and 1970s, large American companies, such as IBM and Motorola, first made Israel into one of their leading development centers, while from the mid-1980s the number of international companies operating in the country has been growing. Alongside these, thousands of local start-ups were founded, some of which went on to become independent multinational firms that are traded on the NASDAQ and compete successfully with the global giants from the Silicon Valley (de Fontenay and Carmel, 2004; Teubal and Avnimelech, 2003).

Since the early 1990s, high-tech industry has played a central role in the Israeli economy, while turning the whole country into what the industry calls 'Silicon Wadi' (the term 'wadi' means a canyon or gorge, and is commonly used in Hebrew and Arabic; de Fontenay and Carmel, 2004). At the end of the 1990s the growth rate of export of high-tech industry was 12 percent, whereas other sectors of export grew at the rate of only of 4 percent (Ha-Poalim Bank, 2000). Furthermore, it employed around 6 percent of all workers in the country, the highest rate for any industrialized nation in that year (Central Bureau of Statistics, 2002). In the first three quarters of 2000, foreign investors made acquisitions of Israeli high-tech firms totaling $12 billion, and since then many more large-scale acquisitions have taken place (de Fontenay and Carmel, 2004). Currently, 43 out of the 50 leading technology giants in the world have a research and development center in Israel.

One way to evaluate the achievements of Israeli high-tech industry is by the number of patents per person in the country. At the start of the 1970s the number of patents in Israel compared to other countries in the Western world was quite low. From the mid-1980s there was tremendous growth in the number of original registered patents and, from 1997 on, only Japan and the USA surpassed Israel (Ha-Poalim Bank, 2000). Some of Israel's achievements in the fields of invention and innovation can be partially attributed to the high ranking of Israeli scientists. *Scientific American's* list of '50 leading' research leaders for the year 2004 includes three Israeli scientists. Four Israelis have recently been awarded the Nobel Prize. Two were awarded in the field of chemistry in 2004 to Professor Aaron Ciechanover and Professor Avram Hersko from the Israel Institute of Technology. The other two prizes were awarded in the field of economics: Professor Robert J. Aumann received the prize in 2005 and Professor Daniel Kahneman, who was born in Israel and received his BA from the Hebrew University of Jerusalem, was named laureate in 2002.

In terms of numbers (the population is currently 6.5 million), Israel's success in the fields of technology and science is striking. However, although it a leading country in technology and science and is perceived as an equal opportunity country, there are disproportionately few women in the fields of science, technology, engineering and mathematics (STEM). Thus, although Israel can be dubbed 'the land of milk, honey and high technology', in the words of Izraeli (1994), women remain to a large extent 'outsiders in the promised land' with regard to their representation in STEM. One notable (and somewhat distorted) indication of this can be seen in the September 2006 edition of *The IT Magazine: The Yearly Israeli Magazine of Business Computation*. A quick glance through the pages of this colorful magazine reveals a conspicuously gendered image of the IT sector in Israel. The cover page of the magazine features a large color photo of a man and three smaller pictures, also all of men. An additional 35 color photos of men grace the inside pages. All these men are CEOs, managers, experts, consultants and academics in the field. By contrast, only two photos of women can be found and these are in advertisements, not content-based material.

This chapter discusses recent data regarding women's representation in these fields in Israel, and then suggests four key explanations for their limited showing in the fields of STEM that take the unique features of the Israeli context into account. I examine the different stages of the life cycle of Israeli women that aid and abet their integration in the fields of STEM. I start with girls' typical experiences in high school, and then turn to young

women's experiences in their mandatory military service. I then discuss the
ways in which specific features of the culture of familialism and motherhood in Israel affect their representation in STEM. Last I analyze the possible role of the Hebrew language in hindering women's advancement in
fields of science and technology. I conclude by presenting a few programs
currently being implemented in Israel to address these issues and to further
women's integration in the fields of STEM.

WOMEN IN STEM IN ISRAEL: SOME DATA/NUMBERS

A 2003 survey conducted by the Ministry of Science explored the basic attitudes and assumptions of the Israeli population regarding women's equal
opportunity education and employment in the sciences. The survey showed
that most people had positive attitudes toward women in the sciences
and responded positively to the statement that 'women's potential abilities
to study and be involved in research in the field of science and technology
are equal to that of men' (Messner-Yaron and Kahanovitch, 2003).
Furthermore, respondents were in favor of women having careers in these
sectors. However, although the public showed a positive and equitable attitude toward women in science and technology, the actual status of women
in Israel in these fields is far from equitable.

Women's Representation in Science and Academia

In the last decade there has been a rise in the number of women enrolled
in Israeli universities. In 2005 women made up 56 percent of the undergraduate student body, 57.4 percent of those at the master's degree level
and 52.8 percent at the PhD level. Thus, although women account for more
than 50 percent of the graduate students as a whole, the figures for the
exact sciences, technology and engineering paint a different picture. For
example, a recent survey (Berlinski, 2005) shows that in mathematics, statistics and computer sciences, the number of women awarded different
degrees ranges between 26 percent and 37 percent, with the lowest percentage for PhDs. In the various branches of engineering, the percentage
of women is even lower, and is around 26 percent for all the engineering
degrees combined.

Recent data show that women and engineering still form an odd couple
in Israel. At the 2006 graduation ceremony at Tel-Aviv University's School
of Engineering, 27 women completed their studies as compared to 296 men
(Grimland, 2006).

Table 6.1   University students by gender and field of studies, 2005
(percentage of women)

Field of studies	BA	MA	PhD
Humanities	66.8	64.5	57.2
Education	85.5	87.5	78.5
Social sciences	66.4	67.4	61.4
Business management	54.9	47.0	50.7
Law	55.4	51.0	39.0
Medicine	50.8	51.2	66.2
Engineering and architecture	26.7	25.7	27.2
Agriculture	59.4	57.5	56.0
Biological science	66.0	63.9	56.8
Physical science	36.7	37.8	37.5
Mathematics, statistics and computer science	34.5	29.5	26.4
Total	55.9	57.3	52.8

Note: The information is taken from a report of the Council for Higher Education.

Despite the fact that the percentage of women graduating from doctoral programs exceeds 50 percent, only 24 percent of the faculty at all levels and research fields (including in the arts, humanities and social sciences) are women. Furthermore, the higher one climbs on the academic ladder, the lower the number of women, and at the highest echelon (i.e. full professors) it is somewhat less than 10 percent (Messner-Yaron and Kahanovitch, 2003). In engineering, mathematics and physics, women make up between 7 percent and 12 percent of the faculty at all ranks; only 4–5 percent of all full professors are women (see Tables 6.1 and 6.2).

Naturally the numbers vary according to the field of research. Whereas the number of women researchers on the whole is higher in the humanities (35 percent of the faculty), social sciences (25 percent), medicine (33 percent) and life sciences (21 percent), their number in the faculty of exact sciences – engineering, mathematics, physics and technology studies – is small (e.g., engineering 12 percent, physics 8 percent). For example, at the Technion (Israel Institute of Technology), Israel's leading school of engineering, the percentage of women faculty members in the Department of Electrical Engineering is only four (8 percent) out of 50 faculty members (Hazzan et al., 2005). The number of full professors is even lower: in 2002 only 4 percent of the full professors in mathematics, computer sciences and statistics in all universities were women (Messner-Yaron and Kahanovitch, 2003) and in the Technion, which for many years produced the country's

Table 6.2   *University faculty by gender and field of studies, 2002*
             (percentage of women)

Field of studies	Lecturer	Senior lecturer	Professor	Full professor	Total
Humanities	49.8	42.9	32.4	19.9	35.6
Education	60.7	52.1	43.4	39.4	50.7
Social sciences	42.8	37.6	18.2	11.6	27.7
Business management	42.1	9.4	14.5	0.00	16.5
Law	17.7	36.5	12.4	17.7	21.1
Medicine	51.5	48.0	33.2	15.8	33.0
Engineering and architecture	19.7	21.1	10.6	4.8	12.1
Agriculture	32.4	21.7	13.3	0.0	13.6
Biological science	33.0	20.8	26.4	14.3	21.1
Physical science	49.9	14.8	7.9	4.2	8.2
Mathematics statistics and computer science	33.0	10.1	8.2	4.0	7.7
Total for 2002 (the data above)	44.7	33.6	21.6	10.6	24.6
Total for 2005*	43.4	36.0	21.4	11.9	24.5

Notes: The information is taken from a report of the National Council for the Promotion of Women in Science and Technology.
* The information is taken from a report of the Council for Higher Education.

scientific and engineering elite, the number of women full professors in 2006 was merely 5 percent in all fields (Churchman, 2006).

Women's Representation in Industry

The high-tech industry in Israel has been growing intensively and both men and women are employed in the field. According to data published by the Chief Scientist in the Ministry of Science and Head Researcher of Israel, the percentage of women working in science and technology in Israel is about 25 percent, whereas women constitute 45 percent of the labor force (Messner-Yaron and Kahanovitz, 2005). These numbers reflect women at different levels; however, in management positions in the fields of technology their numbers are even smaller.

According to data concentrating solely on the high-tech field, the proportion of women working in high technology, in the broadest sense of the term (including non-technology jobs) in the year 2001 constituted about 34 percent of all employees (Central Bureau of Statistics, 2002). More recent data, from the year of 2005, indicate similar numbers (Central Bureau of

Statistics, 2005). According to the Central Bureau of Statistics (2002), high-tech industry is still defined as a 'masculine' field as regards the percentage of women in its ranks. The report, which covers data from 1995 to 1999, further shows that although the number of women employed in the labor force in Israel in general increased in this time period and that the gaps between the percentage of women and men decreased in many fields, their numbers in the high-tech field remained stable, fluctuating between 30 percent and 35 percent, as did the gender gap. Inside high-tech firms themselves more women joined the communication sector, whereas their representation in the sectors of computing and research and development remained small, and did make a meaningful increase in these four years. This proportion of women is similar to many EU countries (European Commission, 2001), but is significantly higher than in countries such as the UK and the Netherlands (Frenkel, 2006).

With regard to managerial positions in high-tech firms, there has been a notable change. For example, a 1999 survey showed that in that year 68 percent of firms from high-tech industry employed at least one woman manager, in comparison with 49 percent in 1996. However, more factories employ at least one female manager in the electronics and electricity sector (76 percent) in comparison with firms in the software sector (60 percent). Furthermore, the number of female managers in the high-tech sector increased from 14 percent in 1996 to 20 percent in 1999. One unexpected and somewhat worrying piece of data shows that as the firms expand from small start-ups to larger companies, the number of women managers decreases in comparison with the number of men managers. In firms that employ over 100 employees, women comprise 18 percent of the managers, whereas in firms that employ up to 29 employees, women comprise 25 percent of the managers (Israel Industrial Union, 2000). Furthermore, according to the data reported by the Chief Scientist in the Ministry of Science and Head Researcher in Israel, in 2005 only 7 percent of the entre-preneurs in Israel were women. Thus although there are hundreds of start-ups in Israel and every year there are dozens more, the number of women launching start-ups is small.

Furthermore, it is interesting to note that although Israel has one of the highest number of patents per person in the world (surpassed only by two big countries; Ha-Poalim Bank, 2000), the percentage of women inventors is low. Between 2000 and 2005, among the patents submitted to the Registrar of Patents less than 6 percent were submitted by women inven-tors (Yaniski-Ravid, 2007).

This on the whole indicates that although women are represented in various ways among the people involved and working in science and tech-nology in Israel, they are still a minority. Furthermore, although there are some indications in the data provided above that call for some optimism in terms of women's representation, there are also indications that in many of the sectors the rate of change of women's entry into prestigious and influential positions has been much slower than expected. In the following section I present some of the unique characteristics of Israeli society and culture which may account for women's limited representation in the sciences and technology.

BARRIERS TO WOMEN'S INTEGRATION IN STEM IN ISRAEL

There is a long list of barriers and hurdles associated with the somewhat limited representation of women in fields of STEM in Israel. Some have worldwide relevance and apply to many countries, whereas others are unique to the Israeli context. Here I examine the impact of the Israeli school system, compulsory military service, and the effects of familialism and motherhood on women's advancement. I then turn to other overarching factors, such as the possible effects of the Hebrew language as contributing to the creation and preservation of the gender gap.

The School System as Affecting Women in STEM

One of the obstacles to women's advancement in the fields of STEM may be rooted in early education. A career in science and technology requires a background in mathematics. In Israel, to be awarded a high school matriculation certificate, which is a prerequisite for higher education, one needs to pass the mathematics examination at the average (3 points), advanced (4 points) or highly advanced (5 points) tracks. As can be seen from Table 6.3, most girls in Israel decide to take low (3 points) or average track math, which is an inherent disadvantage to starting a career in science and technology. However, it is interesting to note that at all levels, the percentage of girls passing and excelling is higher than that of boys. In fact, in 2003, the difference in percentages between boys and girls increased in favor of girls, both in the percentages of students passing the exams and those excelling in them (Churchman, 2006; Messner-Yron and Kahanovitz, 2003, 2005). Girls' higher grades in the lower math tracks indicate that they could probably have succeeded in the advanced or the highly advanced levels, although possibly with somewhat lower grades. This would be to their advantage since many of the fields of science and technology in the higher education system either require higher levels of mathematics even to apply, or give greater weight when calculating the average matriculation test score,

Table 6.3 Achievements in mathematics high school matriculation exams by gender (%), 2003

Gender	Taking the exam				Passing				Excelling			
	3 units	4 units	5 units	Total	3 units	4 units	5 units	Total	3 units	4 units	5 units	Total
Boys	52.8	26.2	21.0	100	86.5	96.5	98.3	91.6	33.0	51.1	64.8	44.4
Girls	57.1	27.8	15.1	100	90.9	97.8	98.6	94.0	44.8	59.9	66.9	52.4

Note: The information is taken from the Ministry of Education website.

to higher math and physics tracks. Thus a high grade in a lower track of mathematics is less advantageous than a somewhat lower grade at a highly advanced level.

The fact that at all levels girls' scores are better than those of boys suggests that girls' innate ability cannot account for for the small proportion of girls choosing to be tested at the higher levels of math. Rather, social and psychological reasons are more likely to lie behind this phenomenon (Messner-Yaron and Kahanovitch, 2005) According to a recent report from the Technion (Churchman, 2006), girls' decisions to study lower levels of mathematics are partially explained by direct and subtle messages conveyed to them by parents and teachers suggesting that 'certain subjects (such as mathematics, physics and computer science) are meant for boys and not for girls'. Although this stereotype is contradicted by the fact that girls score higher on the mathematics high school matriculation exams than boys, unfortunately, most teachers, parents and pupils are not aware of these statistics, and thus it is the stereotype that continues to influence their behavior and girls continue to choose lower levels of studies.

Apart from mathematics, in the field of computer studies the picture is similar. Worldwide surveys indicate that the number of women studying undergraduate-level computer science is constantly decreasing (Galpin, 2002). High school is thought to be a critical point in the computer science pipeline where many female students are lost. Formal and informal data indicate that the percentages of high school girls who study computer science in Israel at the highest level of the matriculation exam remain relatively low. For example, in the years 1998, 1999 and 2000 the percentages of girls who took the highest level of the computer science matriculation exam were 26 percent, 27 percent and 29 percent respectively (Adams et al., 2003).

According to a study by Eidelman and Hazzan (2005), there is a significant difference between the Arab and Jewish sectors in the percentages of female high school students studying advanced level computer science. Specifically, in the sector of the Jewish majority in Israel only 25 percent of those studying high school computer science are female, whereas in the Arab minority sector 50 percent of those studying at the higher level are female.

Two different explanations have been given for these unexpected findings. First, noticeable differences exist in the amount of encouragement Arab female students reported that they receive from various close agents, especially teachers, in comparison to Jewish female students. Arab female high school students reported that they were encouraged more by their mothers (56 percent versus 40 percent), fathers (44 percent versus 40 percent), siblings (44 percent versus 16 percent), friends (44 percent versus 20 percent), and acquaintances who had studied computer science (50 percent versus

20 percent) and – with the greatest difference – by their teachers (56 percent versus 8 percent). One possible explanation for the difference in encouragement is based on findings of other studies that explored cultural and familial differences between Arab and Jewish adolescents. According to these studies, since Arab students are a minority group, as well as a part of an Eastern, collective culture, it is likely that their parents and teachers support higher scholastic achievement in order to help them improve their social status (Peleg-Popko et al., 2003).

Second, the Jewish and Arab sectors in Israel study in separate educational systems. The Arab educational system offers a more limited range of subjects to choose from, including the more conventional and basic subjects (e.g. mathematics, computer science, physics and literature), whereas the Israeli students can choose less conventional subjects (e.g. drama, arts, music, sociology, psychology), as well as the more conventional ones. The limited choice offered to pupils in the Arab sector leads to higher rates of female pupils choosing to study computer science (Eidelman and Hazzan, 2005). Unfortunately, despite the fact that Arab female students make up about half of the computer science classrooms in high schools, according to their self-reports about their future career orientations, this will probably not help to expand the 'shrinking pipeline' in the Arab sector. According to the results of a survey administered to students, most Arab female students have already decided on their future professions and only a small percentage of them consider majoring in computer science, while the majority choose stereotypic female professions (Eidelman and Hazzan, 2005). Thus the better starting point of the female Arab students apparently does not carry over to higher education and industry.

From the above it can be concluded that when female high school students in Israel graduate, in many cases they have already accumulated some disadvantages in terms of their future ability to become integrated into the fields of science and technology. Support and encouragement of teachers and parents are likely to help in promoting girls to aim higher in the fields of mathematics, physics and computer science; however, at this stage such encouragement by authority and educational figures remains weak.

The Israeli Military and its Impact on Women in STEM

In Israel, service in the armed forces is mandatory. Following high school graduation men and women are drafted when they reach the age of 18. This stage in their life cycle has enormous impact on their future careers.

In a recent international competition for 120 novel inventions in the field of technology held by *The Wall Street Journal* in 2004, two Israeli inventions were awarded second and third place. The first firm developed a video capsule that films the intestines and the second developed an ultrasound device (using magnetic resonance imaging – MRI) for the removal of cancerous growths through a non-intrusive procedure. The success of these inventions was attributed by the inventors to their work in the past in the Israeli military in units that develop technological inventions aimed to improve combat (e.g. special missiles, devices for night sight) (Brazilai, 2004). The head of one of these firms stated:

> The medical device we developed is similar in principle to a 'command and control' military device. Now we are trying to develop the future operating room, which will be one that does not involve blood. Thus, the day after the surgery, the patient will be able to go to work.

As can be seen from the news item above, the Israeli military is most influential in affecting the field of high technology and engineering in Israel. A unique characteristic of Israel is the influence of the military in almost every area of private and public life, and the widespread overlap of the military and civilian spheres (Izraeli, 1994; Kimmerling, 1993). As such it can play a central role in determining women's ability to become involved and to progress in the labor force in the fields of high technology, engineering and, to a lesser extent, in science and research. In this section I will first provide a general background about women in the Israeli military, and then discuss the impact of the Israeli military on the high technology field. This section ends with an analysis of the specific impact army service can have on women in the fields of high technology and engineering in Israel.

Women's status in the Israeli military
In Israel, service in the armed forces is mandatory. Men and women are drafted after high school, when they reach the age of 18. The Zionist vision of a 'people's army', the pre-state socialistic ideology (Berkovitch, 1999), and the prolonged Arab–Israeli conflict, leading to the country's pervasive security needs, have all turned Israel into the only Western state with compulsory conscription for both men and women. Mandatory military service for both men and women could signify the construction of a gendered egalitarian citizenship. However, the Israeli military is still a male-dominated territory which values masculinity (Sasson Levi, 2003). Unlike men, women are easily exempt from the army, on the grounds of pregnancy, marriage or religious belief. Thus the law grants priority to a cultural ideology that values women's family responsibilities over their obligations to army service (Berkovitch, 1997; Izraeli, 1997).

Women comprise only 32 percent of the regular army; they serve a shorter term than do men (women are recruited for two years and men for three) and are usually excluded from combat roles. Furthermore, most men who have served in the military are required to serve for 30–40 days per year on reserve duty, at least until the age of 40–45. Women are usually exempt, except for those who have specific skills and training who may be called up to the age of 26 or until they become mothers. (Men do reserve duty and spend around one month per year in the army until the age of 45, whereas women at most times are excluded from reserve duty once they finish their compulsory service.) These structural and organizational differences between men and women limit the range of roles to which women may be posted and constitute explicit barriers to women's advancement to higher ranks in the military (Izraeli, 1997; Cohen, 1997).

Furthermore, the strong link between military service and citizenship in Israel extends the effect of the military on women's status not only to the period of their army service, but in Israeli civilian society more generally. Thus the differential treatment of men and women in the military and women's marginalization generate differential opportunities for mobility, both within the military and in civilian life, that privilege men. The advantages men obtain and derive from military service are converted into advantages in civilian life. Military elites shift easily into roles in civilian elites (e.g. political, managerial, educational, etc.), thus contributing to the sustainability and reproduction of gender inequality (Izraeli, 2001).

The effect of the military on hi-tech industry in Israel
Israel's military is perceived as a hotbed for high-tech entrepreneurs and an important base for the continuing success of the software industry in Israel (Breznitz, 2005; Teubal and Avnimelech, 2003). From 1960 to the present, the military has played a crucial role in the spread of computerization and information technology skills in Israel, thus helping to create an independent industrial sector. According to Breznitz (2005), the military performs various important functions that contribute to the development of the Israeli IT industry. These functions are explained below.

Training and human capital   Young soldiers stay a limited time (up to six years) in the military and do short reserve duty stints. This results in intensive investment in training, and extreme responsibility for R&D is given to very young individuals. This produces highly trained and experienced professionals who form a large pool of trained young people who can join industry thanks to the army.

Collective learning and dissemination of knowledge   The military constitutes a major means of collective learning. Because of the unique structure of reserve duty in Israel, military working teams are composed of former graduates who are civilian experts from a variety of firms and academic institutions, who do their reserve duty alongside active duty soldiers. Since these teams work together in the national interest and with a sense of patriotic camaraderie and mutual trust, they are able to collaborate and share their knowledge in a way that would not be possible outside the military. Furthermore, apart from contributing to the military, the reserve personnel are themselves constantly exposed to the knowledge gathered and created in the military, as well as to the knowledge of their comrades, knowledge they take back to their firms.

Foreign knowledge transfer   The Israeli military plays an important role in the process of exposing the Israeli IT industry to knowledge acquired from foreign software tools and IT companies. The military is often a leader in the acquisition of new tools and state-of-the-art knowledge from abroad, and organizes training courses, hence enabling faster dissemination of the latest software development techniques in Israel.

Social networks and community building   Graduates and reserve personnel of military technological units create dense networks of knowledge, recruitment and venture capital. Professional networks are known to facilitate information spillovers between firms, thereby promoting the spread of the most successful techniques and technologies, organizational structures, and contributing to the rapid movement of talented labor (Saxenian, 1994; Teubal and Avnimelech, 2003). The uniqueness of Israel is that the military serves as the foundation for these dense and large professional high-tech networks. Since Israelis go through several years of military service at a formative stage in their lives, connections with army friends function much as do university connections in the USA, with the added benefit that they are more closely-knit, and that the individuals have observed each other during high-impact work with the military, and can better evaluate each others' capabilities. Therefore, it is common for high-tech start-up founders to recruit a core team from old army friends and acquaintances. Army background also helps employers and investors make selection decisions: data on a person's unit and performance in the army are easily available, and these provide a great deal of information as to a person's ability, work habits and leadership qualities. For example, someone from an elite intelligence unit may be offered a job, or a leadership position in a civilian firm, merely on that basis (Breznitz, 2005).

The effect of the military on women in STEM in Israel
In light of the crucial role played by the Israeli military in the development of the software industry in Israel, it is of great significance to explore how the military affects women's integration into these fields. The military's role

with respect to women's advancement can be seen as a double-edged sword, limiting some opportunities and fostering others. Since the early 1970s, women have been assigned to computer training in the military's computer center (Izraeli, 1994). The army recognized the importance of being able to use young women in technological fields, and has worked towards increasing their numbers (Churchman, 2006). Since young men who can be accepted on software and IT courses often have to be recruited out of a limited pool of candidates who have a low combat profile, the military prefers to recruit a larger number of women for these courses, because they can be drawn from the entire pool of women on active duty. Thus there are a number of programs that enable young women, whether before they enter the army or at the beginning of their service, to acquire an education in these areas.

The percentage of women in many of these courses is often high, and in some courses they are the majority. However, in the more prestigious computing and programming courses, although there have always been women participants, their numbers are more limited (about 20 percent of the participants). There are several reasons for the limited number of women in these courses. First, these courses require higher levels of mathematics and computer science, and, as noted above, Jewish women do not tend to specialize or study the highest levels of these topics in the school system. Thus they are not likely to be accepted on some of these courses. Second, these specialized, 'elite' courses require the participants to sign up for a few extra years of army service. Some young women who have the potential to participate in these courses may be reluctant to sign on for the extra years. Furthermore, although women may be represented in large numbers in the lower ranks of the units specializing in computing and software, there are few women in the higher ranks of these units. For example, data regarding a related field show that women officers in engineering roles are represented mostly at the lower ranks, both professionally and formally (women make up 30 percent of academic professional officers, but only 0.4 percent of the senior academic officers; 29 percent lieutenants, 0 percent colonels) (Messner-Yaron and Kahanovitch, 2003). Moreover, many of the men who serve in these units stay in contact with the units during their reserve duty and work in these units many days each year (up to 40 days per year). The women, on the other hand, as explained above, are not expected to do reserve duty in most cases.

This forms a complex dynamic overall, in which, on the one hand, women's participation in these units enables them to have some access to many of the benefits acquired by service in such units (e.g. training, experience, state-of-the-art knowledge, access to foreign knowledge, and an opportunity for networking). For example, a number of women 'army graduates' today head software and computer service companies (Izraeli,

1994). However, since there are fewer young women in the prestigious computing courses and the higher-ranking echelons, and almost no women do reserve duty, their access to training, experience and knowledge is more limited than that of men. Furthermore, the ability of women in such circumstances to develop social networks – which are so important for access to information and support, as well as to people, places and jobs in civilian society – are more limited (Izraeli, 1997). Moreover, since women barely take part in reserve duty, all the processes of ongoing knowledge accumulation and updates, and their ability to form ties with soldiers during reserve duty (including academics and other graduates working in competing companies) is denied to women. Reserve duty also brings together people from many different walks of life who might otherwise not meet. Serving together creates social bonds of mutual obligation that bypass status differences in civilian life and often extend beyond the service. Etzioni-Halevy (1996), in her study of civilian–military relations in Israel, found that senior officers meet civilian elites and prepare their second careers while still in the military (Izraeli, 2001).

Thus, although the military provides young women with a jumping board to the high-tech and other related fields, the young men in these units gain more tangible and long-term benefits for their future civilian career in related fields.

Ideals of Familialism and Motherhood as Affecting Women in STEM

After going through the military, the next stage for most Israeli women is that of creating their own family, while continuing their studies and starting a career. Despite its post-industrial economy and westernized lifestyle, Israeli society is known for its familialism (Fogiel-Bijaoui, 2002; Remennick, 2006). The family and motherhood continue to play a crucial role, at both the individual and collective levels, and are among the key social values of Israeli society. This is evident in the high marriage rates, the relatively low (albeit growing) divorce rates, and total fertility rates, which are among the highest in the developed industrialized world. Jewish-Israeli women's fertility rates are nationally 2.8 children per woman, ranging from 2.4 in secular families to 7.5 among the Ultra-Orthodox (Remennick, 2006). A recent survey found that Israelis see the ideal family as even larger, with an average of 3.5 children (Bareket, 2005). The Israeli-Jewish pronatalism approach is expressed at both institutional and popular levels and is thought to be driven by various different factors, including religious tradition, the memory of the Holocaust, the loss of life in military conflict and terrorist attacks, and the ongoing demographic competition with surrounding Arab nations (Portugese, 1998; Sered, 2000).

While Orthodox Jews are known for their commitment to fertility, reflecting the biblical commandment to 'be fruitful and multiply', in the secular Israeli community raising a large family is also often represented as a patriotic deed and a contribution to the struggling and developing nation (Berkovitch, 1997). Motherhood is seen as a major ideological icon and a primary identity indicator for most Israeli women regardless of their background and identity (e.g. ethnicity, religiosity, education, employment and career aspirations) (Remennick, 2006). The norm for secular couples is around three children, whereas one child, which is quite popular in other Western countries, is thought of in Israel as unsatisfactory. Childless women carry a lifetime stigma. This pronatalist norm is further institutionalized at the state level through assisted reproductive technologies (ART), which are accessible to all Israeli women since IVF and other expensive treatments are subsidized from public funds (Izraeli, 1994; Kahn, 2000; Remennick, 2000, 2006).

One interesting expression of this cultural ideal can be seen in the way in which motherhood and work are integrated. For example, in Israel there is an extremely limited presence of childless women in the political, economic and academic elites (Herzog, 1999; Frenkel, 2006). A recent list of the 50 most influential women in the Israeli economy drawn up by the prominent newspaper *Ha'aretz* in 2003 included only two childless women. In comparison, according to Hewlett (2002), about 40 percent of the women in the top percentile of wage earners in the USA do not have children (Frenkel, 2006).

As a cultural code, familialism takes for granted an unequal gender division of labor. The woman is constructed as a wife and mother, whose primary responsibility is to bear children, and take care of her home and family. Her paid work is widely accepted as a secondary contribution to the family's livelihood (Fogiel-Bijaoui, 2002). Thus, in the past the widespread gender contract in Israel was one that expected women to do paid labor, but not to have a career. Since the 1970s, however, Israeli public discourse has changed, and the issue of equal opportunities and the opening up of professions and industrial sectors to women has become increasingly important. Nonetheless, overall the cultural ideal that calls for the integration of motherhood and paid labor has not changed (Frenkel, 2006).

This cultural ideal of familialism has an extensive influence on women's aspirations and possibilities for integration in the fields of STEM. Women's expectations of becoming wives and mothers hinder their ability to become full-time employees as engineers, high-tech workers or scientists. For example, a recent survey shows that women in the high-tech industry in Israel in full-time as well as part-time jobs work longer hours than women in all other types of jobs in the labor force (Central Bureau of Statistics, 2002).

Since most women employed in high-tech industry are likely to also have a role as wives and mothers, working long hours can become a difficult demand. This is one of the reasons why women in these fields are poorly represented, and even less so towards the top of the organizational ladder. However, in the unique Israeli context, in which there is also an aspiration to establish an independent national economy and to further the project of nation building through economic development and prosperity, women are also expected to become integrated in the workforce in order to contribute to state productivity (Berkovitch, 2001; Shafir and Peled, 2002).

To enable the successful integration of work and mothering, the state has developed various family-friendly policies (e.g. mostly in the public service sector and unionized workplaces) that allow women to work full time while still caring for their children in the afternoon. Furthermore, a system of subsidized daycare centers for working mothers has developed (Frenkel, 2006). This has led to a widespread gender contract in Israel in which women are expected to do paid labor, and are able to participate in the labor force, but to a more limited extent than men. These cultural norms and structures enable women to take part in the technology and engineering workplace. But on the other hand, their involvement in these fields is generally limited and their ability to climb the corporate ranks is restricted.

Familialism: the case of Israeli high-tech industry
Frenkel (2004, 2006) recently examined the gender performance of Israeli high-tech women as they move between the masculine global culture of the high-tech world and their local Israeli culture, which expects them to combine full-time work (though with limited hours) with their active participation in caring for their children during after-school hours. Her findings show that although women's struggle in the high-tech world seems similar to that of their overseas equivalents, a deeper analysis reveals a distinct Israeli pattern. According to Frenkel (2006), the space created between the two cultural repertoires that shape gender performance in Israel (the masculine high-tech culture and the culture of familialism) is seen as allowing Israeli high-tech women to redefine the meaning of femininity in the workplace. This new femininity posits the image of the woman struggling to juggle active family caring with a career as worthy of imitation and as the cultural heroine of the new economy in Israel. Her examination of the day-to-day practices of women in high-tech industry shows that by openly and demonstratively making use of family-friendly organizational practices (e.g. leaving work early to care for their children), in keeping with the traditional Israeli perception of motherhood and femininity, and by publicly rejecting the claim that by doing so they are less worthy workers, 'hi-tech women at least partially succeed in extracting

themselves from the social role of surrogate men that is imposed on women in other masculine environments, and manage to create a limited space in which to maneuver their doing of gender and their self-classification' (Frenkel, 2006, p. 48). Using this discourse, they manage to challenge the accepted characteristics of both good motherhood and the ideal worker and are able to redefine and manage well both life spheres – work and home – as well as gain social approval and appreciation. This dynamic possibly enables the construction of a new Israeli femininity that neither forgoes family caring nor accepts the marginalization of care givers in the organizational context.

Nonetheless, it is important to note that both Israeli society and the Israeli high-tech sector are not free from gender discrimination and a gendered perception of the image of the ideal worker. However, previous studies have suggested that the tension felt by Israeli career women is slightly less acute in comparison to their counterparts from the American middle class (Lieblich, 1987).

Familialism: the case of science and academia

Among academic scientists and researchers in Israeli academia the ideology of familialism is prevalent as well, and can have serious consequences for women at different critical points in their academic career. One specific unique Israeli aspect I will focus on is the prerequisite that individuals in academic positions spend some time (between one year to a few years) as students or in research position abroad. All Israeli universities require faculty that apply for a tenure track position to have done some of their studies abroad. Because Israel is a small country, it is seen as a necessity for academics to gain some knowledge and experience abroad during or after their PhD studies. This implies that students are expected to get their PhD degrees from universities outside Israel, or if they graduated in Israel, they are expected to do their postdoctoral studies abroad. Leaving for a PhD would mean leaving the country for four to five years at least (most students go to the USA). The requirement for postdoctoral studies is a year or two in the humanities and social sciences and two to four years in the field of natural and exact sciences. This postdoctoral requirement remains a major stumbling block for women.

All Israeli universities have this requirement as a prerequisite for an academic position on the faculty. Since Israeli youth serve in the military (men for three years and women for two years) and at times sign on for a longer period, and then many young people tend to travel or take it easy for a year or two, by the time they reach the stage of a PhD or postdoctoral studies they are likely to be over the age of 30. According to Toren (2000), the average age for women who apply for a faculty position at a university is 33.

At this stage of life Israelis are most likely to have at least one child, if not two or three. According to Toren's striking findings (2000) on women applying for a tenure track position, 78 percent are likely to already have one child (70 percent had their first child before earning their PhD), 50 percent are likely to have a second child as well and 22 percent have a third child (most of the women who chose to have a third child had it after receiving their appointment as lecturer). Although the requirement for postdoctoral studies seems gender-neutral, it is likely to affect women's careers in academia more than men's careers.

While it is accepted, and relatively common, for a wife to accompany her husband on studies or a postdoctoral position abroad, it is much less common for a husband to accompany his wife. This has been suggested to be a major obstacle to women's integration in academia. Furthermore, women who are hired for a tenure track position are likely to have similar conflicts. During their critical years between the degrees of lecturer and the tenured position of senior lecturer they are likely to give birth or to have to take care of young children, for whom in most cases they will be the primary caregivers. During these years they are also expected to be highly productive in academic terms, as well as to attend conferences that take place abroad. These multiple responsibilities are likely to hinder women's achievements as researchers. Although the Israeli universities acknowledge this and grant women (and men) who have had a baby during their pre-tenured period an extra year for tenure, this is still in many cases not enough.

Interestingly, previous research on the number of publications in relation to the number of children showed that childless academics do not publish more than those with children, and mothers of a low number of children do not out-publish those with more children (Toren, 2000). The most prolific publishers are mothers of two children. However, in comparison to men, their publication rates are lower and their advancement rate is slowed at all stages of their academic career (longer time spent between each rank) regardless of their productivity. This has been termed the 'hurdles race' by Moore and Toren (1998), capturing the idea that women in Israeli academia are confronted with gender obstacles at all stages of their academic careers, and not only in the earlier stages.

The Hebrew Language as a Barrier

Another unique aspect of the Israeli context that may subtly affect women's experience on the whole, but more so in fields where their representation is low, is the Hebrew language. According to the Technion report (Churchman, 2006), the Hebrew language plays an important role in constituting women's status and ability to become integrated in the fields of STEM. One central feature characterizing the Hebrew language is its requirement for gender differentiation in relation to every entity that the speaker or writer refers to (including people, but also objects). Furthermore, the generic term used in the Hebrew language is male.

Thus virtually in every university class, training course or discussion, the general term used to refer to the audience and to the profession is male. Apart from the spoken language, all documents in the universities and industry are phrased in the male form, perpetuating the stereotype of 'the scientist', 'the engineer' or the 'technology worker' as a male. The 'solution' usually used is to include a footnote saying that although the language relates to males, it is intended to include females. However, this is a very minimal improvement. Not only does a language reflect existing social, organizational and professional structures, but it also contributes to the nature of these structures and helps stabilize and reproduce the existing order in a manner that implies that these territories (of engineering, science, technology and mathematics) are masculinized.

A recent study of women engineers in Israel lends weight to the argument that language shapes, as well as constitutes, the obstacles and difficulties women encounter in this field. This qualitative study, based on in-depth interviews with women engineers, examined the manner in which Israeli female engineers construct their social lives and the countermeasures that they have adopted to confront the elements that obstruct their integration into the profession (Mordechai, 2004).

A linguistic analysis of the discourse of the women engineers interviewed revealed the use of different, aberrant linguistic patterns. For example, when the women engineers were talking about themselves in first person they would refer to themselves and their actions using the masculine term and not the feminine term (as expected in correct use of the Hebrew language), or using a mixture of the masculine and the feminine terms. These aberrant linguistic patterns, which helped the female engineers obfuscate their gender identity, were most clear-cut especially when discussing their occupation and professional identity. This was evident in a somewhat 'neutral' situation of an interview with the researcher (who was a female); however, it is even more likely to occur in the context of their daily activities and interactions with men (who are the vast majority) in their workplace. These linguistic variations, which are readily distinguishable in Hebrew in comparison to other languages, have not been mentioned in earlier studies in other countries.

According to Mordechai (2004), these linguistic variations are used by women as a coping strategy that enables them to reduce the discrepancy they experience between the pace of the transformation of occupational practices that enable women to work in the profession of engineering, and the slow rate of change in which the gender narrative in the engineering profession is still rooted and constructed on assumptions and imagery of masculinity. Thus the common use of the generic male term in the Hebrew language further signifies to women in fields in which they are a small minority their prolonged (albeit reduced) exclusion from these fields and signals to them that they are better off using the language in an incorrect manner in order to conceal their gendered identity.

CONCLUSIONS AND FUTURE DIRECTIONS

Currently women are present in the field of STEM in the 'land of milk, honey and technology', and to some extent their situation may be better than that of women in other developed and westernized countries. However, their number is still far from being equal to that of men. Many of the possible explanations for the limited representation of women in science and technology in Israel are common reasons that are apparent in other countries (e.g. lack of role models, stereotypes concerning gender and the STEM fields, gender discrimination, masculine norms of the fields of STEM, etc.). However, in this chapter I chose to focus and elaborate only on the unique and particular characteristics of the Israeli context and culture that are likely to hinder women's integration in this field. By reviewing these unique barriers to women's representation in the field of STEM it can be seen that there are various critical stages in the life course of girls and women in Israel that have important implications regarding their tendency and ability to specialize in the field of STEM.

First, the experience of girls in elementary and high school and their choice to refrain from high-level studies in the fields of mathematics, physics and computer science form an initial and critical barrier to their integration in the field of STEM. This barrier has practical implications, since it limits their ability to be accepted to higher studies in these fields, but it also has social implications, strengthening girls' beliefs that STEM is not a suitable field for them. As they leave high school, equipped with somewhat limited knowledge in mathematics, physics and computer science, they are recruited for service in the Israeli military. The experience of young women during their mandatory service in the military enables some of them to gain access to training and experience in R & D in fields of science, computing and technology, as well as some social capital in terms of networks and connections that can assist in their future integration in the civilian labor force in STEM fields. However, the gendered structure of the Israeli army, in conjunction with women's reduced numbers in more prestigious courses and ranks, limits their access to training, knowledge and social capital in comparison to men in the same units.

As their life cycle further advances, most women in Israeli society conform to the social norms of familialism and become wives and mothers. Their responsibility to care for their husbands, children and elderly family members further limits their ability to become fully integrated in science and in the technology industry, and to climb to high ranks in these fields. Last, through all these different stages of the life cycle, the Hebrew language forms a constant and continuous environment which signals to women they are the 'other'. This is likely to become more evident and salient in fields in which women are a small minority, such as the fields of STEM, and furthers their sense of alienation, non-membership and otherness.

Thus, as Israeli women mature from young girls into women and experience the different life stages reviewed above (i.e. high school, military and motherhood), they accumulate disadvantages along the way with regard to their chances of becoming integrated in fields of STEM. In the process these somewhat small disadvantages accumulate and interact to form a larger disadvantage (see Valian, 1998 on the accumulation of small disadvantages) to women in these fields. These particular Israeli dynamics, in conjunction with other more prevalent dynamics and barriers not reviewed in this chapter, work together to form the picture presented above of the limited representation of women in STEM.

It should be noted that the characteristics of Israeli society reviewed above, although they lead to the accumulation of disadvantages to women's advancement in STEM, also give women some advantages and privileges which are not always evident in other countries and contexts. One of the most salient advantages is the possibility women have to integrate motherhood with a professional career in science and high technology, without being forced to give up one of these worlds.

Over the last ten years many different programs have developed in Israel aimed at changing the existing situation and furthering women's representation and advancement in fields of STEM. Some of these programs and their outcomes are described below.

Programs Focusing on High School Education

Since high school education is the starting point for the gender gap in STEM, there are a variety of projects aimed at encouraging girls to study higher levels of mathematics, physics and computer science. One of these is the 'GES project: Girls to Engineering Studies', which is designed to increase the number of high school girls who study mathematics and physics at the level required to enroll in university degree-level engineering studies, as well as to encourage them to consider enrolment for an engineering degree and future employment in engineering and technology. The project is based on several component activities, among them: (a) training math teachers to head the project in their schools; (b) identification of underachieving pupils, and providing help and support to improve their grades and self-esteem; and (c) acquainting target pupils with professions and the courses of study required to enter them.

In schools which took part in this program the number of girls in math classes tripled over a period of three years, with the average grades for girls higher than those for boys (Messner-Yaron and Kahanovitz, 2003). Another project targeted to outstanding high school female pupils, 'Electricity in the Palms of Her Hands', was aimed at changing the perception of electrical engineering in outstanding female high school pupils, using a one-day conference aimed at exposing them to the profession of electrical engineering. A study investigating this initiative found that, if planned properly and thoughtfully, even a single one-day conference can significantly change the perception of electrical engineering among female pupils (Hazzan et al., 2005).

A third project known as 'The Future Generation of Hi-Tech' is an initiative of the Forum of Female Industrialists of the Manufacturers' Association and is run jointly with the Science and Technology Authority of the Ministry of Education and the Commanding Officer of the Women's Corps of the Israeli Military. It is focused on encouraging students in general, and female students in particular, to aim for a career in science and technology. The project began in September 1997 in seven junior high schools and was expanded to more schools in the following years. One class from each school worked in cooperation with an industry which 'adopted' the pupils. In each partnership a special program was developed linking industrial activities to the basic science and technology curriculum of the junior high schools. The program includes activities designed to change the atmosphere in which choices of study tracks and careers are made. Thus it includes counseling activities for students and teachers to raise awareness of the possibilities open to women in industry, field trips to industrial facilities, information activities directed at parents, and meetings with female industrial executives, who lecture on their work and serve as role models for girls.

However, although there are a number of programs comparable to those described above that are aimed at encouraging girls in high school or young women after high school to expand their studies in scientific and technological areas, they are small-scale and subject to budget cuts (Churchman, 2005).

Programs Focused on Military Service

Regarding the integration of women in STEM in the military, the Israeli military has recognized the importance of being able to use young women in the fields of technology and computer science. In order to increase the number of women in these jobs, the military has initiated a few programs. The Women's Corps is responsible for special programs for women, designed to encourage them to go into technological careers. As a part of these programs a few initiatives have been taken. First, women officers and soldiers filling technological positions visit schools to speak to pupils (boys and girls) and teachers on engineering and technological service in the army. These officers and soldiers are instructed to give special emphasis to the role of women in the military. The appearance of female representatives of the military involved in technological activities is aimed at providing a role model for girls before the draft. Second, the army invites pupils to visit military installations to learn about various service options, including technological duties. Girls are separated from the boys, and meet with an officer from the Women's Corps, who encourages them to enter one of the technological frameworks. Despite these activities, the number of women receiving deferments in order to undertake technological studies before their military service is low and has actually declined over the past few years (Messner-Yaron and Kahanovitz, 2003). Furthermore, the military aims to attract young women to technological studies by postponing the military service of girls studying in the practical engineering track at university level, and then enlisting them in professional jobs in the field of technology during their active service.

Programs Aimed at Helping Women who are Mothers

Last, there are some programs designed to help women who are mothers enter academic tracks. For example, in an attempt to provide a solution to the problem of postdoctoral studies abroad, one suggestion has been for Israeli universities to allow postdoctoral research to take place in a different Israeli university and not just abroad. Furthermore, a leading academic institute for exact and natural sciences (The Weizmann Institute) has taken special steps to aid women with their postdoctoral studies abroad. According to its report, one of the problems in traveling abroad with the whole family is also financial, since going abroad for a postdoctoral position demands a strong financial base, particularly if the women have families. Thus the Institute decided to create a precedent by granting a new kind of scholarship awarded for women excelling in science, and is intended to enable them and their family members (husband and children) to go through the postdoctoral period abroad with no financial worries.

Other universities have set up a number of policies that respond to various different aspects of the problems facing women with children. One is the childcare centers that provide relatively full-day service for students and faculty (regardless of the gender of the parent). Another is the policy regarding scholarships for graduate students (master's and PhD) at the Technion: when a woman gives birth she continues to receive her scholarship. If she receives the maximum number of scholarship benefits allotted to her and still needs more time to finish her thesis, she can apply to a special fund and explain why she needs more time and have her advisor confirm this, and ask for additional months of financial aid (Churchman, 2006). Moreover, some universities put extra time on the tenure clock for women and men who have newborn children.

To conclude, there are a variety of projects implemented in Israel aimed at fostering changes in the representation of women in the STEM fields. These programs seem to be helpful; however, they are often limited in terms of the numbers of women participating in them and there are few data on their actual outcomes and success. Nevertheless, with the continuing rapid development of Israel in the fields of technology and sciences it is likely that women will become further integrated in these fields and will be able to enter the promised 'land of milk, honey and high technology' in larger numbers and enjoy the fruits and abundance of these developments.

ACKNOWLEDGEMENT

The author is thankful to Shlomit Rozin for her help in gathering information.

REFERENCES

Adams, E.S., Loftsson, H., Hazzan, O. and Young, A. (2003), 'International perspective of women and computer science', paper presented at SIGCSE 03, Reno, NV, USA.

Bareket, A. (2005), 'New study: Jews in Israel want at least three children', *Ha-aretz*, 5 July.

Berkovitch, N. (1997), 'Motherhood as a national mission: the construction of womanhood in the legal discourse in Israel', *Women's Studies International Forum*, **20**(5–6), 605–19.

Berkovitch, N. (1999), 'Women and citizenship in Israel', *Israeli Sociology*, **2**, 277–318.

Berkovitch, N. (2001), 'Citizenship and motherhood: women's status in Israel', *Y. Peled and A. Ophir (eds), Israel: From Mobilized to Civil Society*, Jerusalem: The Van Leer Jerusalem Institute and Hakibbutz Hameuchad, pp. 206–43.

Berlinski, S. (2005), 'Women in academia. A report presented to the Council for Higher Education', Tel-Aviv, Israel.

Brazilai, A. (2004), 'The missile that landed in the surgery room', *Ha-aretz*, 20 December.

Breznitz, D. (2005), 'Collaborative public space in national innovation system: a case study of the Israeli Military's impact on the software industry', *Industry and Innovation*, **12**(1), 31–64.

Central Bureau of Statistics (2002), *The Development of the Hi-tech in Israel in the years 1995–1999: Labor Force and Wages*, Jerusalem: Israel, Central Bureau of Statistics.

Central Bureau of Statistics (2005), *Data Gathered for International Women's Day*, Jerusalem: Israel Central Bureau of Statistics.

Churchman, A. (2005, 2006), *Women and Men at the Technion: Faculty and Students*, Annual Report, Israel: Technion (Israel Institute of Technology).

Cohen, S. (1997), 'Toward a new portrait of the (new) Israeli Soldier', *Israeli Affairs*, **3**, 77–117.

de Fontenay, C. and Carmel, E. (2004), 'Israel's Silicon Wadi: the forces behind cluster formation', in T.F. Bresnahan and A. Gambardella (eds), *Building High-Tech Clusters: Silicon Valley and Beyond*, Cambridge and New York: Cambridge University Press, pp. 40–77.

Eidelman, L. and Hazzan, O. (2005), 'Factors influencing the shrinking pipeline in high schools: a sector-based analysis of the Israeli high school system', paper presented at SIGCSE '05, 23–27 February, St Louis, MO.

Etzioni-Halevy, Eva (1996), 'Civil–military relations and democracy: the case of the military–political elites' connection in Israel', *Armed Forces and Society*, 22, 401–17.

European Commission Directorate-General for Employment, Social Affairs and Equal Opportunities (2001), *Employment in Europe 2001*, Luxembourg: Office for Official Publications of the European Communities.

Frenkel, M. (2004), *Has the Motherhood Wall Collapsed?*, Tel Aviv: The Women's Network.

Frenkel, M. (2006), 'Reprogramming femininity: gender performance in the Israeli hi-tech industry between global and local gender orders', Working Paper, The Hebrew University, Jerusalem.

Fogiel-Bijaoui, S. (2002), 'Famialism, postmodernity and the state: the case of Israel', *The Journal of Israeli History*, **21**(1–2), 38–62.

Galpin, V. (2002), 'Women in computing around the world', *Inroads–SIGCSE Bulletin*, Special Issue, Women and Computing, 94–100.

Grimland, G. (2006), 'The feminist movement reaches the hi-tech', *Ha-artez*, 25 June.

Ha-Poalim Bank (2000), 'The Israeli hi-tech: the current state of affairs', *Economical Review*, **130**.

Hazzan, O., Levy, D. and Tal, A. (2005), 'Electricity in the palms of her hands: the perception of electrical engineering by outstanding female high school pupils', *IEEE Transactions on Education*, **48**(3), 402–12.

Herzog, H. (1999), *Gendering Politics: Women in Israel*, Ann Arbor, MI: University of Michigan Press.

Hewlett, S.A. (2002), *Creating a Life: Professional Women and the Quest for Children*, New York:Talk Miramax Books.

Israel Industrial Union (2000), *A Report of the Results of a Survey of Women in the Hi-Tech Industry*, Tel-Aviv, Israel.

Izraeli, D.N. (1994), 'Outsiders in the promised land: women managers in Israel', in

N.J. Adler and D.N. Izraeli (eds), *Competitive Frontiers: Women Managers in a Global Economy*, Oxford: Blackwell Publishers, pp. 301–24.

Izraeli, D.N. (1997), 'Gendering women's military service in the Israeli Armed Forces', *Israel Social Science Research*, **12**, 29–166.

Izraeli, D.N. (2001), 'Paradoxes of women's service in the Israeli Defence Forces', in D.N. Izraeli, E. Maman, B. Ari and Z. Rosenhek (eds), *Military, State, and Society in Israel*, London: Transaction.

Kahn, S.M. (2000), *Reproducing Jews: A Cultural Account of Assisted Conception in Israel: Body, Commodity, Text*, Durham, NC: Duke University Press.

Kimmerling, B. (1993), 'Militarism in Israel society', *Theory and Criticism: An Israeli Forum*, **4**, 123–40 (in Hebrew).

Lieblich, A. (1987), 'Preliminary comparison of Israeli and American successful career women at mid-life', *Israel Social Science Research*, **5**(1–2), 164–77.

Messner-Yaron, H. and Kahanovitch, S. (2003, 2005), *Women in Science and Technology in Israel – State of Affairs*, The National Council for the Promotion of Women in Science and Technology.

Moore, D. and Toren, N. (1998), 'Thresholds, hurdles and ceilings: career patterns of women in academia', *Sociological Imagination*, **35**(2–3), 96–118.

Mordechai, A. (2004), *Engineering Lives: Understanding the Ways Israeli Female Engineers Constitute their Social Lives*, MA thesis, Bar-Ilan University, Israel.

Peleg-Popko, O., Klingman, A. and Abu-Hanna Nahhas, I. (2003), 'Cross-cultural and familial differences between Arab and Jewish adolescents in test anxiety', *International Journal of Intercultural Relations*, **27**, 525–41.

Portugese, J. (1998), *Fertility Policy in Israel: The Politics of Religion, Gender and Nation*, Westport, CT: Praeger.

Remennick, L. (2000), 'Childless in the land of imperative motherhood: stigma and coping among infertile Israeli women', *Sex Roles*, **43**(11–12), 821–41.

Remennick, L. (2006), 'The quest for the perfect baby: why do Israeli women seek parental genetic testing?', *Sociology of Health and Illness*, **28**(1), 21–53.

Sasson Levi, O. (2003), 'Feminism and military gender practices: Israeli women soldiers in "masculine" roles', *Sociological Inquiry*, **73**, 440–65.

Saxenian, A. (1994), *Regional Advantage: Culture and Competition in Silicon Valley and Route 128*, Cambridge, MA: Harvard University Press.

Sered, S. (2000), *What Makes Women Sick? Maternity, Modesty, and Militarism in Israreli Society*, Brandeis Series on Jewish Women, Boston: Brandeis University Press.

Shafir, G. and Peled, Y. (2002), *Being Israeli: The Dynamics of Multiple Citizenship*. Cambridge and New York, Cambridge University Press.

Teubal, M. and Avnimelech, G. (2003), 'Foreign acquisitions and R&D leverage in high tech industries of peripheral economies. Lessons and policy issues from the Israeli experiences', *International Journal of Technology Management*, **26**(2–4), 362.

Toren, N. (2000), *Hurdles in the Halls of Science: The Israeli Case*, New York: Lexington Books.

Valian, Virginia (1998), *Why So Slow? The Advancement of Women*, Cambridge, MA: The MIT Press.

Yaniski-Ravid, S. (2007), 'The exclusion of female inventors in the meeting point between the field of property, patents, work and gender discourse', in D. Erez-Barak, S. Yaniski-Ravid, Y. Biton and D. Fogin (eds), *Study of Law, Gender and Feminism*, Tel Aviv: Nevo – Ono Academic College Press.

7. An empirical test of the glass ceiling effect for Asian Americans in science and engineering

Tina T. Chen and James L. Farr

It has been widely hypothesized that Asian Americans face a glass ceiling in their career progression (e.g. Cheng, 1997). Unlike other racial/ethnic minority groups, there are significant proportions of Asian Americans concentrated in professional and technical fields. The often positive images of Asian Americans in general, predominately that of the 'model minority', have led to the prevalent assumption that Asian Americans have overcome structural barriers in the USA and have achieved economic success (Cheng, 1997). In contrast, the cumulative research efforts of researchers in Asian-American studies have found that despite mass media images of Asian Americans as a successful minority group, Asian Americans still encounter barriers in their chances of advancing up the management hierarchy and experience lower returns on education.

The concentration of Asian Americans in professional occupations, such as science and engineering, has often been used to bolster the claim that Asian Americans have overcome structural hurdles in the mainstream economy. This overlooks the fact that although Asian Americans may be highly represented in high-paying professional occupations, they still lag behind their white counterparts in pay and promotions. The model minority label has been used as a 'divide and conquer' strategy. The comparable educational and occupational success of Asian Americans, over and above that of African Americans, Latinos and Native Americans, has generated and sustained the idea of Asian Americans as a 'model' for other minorities (Woo, 1994). This myth suggests that socioeconomic success is within the grasp of any minority member who works hard enough, and those minorities who do not succeed are to blame for their own lack of initiative. This study compares Asian Americans to African Americans in order to provide some evidence regarding whether Asian Americans are really the 'model minority' and have a different experience than the predominant racial minority group in the USA.

Based on aggregate data on educational attainment, occupational distribution and household income, Asian Americans in general have performed as well as whites and have outperformed other minority groups in the USA (Barringer et al., 1993). In 2001, the median household income for Asian Americans was $53 635, compared to $46 305 for non-Hispanic white households, $29 470 for black households, and $33 565 for Hispanic households (DeNavas-Walt and Cleveland, 2001). This aggregate statistic is misleading because when income is adjusted for household size, the income per household member for Asian-American households is $24 933, a lower though not statistically different amount from the income per household member of non-Hispanic white households ($25 751).

The seemingly high overall educational and skill levels of the Asian-American population overshadow the reality that there are still obstacles that even the well-educated Asian Americans face in career mobility (Daniels, 1988; Min, 1995; Takaki, 1990). Research has found that despite higher educational attainment than whites, Asian Americans do not experience the same return on investment (ROI) (US Commission on Civil Rights, 1988, 1992; Woo, 1994). More educated Asian Americans have more difficulty than less educated Asian Americans in achieving income parity with whites (Tienda and Lii, 1987). The racial gap in salary increases with age, with the white male 45-year age group at the top of the income bracket. It is unclear whether this earning differential is due to a glass ceiling (Woo, 1994) or simply a cohort effect. Distinguishing a glass ceiling effect from a cohort effect requires a longitudinal research design, which is incorporated into the present study.

The purpose of the present study is to empirically test for the existence of a glass ceiling barrier for Asian Americans over time using latent growth curve modeling. Prior research on the glass ceiling phenomenon has focused mainly on the experiences of white women (Morrison and Von Glinow, 1990). Theories postulated to explain the existence of a glass ceiling, such as human capital (Becker, 1993), dual labor market theory (Larwood and Gattiker, 1987) and intergroup theory (Alderfer, 1986), have been explored as far as they apply to white women's experiences in organizations. Research on racial minorities in management is sparse, and the bulk of that research focuses on African-American men. Asian Americans have a distinct historical and cultural background from African Americans in the USA and may face different obstacles in their career paths. This study explores both the gender and racial aspects of the glass ceiling phenomenon by comparing men to women and also Asian Americans to African Americans. There is a history of studying race or gender to the exclusion of the other (Karambayya, 1997; Nkomo, 1992). This precludes consideration of the effects of being a double minority – that of being a woman and a minority group member. This study examines whether individuals who are 'double' minorities encounter more barriers in their careers.

THE GLASS CEILING

The US Department of Labor (1991) defines the glass ceiling as 'those artificial barriers based on attitudinal or organizational bias that prevent qualified individuals from advancing upward in their organization into management-level positions'. The concept of a glass ceiling was originally used to portray women's blocked promotion opportunities in corporations (Morrison et al., 1987) and was later applied to ethnic minorities (see US Commission on Civil Rights, 1988; Tang, 1993). It describes a barrier so subtle that it is transparent (invisible), yet so strong that it prevents women and minorities from moving up in the management hierarchy (Morrison and Von Glinow, 1990).

Despite labor laws prohibiting discrimination based on group membership, subtle forms of gender and racial discrimination still exist. It has been found that minorities have limited access to well-paying jobs and have fewer opportunities for promotions (DiTomaso and Smith, 1996). Race still matters, as it influences hiring, job assignment and promotion at all educational levels (Mickelson and Oliver, 1991). Of particular relevance to the present study, economic discrimination against minorities is thought to be greater for the well educated than for the less skilled or uneducated (Becker, 1971).

FOUR CRITERIA FOR A GLASS CEILING EFFECT

The general finding that women and minorities lag behind white men in upward mobility and rewards does not, in itself, prove that a glass ceiling exists. Fewer women and minorities in upper management is not necessarily evidence that a glass ceiling exists, as the disparity can be equally attributable to discrimination or a lack of qualified individuals from those subgroups. Testing a glass ceiling effect requires a longitudinal approach. Thus, few reviews empirically test the presence of a glass ceiling. Additionally, there does not seem to be a consensus or an attempt to come to a consensus on the operationalization of the glass ceiling effect, which makes any tests of such an effect difficult to compare across samples.

A recent attempt has been made to address the lack of a coherent definition and operationalization of the glass ceiling (Cotter et al., 2001). The review of the extant literature on the glass ceiling yielded four criteria that are required in order to define a gender or racial inequality as a glass ceiling effect. Cotter and his colleagues (2001) suggest that a glass ceiling is a specific type of gender or racial inequality that can and should be distinguished from other types of inequality. If the glass ceiling were merely another name for gender or racial inequality, then there is no need for a separate concept. The present study is an effort to test the glass ceiling effect utilizing Cotter and colleagues' (2001) proposed criteria. Maume (2004) extended this line of research using Cotter et al.'s (2001) proposed criteria for a glass ceiling and found support for a gap in managerial attainment between white men and three other subgroups (white women, black men, and black women). Prokos and Padavic (2005) also tested the same criteria on a subsample of the data used in the current study using different analyses and focused solely on gender inequality to the exclusion of race. The present study extends this research and focus on Asian Americans with comparisons to African Americans, as well as looking at the intersection of gender and race.

The first proposed criterion is that a glass ceiling inequality represents a gender or racial difference that is not explained by other job-relevant characteristics of the employee (Cotter et al., 2001). Characteristics such as education, experience, abilities and other job-relevant characteristics, that are components of human capital, should be taken into account when examining outcomes. Earnings and rewards are positively associated with level of human capital (Becker, 1993). Those with higher investments in human capital, through education and training, tend to fare economically and occupationally better than individuals with lower human capital investments.

The second criterion specifies that a glass ceiling inequality represents a gender or racial difference that is greater at higher levels of an outcome than at lower levels of an outcome (Cotter et al., 2001). If the same degree of gender or racial inequality is found at upper and general levels, then the need for a glass ceiling concept is obsolete: there is simply gender or racial inequality (i.e. there is no 'ceiling'). The glass ceiling is not simply about discrimination within hierarchies; rather it is discrimination that increases as one moves up in the hierarchy (Wright et al., 1995).

The third criterion maintains that a glass ceiling inequality represents a gender or racial inequality in the chances of advancement into higher levels, not merely the proportions currently at those higher levels (Cotter et al., 2001). Promotions into higher positions and raises of income are the appropriate independent variables in tests of glass ceiling effects (Stroh et al., 1996). Glass ceilings should be tested in dynamic models that measure change over time, not just static comparisons of outcome levels. Not many studies have actually tested for glass ceilings in promotions or raises since few studies have the necessary longitudinal data. Together with the second criterion, a glass ceiling inequality is restricted to situations where inequalities for promotions to higher levels are stronger than inequalities for promotions to lower levels. The gender/racial gap not only grows but accelerates as individuals move up in the hierarchy.

Criterion four is similar to the third, in that a glass ceiling inequality represents a gender or racial inequality that increases over the course of a career (Cotter et al., 2001). This suggests that career trajectories are the appropriate test for glass ceilings. In combination with the second criterion, a glass ceiling is then limited to when there is a divergence in career trajectories that is greater for those at high levels of outcomes than for those at middle or low levels of outcomes. Constancy in the earnings gap over time implies the absence of a glass ceiling (Morgan, 1998).

CURRENT RESEARCH ON ASIAN AMERICANS IN THE WORKPLACE

Existing research studies on Asian Americans have been few, and those specifically on the glass ceiling effect for Asian Americans have been indirect at best for several reasons. First is a sampling problem: although the Asian-American population is rapidly increasing in the USA, their high concentration in a few urban centers limits the feasibility of research on this subgroup. In addition, compared to other minority groups, Asian Americans are not a politically influential group. They have little representation in legislative and policy-making positions to ensure that their interests are expressed and supported (Cheng and Thatchenkery, 1997). Being perceived as the model minority also undermines the perception that there is a need to address problematic Asian American social issues (ibid.). In conjunction, organizational science is embedded in the problem-solving paradigm and researchers are predisposed to study problems (ibid.). Asian Americans are not considered a 'problem' to be solved due to the model minority perception that as a group they are educationally and economically successful (Woo, 1994).

CURRENT HYPOTHESES

Taken in conjunction with the criteria specified by Cotter and colleagues (2001), a glass ceiling effect should be a racial inequality that is not explained by other job-relevant characteristics of the individual, is greater at higher levels of an outcome than at lower levels of an outcome, increases over the course of a career, and adversely affects the chances of advancement into higher levels.

Predictions

Asian-American career trajectories are contrasted to white males, as the standard against which a glass ceiling effect can be detected is the absence of such an effect, and the white male experience is the most reliable standard for this purpose. If Asian Americans do encounter a glass ceiling, results of analyses should show that after controlling for job-relevant characteristics such as education, training, field, industry and geographic location, Asian Americans: (a) have a lower career trajectory than white males, (b) see differences between salary increase over the career span, and (c) have flatter salary trajectories and those will decelerate more quickly towards the ends of their careers (Figure 7.1).

Method

Participants
Data in this study are part of the Scientists and Engineers Statistical Data System (SESTAT), an integrated collection of three demographic surveys sponsored by the National Science Foundation (NSF). This data system consists of information about a representative sample of individuals who live in the USA and hold a bachelor's degree or higher in a science or engineering field or who are working in a science or engineering job. The data used in this study were part of the licensed SESTAT data, which are not publicly available.

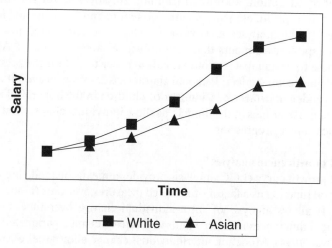

Figure 7.1   Predicted career trajectories for whites and Asian Americans

Design
There were four waves of data collected over a period of seven years (1993, 1995, 1997 and 1999). Probability sampling was used for the SESTAT component surveys. Stratified oversampling by field, level of degree and demographic characteristics was used in order to increase the number of women, underrepresented minorities, the disabled, and individuals in the early part of their careers in the sample. More details on the sampling designs can be found at www.srsstats.sbe.nsf.gov/.

Measures
The self-report survey instruments used to collect the data are available on the SESTAT website at www.srsstats.sbe.nsf.gov. Variables chosen for inclusion in the present study were uniform across the three surveys and all four measurement points. The data were primarily collected by mailed surveys, and non-response was followed up by a computer-assisted telephone interview (CATI) in order to increase response rates.

Variables
The outcome variable of interest is salary. As stated previously, there is some agreement in the literature that promotions into higher positions and raises of income are appropriate tests of the glass ceiling effect (Stroh et al., 1996). Salary has been found to be highly correlated to and account for a high level of shared variance in explaining differential career outcomes (Melamed, 1995). Movement from non-management to management to upper management can be quantified by commensurate pay increases.

Level of education, additional training, employer sector (private, government, non-profit, etc.) and region, job tenure and occupational field are included in the analyses as covariates. These are considered job-related human capital investments that may influence career outcomes. Analyses hold these to be equal across individuals in order to test for the presence of a racial glass ceiling effect. Personal characteristics such as age, citizenship status, gender, marital status, number of children in the household are also included as covariates in the models, as these individual characteristics may influence career progression.

Latent growth curve analysis
Latent growth curve (LGC) analysis provides a means of modeling a developmental function as a factor of repeated measures over time (Duncan et al., 1996). It allows analysis of intra-individual change over time and inter-individual differences in initial status and rate of change parameters (Willet and Sayer, 1994). Modeling interindividual change allows the researcher to ask specific questions about the distribution of individual growth parameters

across individuals in the population and permits prediction of these differences (Willet and Sayer, 1994). Individual-level data are summarized in terms of 'true' initial level of performance (intercept), slope (linear and quadratic rate of change over time) and error (residual) parameters.

Latent growth curve analysis requires three or more occasions of measurement (Duncan et al., 1999). Traditional approaches to studying change, such as difference scores, are limited to analysis of amount of change and give limited information on the rate of change. By incorporating three or more occasions of measurement, LGC analysis is able to provide information on the rate of change, and as the number of occasions of measurement increases, parameter estimates of initial level and change become more precise. More detailed and technical descriptions of this methodology are available elsewhere (McArdle and Epstein, 1987; Meredith and Tisak, 1990; Muthen, 1991; Willet and Sayer, 1994, 1996).

Time-in-study model: analysis of group differences

A time-in-study model that included cohort codes into $k-1$ dummy variables was conducted. There were 12 work experience cohorts included in the analyses. Examining multiple cohorts allowed us to model career outcomes for individuals at different times in their careers. Cohorts 1–10 were grouped in two-year intervals (i.e. Cohort 1 was individuals with one or two years of experience, Cohort 2 included individuals with three to four years of work experience) and Cohorts 11 and 12 were grouped in four-year intervals due to the lower sample sizes in those groups. The dummy coded cohort codes allowed for the detection of fixed effects by cohort group and therefore permitted direct interpretation of cohort differences in initial status and rate of change.

Results

Univariate linear only and linear plus quadratic models were estimated for the samples. Results of these models in the form of fit indices and estimates can be found in Tables 7.1 and 7.2, respectively. The linear plus quadratic model was a better fit to the data (Table 7.1), so further analyses focused on the linear plus quadratic model. A multiple group model (race and gender groups) on the entire sample was estimated to obtain estimates for the different racial and gender groups (Table 7.2). Then a multiple group model with the inclusion of dummy codes for cohorts and covariates was modeled. Partial regression coefficients for the covariates and cohort effects for each racial/gender group are presented in Tables 7.3–7.6.

In overview, cohort effects for all racial/gender groups significantly affected the initial status more often than they affected the linear or quadratic

Table 7.1   Fit indices for time-in-study overall sample models

	χ^2	df	CFI	TLI	RMSEA
Linear only	1182.003	5	0.911	0.894	0.083
Linear and quadratic	50.599	1	0.996	0.978	0.038
Multi-group quadratic	35861.657	9	0.472	−1.112	0.872
Multi-group linear with covariates	6579.861	243	0.918	0.671	0.071

Table 7.2   Parameter estimates for overall and multi-group time-in-study models

	Mean			Variance		
	Est.	S.E.	C.R.	Est.	S.E.	C.R.
Linear & quadratic overall model						
Intercept	5.435	0.015	359.726	4.292	0.863	4.976
Linear	1.52	0.051	29.86	31.97	0.850	37.619
Quadratic	−0.074	0.009	−8.264	0.796	0.034	23.691
White males						
Intercept	5.862	0.020	286.375	5.975	0.212	28.227
Linear	0.253	0.011	23.886	0.265	0.062	4.266
Quadratic	0.012	0.002	7.098	0.014	0.001	13.563
White females						
Intercept	4.549	0.032	142.111	5.377	0.247	21.743
Linear	0.136	0.015	8.965	0.343	0.068	5.057
Quadratic	0.018	0.002	7.575	0.003	0.001	2.863
Asian-American males						
Intercept	5.601	0.049	113.406	4.657	0.524	8.882
Linear	0.199	0.025	7.897	0.245	0.166	1.478
Quadratic	0.024	0.004	5.996	0.010	0.003	3.559
Asian-American females						
Intercept	4.648	0.071	65.285	3.546	0.816	4.348
Linear	0.159	0.047	3.410	0.188	0.265	0.707
Quadratic	0.022	0.007	3.026	0.010	0.005	2.042
African-American males						
Intercept	5.103	0.087	58.895	5.547	1.035	5.360
Linear	0.198	0.049	4.088	0.769	0.341	2.255
Quadratic	0.010	0.007	1.286	0.022	0.006	3.993
African-American females						
Intercept	4.026	0.067	60.218	2.230	0.340	6.553
Linear	0.105	0.032	3.316	0.032	0.099	0.321
Quadratic	0.014	0.005	2.819	0.001	0.002	0.481

Table 7.3   Partial regression weights for all covariates and cohorts, white males

	Est. (intercept)	S.E. (intercept)	Est. (linear slope)	S.E. (linear slope)	Estimate (quadratic slope)	S.E. (quadratic slope)
Age	0.005*	0.001	0.000	0.000	0.000	0.000
Marital status	−0.020	0.058	0.076*	0.029	0.009	0.005
Number of children	0.202*	0.020	0.035*	0.010	−0.004*	0.002
Father's education level	0.012	0.018	−0.002	0.009	0.002	0.002
Mother's education level	−0.215	0.022	0.004	0.011	−0.002	0.002
US citizenship status	0.443	0.115	0.057	0.058	0.004	0.009
Number of degrees	−0.006	0.028	−0.007	0.014	−0.002	0.002
Life science degree	−0.118	0.079	0.096*	0.040	−0.014*	0.006
Physical science degree	0.859*	0.084	0.110*	0.043	−0.011	0.007
Social science degree	−0.516*	0.073	0.021	0.037	−0.005	0.006
Occupation computer	1.529*	0.077	0.002	0.039	0.018*	0.006
Occupation life science	0.005	0.098	−0.083*	0.049	0.015	0.008
Occupational physical science	0.411*	0.102	−0.139*	0.051	0.012	0.008
Occupation, social science	0.602*	0.115	−0.159*	0.058	0.023*	0.009
Computer degree	0.865*	0.082	0.083	0.042	−0.007	0.007
Primary work activity R&D	3.525*	0.064	0.110	0.032	0.005	0.005
Primary work activity teaching	2.125*	0.099	−0.036	0.050	0.009	0.008
Primary work activity management	3.736*	0.065	0.091*	0.033	0.011	0.005
Primary work activity other	4.226*	0.071	0.188*	0.036	0.011	0.006
Employer sector education	−0.033	0.068	0.199*	0.034	−0.026*	0.006
Employer sector government	−0.834*	0.063	0.049	0.032	−0.016*	0.005
Employer region all others	0.633	0.391	0.058	0.198	−0.010	0.032

Table 7.3 (continued)

	Est. (intercept)	S.E. (intercept)	Est. (linear slope)	S.E. (linear slope)	Estimate (quadratic slope)	S.E. (quadratic slope)
Employer region Northeast	0.926*	0.049	0.083*	0.025	−0.005	0.004
Employer region Central	0.308*	0.038	0.031	0.019	0.000	0.003
Executive managerial indicator	0.041*	0.008	0.008	0.004	−0.001	0.001
Total number supervised	0.005*	0.000	0.000	0.000	0.000	0.000
Supervisory work	−0.257*	0.044	−0.121*	0.022	0.019*	0.004
Additional training	0.349*	0.046	0.051*	0.023	−0.005	0.004
DC 1 (Cohort 2, 3–4 years)	0.372*	0.100	0.195*	0.050	0.010	0.008
DC 2 (Cohort 3, 5–6 years)	0.879*	0.089	0.178*	0.045	0.012	0.007
DC 3 (Cohort 4, 7–8 years)	1.110*	0.086	0.162*	0.043	0.008	0.007
DC 4 (Cohort 5, 9–10 years)	1.327*	0.082	0.051	0.041	0.023*	0.007
DC 5 (Cohort 6, 11–12 years)	1.637*	0.087	0.067	0.044	0.018*	0.007
DC 6 (Cohort 7, 13–14 years)	1.815*	0.087	−0.019	0.044	0.026*	0.007
DC 7 (Cohort 8, 15–16 years)	1.875*	0.084	0.094*	0.042	0.008	0.007
DC 8 (Cohort 9, 17–18 years)	1.946*	0.089	0.041	0.045	0.011	0.007
DC 9 (Cohort 10, 19–20 years)	2.061*	0.084	0.004	0.042	0.016*	0.007
DC 10 (Cohort 11, 21–24 years)	2.346*	0.074	−0.052	0.037	0.017*	0.006
DC 11 (Cohort 12, 25–28 years)	0.000	0.000	0.000	0.000	0.000	0.000

Note: * Significant, CR > 2.0.

138

Table 7.4 Partial regression weights for all covariates and cohorts, white females

	Est. (intercept)	S.E. (intercept)	Est. (linear slope)	S.E. (linear slope)	Estimate (quadratic slope)	S.E. (quadratic slope)
Age	0.003*	0.001	0.000	0.001	0.000	0.000
Marital status	-0.159*	0.065	-0.050	0.034	0.010	0.005
Number of children	0.067*	0.032	-0.023	0.017	0.003	0.003
Father's education level	0.109*	0.025	-0.003	0.013	0.002	0.002
Mother's education level	-0.017	0.029	0.004	0.015	0.000	0.002
US citizenship status	0.130	0.165	0.053	0.087	-0.011	0.013
Number of degrees	-0.329*	0.039	-0.084*	0.020	0.007*	0.003
Life science degree	-0.860*	0.103	-0.111*	0.054	0.007	0.008
Physical science degree	-0.403*	0.144	0.010	0.076	-0.005	0.012
Social science degree	-1.161*	0.085	-0.025	0.045	-0.009	0.007
Occupation computer	0.151	0.111	-0.103	0.058	0.021*	0.009
Occupation life science	-0.065	0.121	-0.019	0.063	0.007	0.010
Occupational physical science	0.089	0.171	-0.095	0.090	0.013	0.014
Occupation, social science	0.634*	0.111	-0.183*	0.058	0.028*	0.009
Computer degree	-0.352*	0.113	-0.044	0.059	0.007	0.009
Primary work activity R&D	0.567*	0.122	-0.022	0.064	0.004	0.010
Primary work activity teaching	-0.137	0.135	-0.125	0.071	0.006	0.011
Primary work activity management	0.190	0.118	-0.036	0.062	0.005	0.010
Primary work activity other	0.596*	0.119	-0.003	0.062	-0.007	0.010
Employer sector education	-0.668*	0.081	0.170*	0.042	-0.023*	0.007
Employer sector government	-0.551*	0.089	0.068	0.047	-0.012	0.007
Employer region all others	-2.012*	0.529	0.260	0.227	-0.038	0.043
Employer region Northeast	-0.306*	0.080	0.094*	0.042	-0.011	0.006

Table 7.4 (continued)

	Est. (intercept)	S.E. (intercept)	Est. (linear slope)	S.E. (linear slope)	Estimate (quadratic slope)	S.E. (quadratic slope)
Employer region Central	-0.694*	0.081	0.090*	0.042	-0.014*	0.007
Executive managerial indicator	0.159*	0.048	-0.014	0.025	0.004	0.004
Total number supervised	0.009*	0.001	-0.002*	0.000	0.000*	0.000
Supervisory work	-0.749*	0.062	-0.152*	0.032	0.017*	0.005
Additional training	-0.039	0.068	-0.051	0.035	0.006	0.005
DC 1 (Cohort 2, 3–4 years)	-0.241	0.126	0.056	0.066	-0.001	0.010
DC 2 (Cohort 3, 5–6 years)	0.152	0.122	0.065	0.064	-0.003	0.010
DC 3 (Cohort 4, 7–8 years)	0.328*	0.121	-0.059	0.063	0.011	0.010
DC 4 (Cohort 5, 9–10 years)	0.450*	0.119	-0.039	0.063	0.010	0.010
DC 5 (Cohort 6, 11–12 years)	0.855*	0.128	-0.050	0.067	0.012	0.010
DC 6 (Cohort 7, 13–14 years)	0.845*	0.130	0.022	0.068	-0.004	0.010
DC 7 (Cohort 8, 15–16 years)	1.042*	0.128	-0.035	0.067	0.005	0.010
DC 8 (Cohort 9, 17–18 years)	1.153*	0.144	0.045	0.075	-0.004	0.012
DC 9 (Cohort 10, 19–20 years)	1.480*	0.138	-0.035	0.072	0.003	0.011
DC 10 (Cohort 11, 21–24 years)	1.682*	0.134	0.010	0.070	-0.011	0.011
DC 11 (Cohort 12, 25–28 years)	0.000	0.000	0.000	0.000	0.000	0.000

Note: * Significant, CR > 2.0.

Table 7.5   Partial regression weights for all covariates and cohorts, Asian American males

	Est. (intercept)	S.E. (intercept)	Est. (linear slope)	S.E. (linear slope)	Estimate (quadratic slope)	S.E. (quadratic slope)
Age	0.000	0.002	−0.004*	0.001	0.000	0.000
Marital status	−0.630*	0.132	−0.094	0.075	0.008	0.012
Number of children	0.079	0.050	0.002	0.028	−0.004	0.004
Father's education level	0.140*	0.039	−0.010	0.022	0.005	0.003
Mother's education level	−0.063	0.044	0.005	0.025	0.002	0.004
US citizenship status	−0.606*	0.104	0.088	0.059	−0.010	0.009
Number of degrees	−0.218*	0.046	−0.018	0.026	0.001	0.004
Life science degree	−0.320	0.184	0.036	0.104	−0.019	0.016
Physical science degree	−0.048	0.180	0.034	0.102	−0.012	0.016
Social science degree	−0.792*	0.206	−0.075	0.116	0.000	0.018
Occupation computer	0.477*	0.162	−0.053	0.092	0.015	0.014
Occupation life science	−0.303	0.219	−0.055	0.124	0.016	0.019
Occupational physical science	−0.442*	0.213	0.093	0.121	−0.016	0.019
Occupation, social science	0.354	0.316	0.120	0.179	−0.028	0.028
Computer degree	−0.384*	0.165	−0.028	0.093	0.004	0.015
Primary work activity R&D	0.297*	0.147	−0.030	0.083	−0.002	0.013
Primary work activity teaching	−0.388	0.236	−0.142	0.133	−0.003	0.021
Primary work activity management	−0.288	0.165	0.081	0.093	−0.019	0.015
Primary work activity other	0.601*	0.176	0.127	0.100	−0.033	0.016
Employer sector education	−0.502*	0.139	0.149	0.079	−0.018	0.012
Employer sector government	−0.967*	0.140	−0.009	0.079	−0.012	0.012
Employer region all others	−2.301*	0.740	0.306	0.419	−0.028	0.066
Employer region Northeast	0.097	0.102	0.024	0.056	0.002	0.009

Table 7.5 (continued)

	Est. (intercept)	S.E. (intercept)	Est. (linear slope)	S.E. (linear slope)	Estimate (quadratic slope)	S.E. (quadratic slope)
Employer region Central	−0.115	0.082	0.059	0.047	−0.007	0.007
Executive managerial indicator	0.195*	0.058	−0.009	0.033	0.003	0.005
Total number supervised	0.002*	0.001	0.000	0.000	0.000	0.000
Supervisory work	−0.892*	0.095	0.006	0.054	−0.011	0.008
Additional training	−0.180	0.096	−0.060	0.054	0.005	0.008
DC 1 (Cohort 2, 3–4 years)	−0.984*	0.179	0.072	0.101	0.008	0.016
DC 2 (Cohort 3, 5–6 years)	−0.565*	0.177	−0.040	0.100	0.008	0.016
DC 3 (Cohort 4, 7–8 years)	−0.351	0.184	0.017	0.104	0.007	0.016
DC 4 (Cohort 5, 9–10 years)	−0.249	0.178	−0.010	0.101	0.008	0.016
DC 5 (Cohort 6, 11–12 years)	0.018	0.204	0.043	0.115	−0.002	0.018
DC 6 (Cohort 7, 13–14 years)	0.192	0.208	−0.106	0.118	0.009	0.018
DC 7 (Cohort 8, 15–16 years)	0.652*	0.196	−0.206	0.111	0.028	0.017
DC 8 (Cohort 9, 17–18 years)	0.506*	0.212	−0.173	0.120	0.018	0.019
DC 9 (Cohort 10, 19–20 years)	0.846*	0.204	−0.180	0.115	0.008	0.018
DC 10 (Cohort 11, 21–24 years)	0.480*	0.170	−0.036	0.096	−0.004	0.015
DC 11 (Cohort 12, 25–28 years)	0.000*	0.000	0.000	0.000	0.000	0.000

Note: * Significant, CR > 2.0.

Table 7.6 Partial regression weights for all covariates and cohorts, Asian American females

	Est. (intercept)	S.E. (intercept)	Est. (linear slope)	S.E. (linear slope)	Estimate (quadratic slope)	S.E. (quadratic slope)
Age	0.002	0.002	-0.002	0.002	0.000	0.000
Marital status	-0.128	0.160	0.069	0.116	-0.019	0.018
Number of children	-0.056	0.076	0.059	0.055	-0.013	0.009
Father's education level	0.171*	0.057	0.009	0.041	0.000	0.007
Mother's education level	0.009	0.060	0.083	0.043	-0.010	0.007
US citizenship status	-0.110	0.160	0.046	0.116	-0.011	0.018
Number of degrees	-0.296*	0.080	-0.074	0.058	0.006	0.009
Life science degree	-0.831*	0.219	0.025	0.159	-0.010	0.025
Physical science degree	-0.690*	0.261	0.083	0.188	-0.023	0.030
Social science degree	-0.902*	0.217	-0.091	0.157	-0.003	0.025
Occupation computer	0.487	0.208	0.148	0.150	-0.024	0.024
Occupation life science	0.296	0.260	-0.204	0.188	0.035	0.030
Occupational physical science	0.286	0.325	-0.080	0.235	0.017	0.037
Occupation, social science	0.536	0.302	0.241	0.219	-0.041	0.035
Computer degree	-0.054	0.220	-0.246	0.159	0.040	0.025
Primary work activity R&D	0.144	0.228	0.000	0.165	0.002	0.026
Primary work activity teaching	0.192	0.285	0.047	0.206	-0.034	0.033
Primary work activity management	-0.314	0.234	-0.088	0.169	0.006	0.027
Primary work activity other	0.070	0.236	0.222	0.171	-0.032	0.027
Employer sector education	-10.103*	0.178	0.257	0.129	-0.029	0.020
Employer sector government	-0.485*	0.195	0.167	0.141	-0.032	0.220
Employer region all others	0.040	1.001	-1.021	0.724	0.118	0.115
Employer region Northeast	0.066	0.140	0.122	0.101	-0.017	0.016
Employer region Central	-0.008	0.088	0.041	0.064	-0.008	0.010

Table 7.6 (continued)

	Est. (intercept)	S.E. (intercept)	Est. (linear slope)	S.E. (linear slope)	Estimate (quadratic slope)	S.E. (quadratic slope)
Executive managerial indicator	0.940*	0.280	0.107	0.202	-0.013	0.032
Total number supervised	0.001	0.002	-0.001	0.001	0.000	0.000
Supervisory work	-0.820*	0.143	-0.131	0.103	0.024	0.016
Additional training	-0.343*	0.141	0.279	0.102	-0.044	0.016
DC 1 (Cohort 2, 3–4 years)	0.089	0.242	-0.075	0.175	0.022	0.028
DC 2 (Cohort 3, 5–6 years)	0.308	0.251	-0.091	0.182	0.005	0.029
DC 3 (Cohort 4, 7–8 years)	1.182*	0.250	-0.338	0.181	0.038	0.029
DC 4 (Cohort 5, 9–10 years)	1.024*	0.257	-0.226	0.186	0.013	0.030
DC 5 (Cohort 6, 11–12 years)	1.239*	0.286	0.039	0.207	-0.030	0.033
DC 6 (Cohort 7, 13–14 years)	1.030*	0.303	-0.234	0.219	0.031	0.035
DC 7 (Cohort 8, 15–16 years)	1.341*	0.315	-0.267	0.228	0.018	0.036
DC 8 (Cohort 9, 17–18 years)	1.163*	0.362	0.051	0.262	-0.024	0.042
DC 9 (Cohort 10, 19–20 years)	1.272*	0.331	-0.069	0.239	-0.010	0.038
DC 10 (Cohort 11, 21–24 years)	1.483*	0.330	-0.026	0.239	0.017	0.038
DC 11 (Cohort 12, 25–28 years)	0.000	0.000	0.000	0.000	0.000	0.000

Note: * Significant, CR > 2.0.

slope functions. These results seem to indicate that for white males, white females and Asian-American females, the effect of work experience cohort was positive; the more work experience one had, the higher the initial intercept level. All significant cohort effects on initial status for white males, white females and Asian-American females were positive. The cohort effect for Asian-American males in Cohorts 2–5 were negative ($\beta = -0.892$, -0.565, -0.351, -0.249, respectively). It seems that for Asian-American males, individuals in some younger work experience cohorts (i.e. Cohorts 2–7) had significantly lower initial levels than the first cohort, but later work experience cohorts had higher initial levels than the first cohort.

The effects of cohort on the linear and quadratic slope functions were less consistent. Most cohort effects on the slope functions were insignificant, with the exception of white males. The significance of those results seems more attributable to sample size differences for the various racial/gender subgroups, as white males were the largest subgroup, and accordingly had more statistical power in the analyses. A look at the regression estimates across racial/gender subgroups, although they were not significant, found that a sizeable number of regression estimates on linear slope were in a negative direction, and regression estimates on the quadratic slope were generally positive.

The effect of the individual and work characteristics variables included as covariates varied across racial/gender groups. Predicted trajectories were calculated based on the analyses and charted in two figures, one representing a non-managerial sample and the second representing a managerial sample. Figure 7.2 shows the predicted career trajectories for non-managers. Holding all covariate values constant between all groups, there were still racial and gender inequities in predicted outcomes. White males have higher predicted career trajectories than any other group.

Figure 7.3 shows the predicted career trajectories for all groups if the values for the primary work activity, executive managerial indicator, total number of employees supervised and supervisory work are changed to manager status, but holding all other covariates constant. Figure 7.3 seems to indicate that differences in career outcomes are even greater between white males and other groups when all groups have reached managerial levels. Additional figures for different values on covariates, such as changing the occupational field or the employer sector, are available by request from the author. Although career trajectories varied slightly as a function of changes in these factors, the relative difference between white males and other racial/gender groups did not vary substantially. The most significant differences noticeable by varying covariate values was in changing from a non-manager status to managerial status, and the two figures presented illustrate this phenomenon. The decision was made to present the career

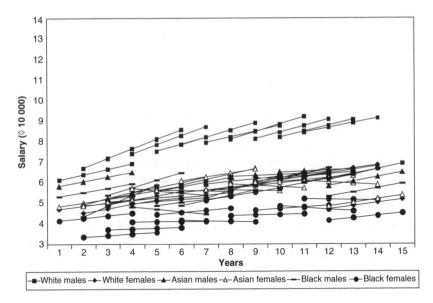

*Figure 7.2   Predicted career trajectories for all cohorts & racial/gender
groups, non-managers*

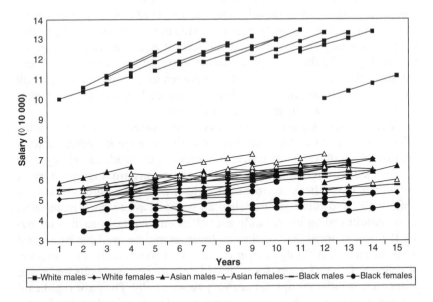

*Figure 7.3   Predicted career trajectories for all cohorts and racial/gender
groups, managers*

trajectories as described above for determination of the glass ceiling effect, as they closely follow the prespecified criteria.

HYPOTHESES

The Glass Ceiling

In summary, it was predicted that if Asian Americans do experience a glass ceiling as defined by Cotter and colleagues' four criteria, results of analyses should show that, even controlling for job-relevant and individual characteristics, (a) Asian Americans in comparison to white males should have a lower career trajectory than white males, (b) the difference between the levels of the trajectories should increase over the career span, and (c) Asian-American trajectories should be flatter and decelerate more quickly towards the end of their careers. Asian-American male and female career trajectories were separately compared to white male career trajectories.

These predicted career trajectories were based on the model estimates with the inclusion of all covariates in the model. The inclusion of these figures was to facilitate the interpretation of the glass ceiling criteria. The predicted career trajectories in Figure 7.2 are the non-managerial examples, and Figure 7.3 shows the predicted career trajectories if the values for the managerial covariates (managerial indicator, supervisory work, number of employees supervised) are changed to managerial status. In both charts it is evident that white males have higher predicted career trajectories than any other group. The most noticeable difference between these two figures is that the difference between white males and all other groups is even larger in the managerial example.

Figure 7.4 is a direct comparison of the predicted career trajectories of white and Asian-American male non-managers only, and Figure 7.5 is a direction comparison of the predicted career trajectories of white male and Asian-American male managers. The difference in levels for Asian-American and white male non-managers can be found in Table 7.7, and the same data can be found for the managerial example in Table 7.8. Figures 7.4 and 7.5 both indicate that Asian-American trajectories are flatter then the predicted trajectories for white males for all cohorts, as white males have steeper positive acceleration in growth across almost all cohorts. Predicted salary level at all four time points across all work experience cohorts shows that the predicted differences between Asian-American males and white males increased over time. In addition, the predicted differences in salary outcomes between white males and Asian-American

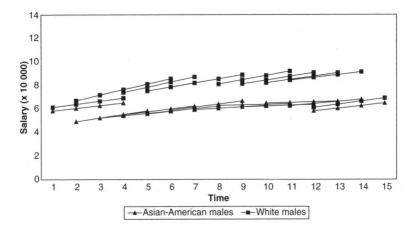

*Figure 7.4   Predicted career trajectories for white males and Asian
American males, non-managers*

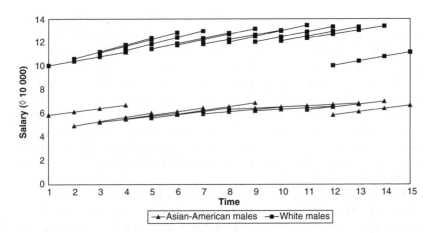

*Figure 7.5   Predicted career trajectories for white males and Asian
American males, managers*

males are much larger in the managerial example. Predicted differences for
the non-managerial trajectories ranged from $3000 to $27000 in the
various cohorts, while the differences between the white males and Asian-
American males' managerial trajectories ranged from $42000 to $68000.

The predicted differences between white males and Asian-American
females were larger than those differences between white males and Asian-
American males. Similar to Asian-American males, Asian-American

Table 7.7   Differences in predicted levels between white male and Asian-American male non-managers

Cohort	Difference Time 1	Difference Time 2	Difference Time 3	Difference Time 4
1	0.303	0.345	0.387	0.429
2	1.784	1.951	2.118	2.285
3	1.969	2.233	2.497	2.761
4	1.910	2.098	2.286	2.474
5	1.955	2.073	2.191	2.309
6	1.966	2.052	2.138	2.224
7	2.030	2.176	2.322	2.468
8	1.806	2.128	2.450	2.772
9	1.950	2.199	2.448	2.697
10	1.710	1.944	2.178	2.412
11	2.174	2.221	2.268	2.315
12	0.303	0.345	0.387	0.429

Note: Numbers should be multiplied by 10 000.

Table 7.8   Differences in predicted levels between white male and Asian-American male managers

Cohort	Difference Time 1	Difference Time 2	Difference Time 3	Difference Time 4
1	4.196	4.291	4.386	4.481
2	5.677	5.897	6.117	6.337
3	5.862	6.179	6.496	6.813
4	5.803	6.044	6.285	6.526
5	5.848	6.019	6.190	6.361
6	5.859	5.998	6.137	6.276
7	5.923	6.122	6.321	6.520
8	5.699	6.074	6.449	6.824
9	5.843	6.145	6.447	6.749
10	5.603	5.890	6.177	6.464
11	6.067	6.167	6.267	6.367
12	4.196	4.291	4.386	4.481

Note: Numbers should be multiplied by 10 000.

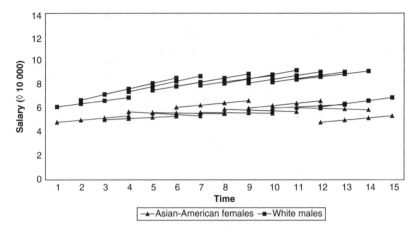

Figure 7.6   Predicted career trajectories for white males and Asian-American females, non-managers

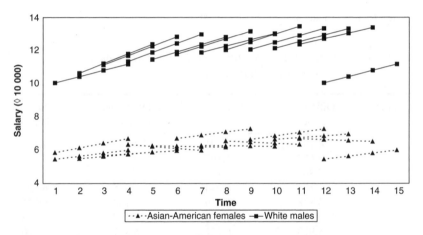

Figure 7.7   Predicted career trajectories for white males and Asian-American females, managers

females had lower career trajectories than white males (Figures 7.6 and 7.7) and this difference in outcomes increases over time (Tables 7.9 and 7.10).

The results seem to indicate differences in predicted outcomes at higher levels (i.e. management levels), which supports the idea that there may be barriers in career advancement, and those more advanced in their careers and in management show more evidence of such an effect. From these analyses, there is evidence supporting a glass ceiling effect for Asian Americans.

Table 7.9   *Differences in predicted levels between white male and Asian-American female non-managers*

Cohort	Difference Time 1	Difference Time 2	Difference Time 3	Difference Time 4
1	1.298	1.382	1.466	1.550
2	1.839	2.181	2.523	2.865
3	2.145	2.505	2.865	3.225
4	1.696	2.250	2.804	3.358
5	1.888	2.259	2.630	3.001
6	1.772	1.932	2.092	2.252
7	2.293	2.587	2.881	3.175
8	2.183	2.618	3.053	3.488
9	2.106	2.215	2.324	2.433
10	2.186	2.369	2.552	2.735
11	2.369	2.661	2.953	3.245
12	1.298	1.382	1.466	1.550

Note: Numbers should be multiplied by 10 000.

Table 7.10   *Differences in predicted levels between white male and Asian-American female managers*

Cohort	Difference Time 1	Difference Time 2	Difference Time 3	Difference Time 4
1	4.596	4.787	4.978	5.169
2	5.137	5.586	6.035	6.484
3	5.443	5.910	6.377	6.844
4	4.994	5.655	6.316	6.977
5	5.186	5.664	6.142	6.620
6	5.070	5.337	5.604	5.871
7	5.591	5.992	6.393	6.794
8	5.481	6.023	6.565	7.107
9	5.404	5.620	5.836	6.052
10	5.484	5.774	6.064	6.354
11	5.667	6.066	6.465	6.864
12	4.596	4.787	4.978	5.169

Note: Numbers should be multiplied by 10 000.

DISCUSSION

Past research on the glass ceiling has focused mainly on white females and African Americans to the exclusion of other minority groups in the USA. In addition, most studies of the glass ceiling have been narrative reviews, or based on aggregate statistics that may obscure the influence of other relevant factors in contributing to inequity in outcomes. The present study was able to include individual, organizational and work-related characteristics as covariates in order to fully account for the influence of each, and comparison of career trajectories across racial and gender groups holding these covariates constant across groups was possible.

Based on the results of the present study, there is evidence supporting a glass ceiling effect for Asian Americans over a seven-year period for individuals at all *stages* of their careers. Asian Americans fulfilled the criteria specified by Cotter et al. (2001) that classify inequality as a glass ceiling effect: Asian Americans had lower predicted career trajectories than white males, this difference in outcome levels increased over time, and Asian Americans' predicted trajectories were flatter and decelerated more quickly over time. This conclusion is speculative based on the current available data, as more research that spans a longer period of time for each work experience group needs to be conducted before any definitive conclusions can be made.

Additionally, it was found that covariates affected different racial/gender subgroups differentially. Regression estimates were not uniformly significant or non-significant across subgroups. The most consistent effect was found for managerial indicators such as primary work activity management, supervisory work, total number of employees supervised, and the executive managerial indicator. These factors consistently resulted in higher initial intercepts for all groups, although the extent of that effect varied across the different racial/gender subgroups. Employer sector (industry/business, education and government) also affected initial levels in that industry was consistently associated with higher initial intercepts.

The present study suggests that the glass ceiling effect is not a phenomenon limited to African Americans or white females. Previous research has focused on those two groups to the exclusion of others, and the inclusion of Asian Americans in the present study found that they do experience what can be defined as a glass ceiling. Despite overwhelming images of Asian Americans in the media achieving economic success superior to other minorities and being the model minority, quantitative evidence demonstrating a glass ceiling effect was found. Despite having high aggregated median incomes, being concentrated in professional and technical fields, Asian Americans have not achieved parity with white males.

STATISTICAL METHODS AND CONSIDERATIONS

Longitudinal modeling of outcome variables allowed for the exploration of career outcomes over a span of seven years. Not many studies have actually tested for glass ceilings in promotions or raises since few studies have the necessary longitudinal data (Cotter et al., 2001). Maume (2004) found support for a glass ceiling effect using longitudinal data for black men and women, and for white women. Prokos and Padavic (2005) used the same sample as the current study but concluded that neither a glass ceiling nor cohort effect accounted for differences in the pay gap between white men and other subgroups. Their methods of analysis differed from this study in that they did not use the same conceptualization of the glass ceiling, nor did they measure intra- and inter-individual change over time. Cotter et al. (2001) argue that a dynamic model allows for examination of changes and trends over time, and can better capture the fluidity of a career, which by definition is a multiple-year phenomenon.

LIMITATIONS

One limitation of the present study was that the seven-year period covered by the study was only a snapshot of a full career trajectory. Future research exploring the glass ceiling and career trajectories should take this even further by following groups for longer periods.

Another limitation of the present study is that the data source was pre-collected by a third party. The advantage of this dataset was that it included large numbers of Asian Americans measured at four time periods and contained a plethora of variables needed to run the analyses prescribed, and such an extensive dataset could not have possibly been collected by a single researcher with limited resources. However, a limitation is that some factors that may be of relevance to career outcomes, such as organizational factors such as mentoring, networking, and socialization or structural barriers, were not assessed.

Last, the inability of existing statistical programs to run complex LGC models with extremely large sample sizes and varied attrition resulted in the need to create a subset of the data from the original dataset. This was not a random subset, but one without missing data. Demographic information from both the original and subset were similar, but reasons for attrition are unknown, and this may have affected the results of the analyses.

FUTURE RESEARCH DIRECTIONS

The current research has found evidence supporting a glass ceiling effect for Asian Americans in the science and engineering fields. The definition and operationalization of the glass ceiling effect was an extension of work by Cotter and his colleagues (2001). This research was an effort to build upon existing research and expand it to include an understudied minority group that has been hypothesized to experience the glass ceiling effect. Similar to Cotter and colleagues (2001), there was evidence of a glass ceiling effect for women. In contrast to their findings, the current findings indicate that there may be a glass ceiling for both Asian-American men and women. Future research on the glass ceiling effect should examine both gender and race rather than one to the exclusion of the other. Furthermore, research that extends beyond the variables captured in this study that may be specific to Asian Americans, such as cultural differences that may lead to different career choices, would contribute significantly to our understanding of the glass ceiling phenomenon for this group.

CONCLUSION

Evidence from this body of research indicates that there is a complex set of factors leading to differential career outcomes for Asian Americans today. The extent to which there are negative outcomes for Asian Americans due to racial inequalities as opposed to actual differences in harder-to-quantify advancement-related variables is undeterminable from this research effort. Present research found that, controlling for a myriad of career-related variables and human capital characteristics, Asian Americans do not fare as well as the media images of the successful model minority would indicate. Asian-American professions still lag behind their white male counterparts in earnings. Indications are that a longitudinal glass ceiling effect exists for Asian Americans at multiple stages of their careers.

ACKNOWLEDGEMENTS

This work would not have been possible without a license agreement from the Science Resources Statistics Division of the National Science Foundation for the use of the restricted data from the Survey of Scientists and Engineers in the years 1993, 1995, 1997 and 1999. The use of NSF data does not imply NSF endorsement of the research methods or conclusions contained in this report.

REFERENCES

Alderfer, C.P. (1986), 'An inter-group perspective on group dynamics', in J.W. Lorsch (ed.), *Handbook of Organizational Behavior*, Englewood Cliffs, NJ: Prentice-Hall.

Barringer, H., Gardner, R.W. and Levin, M.J. (1993), *Asians and Pacific Islanders in the United States*, New York: Russell Sage Publications.

Becker, G.S. (1971), *The Economics of Discrimination*, 2nd edn, Chicago: University of Chicago Press.

Becker, G.S. (1993), *Human Capital: a Theoretical and Empirical Analysis, with Special Reference to Education*, 3rd edn, Chicago: University of Chicago Press.

Cheng, C. (1997), 'Are Asian American employees a model minority or just a minority?', *Journal of Applied Behavioral Science*, 33, 277–90.

Cheng, C. and Thatchenkery, T.J. (1997), 'Introduction: why is there a lack of workplace diversity research on Asian Americans?', *Journal of Applied Behavioral Science*, 33, 270–76.

Cotter, D.A., Hermsen, J.M., Ovadia, S., and Vanneman, R. (2001), 'The glass ceiling effect', *Social Forces*, 80, 655–81.

Daniels, R. (1988), *Asian American: Chinese and Japanese in the United States since 1850*, Seattle, WA: University of Washington Press.

DeNavas-Walt, C. and Cleveland, R. (2001), 'Money income in the United States: 2001', *Current Population Reports*, P60-218, Washington, DC: US Government Printing Office.

DiTomaso, N. and Smith, S.A. (1996), 'Race and ethnic minorities and white women in management: changes and challenges', in J. Tang and E. Smith (eds), *Women and Minorities in American Professions*, New York: State University of New York, pp. 87–110.

Duncan, S.C., Duncan, T.E. and Hops, H. (1996), 'Analysis of longitudinal data within accelerated longitudinal designs', *Psychological Methods*, 1, 236–48.

Duncan, S.C., Duncan, T.E., Strycker, L.A., Li, F. and Alpert, A. (1999), *An Introduction to Latent Variable Growth Curve Modeling*, Mahwah, NJ: Lawrence Erlbaum Associates.

Karambayya, R. (1997), 'In shouts and whispers: paradoxes facing women of color in organizations', *Journal of Business Ethics*, 16, 891–7.

Larwood, L. and Gattiker, U.E. (1987), 'A comparison of the career paths used by successful women and men', in B.A. Gutek and L. Larwood (eds), *Women's Career Development*, Newbury Park, CA: Sage Publications, pp. 129–56.

Maume, D.J. (2004), 'Is the glass ceiling a unique form of inequality?', *Work and Occupations*, 31, 250–74.

McArdle, J.J. and Epstein, D. (1987), 'Latent growth curves within developmental structural equation models', *Child Development*, 58, 110–33.

Melamed, T. (1995), 'Barriers to women's career success: human capital, career choices, structural determinants, or simply sex discrimination', *Applied Psychology: An International Review*, 44, 295–314.

Meredith, W. and Tisak, J. (1990), 'Latent curve analysis', *Psychometrika*, 55, 107–22.

Mickelson, R.A. and Oliver, M.L. (1991), 'The demographic fallacy of the black academic: does quality rise to the top?', in W.R. Allen, E.G. Epps and N.Z. Haniff (eds), *College in Black and White: African American Students in Predominantly White and in Historically Black Public Universities*, Albany, NY: State University of New York Press, pp. 177–95.

Min, P.G. (1995), *Asian Americans: Contemporary Trends and Issues*, Newbury Park, CA: Sage Publications.

Morgan, L.A. (1998), 'Glass ceiling effect or cohort effect? A longitudinal study of the gender earnings gap for engineers, 1982–1989', *American Sociological Review*, **63**, 479–93.

Morrison, A.M. and Von Glinow, M. (1990), 'Women and minorities in management', *American Psychologist*, **45**, 200–208.

Morrison, A.M., White, R.P. and Van Velsor, E. Center for Creative Leadership (1987), *Breaking the Glass Ceiling: Can Women Reach the Top of America's Largest Corporations?*, Reading, MA: Addison-Wesley.

Muthen, B.O. (1991), 'Analysis of longitudinal data using latent variable models with varying parameters', in L.C. Collins and J.L. Horn (eds), *Best Methods for the Analysis of Change*, Washington, DC: American Psychological Association.

Nkomo, S.M. (1992), 'The emperor has no clothes: rewriting "race in organizations"', *Academy of Management Review*, **17**, 487–513.

Prokos, A. and Padavic, I. (2005), 'An examination of competing explanations for the pay gap among scientists and engineers', *Gender and Society*, **19**, 523–43.

Stroh, L.K., Brett, J.M. and Riley, A.H. (1996), 'Family structure, glass ceiling, and traditional explanations for the differential rate of turnover of female and male managers', *Journal of Vocational Behavior*, **49**, 99–118.

Takaki, R. (1990), *Iron Cages: Race and Culture in 19th Century America*, New York: Oxford University Press.

Tang, J. (1993), 'The career attainment of Caucasian and Asian engineers', *Sociological Quarterly*, **34**, 467–96.

Tienda, M. and Lii, D.T. (1987), 'Minority concentrations and earnings inequality: Blacks, Hispanics, and Asians compared', *American Journal of Sociology*, **93**, 141–65.

US Commission on Civil Rights (1988), *The Economic Status of Americans of Asian Descent: An Exploratory Investigation*, Washington, DC: Government Printing Office.

US Commission on Civil Rights (1992), *Civil Rights Issues Facing Asian Americans in the 1990s*, Washington, DC: Government Printing Press.

US Department of Labor (1991), *A Report on the Glass Ceiling Initiative*, Washington, DC: US Department of Labor.

Willet, J.B. and Sayer, A.G. (1994), 'Using covariance structure analysis to detect correlates and predictors of individual change over time', *Psychological Bulletin*, **116**, 363–80.

Willet, J.B. and Sayer, A.G. (1996), 'Cross-domain analyses of change over time: combining growth modeling and covariance structure analysis', in G.A. Marcoulides and R.E. Schumacker (eds), *Advanced Structural Equation Modeling: Issues and Techniques*, Mahwah, NJ: Lawrence Erlbaum Associates, pp. 125–57.

Woo, D. (1994), *The Glass Ceiling and Asian Americans: A Research Monograph*, Washington, DC: US Department of Labor, Glass Ceiling Commission.

Wright, E.O., Baxter, J. and Birkelund, G.E. (1995), 'The gender gap in workplace authority: a cross-national study', *American Sociological Review*, **60**, 407–35.

PART III

Building interest and commitment to STEM

8. Women in mathematics: examining the hidden barriers that gender stereotypes can impose

Jennifer R. Steele, Leah Reisz, Amanda Williams and Kerry Kawakami

> So my best guess, to provoke you, of what's behind [women's underrepresentation in the science and engineering workforce] is that the largest phenomenon, by far, is the general clash between people's legitimate family desires and employers' current desire for high power and high intensity, that in the special case of science and engineering, there are issues of intrinsic aptitude, and particularly of variability of aptitude, and that those considerations are reinforced by what are in fact lesser factors involving socialization and continuing discrimination.
>
> Lawrence H. Summers, President of Harvard University, 14 January 2005

Why are there fewer women than men pursuing and succeeding in prestigious careers in math and scientific domains? This question has captured the attention of researchers and the general public alike. Gender-based discrimination in the workplace is illegal, educational opportunities for women in the sciences seem abundant, and educational reforms have been introduced to help ensure that systematic biases are eliminated. So why is there not an equal number of men and women in top positions in these fields?

At a recent conference designed to discuss issues around diversifying the science and engineering workforce, the president of Harvard University at the time, Lawrence Summers, shared some of his thoughts on the matter. While acknowledging that gender socialization and discrimination might play some role in this gender discrepancy, Summers argued that there were two more influential factors. The first, he suggested, was women's relative lack of drive to put in the long hours needed to succeed in prestigious and lucrative positions:

> The most prestigious activities in our society expect of people who are going to rise to leadership positions in their forties near total commitments to their work . . . it is a fact about our society that that is a level of commitment that a much higher fraction of married men have been historically prepared to make than of married women.

Importantly, the second most central factor, he argued, was women's lesser intrinsic aptitude 'at the high end' of the mathematical ability spectrum. Although his views were not well received by many of those attending the conference and are not completely supported by scientific facts[1], these comments remain representative of a stereotype that continues to permeate our society: the belief that women are simply not as good as men in math and scientific domains.

Gender disparity in the representation of men and women in mathematics, engineering and the physical sciences is indisputable (Crocker et al., 1998; Peter and Horn, 2005; National Science Foundation [NSF], 2004; Stangor and Sechrist, 1998). According to some available statistics, women constitute only about 10 percent of the physical science, math and engineering workforce (C.M. Steele, 1997; Tietjen, 2004), and occupy only 8 percent of tenured and tenure-track positions in mathematics departments (Ripley, 2005) and 13 percent of the positions in chemistry departments (Marasco, 2005) at the top 50 research universities in the USA. Recent statistics at the undergraduate level reveal an increase in the number of women pursuing degrees in math and the physical sciences, and yet women still represent only a fraction of these majors relative to men (Peter and Horn, 2005). According to a 2004 report by the National Science Foundation, roughly 20 percent of the undergraduate and doctoral degrees in physics and engineering were awarded to women. Such facts suggest that the trends in underrepresentation in employment may continue for some time.

Although women's underrepresentation is a fact that cannot easily be disputed, the cause of this discrepancy is often readily up for debate. Contrary to what Summers seemed to suggest, a rich body of research by Jacquelynne Eccles, Janis Jacobs and their colleagues has pointed to the importance of social factors in this discrepancy (Eccles, 1987, 1994; Eccles and Jacobs, 1986; Jacobs and Eccles, 2000), and have particularly highlighted the importance of gendered socialization practices by parents in the domains of science and mathematics (Jacobs and Eccles, 1992; Jacobs et al., 2005; see also J. Steele and Barling, 1996; Tenenbaum and Leaper, 2003). For example, Jacobs and Eccles (1992) found that mothers' gender stereotypes influenced their children's expectations for success in mathematics, which, in turn, affected children's self-perceived ability in this domain. The researchers note that these expectations can lead to self-fulfilling prophecies in which children confirm the expectations of their mothers.

In addition, researchers have found continuing evidence that subtle and overt forms of discrimination *do* take place in the workplace, and some have suggested that discrimination may be more prevalent and/or more damaging in careers where women do not have a substantial voice, due to their lack of numbers (Agars, 2004; Benokraitis and Feagin, 1995; J. Steele et al., 2002; Swim et al., 2001). Ironically, at the same diversity conference where Summers diminished the role that discrimination might play in these gender discrepancies, several female scientists described their personal experiences with discrimination, as well as the discrimination that their research had revealed. Despite the fact that gender discrimination in the workplace seems to be decreasing, such experiences are not unique or uncommon; a report released at the Massachusetts Institute of Technology in 1999 indicated that many of the tenured female faculty in the School of Science felt marginalized and that this feeling was accompanied by a gender discrepancy, favoring men, in the allocation of critical resources including salary and research space.

A rich body of research suggests that socialization and discrimination contribute significantly to the observed gender differences in scientific domains, and in recent years emerging research has highlighted the effect that knowledge of self-relevant stereotypes can have on women in mathematics. Despite Summers's 'best guess' that these discrepancies stem primarily from differences in career ambition and natural ability, it is, in reality, the perpetuation of such beliefs that may serve as a powerful, yet sometimes hidden, barrier to women in these domains. In this chapter we focus on the direct and immediate situational effect that gender stereotypes can have on women who are pursuing higher education and careers in the fields of math, science and engineering by reviewing the growing literature on a process termed 'stereotype threat'. Importantly, in the hopes of acknowledging the many women and organizations that have found ways to overcome these hidden barriers, in this chapter we also review research that has identified institutional and personal means of combating the activation of stereotypes and stereotype threat. The majority of this research has been conducted by social psychologists who have examined these processes in controlled laboratory environments (C.M. Steele et al., 2002); however, several studies have recently provided evidence that stereotype threat effects emerge in real-world settings as well (Keller and Dauenheimer, 2003; J. Steele et al., 2002; Stricker, 1998 as cited in Davies and Spencer, 2005).

It is important to note that our focus on gender stereotyping does not diminish the contribution that various other factors, including, but not limited to, discrimination, gender socialization, and work–family concerns make to these gender discrepancies; our goal is simply to recognize and review the now vast literature that demonstrates the power of the situation to influence our behaviors and attitudes.

GENDER STEREOTYPE DEVELOPMENT

In order to be directly affected by the activation of a gender stereotype, a person needs to be aware that a stereotype exists. Stereotypes, or beliefs about the people in our social world, begin to form at a very early age. The majority of children's first stereotypes are based on gender, as this is one of the first social categories that children consistently recognize (Golombok and Fivush, 1994). Between the ages of 3 and 6, children can usually identify a multitude of gender-based stereotypes, and in many cases children also readily endorse them.

It is not completely clear when or how children develop specific gender stereotypes about math and science, but there is reason to suspect that girls are aware of these particular academic stereotypes from early elementary school (J. Steele, 2003; Shih et al., 1999). In some of our own research, girls in early elementary school (grades 1–4) rated men as being better at math and as liking math more than women (J. Steele, 2003). In another study, girls in late elementary school (grades 4–6) displayed a same-sex bias; specifically, girls rated 'most girls' as being better than 'most boys' at both mathematics and reading and writing, and similarly rated women as being better at reading and writing than men. However, when asked to rate the abilities of men and women in mathematics, this pro-female bias disappeared, with girls rating men and women as comparable in this domain. Importantly, when they received an implicit measure of stereotyping, the Implicit Association Test (IAT; Greenwald et al., 1998; Greenwald et al., 2003), both boys and girls in late elementary school showed a strong gender stereotype. Specifically, both groups of children were quicker to associate male pictures with mathematics and female pictures with reading and writing than the reverse pairings (J. Steele et al., 2007). Although these results do not point conclusively to the emergence of a gender stereotype about *mathematics*, they do indicate that from an early age girls begin to differentially associate male and female with specific academic domains at both an explicit and an implicit, or automatic, level.

It is important to note that it is not clear if these stereotypes are reflected in the actual abilities and performance of women in math and science. Although there is evidence that men outperform women on various standardized math tests such as the SAT-M (Gallagher and Kaufman, 2005), some have argued that this difference is often small, and that the distribution of men's and women's scores often has a great deal of overlap (Hyde, 2005). In addition, there is evidence that females and males have strengths in different areas of mathematics; girls and women excel on tests of arithmetic calculation and memory for the spatial location of objects, whereas boys and men tend to excel on tests of mathematical word problems and memory for the geometric configuration of an environment (Hyde, 2005). A recent review of the literature conducted by Spelke (2005) concluded that girls and boys show equal primary abilities for mathematics and that sex differences only begin to emerge on complex quantitative tasks after elementary school.

Although the evidence regarding differences between men and women on quantitative abilities is somewhat mixed, what *is* clear is that by adolescence and early adulthood, most men and women in North America are aware that a gender stereotype about these domains exists (Crocker et al., 1998). While many actively reject the stereotype, research has now shown that having an awareness of a self-relevant stereotype might be sufficient to diminish performance and reduce one's academic orientation towards stereotyped domains for some women. This can happen through a long-term socialization process and/or through the application of stereotypes by teachers, parents and employers. However, even women who remain very identified with and competent in math and scientific domains are not totally immune to the direct situation-specific effects that stereotypes can have on their performance and identification. It is this situational effect that affects top female students in scientific domains, termed 'stereotype threat', that we review here.

WHAT IS STEREOTYPE THREAT?

In the mid-1990s, Claude Steele and his colleagues, Joshua Aronson and Steven Spencer, put forth a theory of *stereotype threat* (Spencer et al., 1999; C.M. Steele, 1997; C.M. Steele and Aronson, 1995; C.M. Steele et al., 2002). According to this theory, stereotype threat occurs when members of negatively stereotyped groups, such as women in math and science, face the possibility of inadvertently confirming the stereotype about their group. As C.M. Steele and Aronson (1995) explain, 'the existence of such a stereotype means that anything one does or any of one's features that conform to it make the stereotype more plausible as a self-characterization in the eyes of others, and perhaps even in one's own eyes . . .' (p. 797). According to their theory, the possibility of confirming a negative stereotype can be self-threatening and can lead to a disruptive concern that can interfere with performance in the stereotyped domain. Importantly, this concern is most likely to be evoked among people who care about the domain and find it to be self-relevant; in other words it is women who are talented and identified with math and science who are the most likely to show stereotype threat effects.

Spencer et al. (1999) conducted the first studies designed to test the possibility that women's math test performance could be negatively impacted by this situational threat. In one study, male and female math-identified students were asked to take a challenging math test under one of two conditions. In one condition, the stereotype threat condition, participants were told that the math test they were about to take had shown gender differences in the past. In the second condition, the no threat condition, participants were told that the test had previously revealed no gender differences. The latter manipulation was designed to make the stereotype irrelevant for women, and therefore eliminate stereotype threat. Consistent with their expectations and with the theory of stereotype threat, women's math test performance was worse than men's when the stereotype was relevant. Importantly, however, these researchers demonstrated that when the test was described as showing no gender differences, women's performance was not depressed relative to men's.

Stereotype threat effects have now been shown to emerge with a host of stereotyped group members including African Americans (C.M. Steele and Aronson, 1995), Latinos (Aronson et al., 1998; Gonzales et al., 2002), and low SES students (Croizet and Claire, 1998) on purported tests of intellectual ability, the elderly on memory tasks (Chasteen et al., 2005; Levy, 1996), and white students on purported tests of natural athletic abilities (Stone et al., 1999; see Wheeler and Petty, 2001 for an additional review). White men have even produced stereotype threat effects on a test of mathematical abilities when they were reminded of a positive stereotype for Asian Americans in this domain (Aronson et al., 1999). However, due to the importance of mathematical skills in the pursuit of higher education, as well as the relative abundance of math-oriented students on university campuses, math-identified women have been one of the most studied groups in stereotype threat studies.

This extensive research on women in mathematics has made it clear that stereotype threat can be induced by a variety of contextual factors. Building on research with various racial groups, stereotype threat effects have now been shown to emerge when a math test is described as being diagnostic of ability (Martens et al., 2006; Marx et al., 2005), as opposed to non-diagnostic of ability. In addition, women's math test performance can be affected by the ratio of men to women in a testing situation (Inzlicht and Ben-Zeev, 2000), social comparison information (Davies et al., 2002; Reisz et al., 2007), and implicitly activated identities (Ambady et al., 2004; Shih et al., 1999).

In one interesting demonstration, Inzlicht and Ben-Zeev (2000) induced stereotype threat by having female participants take a math test in a mixed-sex (with two men), as opposed to a single-sex (with two other women), group. Women who were the only female test taker in their group underperformed on the math test relative to women who were in the room with two other women. These researchers also demonstrated that this effect occurred only for women's math test performance; women who were asked to take a verbal test instead were unaffected by the gender composition of the room.

In a second study, Inzlicht and Ben-Zeev (2000) showed that the detrimental effect of performing as the minority woman in a stereotyped domain was proportional to the number of males in the group with whom they wrote the math test. Female participants in a mixed-sex majority condition (two women, and one man) experienced more moderate problem-solving deficits than female participants who wrote a math test in a mixed-sex minority condition (two men and one woman). The gender make-up of an environment alone, then, can determine whether gender stereotypes will be activated, and this activation may in turn cause women to experience performance deficits in stereotyped domains such as mathematics.

In our own research, we have found that being presented with information about a male math 'superstar' can similarly depress the performance of math-identified women (Reisz et al., 2007). Previous research has demonstrated that learning about successful others in domains of great importance to us can deflate our feelings of ability, if we believe that we can no longer achieve similar success (Lockwood and Kunda, 1997). Building on these findings, we reasoned that an unattainable social comparison might be particularly threatening if it helps to confirm a negative, self-relevant gender stereotype. We also predicted that such a comparison might not be deflating if it helps to disprove a relevant gender stereotype. To test this possibility, we asked math-identified female undergraduates to read about an extremely gifted first-year math major who was either male (stereotype confirming) or female (stereotype disconfirming). Participants were subsequently asked to take a challenging math test in what they believed to be an unrelated study. In line with our predictions, math-identified women who read about a highly gifted first-year male math student performed more poorly on a subsequent math test than women who read about an identically gifted female math student, or women who read a neutral story.

Stereotype threat can also be induced by simply activating gender stereotypes – even if they are not domain relevant. For example, Davies et al. (2002) found that exposing women to gender-stereotypic television commercials implicitly primed female stereotypes, leading math-identified women to subsequently underperform on a math test (Study 1) and avoid math in favor of verbal items on an aptitude test (Study 2). Further analyses revealed that the level of stereotype activation among the female participants mediated the effect of commercial type on subsequent math test performance, with higher levels of stereotype activation leading to worse performance on the test.

In short, there appear to be multiple, seemingly minor variations to a testing environment that can result in women's underperformance in mathematics. Interestingly, there is reason to believe that similar effects can emerge even when a concern about confirming a negative stereotype is not explicitly induced. In two studies conducted by Ambady et al., activating the social category female through the subliminal presentation of words such as 'girl', 'grandma' and 'skirt' led women to underperform on a challenging math test relative to women who were subliminally presented with neutral words of comparable length (Ambady et al., 2004). Similarly, women in a study by Shih et al. (1999) had decreased math test performance after filling out a one-page questionnaire that subtly reminded them of their gender identity.

Taken together, this research provides strong support for the situational influence that stereotypes can have on women's math test performance. Importantly, the studies demonstrate that stereotype threat can be evoked by a host of situational cues, including test description, gender composition of the room, as well as various subtle and overt factors that make women's gender salient. When considering the effect of stereotypes on women in math and scientific domains, it is important to note, however, that math test performance is not the only potential casualty. Models of achievement-related decisions point to the importance of women's attitudes towards math and science in predicting women's willingness to pursue advanced degrees and careers in these domains (Eccles, 1987; Stangor and Sechrist, 1998), and research has now established that stereotype threatening situations can similarly influence women's identification with these domains.

STEREOTYPE THREAT AND DOMAIN IDENTIFICATION

According to C.M. Steele (1997), to be academically successful a person must *identify* with their field(s) of study in such a way 'that one's self-regard significantly depends on achievement in those domains' (p. 616). Unfortunately, theory and research now support the fact that stereotypes can undermine this identification in several ways. First and foremost, people can simply avoid the domain in which they are stereotyped (C.M. Steele et al., 2002). Women have many occupations and majors available to them, and one of the ways to overcome the risk of being negatively stereotyped is simply to avoid math and science. Clearly there are unfortunate consequences for both the individual and the group when this strategy is adopted; women do not get the opportunity to learn and excel in these domains, which can limit their long-term career options and ultimately serve to confirm the stereotype. Less drastic, yet similarly detrimental responses include psychological *disengagement* (Crocker et al., 1998) and *disidentification* (C.M. Steele et al., 2002) from the domains. *Disengagement* has been described as a short-term strategy in the face of stereotype threatening situations, whereas *disidentification* is a long-term or chronic response. When feelings of stereotype threat arise, research suggests that women may start to create a psychological distance between the importance that they place on excelling in the domain and their self-concept as a way to protect themselves from future threats to self-esteem (disengagement); this may result in women ultimately leaving these fields of study (disidentification).

At least two studies provide evidence of the situational impact of stereotypes on women's identification. In the previously described research conducted by Davies et al. (2002), women who were exposed to gender-stereotypic television commercials not only underperformed on a math test, but they also reported more interest in majors and careers that involve verbal skills (such as journalism and communications), and significantly less interest in majors and careers that involve quantitative skills (such as engineering and computer science), relative to women who had viewed non-stereotypical commercials. Women who viewed stereotypical commercials also showed a marked preference for verbal over quantitative fields of study that did not emerge for women in a neutral, 'non-threatened' condition.

Additional research has revealed that stereotypes do not need to be explicitly made salient in order to have an effect on women's self-reported interest in quantitative and verbal domains. J. Steele and Ambady (2006) demonstrated that subtle gender primes could shift women's attitudes in stereotype-consistent directions. Women who were subliminally primed with female-related words (Study 1a) or who were reminded of their gender identity through the completion of a one-page questionnaire (Study 1b) subsequently reported a preference for arts-related academic activities (i.e. writing an essay, analyzing a poem) over math-related academic activities (i.e. solving an equation, completing a geometry problem-set), whereas women in control conditions reported an equal interest in both domains.

MEDIATORS OF STEREOTYPE THREAT

If we hope to combat this 'threat in the air', it is important to identify the process through which stereotype threat effects emerge. Early theorizing suggested that anxiety was a key mediator of stereotype threat effects; however, solid evidence based on self-report measures has been inconclusive

(C.M. Steele et al., 2002). Spencer et al. (1999) provided partial support for the role of anxiety in stereotype threat effects. In one study, Spencer et al. found that women who were expecting to take a challenging math test described as showing gender differences reported more anxiety before the test than women who were told the test showed no gender differences. However, the full test for mediation was not statistically reliable, leaving some lingering doubt about the role of anxiety in these effects. In addition, several other studies (see C.M. Steele et al., 2002, for a review) found little or no evidence of increased anxiety among stereotype-threatened participants, despite the fact that the expected performance decrements emerged.

Since those early experiments, there has been new evidence that a variety of mechanisms, and/or some combination of these mechanisms, might result in stereotype threat. Researchers examining stereotype threat effects on women's math test performance have uncovered multiple potential affective and cognitive processes that might mediate these effects, including arousal (Ben-Zeev et al., 2005a; O'Brien and Crandall, 2003), dejection emotions, negative thinking, and a prevention (i.e. wanting to 'not fail') as opposed to a promotion (i.e. wanting to 'succeed') self-regulatory focus (Cadinu et al., 2005; Keller and Dauenheimer, 2003; Seibt and Förster, 2004), reduced working memory capacity (Schmader and Johns, 2003), the attempted suppression of stereotypes (Spencer et al., 2007) and stereotype activation (Ambady et al., 2004; Davies et al., 2002).

While it is beyond the scope of this chapter to describe the details of each of the studies examining these mediational processes (see C.M. Steele et al., 2002 for a partial review), it is important to note that these studies provide some initial indication of strategies for overcoming stereotype threat. Research on the role of arousal provides evidence that stereotype threat effects can be eliminated when women are provided with the opportunity to attribute the source of their arousal to another plausible source (Ben-Zeev et al., 2005b; see also Brown and Josephs, 1999, who made use of a self-handicapping misattribution paradigm to alleviate stereotype threat). In addition, research examining thought suppression (Wegner, 1994) in conjunction with the findings of Spencer et al. (2007) suggests that women in stereotype-threatening situations might overcome repeated attempts to suppress stereotype activation by substituting another thought. In one study, stereotype-threatened women showed improved performance when they were told to think about a valued identity each time a stereotype-related thought came to mind during a challenging math test (Spencer et al., 2007).

Finding ways of overcoming stereotype threat has not been the goal of most researchers examining mediational processes, and yet this work provides initial suggestions for how to allay threatening environments.

Building on these and other findings, some researchers have begun to specifically examine whether short-term or long-term interventions and strategies can be introduced to help counteract these situational threats. In an attempt to better understand this phenomenon, researchers have also begun to identify individual differences in people's tendency to be affected by the possibility that they might confirm a negative stereotype about their groups. The findings of these studies are reviewed below.

OVERCOMING STEREOTYPE THREAT

At first glance, it would seem that one of the best ways to overcome feelings of threat associated with being stereotyped is to become extremely skilled in the domain. Spencer et al. (1999, Study 1; see also O'Brien and Crandall, 2003) demonstrated that stereotype threat effects only emerge when math-identified women are presented with a *challenging* test of their mathematical abilities; in their research, such gender differences did not emerge when men and women were presented with an easier test of mathematical prowess. As test difficulty is dependent on skill level, women who are exceptionally skilled may face less concern about inadvertently confirming a negative stereotype about their group, simply because these women might not be as challenged by situations in which higher math abilities are expected.

This route to overcoming stereotype threat is a tenuous one, however, as any person striving to be successful in higher education should ultimately face challenges, no matter what their skill level. And as C.M. Steele (1997, p. 618) explains,

> For the advanced female math student who has been brilliant up to that point, any frustration she has at the frontier of her skills could confirm the gender-based limitation alleged in the stereotype, making this frontier, because she is so invested in it, a more threatening place than it is for the nonstereotyped. Thus, the work of dispelling stereotype threat through performance probably increases with the difficulty of work in the domain, and whatever exemption is gained has to be rewon at the next new proving ground.

Even a very talented female scientist would need to disprove the stereotype by re-establishing her skills and ability in each new context that she encountered; if she faltered, even slightly, she would again risk being viewed as representative of her gender group, instead of as an individual.

At a societal level, another obvious way to overcome stereotype threat would be to dispel the stereotype entirely. This, again, is difficult given the staggering statistics about women's underrepresentation in these domains.

Although these statistics alone hardly provide concrete evidence that women are not as skilled at, interested in, or dedicated to these domains as men, they do provide solid evidence of a gender difference. As more women enter these educational domains, it is likely that this stereotype will be dispelled; in the meantime this strategy alone is not a viable possibility.

Given the inherent limitations to these approaches, researchers have theorized and demonstrated more viable routes to help combat the threat that stereotypes can impose. Stereotype threat is a *situation*-specific phenomenon and accordingly some theory and research has focused on ways to alter educational environments to reduce the possibility that stereotyped group members feel concern that they will be viewed through a stereotyped lens (McIntyre et al., 2003; C.M. Steele, 1997; C.M. Steele et al., 2002). In addition, recent research has demonstrated that specific *personal interventions* can be used to help eliminate the effect that stereotypes can have on women's math test performance (Ambady et al., 2004; Croizet et al., 2001; Martens et al., 2006; Shih et al., 1999). Finally, a third line of research has sought to determine *individual differences in susceptibility and responses to stereotype threat* (Pronin et al., 2004; Schmader, 2002; Schmader et al., 2004; J. Steele, 2003; J. Steele et al., 2007). Research based on each of these three paths is described in greater detail below.

SITUATIONAL INTERVENTIONS

According to C.M. Steele (1997), there are situational changes that can be put in place in educational and occupational settings to reduce the probability that women will feel concern about being viewed stereotypically. Steele specifically outlines three 'wise schooling' strategies that can help women who are both domain identified and non-identified. The first strategy of wise schooling is to build optimistic teacher–student relationships. Stereotypes can lead women to feel concerned that their teachers or employers will question their abilities; accordingly it is vital that this possibility be explicitly disavowed in any mentoring context. Additional strategies include emphasizing challenge over remediation when there is a need for skill building and focusing on the malleability of intelligence through experience and training. Previous research has found that negative feedback provided to boys often focuses on their poor behavior or lack of effort, whereas negative feedback given to girls often emphasizes intellectual shortcomings (Dweck et al., 1978). These different types of feedback implicitly convey the view that boys have the potential to succeed with sufficient effort whereas girls are inherently limited. By focusing on the expandability of human intelligence in stereotype-threatening contexts, girls and women will have a greater potential to thrive.

For women who are already invested in the domain of mathematics, there are additional institutional interventions that can help to reduce the probability that they will disidentify with the domain. First, it is important to 'affirm domain belongingness' by explicitly reinforcing that women are welcome and accepted in mathematical and scientific contexts. Clearly this needs to be done appropriately, to ensure that this affirmation does not inadvertently serve to activate stereotypes. Second, it is important to value multiple perspectives in the classroom or work environment. Finally, C.M. Steele (1997) suggests that it is critical to provide women with positive role models. Female mathematicians who have been able to flourish despite their membership in a negatively stereotyped group carry with them the encouraging message that these obstacles can be overcome.

To date the majority of research that has been conducted on 'wise schooling' practices has focused on racial minority group members as opposed to women in math and science (C.M. Steele et al., 2002). However, there is no reason to believe that similar strategies and interventions would not be equally successful with women in mathematics. And there is some laboratory-based research to support this possibility. For example, several studies have demonstrated that providing information about a successful role model can effectively combat stereotype threat effects (Marx and Roman, 2002; Marx et al., 2005; McIntyre et al., 2003). In one study, researchers buffered threat-induced performance deficits in undergraduate women by explicitly portraying the female experimenter as highly competent in mathematics. In contrast, portraying the female experimenter as having a low level of competence in math resulted in poorer math test performance (Marx and Roman, 2002, Study 2). In other research, reminding participants of other domains in which women have succeeded alleviated the effects of stereotype threat on a subsequent math test (McIntyre et al., 2003). These findings provide some laboratory-based support for the importance of positive role models in reducing the debilitating effects that stereotype threat can have on women's math performance.

In short, theorizing and research suggest that there are ways that educational institutions and organizations can combat stereotype threat. Importantly, these contextual interventions can work in conjunction with policies designed to foster work–family balance and combat group-based discrimination. However, individuals who find themselves in stereotype-threatening situations are not often in a position to change their environments; accordingly, it is important to acknowledge interventions that can be implemented at an individual level that help to combat stereotype threat effects.

PERSONAL INTERVENTIONS

Researchers have examined the use of *self-affirmation* as a way for an individual to combat stereotype threat (Croizet et al., 2001; Martens et al., 2006). According to the theory of self-affirmation, one of our primary social motivations as individuals is self-integrity maintenance. Early self-affirmation research has demonstrated that when people are faced with a threat to their self-integrity (i.e. after receiving negative feedback), they will look to affirm themselves as a way of dealing with or overcoming this threat (C.M. Steele et al., 1993; Fein and Spencer, 1997). If stereotype threat presents a threat to self-integrity for people who are highly identified with a given domain, then affirming their identity by recruiting other positive aspects of the self should alleviate that threat.

To test this possibility Martens et al. (2006, Study 1) asked math-identified women to take a math test under stereotype-threatening or non-stereotype-threatening conditions. They then provided half of the stereotype-threatened women with the opportunity to affirm themselves prior to taking the test, by asking them to write about an important personal value. As expected, stereotype-threatened women who affirmed an important part of their identity subsequently performed as well as non-stereotype-threatened women, and significantly better than threatened women who did not self-affirm on a challenging test of their mathematical abilities. Similar results emerged in another study by Croizet et al. (2001) in which women's student identity was affirmed in a stereotype-threatening situation. Stereotype-threatened women who were led to believe that they were more intellectually curious and helpful than other students (a self-affirmation manipulation) just before completing a challenging math test performed as well as women in a non-stereotype-threatened condition. Such results suggest that one way to alleviate stereotype threat is to affirm the self by recruiting information central to the person's being, such as a key value or characteristic. As Croizet et al. note, to be effective, this information needs to be 'at least as important to the individual's perception of self-adequacy as are the negative images inherent in the threat' (C.M. Steele, 1988, p. 291).

In our own work, we have found *individuation* to be another means of combating the effects of stereotype activation on women's math test performance (Ambady et al., 2004). After being primed with the concept 'female' or with neutral words, undergraduate women were given a questionnaire designed to either provide them with the opportunity to think about their uniqueness (the individuation manipulation) or designed to serve as a filler task (control condition) before taking a challenging math test. We hypothesized that women who thought about their uniqueness would gain some distance from group-based stereotypes, thus rendering the negative stereotype about women's inferior math ability irrelevant in the testing situation. As expected, women in the individuation condition performed better than gender-primed women who were not individuated, and performed as well as women who were not gender-primed.

It is important to note that in each of these studies, participants were unaware of the intended results of the experimental manipulations. It therefore remains unclear whether women in a scientific occupation or major could combat stereotype threat by generating self-affirming or individuating thoughts in situations where they realize that they might be affected by stereotype threat. This research similarly does not determine whether women who succeed in math and scientific domains already make use of these strategies. Nonetheless, these results provide some initial indication that individual-based interventions can be introduced to combat the effects of stereotype threat.

Another way that women might overcome stereotypes is through the activation of other group identities that are not negatively stereotyped. The self-concept is composed of a diversity of social identities and each of these identities may have different, even opposing, stereotypes associated with them (Shih et al., 1999). For example, a woman majoring in mathematics may also be a soccer player, a musician, a practicing Catholic, and an Asian American. Not all of these identities will be salient at a particular moment in time, however; the working self-concept is believed to be those aspects of our identities that are salient to us at a given moment (Markus and Wurf, 1987). When taking a math test that has been described as previously showing gender differences, a woman's gender identity becomes salient, which induces concerns related to confirming a negative math stereotype. However, subtly reminding this woman of her positively stereotyped Asian identity might help to combat these effects.

To test this possibility, Shih et al. (1999) recruited Asian-American women and asked them to complete a one-page questionnaire followed by a challenging math test. The questionnaire included items that were designed to subtly remind women of either their positively stereotyped racial identity (i.e. 'Do your parents or grandparents speak any languages other than English?'), their negatively stereotyped female identity (i.e. 'Do you prefer co-ed or single-sex dormitories?'), or in a control condition, no particular identity (i.e. 'Would you consider subscribing to cable television?'). Consistent with societal stereotypes, participants in the Asian-prime condition performed significantly better on the math test than women in the female-prime condition, relative to participants in the control condition. These results are particularly intriguing as no direct mention of the stereotypes themselves was ever made; Asian-American women were only reminded of aspects of their *identities*. However, caution would need to be used in adopting this as a strategy to combat stereotype threat. Subsequent research has shown that if people are made blatantly aware of their positively stereotyped identities, their performance can actually be impaired, likely due to a concern about whether they will be able to live up to the stereotype (Cheryan and Bodenhausen, 2000; Shih et al., 2002).

One final, albeit less practical, strategy that we have examined in our research involves having participants physically approach mathematics (Kawakami et al., 2007). Social psychological research on approach–avoidance behaviors has demonstrated a general facilitation for approaching liked objects and avoiding disliked objects (Chen and Bargh, 1999; Solarz, 1960). Importantly, this body of research has also shown that for neutral attitude objects as well as social categories, people can develop a greater liking for items that they approach as opposed to avoid (Cacioppo et al., 1993; Förster and Strack, 1997; Kawakami et al., in press; Priester et al., 1996). Building on this literature, we examined whether training women to approach math-related objects would result in a more positive attitude and orientation towards this domain.

Unlike the majority of stereotype threat research, we recruited women who were not particularly identified with mathematics. Non-identified women in an experimental condition received extensive practice in approaching math-related pictures on a computer screen by pulling a joystick towards themselves, whereas women in a control condition were asked instead to move the joystick to the side (right or left). In line with our predictions, women who were trained to approach math-related objects were subsequently quicker to associate math with self-related words on an implicit measure of math identification. In addition, they attempted more questions on a challenging math test than women in a control condition. These findings suggest that one way to increase women's participation in domains such as mathematics may simply be to encourage women to approach these domains. In this study, 'approach' involved a very basic-level process (a simple, repeated arm movement); however, these findings suggest the possibility that a variety of approach behaviors such as female-friendly teaching formats and classroom environments that challenge avoidance orientation and draw otherwise unidentified women in, could have a profound impact on women's orientation towards this domain.

INDIVIDUAL DIFFERENCES IN SUSCEPTIBILITY AND RESPONSES TO STEREOTYPE THREAT

In addition to identifying situational and personal interventions aimed at combating stereotype threat, researchers have also attempted to identify individual differences that might moderate women's susceptibility to stereotype threat effects in mathematics, as well as long-term strategies that women in these domains adopt. It is important to reiterate that one set of strategies aimed at dealing with the risk of confirming a negative stereotype is simply to avoid, disengage or disidentify with the stereotyped domain. These strategies no doubt contribute to the current underrepresentation of women in math, science and engineering; however, it is clearly not the ideal strategy if we wish to increase the number of women in these fields. Of greater interest are those individual differences and strategies that allow women to remain engaged with these fields of study.

Schmader and her colleagues have found that women's identification with their gender group, as well as their willingness to endorse gender stereotypes, moderate stereotype threat effects (Schmader, 2002; Schmader et al., 2004). In one study, Schmader (2002) asked women and men to take a challenging math test under one of two conditions: participants in the stereotype threat condition were told by a male experimenter that the researchers were interested in women's performance relative to men, whereas participants in the control condition were told that the researchers were interested in the individual performance of women and men. Schmader then used previously collected information about participants' gender identification to examine whether stereotype threat effects would be more pronounced for women who were highly identified with their gender group. In line with her predictions, Schmader found that women high in identification with their gender group, as indicated by their agreement with statements such as 'Being a woman is an important reflection of who I am' (Luhtanen and Crocker, 1992), were more susceptible to this stereotype threat manipulation than women who reported a low level of gender identification. Although not conclusive given the experimental design, these findings suggest that one way women might overcome the threat that gender stereotypes can impose is to simply reduce the extent to which their gender identity is central to their self-concept.

In line with these data, Pronin et al. (2004) investigated the possibility that female math majors selectively reject only those aspects of femininity that might be perceived as hindering their ability to succeed in mathematics, a process they have termed *identity bifurcation*. In one study, Pronin et al. (Study 1) asked women enrolled in undergraduate math classes to rate the extent to which various characteristics applied to them and were important to their sense of self. These items included characteristics that were pre-tested to be feminine and stereotypically associated with a lack of potential in mathematics (i.e. emotional, flirtatious, family-oriented), feminine and not associated with a lack of math potential (i.e. sensitive, nurturing, fashionable), and masculine (i.e. competitive, aggressive, analytical). Consistent with their predictions, women who had previously taken a large number of courses in mathematics only rated the traits that were feminine and stereotypically associated with a lack of potential in mathematics (and not the traits that were feminine and not associated with a lack of math potential or masculine traits) as less representative of themselves than women with less exposure to courses in mathematics. These findings suggest that one way some women might overcome stereotype threat is by rejecting, at least temporarily, certain aspects of femininity (such as wearing make-up or flirting).

Finally, we have suggested that a related process, termed *stereotype stratification*, might emerge among targets of negative stereotypes (J. Steele, 2003; J. Steele et al., 2007). The term *stereotype stratification* is used to refer to the process of 'cognitively viewing oneself as a member of a subgroup to which the stereotype does not apply' (J. Steele, 2003, p. 2590). For example, girls might develop a gender stereotype that is specific to women (an age subgroup to which they do not currently belong), whereas boys might develop a global gender stereotype about mathematics. In an initial demonstration of this possibility, girls in early elementary school were asked to rate how good they found boys, girls, men and women to be at mathematics. Consistent with this theory, girls rated boys and girls as having comparable abilities, but rated men being better at math than women (J. Steele, 2003). In a subsequent study, boys and girls were asked to draw a picture of a gender-unspecified mathematician who was described as being either an adult or a child. Again consistent with our expectations, boys drew a male mathematician regardless of whether they were asked to draw a child or an adult. By contrast, the gender of girls' drawings depended on the age of the mathematician described; girls were more likely to draw a child mathematician who was female and an adult mathematician who was male (J. Steele, 2003). These findings suggest that girls might be redefining this stereotype in a way that is temporarily self-protective.

Although it is unclear whether these individual and group differences reflect protective strategies that have been adopted, it should be noted that there are potential costs associated with adopting any of these strategies in an attempt to overcome stereotype threat. Women who distance themselves from their gender group, or from specific aspects of their gender identity, might lose the psychological protection that group membership can often afford. Alternatively, by redefining the stereotype in the short term, girls might find themselves more susceptible to stereotype-threatening situations as they move into womanhood. In addition, each of these strategies might increase women's likelihood to stereotype other women who have not adopted a similar approach. Nonetheless, these data provide some interesting insight into the ways that successful female mathematicians and scientists might deal with stereotype-threatening situations.

CONCLUSION

This chapter began with a seemingly straightforward question: Why are there fewer women than men pursuing and succeeding in prestigious careers in math and scientific domains? The goal of this chapter was not to review the multitude of potential factors that contribute to this gender discrepancy; instead, we set out to review the growing literature examining the situational impact of gender stereotypes on women's math test performance and their identification with this domain. What is clear from this literature is that gender stereotypes can have an immediate and consequential effect on women's performance and identification with the field of mathematics. Importantly, this literature also suggests that there are strategies that can be adopted by institutions and individuals to help combat this situational threat. Although this literature provides some insight into our initial question, future research is needed to determine the conditions under which stereotype threat emerges in naturalistic settings, and importantly, to better understand how successful women in these fields have been able to surmount these potential obstacles.

One final question to emerge from this literature is whether it is beneficial or detrimental for women in the sciences to learn about stereotype threat. There is research to suggest that knowledge in this case is beneficial. Johns et al. (2005) found that women in an experimental condition who received a 'teaching intervention' designed to educate them about stereotype threat performed better than other women in a math testing situation. In addition, the more the women in the experimental condition attributed any anxiety they felt to gender stereotypes, the better they performed. This was in contrast to women who took the test without first learning about stereotype threat; the more the women in this control group made attributions to gender stereotypes, the *worse* they performed. In short, this research provides some indication that educating women might provide one strategy to reduce the situational impact of stereotypes on women in mathematics.

Although women continue to be underrepresented in math and scientific domains, there is great hope for the future. Women have made steady progress in their representation in these domains, and these numbers will undoubtedly continue to climb. As more women enter these fields, stereotypes will likely cease to be a hidden barrier to be confronted. And through continued research aimed at understanding stereotype threat, we will, we hope, have more information to share on how this current obstacle can best be overcome.

ACKNOWLEDGEMENT

The research reported in this paper was supported by a Social Science and Humanities Council of Canada (SSHRC) research grant to the first author.

NOTE

1. In a critical review of the scientific data on sex differences in cognitive abilities, renowned developmental psychologist Elizabeth Spelke (2005, p. 956) concluded that 'research on the cognitive abilities of males and females from birth to maturity does not support the claim that men have a greater intrinsic aptitude for mathematics and science'.

REFERENCES

Agars, M.D. (2004), 'Reconsidering the impact of gender stereotypes on the advancement of women in organizations', *Psychology of Women Quarterly*, **28**, 103–11.

Ambady, N., Paik, S.K., Steele, J., Owen-Smith, A. and Mitchell, J.P. (2004), 'Deflecting negative self-relevant stereotype activation: the effects of individuation', *Journal of Experimental Social Psychology*, **40**, 401–8.

Aronson, J., Quinn, D.M. and Spencer, S.J. (1998), 'Stereotype threat and the academic underperformance of minorities and women', in J.K. Swim and C. Stangor (eds), *Prejudice*, San Diego, CA: Academic Press, pp. 83–103.

Aronson, J., Lustina, M.J., Good, C., Keough, K., Steele, C.M. and Brown, J. (1999), 'When White men can't do math: necessary and sufficient factors in stereotype threat', *Journal of Experimental Social Psychology*, **35**, 29–46.

Benokraitis, N.V. and Feagin, J.R. (1995), *Modern Sexism*, 2nd edn, Englewood Cliffs, NJ: Prentice-Hall.

Ben-Zeev, T., Fein, S. and Inzlicht, M. (2005a), 'Arousal and stereotype threat', *Journal of Experimental Social Psychology*, **41**, 174–81.

Ben-Zeev, T., Carrasquillo, C.M., Ching, A.M.L., Kliengklom, T.J., McDonald, K.L., Newhall, D.C., Patton, G.E., Steward, T.D., Stoddard, T., Inzlicht, M. and Fein, S. (2005b), '"Math is hard!" (Barbie, 1994). Responses of threat vs. challenge-mediated arousal to stereotypes alleging intellectual inferiority', in A.M. Gallagher and J.C. Kaufman (eds), *Gender Differences in Mathematics*, New York: Cambridge University Press, pp. 48–72.

Brown, R.P. and Josephs, R.A. (1999), 'A burden of proof: stereotype relevance and gender differences in math performance', *Journal of Personality and Social Psychology*, **76**, 246–57.

Cacioppo, J.T., Priester, J.R. and Berntson, G.G. (1993), 'Rudimentary determinants of attitudes: II. Arm flexion and extension have differential effects on attitudes', *Journal of Personality and Social Psychology*, **65**, 5–17.

Cadinu, M., Maass, A., Rosabianca, A. and Kiesner, J. (2005), 'Why do women underperform under stereotype threat? Evidence for the role of negative thinking', *Psychological Science*, **16**, 572–8.

Chasteen, A.L., Bhattacharyya, S., Horhota, M., Tam, R. and Hasher, L. (2005), 'How feelings of stereotype threat influence older adults' memory performance', *Experimental Aging Research*, **31**, 235–60.

Chen, M. and Bargh, J.A. (1999), 'Consequences of automatic evaluation: immediate behavioral predispositions to approach or avoid the stimulus', *Personality and Social Psychology Bulletin*, **25**, 215–24.

Cheryan, S. and Bodenhausen, G.V. (2000), 'When positive stereotypes threaten intellectual performance: the psychological hazards of "model minority" status', *Psychological Science*, **11**, 399–402.

Crocker, J., Major, B. and Steele, C.M. (1998), 'Social stigma', in D.T. Gilbert, S.T. Fiske and G. Lindzey (eds), *The Handbook of Social Psychology*, 4th edn, Vol. 2, Boston, MA: McGraw-Hill, pp. 504–53.

Croizet, J.C. and Claire, T. (1998), 'Extending the concept of stereotype threat to social class: the intellectual underperformance of students from low socioeconomic backgrounds', *Personality and Social Psychology Bulletin*, **24**, 588–94.

Croizet, J.C., Desert, M., Dutrevis, M. and Leyens, J.P. (2001), 'Stereotype threat, social class, gender and academic under-achievement: when our reputation catches up to us and takes over', *Social Psychology of Education*, **4**, 295–310.

Davies, P.G. and Spencer, S.J. (2005), 'The gender-gap artifact: women's underperformance in quantitative domains through the lens of stereotype threat', in A.M. Gallagher and J.C. Kaufman (eds), *Gender Differences in Mathematics*, New York: Cambridge University Press, pp. 172–88.

Davies, P.G., Spencer, S.J., Quinn, D.M. and Gerhardstein, R. (2002), 'Consuming images: how television commercials that elicit stereotype threat can restrain women academically and professionally', *Personality and Social Psychology Bulletin*, **28**, 1615–28.

Dweck, C.S., Davidson, W., Nelson, S. and Enna, B. (1978), 'Sex differences in learned helplessness', *Developmental Psychology*, **14**, 268–76.

Eccles, J.S. (1987), 'Gender roles and women's achievement-related decisions', *Psychology of Women Quarterly*, **11**, 135–72.

Eccles, J.S. (1994), 'Understanding women's educational and occupational choices: applying the Eccles et al. model of achievement-related choices', *Psychology of Women Quarterly*, **18**, 585–609.

Eccles, J.S. and Jacobs, J.E. (1986), 'Social forces shape math attitudes and performance', *Signs*, **11**, 367–80.

Fein, S. and Spencer, S.J. (1997), 'Prejudice as self-image maintenance: affirming the self through derogating others', *Journal of Personality and Social Psychology*, **73**, 31–44.

Förster, J. and Strack, F. (1997), 'Motor actions in retrieval of valenced information: a motor congruence effect', *Perceptual and Motor Skills*, **85**, 1419–27.

Gallagher, A.M. and Kaufman, J.C. (2005), 'Gender differences in mathematics: what we know and what we need to know', in A.M. Gallagher and J.C. Kaufman (eds), *Gender Differences in Mathematics*, New York: Cambridge University Press, pp. 316–31.

Golombok, S. and Fivush, R. (1994), *Gender Development*, New York: Cambridge University Press.

Gonzales, P.M., Blanton, H. and Williams, K.J. (2002), 'The effects of stereotype threat and double-minority status on the test performance of Latino women', *Personality and Social Psychology Bulletin*, **28**, 659–70.

Greenwald, A.G., McGhee, D.E. and Schwartz, J.L.K. (1998), 'Measuring individual differences in implicit cognition: the implicit association test', *Journal of Personality and Social Psychology*, **74**, 1464–80.

Greenwald, A.G., Nosek, B.A. and Banaji, M.R. (2003), 'Understanding and using the Implicit Association Test: I. An improved scoring algorithm', *Journal of Personality and Social Psychology*, **85**, 197–216.

Hyde, J.S. (2005), 'The gender similarities hypothesis', *American Psychologist*, **60**, 581–92.

Inzlicht, M. and Ben-Zeev, T. (2000), 'A threatening intellectual environment: why females are susceptible to experiencing problem-solving deficits in the presence of males', *Psychological Science*, **11**, 365–71.

Jacobs, J.E., Davis-Kean, P., Bleeker, M., Eccles, J.S. and Malanchuk, O. (2005), 'I can but I don't want to: the impact of parents, interests, and activities on gender differences in math', in A.M. Gallagher and J.C. Kaufman (eds), *Gender Differences in Mathematics*, New York: Cambridge University Press, pp. 246–63.

Jacobs, J.E. and Eccles, J.S. (1992), 'The impact of mothers' gender-role stereotypic beliefs on mothers' and children's ability perceptions', *Journal of Personality and Social Psychology*, **63**, 932–44.

Jacobs, J.E. and Eccles, J.S. (2000), 'Parents, task values, and real-life achievement-related choices', in C. Sansone and J.M. Harackiewicz (eds), *Intrinsic and Extrinsic Motivation*, San Diego, CA: Academic Press, Inc., pp. 405–39.

Johns, M., Schmader, T. and Marten, A. (2005), 'Knowing is half the battle: teaching stereotype threat as a means of improving women's math performance', *Psychological Science*, **16**, 175–9.

Kawakami, K., Phills, C., Steele, J.R. and Dovidio, J.F. (in press), '(Close) distance makes the heart grow fonder: improving implicit racial attitudes and interracial interactions through approach behaviors', *Journal of Personality and Social Psychology*.

Kawakami, K., Steele, J.R., Cifa, C., Phills, C.E. and Dovidio, J.F. (2007), 'Approaching Math Increases Math = Me, Math = Pleasant, and Perseverance at Math', unpublished manuscript.

Keller, J. and Dauenheimer, D. (2003), 'Stereotype threat in the classroom: dejection mediates the disrupting threat effect on women's math performance', *Personality and Social Psychology Bulletin*, **29**, 371–81.

Levy, B. (1996), 'Improving memory in old age through implicit self-stereotyping', *Journal of Personality and Social Psychology*, **71**, 1092–107.

Lockwood, P. and Kunda, Z. (1997), 'Superstars and me: predicting the impact of role models on the self', *Journal of Personality and Social Psychology*, **73**, 91–103.

Luhtanen, R. and Crocker, J. (1992), 'A collective self-esteem scale: self-evaluation of one's social identity', *Personality and Social Psychology Bulletin*, **18**, 302–18.

Marasco, C.A. (2005), 'Women faculty makes little progress', *Chemical & Engineering News*, **83**, 38.

Markus, H. and Wurf, E. (1987), 'The dynamic self-concept: a social psychological perspective', in M.R. Rosenzweig and L.W. Porter (eds), *Annual Review of Psychology*, Vol. 38, Palo Alto, CA: Annual Reviews, pp. 299–337.

Martens, A., Johns, M., Greenberg, J. and Schimel, J. (2006), 'Combating stereotype threat: the effect of self-affirmation on women's intellectual performance', *Journal of Experimental Social Psychology*, **42**, 236–43.

Marx, D.M. and Roman, J.S. (2002), 'Female role models: protecting women's math test performance', *Personality and Social Psychology Bulletin*, **28**, 1183–93.

Marx, D.M., Stapel, D.A. and Muller, D. (2005), 'We can do it: the interplay of construal orientation and social comparisons under threat', *Journal of Personality and Social Psychology*, **88**, 432–46.

Massachusetts Institute of Technology (1999), *A Study on the Status of Women Faculty in Science at MIT*, Faculty NewsLetter, **10**(4), 1–20.

McIntyre, R.B., Paulson, R.M. and Lord, C.G. (2003), 'Alleviating women's mathematics stereotype threat through salience of group achievements', *Journal of Experimental and Social Psychology*, **39**, 83–90.

National Science Foundation (2004), *Women, Minorities, and Persons with Disabilities: 2004* (NSF Document No. nsf04317).

O'Brien, L.T. and Crandall, C.S. (2003), 'Stereotype threat and arousal: effects on women's math performance', *Personality and Social Psychology Bulletin*, **29**, 782–9.

Peter, K. and Horn, L. (2005), *Gender Differences in Participation and Completion of Undergraduate Education and How They Have Changed Over Time* (NCES Publication No. NCES 2005169), Washington, DC: Institute of Education Sciences.

Priester, J.R., Cacioppo, J.T. and Petty, R.E. (1996), 'The influence of motor processes on attitudes toward novel versus familiar semantic stimuli', *Personality and Social Psychology Bulletin*, **22**, 442–7.

Pronin, E., Steele, C.M. and Ross, L. (2004), 'Identity bifurcation in responses to stereotype threat: women and mathematics', *Journal of Experimental Social Psychology*, **40**, 152–68.

Reisz, L., Steele, J. and Kawakami, K. (2007), ' "If she can do it, so can I! If he can do it ... Can I?" The effect of cross-sex social comparisons on the math test performance of women in the sciences', unpublished manuscript.

Ripley, A. (2005), 'Who says a woman can't be Einstein?', *Time*, March, 35–44.

Schmader, T. (2002), 'Gender identification moderates stereotype threat effects on women's math performance', *Journal of Experimental Social Psychology*, **38**, 194–201.

Schmader, T. and Johns, M. (2003), 'Converging evidence that stereotype threat reduces working memory capacity', *Journal of Personality and Social Psychology*, **85**, 440–52.

Schmader, T., Johns, M. and Barquissau, M. (2004), 'The costs of accepting gender differences: the role of stereotype endorsement in women's experience in the math domain', *Sex Roles*, **50**, 835–50.

Seibt, B. and Förster, J. (2004), 'Stereotype threat and performance: how self-stereotypes influence processing by inducing regulatory foci', *Journal of Personality and Social Psychology*, **87**, 38–56.

Shih, M., Ambady, N., Richeson, J.A., Fujita, K. and Gray, H.M. (2002), 'Stereotype performance boosts: the impact of self-relevance and the manner of stereotype activation', *Journal of Personality and Social Psychology*, **83**, 638–47.

Shih, M., Pittinsky, T.L. and Ambady, N. (1999), 'Stereotype susceptibility: identity salience and shifts in quantitative performance', *Psychological Science*, **10**, 81–4.

Solarz, A.K. (1960), 'Latency of instrumental responses as a function of compatibility with the meaning of eliciting verbal signs', *Journal of Experimental Psychology*, **59**, 239–45.

Spelke, E.S. (2005), 'Sex differences in intrinsic aptitude for mathematics and science? A critical review', *American Psychologist*, **60**, 950–58.

Spencer, S.J., Iserman, E., Davies, P.G. and Quinn, D. M. (2007), 'Suppression of doubts, anxiety, and stereotypes as a mediator of the effect of stereotype threat on women's math performance', unpublished manuscript.

Spencer, S.J., Steele, C.M. and Quinn, D. (1999), 'Stereotype threat and women's math performance', *Journal of Experimental Social Psychology*, **35**, 4–28.

Stangor, C. and Sechrist, G.B. (1998), 'Conceptualizing the determinants of academic choice and task performance across social groups', in J.K. Swim and C. Stangor (eds), *Prejudice: The Target's Perspective*, San Diego, CA: Academic Press, pp. 105–24.

Steele, C.M. (1988), 'The psychology of self-affirmation: sustaining the integrity of the self', in L. Berkowitz (ed.), *Advances in Experimental Social Psychology*, Vol. 21, New York: Academic Press, pp. 261–302.

Steele, C.M. (1997), 'A threat in the air: how stereotypes shape intellectual identity and performance', *American Psychologist*, **52**, 613–29.

Steele, C.M. and Aronson, J. (1995), 'Stereotype threat and the intellectual test performance of African Americans', *Journal of Personality and Social Psychology*, **69**, 797–811.

Steele, C.M., Spencer, S.J. and Aronson, J. (2002), 'Contending with group image: the psychology of stereotype and social identity threat', in M.P. Zanna (ed.), *Advances in Experimental Social Psychology*, Vol. 34, San Diego, CA: Academic Press, pp. 379–440.

Steele, C.M., Spencer, S.J. and Lynch, M. (1993), 'Self-image resilience and dissonance: the role of affirmational resources', *Journal of Personality and Social Psychology*, **64**, 885–96.

Steele, J. (2003), 'Children's gender stereotypes about math: the role of stereotype stratification', *Journal of Applied Social Psychology*, **33**, 2587–606.

Steele, J. and Ambady, N. (2006), '"Math is Hard!": The effect of gender priming on women's attitudes', *Journal of Experimental Social Psychology*, **42**, 428–36.

Steele, J. and Barling, J. (1996), 'Influence of maternal gender-role beliefs and role satisfaction on daughters' vocational interests', *Sex Roles*, **34**, 637–48.

Steele, J., James, J. and Barnett, R. (2002), 'Learning in a man's world: examining the perceptions of undergraduate women in male-dominated academic areas', *Psychology of Women Quarterly*, **26**, 46–50.

Steele, J., Williams, A., Reisz, L. and Shapiro, D. (2007), 'Children's implicit and explicit gender stereotypes about mathematics', unpublished manuscript.

Stone, J., Lynch, C.I., Sjomeling, M. and Darley, J.M. (1999), 'Stereotype threat effects on Black and White athletic performance', *Journal of Personality and Social Psychology*, **77**, 1213–27.

Summers, L. (2005), 'Remarks at NBER conference on diversifying the science and engineering workforce', 14 January, retrieved 25 March 2006 from http://www.president.harvard.edu/speeches/2005/nber.html.

Swim, J.K., Hyers, L.L., Cohen, L.L. and Ferguson, M.J. (2001), 'Everyday sexism: evidence for its incidence, nature, and psychological impact from three daily diary studies', *Journal of Social Issues*, **57**, 31–53.

Tenenbaum, H.R. and Leaper, C. (2003), 'Parent–child conversations about science: the socialization of inequities?', *Developmental Psychology*, **39**, 34–47.

Tietjen, J.S. (2004), 'Why so few women, still?', *IEEE Spectrum*, **41**, 57–8.

Wegner, D.M. (1994), 'Ironic processes of mental control', *Psychological Review*, **101**, 34–52.

Wheeler, S.C. and Petty, R.E. (2001), 'The effects of stereotype activation on behavior: a review of possible mechanisms', *Psychology Bulletin*, **127**, 797–826.

9. Attracting the engineers of 2020 today

Susan Staffin Metz

INTRODUCTION

> Women have emerged as the most educated segment of our society over the past quarter century, but large numbers still view technical fields as off-limits. Imagine the infusion of knowledge and creativity if they were to choose science or engineering at the same rate that they have opted for business, law or medicine. (Building Engineering and Science Talent, 2004, p. 2.)

Women of all ethnicities are underrepresented significantly throughout the continuum of engineering education and professional practice despite 30 years of research, programming, reports and discussion among the engineering community across all sectors. Why do women continue to opt out of engineering and in fact never consider the field as a possible career choice? Funded by public and private foundations, industry and government, significant research has been conducted to understand how to engage women in the engineering enterprise. National initiatives and local programming have been implemented to increase preparedness, improve awareness, assess academic climate, improve curriculum and pedagogy, increase scholarships and fellowships, and generate enthusiasm to attract and retain women in the engineering profession.

Many factors dissuade women from engineering, particularly the traditional and pervasive stereotypes evident in common sources of information pertaining to what engineers do and who engineers are. Since engineering is virtually absent from the curriculum in K-12 education in the USA, as well as from the mass media, there is a greater reliance upon other information sources. It is imperative that organizations and people who are the purveyors of information about engineering be diligent about conveying knowledge that includes rather than excludes students of all demographics from the field.

WOMEN ARE PREPARED TO STUDY ENGINEERING

Although many female high school students are prepared to pursue an engineering degree, most simply choose not to. They have taken the upper level math and science classes necessary to major in engineering in college (see Table 9.1). In 2000, most public high school graduates of both genders took biology to fulfill their science requirement. Females were more likely to have taken chemistry and biology, while males were more likely to have taken physics. Males were slightly more inclined to have taken calculus than females while females were more inclined to have taken analysis/ pre-calculus and algebra II than males (CPST: NCES, 2006). From an overall standpoint, females and males are equally prepared upon graduating high school to enter a college engineering program.

In terms of standardized math testing, very little difference exists between genders in performance. The average score for 17-year-old girls on the National Assessment of Educational Progress (NAEP) in 2004 was 305 compared to 308 for boys. In 2004, 61 percent of male 17-year-olds compared to 57 percent of females of that age scored above 300. Interestingly, their performances have changed very little over the last three decades. It is assumed that graduates with this proficiency generally have the skills needed for freshman engineering courses. There is only one level higher, and only 5 percent of females and 9 percent of males score at this proficiency level. Standardized Achievement Test (SAT) scores continue to show only a slight gap between genders. While mathematics SAT scores for both males and females have increased over the past decade, these scores have remained close. In 2005, the average score for males was 538 compared to the female average of 504.

As we move further along the educational continuum, the number of engineering-interested students falls significantly below the number of engineering-ready students. Interest in engineering and other fields can be

Table 9.1   High school students math and science course completion, 2000

	Males	Females
Biology	89.0	93.3
Chemistry	58.0	65.7
Physics	34.2	29.0
Algebra II	64.8	70.5
Analysis/pre-calc.	25.4	27.9
Calculus	12.2	11.1

Source: Commission on Professionals in Science and Technology: NCES (2006).

assessed by reviewing PSAT (Preliminary SAT) data which provide the opportunity for students to indicate their intended college major. Among 1.4 million high school juniors taking the PSAT in 2004–5, only 8.3 percent indicated that they planned to major in engineering. Disaggregating the data by gender shows that 16.3 percent of males selected an interest in engineering compared with a mere 1.9 percent of females (CPST: College Board, 2006).

Furthermore, while the number of both genders enrolling in engineering has slightly declined since 1994, the drop in enrollment for women has been greater. In fall 2004, full-time first-year students declined by 1.6 percent for men and 2.6 percent for women from two decades ago. The proportion of women among total undergraduate engineering enrollments steadily increased from 1984 to 1999, but has been on a slightly downward trend since that period, as illustrated in Figure 9.1 (CPST: EWC, 2006).

The decline of women in college engineering programs is especially alarming in light of the fact that in 2004, women earned nearly half of all degrees in law (48 percent) and medicine (46 percent), 41 percent of the masters in business administration, 36 percent of PhDs in natural science, but only 18 percent of the engineering doctorates (CPST: EWC, 2006).

It is critical that our nation cultivates the scientific and technical talents of all its citizens, not just of those who have traditionally worked in science,

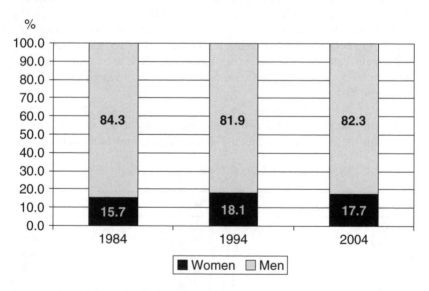

Source: Commission on Professionals in Science and Technology (2006). Data derived from the Engineering Workforce Commission.

Figure 9.1   Total undergraduate engineering enrollment of women

technology, engineering and mathematics (STEM) fields. In 2010, women will earn more degrees than men at every level of higher education from associate to doctoral degree (Building Engineering and Science Talent, 2004). At the baccalaureate level, women already dominate the ranks, earning 56 percent of the undergraduate degrees in 2002 (CPST: NCES, 2006). The US workforce of scientists and engineers no longer mirrors the national profile. White males comprise nearly 70 percent of the science and engineering workforce, while white females comprise only 15 percent of this group. African Americans, Hispanics and Native Americans make up 24 percent of the population collectively but only 7 percent of the science and engineering workforce (Congressional Commission, 2000). Significantly greater numbers of scientists and engineers must come from the talent pool comprised of this new majority to expand our capacity for innovation (Jackson, 2002). Given the demographics of the US workforce, which predicts that, by 2010, 67 percent of the entrants into the workforce will be women and minorities, it is imperative that engineering present itself to attract capable students from all demographic groups (Business Round Table, 2005).

ENGAGEMENT IS CRITICAL

How do we engage students, particularly women and minorities in the USA, in the engineering enterprise? A recent study by Jolly et al. (2004) proposes a trilogy of closely entwined characteristics that are necessary for students to advance in the sciences and quantitative fields. The trilogy includes:

- *engagement*: an orientation to the sciences and/or quantitative disciplines demonstrated by awareness, interest and motivation;
- *capacity*: the knowledge and skills needed to advance to increasingly complex content in the sciences and quantitative disciplines;
- *continuity*: access to institutional and programmatic opportunities, material resources and guidance that support advancement to increasingly complex content in the sciences and quantitative disciplines.

While the level of each characteristic may vary, all three are required for one who pursues an engineering career. If engagement is lacking, there is no desire to develop understanding. If capacity is lacking, there are no basic skills on which to build knowledge and interest. If there is no continuity, students are unable to apply the knowledge learned.

Applying the engagement, capacity, continuity (ECC) model to women in engineering offers some fascinating insight. Continuity has increased as a result of Title IX, which provides for equal opportunities in school for young men and young women, at least for predominantly white upper- and middle-class students. Students attend the same schools and have access to the same high school courses, and an increasing number of advanced and AP courses. They also have equal access to colleges and funding opportunities. As mentioned previously, capacity in mathematics is very similar and is improving for both male and female students in this demographic group. Standardized achievement test scores in mathematics are higher and gender differences are nearly nonexistent in mathematics course taking, with the exception of the SAT mathematics test (Jolly et al., 2004).

Girls graduate from high school with skills and knowledge equivalent to those of their male peers but substantially fewer girls continue in engineering and science, which suggests distinct differences in engagement between boys and girls. Recent increases in girls' enrollment in STEM courses and their rising achievement overall have not corresponded to increases in their participation in the physical science and engineering fields (Clewell and Campbell, 2002). Research indicates that female high school students are less interested than male students in science and engineering education and in their related careers (Xie and Shauman, 2003). Therefore, while it remains important to improve continuity and capacity for all students, engagement is the key to getting more women involved in engineering.

Engagement is the focus of this chapter and requires further exploration. Jolly et al. (2004) argue that the most successful engagement facilitates positive attitudes and motivation for increased knowledge and understanding. There are several aspects of engagement that can individually serve this purpose: emotional engagement, vocational engagement, cognitive engagement and behavioral engagement. Evidence suggests that the two types of engagement most influential to women in this context are: (1) emotional engagement (Fredericks et al., 2004), defined as a positive reaction to people, content and environment in the academic setting, and a view of the discipline as fun, intriguing and intellectually rewarding; and (2) vocational engagement as having a perspective of the profession as fulfilling to an individual's aspirations with a variety of longer-term rewards (Jolly, 2002).

PUBLIC UNDERSTANDING OF ENGINEERING

Neither women nor men will choose engineering for the right reasons unless both the profession and engineering educators can reach out to a broad population with a full portrait of the richness of culture and practice
(Adelman, 1998, p. 85).

Unless society fully and accurately understands the field of engineering, the USA will remain unable to attract a diverse, world-class engineering workforce necessary to ensure the nation's continued leadership in engineering innovation (Duderstadt, 2004). The National Academy of Engineering identified the necessity for improved public awareness of engineering, which will result in more technical literacy among decision makers, more technical literacy in the general public, and more and better-prepared students in engineering (Davis and Gibbin, 2002). In 2003, the American Association of Engineering Societies (AAES) commissioned a Harris Poll to determine the public's understanding and attitudes toward engineering and engineers. According to the poll, 66 percent of Americans feel they are 'not very or not at all well informed about engineering and engineers'. Women were less interested in engineering than men, with 28 percent indicating they were 'very or somewhat' interested compared with 53 percent of men (AAES/Harris Poll, 2003). Increased public knowledge and awareness of science and engineering has the potential to influence people's understanding of who scientists and engineers could be. Improving technological literacy would also broaden society's understanding that women, underrepresented minorities and persons with disabilities are capable of and should be encouraged to contribute to the scientific enterprise in equal measure (Congressional Commission, 2000).

CAREER IMAGE CONFLICTS WITH CONTEMPORARY VALUES

> It is important to see the particular ways in which the image of a scientific career conflicts with contemporary values. It divides girls and boys. The boys, when they react positively, include motives which do not appeal to the girls – adventure, space travel, delight in speed and propulsion; the girls, when they react positively, emphasize humanitarianism, and self-sacrifice for humanity which do not appeal to the boys. The girls reject science . . . as a possible form of work for themselves, [since it is] concerned with things rather than with people . . .
>
> (Mead and Metraux, 1957, p. 387)

The research cited above was based on an analysis of a nationwide sample of essays written by high school students in response to questions asked at 145 schools in the USA consisting of 35 000 students. Nearly 50 years have passed since this finding was revealed and change has been extraordinarily slow. It is essential that we project a more positive, contemporary image of engineering, science and technology in order to make these careers more attractive to all Americans, particularly women given their growing majority status in the workforce.

Using a sample of first-year engineering students at three universities in South Africa, Jawitz and Case (1998) found that females, more often than males, named 'social identity' or making a contribution to the community or country, working as a team, wanting to be different, or to prove oneself significantly as a primary draw to the field. Attraction to the kind of work female students think engineers do within specific applications draws women to engineering majors. Examples include helping people and society, building and designing, improving the environment, and exploring outer space (Goodman et al., 2002).

Significant similarities and differences between male and female perceptions are illustrated in Anderson and Gilbride's (2005) study of 2500 Canadian high school students. They found that males and females acknowledged that engineering heavily involves mathematics, the use of machinery and can be a high-paying job. In fact, females ranked 'uses lots of machinery' as their second overall statement compared to males, who ranked that statement fourth. The researchers contend that this perception may discourage women from pursuing engineering since they have been traditionally discouraged from jobs that involve heavy machinery and/or manual labor. Another striking finding was that neither female nor male students thought that engineering was a career that would be interesting for women, with a mere 3 percent of males and 6 percent of females reporting this sentiment. Forty-four percent of the male students viewed engineering as an exciting, creative career, while only 23 percent of female students viewed engineering the same way.

Margolis and Fisher's book *Unlocking the Clubhouse* (2002) further illuminates a young woman's decision-making process regarding a career in technology. In researching a student's decision to major in computer science, they found that women consider numerous factors, while men consider only a few of these factors. 'Computing with a purpose', the concept of using the computer as a tool to enable processes and solutions that impact human and social contexts, make the study of computer science compelling and meaningful to women. Nearly half (44 percent) of the women interviewed and only 9 percent of the men link their interest in computing to areas outside of the hardware and software.

The image of a computer science student was another aspect that Margolis and Fisher explored. They asked male and female students to provide descriptions of the typical computer science student. About 50 percent of all respondents said that the image of the computer science student 'is not me'. Gender differences are telling, with 69 percent of the female and 32 percent of male computer science majors viewing themselves as different from most of their peers since their life does not revolve around the computer. Consequently, nearly two-thirds of the women question whether they belong in computer science because they do not identify with the typical male computer science student.

This raises an interesting issue. Who are the students who belong in the technical professions? If we buy into the stereotypes, we will limit the type of student who engages in these careers. Students who do not identify with the classic stereotypes are uncertain if they belong. That is why it is imperative to expand the perception of engineers and engineering.

What strategies are necessary to convey that message successfully? Recently, a study was conducted by WGBH Educational Foundation (2005) to better understand what attracts high school women to engineering. The study states the following key issues and findings:

- High school girls believe that engineering is for people who love math and science. They don't have an understanding of engineering, show an interest or think it is for them. They perceive engineering as a profession for men.
- Engineering is portrayed as very challenging and stresses the importance of superior math and science skills. Messages do not include benefits and rewards of being an engineer.
- Professional interests for girls hinge on relevance – the job is rewarding and the profession is for someone 'like me'.
- Career motivators for high school girls include: enjoy their job, have a good work environment, make a difference, earn a good salary, and have flexibility.
- High school girls react positively to personal and informational stories.

These high school girls tell us that it is important to:

- share more stories of how people's lives have been affected by engineers;
- stress how engineering is not just about drafting and cars – it can be about social issues, and third-world countries becoming better and citizens happier;
- talk about hands-on fun, that it's not sitting in a cubicle all day, but it's traveling the world, making a difference, seeing your creations come to life;
- emphasize that engineers not only make good money, but contribute to the well-being of the human race.

It is imperative to listen to what high school girls are telling us and to focus on the implications of this study. A broader range of practices and the prospect of truly making a difference in people's lives must be captured in the image of engineering if we hope to attract women to the field. This is not a stretch. It is very much a part of the essence of engineering. We must do a better job of conveying the engineering story. We must also enhance this type of research by conducting additional studies to assess if these messages are consistent across all demographic groups of women.

ATTRACTING STUDENTS WITH DIVERSE INTERESTS TO ENGINEERING

Solutions of societal problems require that [science and mathematics] be applied in innovative ways with consideration of cultural differences, historical perspectives and legal and economic constraints among other issues. We aspire to engineers in 2020 who will remain well grounded in the basics of mathematics and science, and who will expand their vision of design through a solid grounding in the humanities, social sciences and economics. Emphasis on the creative process will allow more effective leadership in the development and application of next-generation technologies to problems of the future.

(National Academy of Engineering, 2004, p. 49)

How does this vision contrast with the stereotypes, common perceptions, and current messages prevalent in society? *The Engineer of 2020* (National Academy of Engineering, 2004) emphasizes the versatility of an engineering education and enthusiastically demonstrates the intrinsic reward of improving the quality of life for people. Although many engineers pursue career paths in fields that are considered more traditional, a significant number use their engineering education to pursue careers in law, medicine, business and education. The opportunities offered by an engineering education are numerous and diverse, but young people, their parents and counselors remain unaware of this. Key attributes of an engineer depicted in *The Engineer of 2020* include strong analytical skills, practical ingenuity, creativity, communication, business and management, leadership, high ethical standards, professionalism, dynamism, agility, resilience, flexibility and lifelong learners (National Academy of Engineering, 2004). This litany of attributes would attract a broad spectrum of students. The combination of these attributes and multiple career opportunities is a far cry from the traditional and linear descriptions of engineering that must be dispelled. Wouldn't more students be attracted to engineering if they truly understood and embraced this concept? How messages are crafted and presented cannot be underestimated when it comes to attracting or repelling students from the profession.

WHAT MESSAGES ARE WE SENDING?

As we continue to discuss the need to improve the portrayal of engineering, it is necessary to recognize that there is much good work being done regarding this issue on national and local levels. There is a multitude of outreach programs, websites and publications that should be applauded for their effort to increase awareness among students, parents and educators about the broad range of career opportunities in engineering. However, a great deal of inconsistency remains and it is important to identify existing problems so they can be effectively addressed. Only then can we eliminate 'sending the wrong messages' as one of the factors that deters women from pursuing engineering study. This is a solvable problem that will take comparatively far fewer resources, political will, culture change and systemic transformation than other factors that deter women from the field. Every organization that seeks to improve the representation of women of all ethnicities needs to become guardians of their 'engineering messages'.

On the Internet, therefore, a potential engineering student could be turned off from engineering after reading just a few sentences about the field if it feeds into the stereotypes that are entrenched in our culture, often negative and extremely limiting. Women are disproportionately and adversely affected by this experience. The number of teenagers using the Internet has grown 24 percent in the past four years and 87 percent of those between the ages of 12 and 17 are online (Lenhart et al., 2005). In 2006, 71 percent of adult women and 74 percent of adult men are Internet users. Disaggregating the data by race and ethnicity reveals that 73 percent of Internet users are white, non-Hispanic, 61 percent black non-Hispanic and 76 percent English-speaking Hispanic (Pew Internet and American Life Project, 2006). With such a high level of Internet users, it is not surprising that a website is increasingly the place where people get that vital first impression.

Descriptions of engineering on popular websites present messages that deter students, particularly women and minorities, from engineering based on the research cited in this chapter. This problem is compounded by the high degree of Internet usage combined with the millions of web pages that exist on the subject. We need to be particularly concerned about mass-market websites and other forms of media that address the mainstream target populations in which other information sources such as mentors and educators may be absent. Conversely, if those messages are well crafted, students will likely continue to the next tier of information, perhaps to websites of organizations specifically affiliated with engineering. This tier might include professional societies, university schools of engineering and other non-profit groups. Attracting students to engineering who are largely unfamiliar with the field is a challenge, especially when students and their

advisors are inclined to rely on traditional stereotypes to fill in the information gaps. Often, a website, article, presentation or other communication
has limited potential to spark enough interest in the field to encourage a
prospective engineering student to seek more information. If the message
fails, the student is likely lost to another profession.

   Three websites are used as case studies to explore the importance of
presenting engineering in an informative and interesting way that opens
options and generates excitement. The CollegeBoard.com website was
chosen because it appears on the first Google page when a search for college
majors is performed. In addition, the site is used by millions of parents and
students interested in college regardless of field, since registration for SAT
tests is handled through this site. WorldWideLearn.com was selected
because it is listed on the second Google page when requesting a search
on college majors. The Professional Practice component of the ASME
(American Society of Mechanical Engineers) website was also selected
because it provides information to students who are interested in finding
out more about engineering. These students have presumably explored
general college majors and they are seeking the next tier of information,
specifically regarding engineering. The discipline of mechanical engineering was chosen as the target for discussion, since it is the engineering discipline that graduated the most bachelors' degrees in 2005, and it has the
lowest representation of women graduates in a major engineering field
(CPST, 2005). Moreover, this component of the ASME website was chosen
because ASME recently made the decision to dramatically edit the content
to be inclusive of a more diverse student population. Consequently, much
of what is described in this section may no longer appear on the website,
depending on the timing of this publication. However, the former ASME
Professional Practice content serves as an extremely useful teaching tool to
others who are reviewing their websites' content with the goal of ensuring
that their messages appeal to a broad group of students.

   To enhance the analyses of the websites used as case studies, ten successful men and women who have mechanical engineering degree(s) were
asked to give their reaction to the website content. These individuals
include mechanical engineering college faculty, department chairs and
deans, and executives from industry and non-profit organizations. This
mechanical engineers' survey (MES) is not a scientific qualitative study, but
it provides some relevant and enlightening insight for further exploration.

CollegeBoard.com

The College Board website is a large repository of information on colleges,
careers, college majors, financial aid and standardized testing. The users are

typically students, parents and educators across a wide spectrum of interests. The site offers a tremendous opportunity to attract a broad segment of the student population to engineering, but only with well-developed messages. Under the link to mechanical engineering www.collegeboard.com/csearch/majors_careers/profiles/majors/14.1901.html, there is a brief description of what type of work engineers do, a quote from an engineering student and other relevant information. One section is designed to help users assess a major field of study as illustrated below:

Are You Ready To . . .?
- Rely on your math skills
- Master difficult scientific concepts
- Work on your own and in groups
- Write lab reports and research papers
- Take on a heavy course load
- Spend five years as an undergrad, if you're like many majors trying to squeeze in course work and a co-op (internship)

It Helps To Be . . .
A fan of science and math, a creative problem solver, and someone who likes to take things apart to find out how they work.

In response to this assessment, one MES participant, whose sentiment was shared by others stated,

These bullets stress the wrong things, the least interesting aspect of the field. And I'll bet that the number of research papers written in a four-year curriculum is extremely low in comparison to many other majors. I do like the wording, 'fan of math and science'. If someone hates math and science, then they should know that engineering is not for them. But you don't have to LOVE math and science to be an engineer.

Others noted that, in fact, many college majors require a heavy course load as well as the need to master difficult concepts. Co-op programs in any field typically take five years of undergraduate education to complete. Alternatively, the focus of the text should be on readiness to work in teams to assess and solve interesting problems, to learn more about the physical world around you, and to learn the fundamentals of math and science so you can use them as tools to create products and processes. Why intimidate students? Let college admissions officers weed out students who do not have the academic ability and the motivation to succeed in engineering. Engineering will lose every time if messages feed into a lack of confidence, lack of knowledge, and uncertainty, all of which are common among aspiring college students.

WorldWideLearn.com

www.worldwidelearn.com presents itself as the *World's Premier On-Line Directory of Education*. The section about mechanical engineering (www.worldwidelearn.com/online-education-guide/engineering/mechanical-engineering-major.htm) offers information to help students decide whether or not to pursue this major. Here is an excerpt from the web page:

> Evaluate your potential future as a mechanical engineering major by asking yourself these questions:
>
> - How are your grades in math and science? If you struggle, choose another specialty. If you do well and ask for more, mechanical engineering might be the right choice.
> - Do you have a curiosity about how things work? Have you found yourself taking things apart and putting them back together? This curiosity is a natural attribute of the mechanical engineer.
> - If you live to discover new or better ways to do things, you are definitely on the right track.
> - Are computer games, mazes, and jigsaw puzzles fun for you? What could be better than doing work you enjoy?
> - Do people turn to you for advice or trust your decisions? That means you think clearly and have demonstrated decision-making abilities in the past. It is an important requirement for a mechanical engineer.

In the absence of accurate information and a breadth of understanding of the profession, students examine the website for reasons to engage or disengage. This description is extraordinarily limiting and would fit just a small group of students. If taken literally, it would turn away thousands of potentially successful engineering students. The statements, 'if you struggle, choose another specialty. If you do well and ask for more, mechanical engineering might be the right choice' are arrogant and inaccurate. One MES respondent said, 'I have found that some of my best students struggle with math and science. They learn math and science and are able to use them as tools, but they often do not have an immediate gift of understanding.' Take, for instance, a student who worked exceedingly hard to get an A in an advanced math course and she is happy that the course is over. She 'struggled' and she 'is not asking for more math courses'. Does that mean she should not consider mechanical engineering as a major? A student should not even be put in the position of having to assess this circumstance. The characteristics identified on this web page should be broad enough to engage a variety of academically qualified students. Wouldn't the field of engineering and society benefit from students who are motivated to enroll in numerous math and science courses to obtain an engineering degree, but also have a passion for politics, law or journalism? This could lead to a national leader with an engineering background, of which there are far too few.

MES respondents also offered helpful insight regarding the second bullet, 'Have you found yourself taking things apart and putting them back together? This curiosity is a natural attribute of the mechanical engineer.' One professor said, 'I'm not one of those people who has taken everything apart, and wouldn't consider myself extremely hands-on. Students reading this could easily think, "Gee, I haven't taken my car apart and rebuilt my engine . . . I guess that mechanical engineering is not for me." '. The third bullet, exclaiming, 'If you live to discover new or better ways to do things, you are definitely in the right track', further narrows the playing field. The words 'live to' represent an extreme interest held by very few students.

The question posed in the fourth bullet, 'Are computer games, mazes, and jigsaw puzzles fun for you? What could be better than doing work you enjoy?' surprised several MES respondents. They did not understand this connection to mechanical engineering. One respondent disliked computer games, another loved sailing and tennis, and a third loved cooking and skiing. This descriptor is simply an endorsement of a stereotype that describes some people who major in mechanical engineering and many people who do not pursue this career. Presumably, it does not describe countless others who would major in the discipline if it were portrayed differently.

The last characteristic identified in this section could apply to most fields of study. 'Do people turn to you for advice or trust your decisions? That means you think clearly and have demonstrated decision-making abilities in the past. It is an important requirement for a mechanical engineer.' It is also a statement that is very intimidating and somewhat inappropriate for students who are young and impressionable teenagers. How many people do you know who typically turn to teenagers for their advice or trust their decisions? Students should not be made to feel excluded from an engineering pursuit because of unrealistic, largely inaccurate characteristics. We cannot afford to eliminate students who may be well suited to an engineering career, which is why each word in these messages is so critical.

ProfessionalPractice.Asme.org

ASME hosts a Professional Practice Curriculum website (www. professionalpractice.asme.org/ppc_pages/courses.htm), which was developed by senior engineers, managers and faculty leaders for students and early-career engineers and engineering students. Contained within the site is a module entitled 'Why Major in Engineering?' As mentioned in the introduction to this section, ASME (American Society for Mechanical Engineering) is revamping this component of its website with the goal of attracting a more diverse and extensive student population to its discipline. The definition of diversity in this case goes beyond the traditional gender and race/ethnic focus to include students with an interest in applying their mechanical engineering degree to a wide range of professions.

In reviewing the content of this website, let us first consider the beginning of the introduction to the ASME module 'Studying Engineering': 'Unlike the doctor, his life is not a life among the weak. Unlike the soldier, destruction is not his purpose. Unlike the lawyer, quarrels are not his daily bread. To the engineer falls the job of clothing the bare bones of science with life, comfort, and hope' (Herbert Hoover, 31st President of the United States and Mining Engineer). Although engineering is proud of having a US president represent its field, the quote completely excludes women and does not illuminate the current state of engineering satisfactorily.

The text continues:

> Since you are reading this module, you are probably wondering, 'Is majoring in engineering right for me?' The short answer: 'Of course it is!' However, engineering is not for everyone, so it's useful to examine the things that set the engineer apart from other professionals. Who are these people known as engineers? Let's investigate. The most common conceptions (and some misconceptions) of what it's like to major in engineering include:
>
> • It's hard.
> • It's a lot of work.
> • It involves a lot of math.
> • It drains you of humor, fashion sense, and the ability to live for extended periods without being attached to a computer.
>
> The first three conceptions are – for better or for worse – largely correct, but worth the effort. The fourth conception is false, although the computer, as we know, has actually revolutionized the engineering analysis process. As to fashion, we might say that engineers lead the way in fashion every twenty years or so, when our wardrobes happen to come back into fashion. And while not everyone can appreciate the subtle intricacies of engineering humor, an engineering joke can usually get the other inmates at the computer lab chuckling.

A nine-sentence nerd-bashing joke follows and ends the introductory section.

Based on a review of this section, the MES respondents commented: 'Some classes are hard, some are easy, some are interesting, some are boring. Some hard ones can be interesting and some easy ones can be boring. I think this is true for any major. It does require more math than some majors but less than others.' The lack of information about the extraordinary contributions to society by engineering is problematic. The research reviewed substantiates that the appeal to students, particularly women, stems from the critical role engineers play in identifying and addressing our society's most challenging problems. In fact, a woman faculty member who participated in the MES gave this response, 'Hard, math, and makes you a nerd but NOTHING that describes what mechanical engineers do – nothing about serving society or building products. This one in particular will drum all women out of the field.'

The first two bullets 'It's hard' and 'It's a lot of work' can be said about many college majors. In addition, for a student who is inclined toward math and science, the more difficult college majors may be English and history. The more important point, though, is that we are also trying to attract students majoring in English, history and many other subjects to engineering because technical literacy is essential in our globally competitive and technologically sophisticated world.

The third bullet, 'It involves a lot of math', is true to some extent, but an MES respondent points out, 'I never liked math but I loved heat transfer.' Engineers don't necessarily love math and science. What they love is what the knowledge of math and science allows them to do. The fourth bullet about fashion feeds into the long-held stereotype about engineers being geeks and nerds. Even though this is supposed to be funny, do we need a reminder? Can we not find other descriptors that are more engaging for all students?

The ASME website content continues with the question, 'Why is being an engineer so great?' The response is: 'Engineers make real money.' While no one would argue that a good salary is unattractive to prospective students of all majors, this is certainly not the primary reason why a student would select engineering as a field of study since there are many other math- and science-based fields with equally good or potentially better salaries. A brief discussion about the average starting salary and median incomes compared to some other fields would suffice.

The next website section, 'Who is an Engineer?' lauds the versatility of an engineering education and then proceeds to list 21 relatively well-known people with engineering degrees who are artists, astronauts, musicians, leaders of countries, chief executives of industry and television personalities. Although this content has the potential to attract students with varying career interests and is well intended, the predominantly white male list includes one woman, one African-American man, and one Hispanic man. This sends a clear message to women and underrepresented minorities that engineering is not for them.

In 'How to Recognize Your Engineering Potential', the personality of an engineer is discussed in an attempt to help students assess whether they should consider engineering as a college major and career. The text reads:

> Not everyone is cut out for engineering. Although there is no personality test to determine with 100 percent accuracy who will be a successful engineer and who will not, the ASME Career Life Guide has suggested that there are some 'highly-desired personal qualities' that indicate that engineering could be right for you:
>
> - accuracy
> - adaptability
> - ability to work under pressure
> - careful
> - committed
> - cooperative
> - creative
> - decisive
> - energetic
> - ability to get along with other people
> - good communication
> - an independent worker
> - methodical
> - organized
> - receptive
> - reliable
> - self-confident
> - self-motivated
> - thoughtful
>
> This makes it sound like the prospective engineer needs to be a perfect human being. Of course that's not true. The successful engineer, of course, will have a well-rounded personality and an aptitude for technical material. But merely being proficient in math and science courses will not an engineer make. As one recruiter of engineering graduates has said, what he's hunting for, besides academic ability, is an insatiable curiosity about how physical objects work and an irresistible urge to tinker with things until they do indeed work. Does this sound like you?

Simplifying the description of how to recognize your potential as an engineer while keeping the descriptors broad-based is the better approach in order to avoid alienating prospective students from engineering at this early stage of career development. Consider this alternative:

> There is no personality test to determine with 100 percent accuracy who will be a successful engineer and who will not since there are so many career options for engineers. However, use the questions below as a guide to see if majoring in engineering may be a good fit for you.
>
> Do you . . .
>
> - enjoy assessing and solving problems?
> - do well in math and science?
> - have a curiosity about the way things work?
> - have an interest in working in teams?
> - look at the world around you and want to make things better?
> - communicate well or want to learn how to communicate well?

If you answered yes to most of the questions, engineering may be the perfect college major for you.

Finally, the illustrations used on a website also tell a story. The sections of this website that were reviewed include five pictures. Two of the pictures depict white men working with equipment, a third shows a white man holding a CD-ROM, and a fourth illustration shows the back of a white man's head with a computer screen in the background. The only illustration of a woman includes a close-up of her face. There is no depiction of a diverse group of people working together or individuals of different genders or race working on interesting things.

BEWARE OF FUELING STEREOTYPES

Attracting the engineer of 2020 will require many initiatives, including a mass marketing effort that goes beyond websites, public television stations, engineering professional societies, trade magazines and outreach efforts supported by engineering colleges. It is important to find ways to infiltrate mass media and mainstream news that target large segments of the population, generally unfamiliar with engineering. For this reason, when a 'teachable moment' arises, we need to capitalize on the opportunity.

As an example of a lost opportunity to dispel stereotypes and present science and engineering in a favorable light, *TIME Magazine*, a mainstream well-respected magazine, published its 13 February 2006 issue with the cover story, 'Is America Flunking Science?' The cover depicted a young white boy in front of a science lab bench with a charred and somber expression on his face as he contemplated the exploded glass beaker. The cliché 'a picture is worth a thousand words' could not be more true and more damaging in this case. For those who saw this *TIME Magazine* cover but did not read the articles in that publication, it merely reinforces long-held stereotypes. For those who did go on to read the articles articulating a real concern about the USA losing its edge in science, about who will practice science in the future, and about the lack of well-educated science teachers, they may have come across other references driving biases deeper.

One case in point appeared in an article from the same *TIME* edition entitled, 'Looking for a lab-coat idol' (Keegan, 2006). The article develops the issue that kids are naturally inquisitive about science when they are young but lose that curiosity later on in school. It raises the question of what can be done to nurture rather than squelch that curiosity. Keegan (2006) quotes John Hennessy, president of Stanford University, who is an advocate of increasing diversity in engineering and science and has spoken on this subject on many occasions. Yet, while making a valid point concerning the lack of role models, he sends the message that girls are tangential to science when he states, 'In the US, about 50,000 students take part in the [science] fairs. We have [TV] shows about doctors, lawyers, and politicians. Where are our role models of scientific innovation? We need Eddie the Engineer or Sam the Scientist.' Could Sam have been Samantha? When young women remain significantly underrepresented in engineering and science, we have to be less obtuse, more direct and more cautious about what we say, especially when those making the statements are prominent leaders and whose statements are included in *TIME Magazine*.

In 2005, Lawrence Summers, the president of Harvard University, speaking before the National Bureau of Economics Research Conference, stated that women may be innately inferior to men in math. Although everyone is entitled to an opinion, or entitled to be provocative, as Mr Summers maintained after the speech, the president of a university never speaks entirely as an individual, especially when that institution is Harvard. Whatever is said, you must be aware of the ramifications of your words (Fish, 2005). In response to Summers' comment, Denice Denton (2005), former chancellor of UC Santa Cruz whose field of research was electrical engineering writes,

> The key point is that the US is facing a crisis of global economic competitiveness. It is essential that we draw on all of the human capital in this country. We simply cannot afford to shut out more than half the population from the kind of work that will power . . . our country's economy and enhance our competitive edge. To this end, presidents of our most highly respected universities have a responsibility to provide leadership nationally at this critical time. And Harvard has a special responsibility to lead, because of its unique place in higher education. All of us dedicated to equal opportunity would expect no less.

The worldwide firestorm that was set off as a result of Mr Summers' comment, largely among the academic community, was ironically beneficial to the cause since it raised awareness. In response, Harvard took action to examine its own environment related to women in science, followed by other universities that adapted Harvard's well-publicized model. Unfortunately, despite the rigorous debate that ensued on university campuses over Mr Summers' comment, the general public, which was not necessarily engaged in the follow-up discussions, was probably more aware of the reinforcing of a stereotype confirming a misconception. How many parents asked themselves, 'Do I want my daughter majoring in a field that is biased against women?' What are female students asking?

When a technology company advertises in mainstream media, it is presented with a rare opportunity to make an impact on a broad population outside the engineering community. That is why it was very disappointing to see a full-page color ad by CDW-G, a company that specializes in computer solutions depicting nine white male college students in front of what looks like a fraternity house with the caption 'We're getting technology to the people who shape the future'. The ad is targeted to college faculty who use technology in the classroom as a teaching tool. This ad was placed in the *Chronicle of Higher Education* several times in February and March of 2006. The *Chronicle* is arguably the most widely read weekly newspaper among the higher education community regardless of field. This represents a cross-section of faculty in many technical and non-technical disciplines. CDW-G had the opportunity to show a diverse group of students in this picture, dispelling stereotypes of students and technology. Instead, every English, sociology, history and fine arts professor who leafed through the *Chronicle of Higher Education*'s (2006) pages caught a glimpse, even if only subliminally, of this image revealing the message that no people of color or women are connected with technology.

Accurate information about engineering and who is suited to be an engineer needs to be instantly effective when the opportunity presents itself. People affiliated with engineering should be diligent about reviewing content that is on websites and in print to ensure consistency and inclusiveness of messages. Review your own organization's websites and contact other organizations who display content that should be edited. It is critical that we safeguard the information we deliver. We all benefit. Colleges and universities should consider devoting a segment of their website to properly educating students, parents and educators about engineering. This needs to be done both on the engineering school website and at the link preceding the engineering school website to encourage navigation in that direction. Since Americans acknowledge that they know relatively little about engineering (AAES/Harris Poll, 2003), providing thorough and accurate information is just one major tool aimed to increase interest in the field. We need to capitalize on this opportunity.

IF WOMEN ENROLL IN ENGINEERING, WILL THEY STAY?

> Not only do the social dimensions of an engineering career need to be emphasized in the publicity aimed at these students, but curricula and workplace experiences need to build on and sustain the differing initial motivations in order to retain these students in the profession.   (Jawitz and Case,1998, p. 239)

Let's imagine that a publicity campaign for the field of engineering has been so successful that all members of society embrace the profession. Women of all ethnicities are academically prepared to enter engineering study in college and choose to do so because they understand that having an engineering education is synonymous with being a well-educated person in the twenty-first century regardless of their ultimate career path. Many are now driven to contribute to a world plagued with problems relating to healthcare, security, environment, energy, city infrastructures, knowledge management, and more. They are eagerly anticipating the start of their freshmen year in one of the many terrific engineering schools in the USA.

If this scenario ever becomes a reality, the engineering community will still need to focus on how to retain these academically talented students who are motivated by factors that are somewhat different than those of traditional engineering students. Can engineering educators deliver a curriculum with modifications to incorporate contemporary motivational factors? Many programs are currently faced not only with high attrition, but women are leaving with stronger grades than the men who stay (Adelman, 1998). One problem is that many engineering degree programs assume that students decide they want to be engineers by age 17 when they are simply not ready to narrow their choices. Then they tackle the typically jam-packed engineering curriculum, which precludes participation in other areas of interest. Not surprisingly, when confronted with choosing between interests, engineering – a white-male-dominated profession, surrounded by less than auspicious stereotypes – loses every time, particularly among women and people of color (Muller and Metz, 2002).

The Accreditation Board for Engineering and Technology (ABET) 2000 criteria have set the framework for a potentially more innovative curriculum with more latitude by focusing on student outcomes instead of required courses. Many engineering schools are making their curriculum more appealing by:

- integrating engineering design courses in freshmen and sophomore years;
- including teamwork experiences in courses;
- offering opportunities for undergraduates to do research with faculty;
- providing support centers for faculty seeking to improve teaching methods;
- employing various forms of technology in the classroom to improve pedagogy.

However, since college curriculum is slow to change, attracting students motivated to be engineers by completely different factors may require a more whole-scale transformation. Ilene Busch-Vishniac (Busch-Vishniac and Jarosz, 2004) and her colleagues are asking the question, 'Is it possible to uphold the rigor of an engineering education with regard to the fundamentals (which could be defined differently) and integrate substantial cultural, economic, political, psychological and communications components to attract a diverse population to the profession?' In fact, should we be educating students to have a core engineering education whose primary areas of interest lie in other fields such as law, politics, medicine and journalism, among others?

Service learning is an emerging area that has the potential to attract students who are motivated to become engineers in order to make a difference in the world. Students involved in service learning work as a team to define, design, build and test engineering solutions to assist local agencies in providing much-needed care to people within their jurisdiction. This real-world opportunity provides undergraduates with first-hand experience to witness the positive impact of their work on humanity.

As research indicates, service learning attracts women and underrepresented minorities in disproportionate numbers. An effective example of service learning is Engineering Projects in Community Service (EPICS), initiated at Purdue University in 1995. According to EPICS founders Coyle et al. (2005), EPICS places a strong emphasis on teamwork, communication and commitment. Under the program, undergraduates earn academic credit for their contributions to long-term team-based design projects that deliver innovative, technology-based solutions to problems identified by not-for-profit organizations in the community (Coyle et al., 2005). As a result, EPICS has become quite effective in encouraging women to pursue study in engineering and computer science. Between 1996 and 2001, enrollment of female students in electrical and computer engineering (ECE) and mechanical engineering (ME) majors at Purdue ranged from 10 to 12 percent women , while the representation of women in these fields in EPICS was 20 percent. In spring 2001, 33 percent of the computer science (CS) students in EPICS were women, compared with 11.5 percent of the total undergraduates in CS at Purdue. In the first three years of the program, during which 20 percent of the students in EPICS were women, approximately 30 percent of the team leaders were women. EPICS has become a popular service learning model with 2000 students having participated in the program thus far at Purdue. Additionally, 15 other universities have adopted this program and a growing number of engineering schools now require service learning as part of the curriculum or offer it as an elective (Selingo, 2006). The EPICS founders hypothesize that expanding an engineer's core competencies to include the broad spectrum of skills associated with engineering design may contribute to attracting a population of engineering professionals who are gender and ethnically diverse.

An exciting option for those students who seek an experience outside the USA, is 'Engineers Without Borders' (EWB, 2006), a non-profit humanitarian organization established to partner with developing communities to improve their quality of life. EWB engages and trains internationally responsible engineers and engineering students to implement sustainable projects in developing communities worldwide. The objective of EWB is to educate a new generation of engineers who will benefit from witnessing the many facets of engineering solutions to problems in developing communities. EWB offers effective training beyond the technical skills obtained through basic education and the education of host-community partners. EWB-USA, for example, promotes a new perspective for the engineering community by providing unique opportunities for engineers to work in partnership with a variety of stakeholders including community officials, social scientists, public health officials, economists, business owners, and international development organization officials. There are currently 108 student chapters of EWB in the USA, most of which are based at colleges and universities.

CONCLUSION

The recent publication *Changing Our World: True Stories of Women Engineers* (Hatch, 2006), offers a compelling description of the field of engineering:

> Even though engineering plays a critical role in nearly all aspects of our lives, the work of an engineer can seem like a mystery to those outside the profession. But it's really very straightforward. First, engineers see an opportunity to improve people's quality of life. They gather information, brainstorm ideas with teams of people and study possible solutions. The best options are selected based on cost, ease of use, impact on the environment and other factors. Communicating the solution through writing and speaking to groups is the next step. Finally, they work with creative interesting people in other professions to oversee the building or implementation of their idea. Engineering is the way dreams become reality.

This is a very visual and broad based description of engineering. It serves to open up possibilities, not simply to feed the stereotypes that exist and impose limits. The broader the description, the greater the appeal to more students with a wide range of interests. Most people do not think of engineers working as educators, entrepreneurs, consultants, researchers, technical sales and marketing executives, lawyers, doctors, dentists, journalists, politicians and business executives. Clearly there is considerable work to be done to attract women to the field of engineering. Madison Avenue has taught us that consistent messages across all forms of media can make an impact on the public's perspective and attitude. Messages matter. We need to transform engineering messages to be a benefit and not a liability.

REFERENCES

AAES/Harris Poll (2003), 'American perspectives on engineers and engineering: final report', retrieved on 18 July 2006 from www.aaes.org/harris_2004_files/frame.htm.

Adelman, C. (1998), *Women and Men on the Engineering Path: A Model for Analyses of Undergraduate Careers*, US Department of Education and the National Institute for Science Education (ISBN 0-16-049551-2), Washington, DC: US Government Printing Office.

Anderson, L.S. and Gilbride, K.A. (2005), 'IMAGE of engineering among Canadian high school Students', *Proceedings of the 8th UICEE Annual Conference on Engineering Education*, Kingston, Jamaica: UNESCO, International Centre for Engineering Education, pp. 1–4.

'ASME Professional Practice Curriculum On-Line', retrieved on 25 June 2006 from www.professionalpractice.asme.org/transition/studying/index.htm.

Building Engineering and Science Talent (2004), 'The talent imperative', San Diego, CA, retrieved 30 June 2006 from www.bestworkforce.org.

Busch-Vishniac, I.J. and Jarosz, J.P. (2004), 'Can diversity in the undergraduate engineering population be enhanced through curricular change?', *Journal of Women and Minorities in Science and Engineering*, **10**(3), 255–81.

Business Round Table (2005), '*Tapping America's potential: the education for innovation initiative*', July 1 retrieved 30 June 2006 from www.businessroundtable.org//publications/publication.aspx?qs=2AF6BF807822B0F1AD1478E.

Chronicle of Higher Education (2006), CDW-G Advertisement, 31 March, p. A5.

Clewell, B.C. and Campbell, P.B. (2002), 'Taking stock, where we've been, where we are, where we're going', *Journal of Women and Minorities in Science and Engineering*, **8**, 265–84.

'College Board: Major: Mechanical Engineering', retrieved 9 July 2006 from www.collegeboard.com/csearch/majors_careers/profiles/majors/14.1901.html.

Commission on Professionals in Science and Technology: EWC (2005), data derived from the Engineering Workforce Commission, *Engineering and Technology Enrollments*, Fall 1984 through Fall 2004.

Commission on Professionals in Science and Technology (2006), retrieved on 30 June 2006 from www.wepan.org. Data derived from National Science Foundation, *Science and Engineering Doctorate Awards: 2004*; National Center for Education Statistics, *Digest of Education Statistics, 2004* and previous editions; American Bar Association, *J.D. Enrollment & J.D. Degrees Awarded (Total/Women/Minorities) 1984–2004*; and Association of American Medical Colleges, *FACTS – Applicants, Matriculants and Graduates*.

Commission on Professionals in Science and Technology: College Board (2006), retrieved on 30 June 2006 from www.wepan.org. Data derived from College Board, *2005 College-Bound Seniors*.

Commission on Professionals in Science and Technology: EWC (2006), retrieved on 30 June 2006 from www.wepan.org. Data derived from Engineering Workforce

Commission, *Engineering and Technology Enrollments*, Fall 1984 through Fall 2004.

Commission on Professionals in Science and Technology: NCES (2006), retrieved 30 June 2006 from www.wepan.org. Data derived from the National Center for Education Statistics, *Digest of Education Statistics*, 2004, NCES2006005, October 2005.

Congressional Commission on the Advancement of Women and Minorities in Science, Engineering and Technology Development (2000), *Land of Plenty: Diversity as America's Competitive Edge in Science Engineering and Technology*.

Coyle, E.J., Jamieson, L.H. and Oakes, W.C. (2005), 'EPICS: engineering projects in community service', *International Journal of Engineering Education*, **21**(1), 139–50.

Davis, L.A. and Gibbin, R.D. (eds) (2002), *Raising Public Awareness of Engineering*, Washington, DC: The National Academies Press.

Denton, D.D. (2005), 'President Summers' remarks offer global teachable moment', *UC Santa Cruz Currents*, **9**(22), 31 Jan.–6 Feb., retrieved 18 July 2006 from http://currents.ucse.edu/04-05/01-31/opinion-denton.asp.

Duderstadt, J.J. (2004), 'Making the case for enhanced federal investment in engineering research and education', retrieved 30 June 2006 from www.nsf.gov/attachments/104206/public/Final_Case.doc.

'Engineers Without Borders', retrieved 10 July 2006 from www.ewb-usa.org.

Fish, S. (2005), 'Clueless in academe', *Chronicle of Higher Education*, 23 February, retrieved 8 July 2006 from http://chronicle.com/jobs/2005/02/2005022301c.htm.

Fredericks, J.A., Blumenfeld, P.C. and Paris, A.H. (2004), 'School engagement: potential of the concept, state of the evidence', *Review of Education Research*, **74**, 59–109.

Goodman, I.R., Cunningham, C.M. and Lachapelle, C. (2002), *The Women's Experiences in College Engineering (WECE) Project Final Report*, Cambridge, MA: Goodman Research Group, Inc.

Hatch, S. (2006),. *Changing Our World: True Stories of Women Engineers*, Reston, VA: American Society of Civil Engineers.

Jackson, S.A. (2002), 'The quiet crisis: falling short in producing American scientific and technical talent', San Diego, CA: Building Engineering and Science Talent, retrieved 30 June 2006 from www.bestworkforce.org.

Jawitz, J. and Case, J. (1998), 'Exploring the reasons South African students give for studying engineering', *International Journal of Engineering Education*, **14**, 235–40.

Jolly, E.J. (2002), *Confronting Demographic Denial: Retaining Relevance in the New Millennium*, Washington, DC: ASTC Dimensions.

Jolly, E.J., Campbell, P.B. and Perlman, L. (2004), 'Engagement, capacity and continuity: a trilogy for student success', GE Foundation, retrieved 18 July 2006 from www.campbell-kibler.com.

Keegan, R.W. (2006), 'Looking for a lab-coat idol', *TIME Magazine*, 13 February, Time, Inc., retrieved 26 July 2006 from www.time.com/time/archive/preview/0,10987,1156600,00.html.

Lenhart, A., Madden, M. and Hitlin, P. (2005), 'Teens and technology: youth are leading the transition to a fully wired and mobile nation', *Pew Internet and American Life Project*, retrieved 26 July 2006 from www.pewinternet.org/PPF/r/162/report_display.asp.

Margolis, J. and Fisher, A. (2002), *Unlocking the Clubhouse*, Cambridge, MA: MIT Press.

Mead, M. and Metraux, R. (1957), 'Image of the scientist among high school students', *Science*, **126**, 384–90.

Muller, C.B. and Metz, S.S. (2002), 'Burying the pipeline and opening avenues to engineering', *PRISM*, December, 72.

National Academy of Engineering (2002), *Raising Public Awareness in Engineering*, Washington, DC: National Academy Press.

National Academy of Engineering (2004), *The Engineer of 2020: Visions of Engineering in the New Century*, Washington, DC: The National Academy Press.

Pew Internet and American Life Project (2006), 'Demographics of Internet users February 15–April 6, 2006 tracking survey', retrieved 23 July 2006 from www.pewinternet.org/trends/User_Demo_4.26.06.htm.

Selingo, J. (2006), 'May I help you?', *PRISM*, Summer, 40–45.

WGBH Educational Foundation (2005), *Extraordinary Women Engineers Final Report*, Reston, VA: American Society of Civil Engineers.

'World wide learn: guide to college majors in mechanical engineering' (2005), retrieved 25 June 2006 from www.worldwidelearn.com/online-education-guide/engineering/mechanical-engineering-major.htm.

Xie, Y. and Shauman, K. (2003), *Women in Science*, Cambridge, MA: Harvard University Press.

10. Developing career commitment in STEM-related fields: myth versus reality

Helen M. Madill, Rachel G. Campbell, Dallas M. Cullen, Margaret-Ann Armour, Albert A. Einsiedel, Anna-Lisa Ciccocioppo, Jody Sherman, Leonard L. Stewin, Stanley Varnhagen, T. Craig Montgomerie, Cynthia J. Rothwell and Wendy L. Coffin

Karen[1] knew by the time she started high school that engineering was high on her list of career options. Throughout high school, summer positions with her father's engineering firm gave her a good idea of the extent and variety of engineering careers, so she knew she wanted to enter civil and environmental engineering in university. She did well in her course work and did a co-op year with one of Canada's leading engineering firms. There she gained experience that was directly related to her studies, made good connections, and developed her technical skills. Karen graduated with the professional engineering association's leadership award, found an exciting job with a large civil engineering firm, and was soon engaged in a major project. She quickly became immersed in the real-life issues of civil and environmental engineering and, despite the long hours, thrived on the challenge. She continued to enjoy being part of a team and although sometimes colleagues might question her abilities, she did not perceive any gender-related discrimination in the workplace. Karen had always believed in her abilities and presented herself with confidence. She received a number of promotions within her first five years with the firm and was now poised to take the lead on a special section of a large international contract. The opportunity to travel and to work in another culture was further confirmation for Karen that civil engineering was definitely the right choice.

Karen's experiences since graduating from high school read as if they are too good to be true – and unfortunately they are. Karen's profile is based on a collection of success experiences from participants in our research program, but any difficulties or challenges have been glossed over. While Karen may be typical of a select group of young women whose careers are highlighted on science, technology, engineering and mathematics (STEM) related websites or in professional newsletters, these women's careers do not represent the norm. If Karen's experience were the reality of career decision-making and commitment, there would be no need for this chapter. Rather, Karen's fictitious profile is a reflection of people's beliefs – beliefs that often keep them from reaching their goals when their experiences fall far short of the ideal. The young women who graduate from high school and base their expectations on such accounts are falling prey to a myth. Any projection that is based on a straight line of successes fails to account for the uncertainties of real life. Believing in such mythologies may lead students, employers and administrators astray, or enable policy makers to preserve the status quo, comfortable in their assumptions that nothing more needs to be done! Individual career paths are much more heterogeneous and diverse than people believe. Women, in particular, must take numerous contingencies into account when making career-related decisions.

The majority of the students and professionals who participated in our investigation of career decision-making in STEM fields did not have such unequivocally positive experiences as Karen. For example, whereas Karen had no problem identifying her career focus before entering university, we found it was quite common for students to be undecided about their career choice in the third year of their general science degrees. While Karen happily entered the same profession as her father, several students described the difficulties they were having 'living another's dream'. Karen made the transition from high school to university without any difficulties, but most of our students described encountering big differences that had to be negotiated (e.g., workload, teaching/learning approach, size of classes). Once through her undergraduate degree and in her first position, Karen adjusted quickly and did well. She did not face the difficulties that several of our new graduates reported in their first professional positions, where isolation and workload differed greatly from what they had expected. Finally, Karen was quickly promoted and after five years was in line for a leadership position within an international project. For our professionals, promotion was rarely quick and never assured. As a result, they had changed companies, actively sought positions that led to further opportunities, and networked to achieve their goals.

The continued need to engage with women's careers in STEM fields is reflected in labour market statistics. In Canada, the location of the research presented in this chapter, women's share of the labour force has changed between 1991 and 2001, but increasing the proportions of women has been slow, even declining in computer and information systems (see Table 10.1).

*Table 10.1   Women's share of the Canadian labour force: 1991, 1996
            and 2001*

Discipline	1991 (%)	1996 (%)	2001 (%)
Life sciences	25.54	28.64	34.74
Physical sciences	19.29	24.40	28.07
Computer and information systems	34.0	29.51	27.60
Technical occupations related to natural and applied sciences	15.45	15.50	20.41
Engineering	6.39	8.03	11.12
Total labour force	45.02	45.94	46.75

Source: CCWESTT (2006).

Our interdisciplinary research team undertook three studies between 1994 and 2004 to obtain a better understanding of women's career decision-making in STEM fields and gain insight into the slow progress that is evident in Table 10.1. A brief summary of those studies, two longitudinal studies and a cross-sectional study, is presented below.

STUDY 1 (1994–97): ATTRACTING FEMALES TO SCIENCE CAREERS: HOW WELL DO SPECIAL INITIATIVES WORK?

In 1994, qualified applicants (young women who had completed Grade 11) to the University of Alberta's Women in Scholarship, Engineering, Science, and Technology (WISEST) Summer Research Program (WSRP) were randomly assigned to one of three groups: the WSRP cohort ($n = 46$), who were paid research assistants in science or engineering labs; the Discovery cohort ($n = 40$), who attended a one-day science career workshop; or the Control cohort ($n = 68$), who received no intervention. Participants completed phone surveys which included questions about their career aspirations, summer activities, study and work plans in 1994, 1995 and 1996. There were no significant differences between the three groups in their career interests or values. However, the WSRP cohort perceived that their experience was an important factor in selecting (or not selecting) science because they were able to evaluate their expectations of 'being a scientist' against the day-to-day reality of work in a science laboratory. They also perceived that their campus experience made their transition to a large university easier and that they were more likely to find summer jobs that were related to their fields of study (for further details see Madill et al., 1997; Madill et al., 2000b).

STUDY 2 (1997–2000): I LIKED SCIENCE, BUT NOW WHAT DO I DO? YOUNG WOMEN'S PERSPECTIVES FOLLOWING HIGH SCHOOL

Twenty-six focus groups ($n = 123$) were conducted with women enrolled in science and science-related fields in six college, university, and technical institute programs in Alberta, Canada. The sample included students returning to post-secondary education after several years in the work-force and students with children. Findings indicate that family members (particularly parents), friends and people in the discipline of interest fre-quently influenced participants' field choices and career decisions. Both positive and negative work experiences were powerful influences in shaping participants' career decisions; hands-on experience was especially valuable. For mature students both the cost and length of programs also played a part. Financial concerns were consistently reported as barriers. Finding employment with an undergraduate degree in their field of study was often expected to be difficult. Female role models (teachers, instructors, man-agers) were understood to be important, but not always viewed positively. Several of the younger participants appeared to resent being asked to address gender differences or gender-related issues, arguing that this was all in the past. For those who had encountered gender-related issues in co-op, internship, or summer work-related experiences it was a different matter; women in technical programs were also more likely to be concerned about how they would be treated in their fields once they were employed (for further details see Ciccocioppo, 1999; Ciccocioppo et al., 2002; Madill et al., 2000a).

STUDY 3 (2002–2003): WOMEN'S VIEWS OF THEIR OPPORTUNITIES IN THE NEW ECONOMY

To obtain information about the factors that impact women's career com-mitment, to explore the transition from education to employment, and to test a model developed from Studies 1 and 2, focus groups and interviews were conducted using a semi-structured format with senior students ($n = 49$, nine focus groups, eight interviews), new graduates ($n = 17$, all interviews), and experienced professionals ($n = 21$, all interviews). Data from these three groups were then formatted separately and used as the basis for three nominal group processing exercises in which individuals at each of these three career stages met to determine STEM priorities for the issues identified in the individual and group interviews. The data were categorized according to thematic categories from the model presented in Figure 10.1.

From the work that we completed in Studies 1 and 2 it was evident that career decision-making was not a linear process. Individual differences abound and, as can be seen in the profiles that are presented throughout this chapter, personal situations and experiences have differing impacts on women at different phases of their career decision-making. Field choice and career commitment are influenced by personal experiences (pivotal experiences) that can reach back to grade school and forward to pre-retirement. Aspirations are modified to accommodate the circumstances and contingencies that women have to juggle and attempt to balance. Decisions may be revised, but an initial interest in science may be maintained and pursued when opportunity permits. There appears to be an interesting interplay between pivotal experiences, the acquisition of strategies and skills, and the use of resources that can have positive or negative effects on women's career decision-making and career commitment, particularly at the transition points in the decision-making process (high school to postsecondary education, undergraduate to graduate work, the first professional experience, subsequent personal and career-related decisions related to women's role functions).

In this chapter, we will address several myths using examples from the three studies and profiles of fictitious people (developed from participants' contributions) which exemplify the barriers and constraints young women face. We will emphasize how research findings (ours and those of others) and theories of career decision-making can enhance our understanding of women's experiences and help us develop realistic intervention and policy options. While there are undoubtedly a great many myths about career decision-making, the following are examples that members of the research team have encountered. Our experiences as academic staff or graduate teaching assistants working at large, research-intensive universities or a technical institute, or as psychologists specializing in career counselling in university settings in Alberta, Canada, also contributed to the identification of these prominent myths:

- Recruitment is the real issue.
- I should know what I want to do – everyone else does.
- Once I get a degree everything will fall into line.
- Who knew you had to work with so many people?
- I'll be an executive, a mother, have an exciting social life . . . won't I?

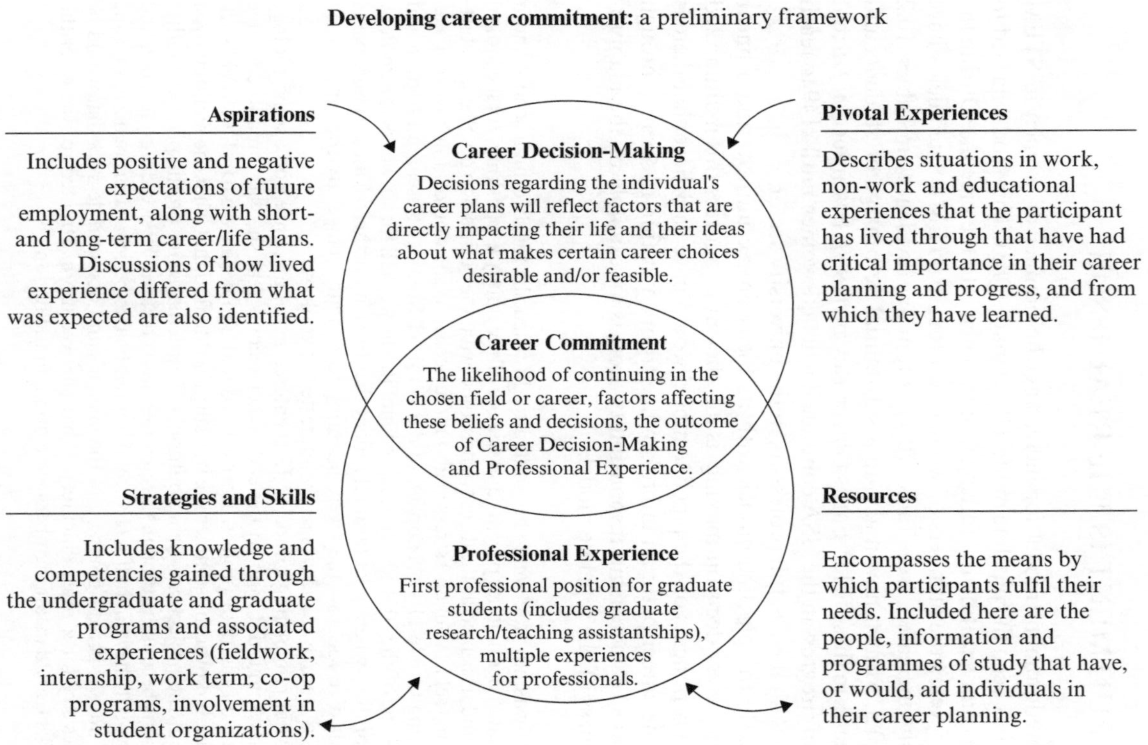

Developing career commitment: a preliminary framework

Aspirations

Includes positive and negative expectations of future employment, along with short- and long-term career/life plans. Discussions of how lived experience differed from what was expected are also identified.

Career Decision-Making

Decisions regarding the individual's career plans will reflect factors that are directly impacting their life and their ideas about what makes certain career choices desirable and/or feasible.

Career Commitment

The likelihood of continuing in the chosen field or career, factors affecting these beliefs and decisions, the outcome of Career Decision-Making and Professional Experience.

Pivotal Experiences

Describes situations in work, non-work and educational experiences that the participant has lived through that have had critical importance in their career planning and progress, and from which they have learned.

Resources

Encompasses the means by which participants fulfil their needs. Included here are the people, information and programmes of study that have, or would, aid individuals in their career planning.

Professional Experience

First professional position for graduate students (includes graduate research/teaching assistantships), multiple experiences for professionals.

Strategies and Skills

Includes knowledge and competencies gained through the undergraduate and graduate programs and associated experiences (fieldwork, internship, work term, co-op programs, involvement in student organizations).

Figure 10.1 Model of career commitment, derived from Studies 1 and 2

- Women just aren't cut out for the sciences and engineering.
- Everything is equal now so stand on your own two feet.

RECRUITMENT IS THE REAL ISSUE

The predominant model for increasing the number of women in STEM fields has been the pipeline model (Berryman, 1983). This model has led to a focus on recruitment – forcing more women into the pipeline. During the past 15 years the numbers of women working in STEM-related fields have steadily increased (see Table 10.1). From the evidence in Tables 10.2 and 10.3, women now make up a substantial percentage of students and graduates in these fields, but as Glazer-Raymo (1999) has argued, if current rates of progress in the USA continue it will take women until 2149 to reach parity with men as full professors in the university sector.

Clearly the pipeline model, with its focus on recruitment and a linear view of career decision-making, is insufficient to address this multifaceted issue. Proponents of the pipeline model would have us believe that there is only one career path: an unbroken line from education in science through positions of increasing responsibility. Lori is an example of the inappropriateness of the pipeline model.

Lori was not sure what she wanted to do when she finished high school and it irritated her that her parents and friends of the family kept asking. As she looked around it seemed as if all her friends knew what they wanted to do. She was starting to feel left out and stressed about the decisions she would soon have to make. During Grade 11 Lori applied to the WISEST Summer Research Program and was one of the 50 students accepted into it. She worked for six weeks in a zoology laboratory where pika (a small rodent that lives in northern Canada) were being studied to see how they were adapting to climate change. By the time her six weeks were over she was really interested in zoology.

After completing Grade 12 Lori entered general science, took some zoology courses, and did well. At the end of her second year she was hired to continue work on the pika project. Lori was excited about being part of the fieldwork team, but over the summer she was surprised to find that what she really enjoyed about the project was being outdoors. The actual work on the pika was rather tedious because, although the creatures looked cute, they were hard to catch and bit you if they got half a chance! After her field experience Lori realized that she did not see herself going on to the master's and doctoral degrees that would be necessary for a research career. What she was more attracted to was what the Parks Canada staff members were doing in the region.

According to the 'pipeline' analogy, Lori has been 'lost', since her interests have led her out of the zoology laboratory into which she was recruited. But Lori has not been lost, nor has her education been wasted. Indeed, this

Table 10.2   Women's share of enrolment in STEM-related disciplines in Canada, 2003–2004

	Undergraduate enrolments	Graduate	
		Master's	Doctoral
Agricultural, natural resources and conservation	57.5% (*n* = 8527.9)	56.9% (*n* = 2327.1)	42.3% (*n* = 892)
Architecture, engineering and related technologies	22.1% (*n* = 59 932.0)	28.5% (*n* = 11 080.6)	19.3% (*n* = 4773.1)
Mathematics, computer and information sciences	25.3% (*n* = 29 774.1)	38.1% (*n* = 4448.9)	27.6% (*n* = 1823)
Physical and life sciences, and technologies	58.1% (*n* = 70 108.1)	52.3% (*n* = 7636.9)	40.6% (*n* = 6813.7)

Source: CAUT (2006).

Table 10.3   Women graduates in STEM-related disciplines in Canada, 2003

Discipline	BSc	MSc	PhD
Agricultural, natural resources and conservation	57.9% (*n* = 2223)	55.8% (*n* = 862)	38.3% (*n* = 141)
Architecture, engineering and related technologies	25.8% (*n* = 12 300)	27.6% (*n* = 3730)	16.9% (*n* = 537)
Mathematics, computer and information sciences	28.1% (*n* = 7855)	44.7% (*n* = 1571)	17.3% (*n* = 208)
Physical and life sciences, and technologies	61% (*n* = 11 442)	51.5% (*n* = 2130)	34.9% (*n* = 1039)

Source: CAUT (2006).

type of interpretation is 'the major conceptual limitation in the literature on women in science' (Xie and Shauman, 2003, p. 7). It is inappropriate to suggest that there is only one source of input, one route to follow, and one destination. In fact, many career development theorists have shifted away from the importance of staying 'on course' with a career plan and have begun writing about the important role that chance can play in making a career decision.

Patton and McMahon (1999) developed a systems theory framework of career development, which depicts the various influences relevant to an individual's career development in a circular model, including the importance of the individual system, the contextual system in which the individual exists, the process of change over time, and the role of chance. They note that chance can have a profound influence in the course of an individual's career planning, and that it is important to acknowledge this in our understanding of career development. 'Given the complexity of influences in relation to career development, it is unreasonable to assume that the individual's career development will always be planned, predictable, or logical' (p. 166). Similarly, Mitchell et al. (1999) used the term 'planned happenstance' to describe 'the creating and transforming of unplanned events (chance) into opportunities for learning' (p. 117). This perspective is diametrically opposed to the popular notion in the career development literature that chance is to be eliminated from career decision-making. Using 'planned happenstance' theory, career indecision may be positively reframed as 'open-mindedness' (Mitchell et al., 1999).

Other scholars have examined career decision-making specifically from the vantage points of women's career development and career development in science-related fields. Jacobs (1999, p. 137) noted that career aspirations

> are not stable as assumed. Occupational choices shift frequently and often cross sex-typed boundaries . . . The great majority of young women change the specific occupation to which they aspire, and among these changes, there was little connection between early aspirations, later aspirations, and subsequent occupational choices.

In contrast, Tai et al. (2006) showed that experiences as early as Grade 8 may have an important impact on field choice and career plans.

All of the Grade 11 students in our Study 1 ($n = 149$) aspired to enter science or science-related fields (engineering, health sciences, agriculture); three years later 75.8 per cent remained in science-related fields. Thirty had shifted to other fields, including social sciences, business and education. Those in the health sciences, social sciences and education continued to use their original science-related interests, indicating a fairly strong relationship between aspirations and field choice. When it comes to occupational choice, however, personal situational determinants come into play. Here is but one example:

> I worked in offices for 4–5 years, and I didn't like it. There was something missing, but I did not know what . . . I had already begun in science, but I had left school and went back in accounting because my father used to always [say], 'what are you going to do with sciences? You're just wasting your time. Business is what it's all about.' So when I decided to go back to teach, I decided to go back to sciences, because that was my initial love, so I'm back.

Several older participants in Study 2 explained that their desire to enter a science-related career following high school was not realized due to financial or family pressures. However, when the departments or companies where they were employed downsized or closed, they used their severance packages to enter a two-year laboratory technology program. This enabled them to return to a science-related field, spend a relatively short (but intense) time as students, and assured them of employment at the end of their studies. The opportunity to start afresh allowed them to revisit their original field of interest – science – even if they had to tailor that interest to fit certain personal and situational determinants (e.g., severance arrangements, government support programmes, family responsibilities, location). These participants had established a commitment to a field (science) that laid the foundation for their eventual career choice.

These experiences reflect the process of recycling that Super (1990) later incorporated into his original career development framework to explain how individuals whose original career choice was not fulfilled returned to their initial career aspiration or field of interest when the opportunity arose. Rather than a linear, pipeline model, we support the life span and life course perspectives on career decision-making, such as those proposed by Super (1990) and Xie and Shauman (2003). These models enable one to account for the multiple transitions and personal situational determinants that affect an individual's career path.

I SHOULD KNOW WHAT I WANT TO DO – EVERYONE ELSE DOES

A major motivator for students entering university is the promise of a fulfilling career (Orndorff and Herr, 1996). Students who are encountering increased burdens of debt are expecting to obtain valuable career experience and to complete a degree that is marketable once they graduate (Ciccocioppo, 1999). Despite these motivators, many first-year students are tentative in their career choice (Ciccocioppo, 2005; Dale and Zych, 1996; Li, 1996; Orndorff and Herr, 1996).

> Carol did not particularly like high school: she did well enough, but usually found other activities more interesting than her schoolwork. 'Teachers always told my parents that I had the potential to go on to university and if I focused on my studies I would really do well, but I didn't know what I wanted to do after high school. How was I to know what to focus on?'
>
> Although Carol liked playing sports, she did not see herself being a physical education teacher, but that was the only thing the student counselor suggested. Many of Carol's friends were planning to go to university and her best friend was going into science, so Carol decided to do the same.
>
> Carol was excited and a bit scared when she entered general science, but she was with her friends so there was plenty of support. At the end of her second year, she was no further ahead in her career decision-making. Then she heard

about a UA: WiSE (University of Alberta Women in Science and Engineering Career Fair. She had been to career fairs in high school and had not found them very useful. However, the UA: WiSE event was different: a number of women from various science, engineering and technology fields spoke and then answered questions about what it was like to work in each field.

Carol was delighted to discover that her lack of direction was not unusual. There were other science students, some in their third and even their fourth years, who did not know how they were going to use their degrees once they got them. Carol did not leave her first UA: WiSE meeting with *the answer*, but what she did gain was a resource group; people who were trying to answer career-related questions similar to the ones that she was asking.

Throughout our research, young women have expressed their concerns about not knowing what they want to do and the pressure that people around them, particularly family, are placing on them to decide. They have a sense that everyone knows what they want to do except them, a view that is reinforced by traditional ideas of careers, as reflected by the pipeline model, that suggest a linear pathway. Mitchell et al. (1999) discussed how, in North American culture, decisiveness in career planning is the expectation, and an undecided person is seen as someone who is 'wishy-washy'. The authors suggest, however, that indecision about long-term career plans is appropriate given the uncertainty of the future. Given that young women's career paths are often anything but linear, a more appropriate way to conceptualize career development is to use what Super (1990) identified as different phases within a career cycle.

Super (1980) viewed career development as a dynamic process: 'the decision points of a life career reflect encounters with a variety of personal and situational determinants' (p. 294). Interests are shaped by our developing values, opportunities to implement our self-concept, and a series of personal and situational determinants that are not necessarily unique to us, but that we likely deal with in unique ways. Super proposed that the 'Exploration' phase of our career cycle included identification of a vocational preference or preferences, followed by a trial period with little commitment (possibly in our early to mid-20s). It is not until the 'Establishment' phase, when we make a trial commitment, that our career choice is likely to stabilize (possibly in our mid-20s through early 30s) (Super, as cited in Herr and Cramer, 1979). Ciccocioppo's (2005) research findings supported this assessment, particularly the early phases that Super proposed. An exploratory stage, wherein one experiments with options, is most apparent in the words of students, particularly as they finished high school and entered university.

Near the end of their university studies many of the young women in our research had solidified career goals, as proposed by Super's trial period, while others remained in an exploratory phase in which the options remained broad. Senior students, particularly those not in technical or professionally oriented programs (e.g., not engineering or science education) often expressed concern about how they would use their degrees:

> Yeah, I think I'd like to be able to have somebody to talk to about what options there are for jobs. Dr. A said basically that there's so much stuff you can do with a science degree, but if you don't know where to start, then it's really hard to know what you can do. Like, you have nowhere to look or nowhere to go. So it would be nice to have a few options or a few examples of things, and then to move on from there.

In contrast, others came to university with a clear idea of where they wanted to go (predominantly medicine). Many of these young women, however, hit roadblocks that forced them to reassess their paths and look for alternatives. Early foreclosure upon 'a career' can leave students without options if they do not achieve their one and only goal, and choosing an alternative may look like failure. For others, however, the blocking of one path forced them to reassess their interests and examine a broader range of options, options often not considered earlier because they were unknown or not encouraged:

> When I started my science degree, I really wanted to go into medicine, like everybody else! So that's where I was aiming, when I started my degree . . . I worked my butt off and I got average grades. So it was pretty stressful. Anyway, I'm happy with where my career's going now. (Recently started a two-year after-degree program in a health-related field)

A critical aspect for participants in solidifying their field of interest and ultimate career choice was the opportunity to gain experience in the field (co-op or summer positions). Such experiences gave them critical knowledge of what to expect in the workplace, what different types of work involved, and the diversity of jobs in each field. For several participants this included realizing they were no longer interested in jobs that had attracted them initially. One participant who was enrolled in a technical program stated:

> I think our co-op and practicum experience throughout our 2-year program has opened my eyes to the different fields that you can go into. When I first came in here, my intention of working in this program was being in a laboratory setting. I've done my co-op and my practicum in that kind of setting, and now I know that's something I don't want to do. For other girls in our program, they've done different co-ops and practicums [*sic*] at different places, and it gets you to look at all the different things you could do. But prior to that, I didn't have any experience.

For others, the opportunity to gain hands-on experience gave insight into new areas that they might want to pursue, a chance to develop technical skills, the opportunity to see how their skills would actually be used, opportunities to make contacts with individuals in the field, and the chance to experience different types of organizations (academia, industry, government). The importance of these work experiences was also identified by the experienced professionals when they reflected back on their early careers. As one stated, 'Once I started research, I really loved it! . . . So there was no question once I got into my research; it was definitely the stuff that I wanted to do.'

It is important also to note that concerns over career choice are not finalized once education is completed or when one moves into her first professional position. Rather, individuals face multiple points of transition throughout their careers (Super, 1980). An additional complication is the popular idea that young people entering the workforce can expect to have multiple careers over their lifetime (Taylor, 2005). Brown (2000) noted that 'employment security is no longer tied to an organization, but rather to the individual's career management and resilience skills . . . Life changes and career changes often go hand in hand, offering the skilled and flexible worker opportunities to use these changes for personal advantage.'

ONCE I GET A DEGREE EVERYTHING WILL FALL INTO LINE

Young people often believe that once they complete qualifications in a professional field they will be virtually guaranteed employment. Co-op experiences may lead to a job offer, but career-wise individuals still need to know where they are headed (or would like to go). The Meyerhoff Scholar's Program (Staples, 2006) is a successful example of engaging students in collective problem solving during their educational experience in a similar manner to teams of scientists. Such experiences have been shown to enable a diverse group of students to succeed in science and be sought after for positions following graduation. Staples stated 'the Meyerhoff model shows that a vibrant, well-structured science program can produce large numbers of students who excel and remain in the field' (86 per cent of Meyerhoff participants graduate, p. 2). As Alex's profile reflects, decisions remain tentative, particularly in transitional periods, and are strongly affected by positive and negative experiences:

After completing her computing science degree, Alex was hired by a large organization. She knew something about the company and the people who worked there, so it seemed like the perfect opportunity. Now, after a year, Alex is not convinced she made the right choice. Although she realizes her current position is a fairly good one, and the company is large enough that, unlike some of her friends, she has a sense of job security, she feels very isolated in her job. In university she had a big group of female friends – now she works only with men. She never thought this would make much difference, but she finds that communicating with, and asking for advice from, men who are often much older than she is can be intimidating and awkward.

Now, it seems there were aspects of an organization – beyond salary and job description – that she should have considered before deciding. The numbers of hours expected, for example, are far beyond what she had anticipated. University had meant long hours, but now it is long hours with no friends to work and socialize with! To 'get ahead' she feels that she has to put in these hours, but Alex is now asking herself 'How can I work this much and still have a life?' Although her co-op placements had helped her to develop teamwork skills, she is finding that she is not very confident presenting, and arguing for, her ideas in a boardroom of her superiors. In fact she worries that her nervousness is affecting whether people really hear her ideas.

Enrolment in a Meyerhoff-type program might have given Alex additional confidence when she faced the transition into employment. As participants in our research described their transitions (e.g., from post-secondary education to their first position), the impact of work-related experiences became readily apparent. Although we did not measure organizational commitment *per se*, graduate students and experienced professionals like Alex perceived their positive and negative early experiences with management in the organizations they worked for, as pivotal in their career decision-making (Study 3; Ciccocioppo, 1999; Madill et al., 2003).

While organizational commitment and career commitment are viewed as separate concepts within the literature, from the point of view of our participants these concepts appear complementary. Work experiences, for example, were strongly related to affective commitment (overall job satisfaction, perceived organizational support, organizational justice). Indeed a lack of satisfaction with a particular position or organization could lead to individuals leaving a field entirely.

The impacts of these experiences were relayed by the experienced professionals, 17 (of 21) of whom identified the transition from school to their first (post-student) professional position as difficult. The women found the positions differed from their expectations and that they were one of the few (or only) women in their section, unit, or team. For recent graduates, the issues were how the positions differed from what they had expected, the lack of support and guidance in the workplace, the long hours, the pressure to produce results, and unclear job expectations. One experienced professional explained the difference between reality and expectation in her first professional position this way:

> I wanted to get the best kind of salary, but I was quite a timid, naïve, trusting person, so I didn't know how to play any of the political games. I don't really respond to those as well; I'm a very factual person, engineer, scientist. I believe we come out with those skills, and we don't have – if you haven't been brought up in a home or an environment that you learn to be able to work the politics. I've always believed that what you say, you base it on facts, and then decisions are made from there. But that's, of course, not how politics works in employment.

After studying the development of organizational commitment, Meyer et al. (1991) concluded that organizational commitment 'is associated with both positive experiences prior to and following entry into an organization' (p. 731). Access to accurate information and job quality, both of which are within organizational control, have an impact on affective commitment. One of our participants described the powerful effect that organizational practices had on her career decision-making:

> I think it was about the second year of my graduate degree when I started seeing how difficult it was to get in and how many hoops you have to jump through in getting a position with academia. I don't have a lot to go on, to compare with other situations. So it's hard to say, but I know that in academia, it's very difficult to get any respect as a researcher, even after you've been hired. You're a junior researcher, you're an assistant professor; you have no say in what happens. And there's a lot of pressure to produce, to be a good teacher, to contribute to the department. Our department has hired a lot of new professors during the time I've been here, and they all work ridiculous hours. They work 80-hour weeks, 12 hours a day, 7 days a week, and I'm not interested in that. So I started seeing that in my second year. By third year, I realized there was no way I'm willing to put myself through that. Then I started realizing I wasn't actually that interested in research in itself, so that helped cement the decision not to continue.

WHO KNEW YOU HAD TO WORK WITH SO MANY PEOPLE?

Successful entry into the STEM workforce depends upon more than technical skills. Participants in Study 3 were unanimous in their views of the importance of self-confidence and 'soft skills' – people skills, communication and presentation skills, and teamwork. These interpersonal skills were critical to later career commitment. Effective communication is particularly important in 'a climate of corporate change' (Cooper and Lewis, 1999, p. 41). Further, Hughes et al. (2003) noted that well-educated women employees were particularly responsive to their employers' attempts to develop a positive workplace climate.

> Looking back, Victoria saw herself as a tomboy. She always loved finding out how things worked and getting her hands dirty. Her parents encouraged her to explore these interests and delighted in her abilities. Vicki indicated that she 'didn't know that women weren't supposed to be good at math!' Ultimately she chose engineering as she thought that this field would give her the most breadth and flexibility when it came to getting a job.
>
> After her first year of university she chose mechanical engineering because it seemed to be the area where she would have a chance to see how things really worked. But the opportunity to get in there and make things work was missing until her final year when she had the chance to complete a short practicum.
>
> It was not until she was working that Vicki became really happy with her field. Upon graduation she found a position with a mid-size organization that designed and repaired major pieces of equipment, such as drilling rigs. The work was great, but for the first time being a woman seemed to matter. She learned that to get ahead in this man's world, she had to stand up for herself and to prove herself. Once she was able to demonstrate that she 'could handle the technical stuff' her male colleagues became some of her biggest supporters.
>
> One of the first things she had to learn was to communicate in the style that was used in this business; a no-nonsense approach that was evident in the direct and unemotional way that the men around her went about their business. The emphasis was on getting the job done, not on people's attitudes or feelings.

Like Vicki, students and professionals we have spoken with identified a range of skills needed in the workplace that went beyond the knowledge that they had acquired through their undergraduate coursework. These included confidence in using their skills, making presentations, and contributing as team members (particularly as young members, or as the only woman on the team). Senior students and new graduates placed interpersonal skills within the top five strategies and skills essential for employment. Undergraduates indicated that large classes were not conducive to the development of these soft skills; when and if these were acquired, it was through student leadership roles or membership in special interest groups. These students were not entering the workforce afraid that their technical skills were lacking, but questioning whether they had the interpersonal skills needed for success.

Experienced professionals, when discussing what would lead to a successful career, also stressed the importance of interpersonal and social skills:

> To tell you the truth, when you get people, no matter what gender they are, into a company, the technical capabilities of somebody to succeed in the workplace is really just the ante – it's the table stakes. My observation is whether people succeed in companies is their ability to deal with people and communicate and get along and work in teams and all those kinds of things.

Critical examples of the skills experienced professionals believed to be necessary included the ability to work in a team, written and oral communication skills, the ability to be self-motivated, the ability to be adaptable to new
environments, the ability to present information and answer questions on
your feet, having organizational and time-management skills, and being
able to 'say no'.

Our experienced professionals stressed the importance of self-confidence
and considered this factor as one of the most critical skills that a woman
can develop. Students in our studies also recognized the importance of
developing their self-confidence. One young woman in Study 1 stated:

> I know I'm very doubtful of what I know. I know that if I think I know some-
> thing, I know it inside out, because otherwise, I'm wary of whether or not I'm
> ready for a test, or whether or not I understand. And guys don't seem to be the
> same way. They seem to be very confident, very strong in themselves, and they
> don't seem to need the social interaction the way girls do . . .

Importantly this 'lack of confidence' does not just disappear or get rectified
with time, as two of our professionals identified:

> I had 'confidence training'! We all need confidence training! In fact, I'm 34 now,
> and I don't think I built my confidence until the last year or two; that's pretty
> sad.

> I was a workaholic because I didn't have confidence I was succeeding, so that's
> what I did to succeed. See, confidence is huge – huge!

Yet the development of self-confidence cannot be done in isolation; it
requires feedback and reinforcement from others. Programs such as the
WISEST Summer Research Program work to create opportunities for the
development of confidence, as one professional identified:

> One of the great things that you get to do sometimes is pull one of those [young
> women] aside and give them some experiences that build that confidence. I think
> the WISEST program is tremendous for that, because it gives them experience
> very early on that is real technical experience, so when they go for job interviews,
> they already have technical experience after their first year, and that tends to
> build on itself. So I think that's one of the tremendous things that's a by-product
> of the WISEST program, is you build confidence early; not just interest, but
> confidence, and the two go hand-in-hand, and success builds on success.

The critical importance of confidence can be seen in research that links perceptions of self-efficacy and commitment to a position. Super and Sverko
(1995), for example, noted 'that an important aspect of satisfaction is *self-
perceived efficacy* in performing a role' (p. 33, emphasis added). While

positive experiences build or reinforce self-efficacy, negative experiences can have a powerful cumulative effect on the desire to continue in a role, field, or career choice (Etzkowitz et al., 2000).

I'LL BE AN EXECUTIVE, A MOTHER, HAVE AN EXCITING SOCIAL LIFE . . . WON'T I?

After decades of research examining women's career development, it has become apparent that 'it is still very difficult for women to have it all; career and family' (Xie and Shauman, 2003, p. 153). These authors found that marriage and parenting was a disadvantage to women's careers but not to men's careers, after controlling for a number of factors. Among scientists, women were more likely than men to be partners in a dual-career marriage and 'although some of the gender differences are attributable to the advantages that marriage and parenthood bestowed upon men, they clearly suggest that being married and having children create career barriers that are unique to women scientists' (p. 210). The idea that work and family should be separate and that the ideal career is only represented by a continuous full-time commitment still must be challenged (Cooper and Lewis, 1999). Vicki's predicament speaks to this dilemma.

It has been 10 years since Vicki graduated with a BSc in electrical and computer engineering and completed her professional registration requirements. Recently her supervisor began pressuring her to move into a management role. Vicki has mixed feelings about this. Management would present new challenges and it would take advantage of her excellent interpersonal skills. But from what she has seen, taking that step also means leaving behind the technical aspects of her current responsibilities. Because the technology changes quickly in her field it would be very hard to catch up if she decided that the move had been wrong.

Moving into management would also mean longer hours and more traveling. Vicki is married and she realizes that, at 33, if she is going to have children as she has always planned, a more involved role might not be such a good fit. She and her husband have discussed this a great deal, and although he is very supportive and listens, he just does not seem to understand the dilemma she is facing. When she looks around the office for other women to talk to, she realizes that the only ones who have children are the secretaries and the administrative assistants whose lives seem so different from hers.

Vicki's dilemma is not an uncommon one and reflects research findings that women's careers are 'relational' in nature (Crozier, 1999; Lalande et al., 1998; Mainiero and Sullivan, 2005). Women's 'career decisions were normally part of a larger and intricate web of interconnecting issues, people and aspects that had to come together in a delicately balanced package . . . we saw women making decisions about their career options after considering the impact their decisions will have on others' (Mainiero and Sullivan, 2005, p. 111). Their ABC Model of Kaleidoscope Careers has three key parameters: authenticity (being true to oneself); balance (juggling multiple role demands); and challenge (sufficient to maintain interest in the career role). Not unlike Super's (1990) Life Career Rainbow, O'Neil and Bilimoria's (2005) three-phase model, and Nash and Stevenson's (2004) 'kaleidoscope strategy', Mainiero and Sullivan divided careers into stages and demonstrated that certain issues assumed prominence at different points over the life span. In the early-career stage, goal achievement and challenge are the key elements while balance and authenticity are secondary. In the mid-career stage, establishing a balance between working and home/family and relational demands is the key, and challenge and authenticity are secondary considerations. In the late-career stage, authenticity is the central element, challenges are accepted, but on the women's 'own terms'; balance remains important, but it becomes secondary. In comparison, men's careers were more linear or sequential; initially career concerns were related to the self and challenge was the key element, with balance and relational concerns coming in the later career stage. The multiplicity of elements (working and family roles) that women strove to balance in their mid-career stage was not evident.

Although Mainiero and Sullivan (2005) argued that balance becomes a major concern during mid-career, our research found it to be a salient issue for participants across the career spectrum. Intimately tied to the questions of balance was a need to plan and a concern with 'wasted' time. As one young woman stated:

> That's the whole thing with school: you don't know how to balance your life out. I took a year off in-between high school and college, and I shouldn't have wasted it, but I kind of did. Now, the way I'm looking at it, I'm going to be in school for at least 4 or 5 more years, and you just don't know when to settle down and do what you want to do before you have to – I don't know . . . It's just a concern, 'cause you want a family, but you want to travel, but you want a good job, and you want to go to school. There's just so much to do in so little time.

The centrality of these concerns becomes increasingly prominent with career progress. For a number of the women who were in their early careers these questions were critical. One young woman stated:

> What I'm more concerned about is how do you balance work with your family life; like, how do you make the decision when it comes to time whether you're going to take your maternity leave, or take half of it, or come back full-time or part-time, and there's no one there who's dealt with any of that.

A number of women in their early professional careers felt there was no clear information or role models. The role models of successful careers that were available were individuals who worked extremely long hours and were highly dedicated to their careers, but whose lives lacked the balance that these women wanted to achieve.

Our research participants with established STEM careers, however, were the group who most frequently identified the issue of balance:

> I think it can be done, but to me, my career has always been really important; it's really a big part of who I am and how I get my personal satisfaction. So I guess my advice would be I don't think that you can have it all; I think you need to make some compromises. [Everyone] can't be Martha Stewart and have a full-time high responsibility job; I don't think it's possible.

It is important to note here that the experienced professionals whom we interviewed were those who remained in STEM careers. Arguably those most directly affected by the difficulty of balance are no longer in these careers.

WOMEN JUST AREN'T CUT OUT FOR THE SCIENCES AND ENGINEERING

Much has been written about women's lack of suitability for careers in STEM. Researchers have commented upon the negative effects of competitiveness, culture, traditions, and climate on women's career success (Byrne, 1993; Etzkowitz et al., 2000; Xie and Shauman, 2003). Competitiveness played a part in Jessica's experience and although it was a negative experience, the overall outcome was positive for her.

> Jessica found her calling in her first year of university. It was environmental biology. Although she wasn't sure of her exact area of focus, the intricate systems of small mammals amazed her. After talking with some teaching assistants, she decided to pursue a PhD to have a career in research. Near the end of her degree she was awarded a summer studentship. Before she commenced the studentship, the Council notified recipients of a newly revised pay scale and she approached her supervisor to alter her contract accordingly. To her surprise her supervisor informed her that he planned to use the additional monies to hire another summer student, a male, and that she was expected to work with this student and show him the ropes. She was appalled by the lack of ethical behaviour this researcher displayed, but she acquiesced as she saw no way of dealing with the power differential. She completed the summer studentship and obtained her BSc, but she abandoned her aspirations for a research career and embarked upon studies that would lead to admission to veterinary medicine, a field with ethical standards, and one where she could operate as a sole practitioner.

Many of the barriers that we have discussed above are, to differing degrees, not only faced by women. Men also find that the career expectations they held upon entering post-secondary education, their first professional positions, or their dreams of climbing the corporate ladder are not met by the actual experience. Increasingly men face demands (and desires) to become more involved in family life. The difference for women is that each of these concerns is underscored with a social perception that perhaps they face these issues because they don't 'fit'.

Across the career spectrum, women we have interviewed have indicated a range of similar experiences and expectations that the sciences, and engineering in particular, are a 'guy thing'. As one woman from Study 1 stated:

> As far as I understand it, chem tech is still a male-dominated field out there . . . There's also the handyman thing, too, I think. Because most men have tinkered all their lives – you know, they're raised differently than we are – they're kind of mechanical. Not that we're not, but they're expected to be, and we're expected not to be . . . It's the perception that men are better at tinkering, better at math . . .

A number of the women revealed these types of self-defeating beliefs, some of whom discussed behaving in conjunction with these beliefs – either in their expectations of themselves or of other females. One stated, 'I find the guys – I trust their judgment a little more, because – I don't know why, but I do.'

Coping with these gendered expectations then becomes critical. One strategy is to ignore gender:

> Never, ever, do I highlight that I'm a female. Never do I identify the fact that I'm a female, or different. There are a lot of power and politics at my level, and if you're male, you'd probably use that, but I don't use female power ploys. (Female engineer in Alberta Oil Industry, cited in Miller, 2004, p. 66)

The perceptions of oneself as gendered in a non-traditional field such as engineering must be carefully managed. You are different. You must take responsibility for that difference and work to blend in. This is reflected in Poggio's (2000) finding that women working on a building site felt continually forced to prove themselves – indeed their technical skills were of secondary importance to exhibiting the 'required' behaviour, which involved a contradictory position of being at once assertive yet not challenging their male co-workers (p. 388).

The experienced professionals in our research expressed similar sentiments. Transition into the workplace brought the realization that they would have to 'prove themselves'; gaining a better understanding of gender roles, and the need to balance masculine and feminine approaches, was a critical strategy for their career progression. A notable example of the way one woman played with these expectations reflects their salience:

> I found that if sometimes I made a point of not smiling, some men couldn't stand it. They would be almost dancing around me, trying to make me smile, because they wanted me to conform to their expectations of a woman – and I wouldn't smile! Yeah, I had to learn not to – it was really, you had grown up to be a feminine woman, and to be nice and polite and defer to everybody, and you really had to get over that. It's not a successful strategy at all! Know what you want, know who you are, ask for what you want. That's hard to pick up if you've never been told that.

Dealing with the gender expectations of the men they worked with became critical to their success. They learned to fit into the behaviour patterns of the men around them, particularly developing masculine communication styles, avoiding 'personal' or caring relationships with co-workers/clients/students, and finding ways to fit into aggressive workplaces.

Did Jessica lack the ambition to complete her original career choice, as Fels (2004) suggested, abandoning her original choice because she wasn't cut out for science? Or, when faced with values that differed markedly from her own, did her shift reflect seeking a career that in her mind was more compatible with her values? She perceived her supervisor's behaviour as typical of research in her field of interest and altered her course of action given the personal and situational determinants she faced. As Seta et al. (2000) noted, '[i]f your work life reflects your values and interests, it is more likely to be compatible with your other identities such as parent, community leader, and participant in recreational activities' (p. 450).

EVERYTHING IS EQUAL NOW SO STAND ON YOUR OWN TWO FEET

Williams and Emerson (2001) suggested that once women occupy 30 per cent of the workforce in a particular field they might have reached sufficient critical mass to have an impact on developments and policies in that field, leading to important changes. Evidence in Table 10.1 shows that women have made significant gains, having exceeded the 30 per cent level in the life sciences and that they are coming close to reaching that level in physical sciences, and computer and information technologies. However, these figures represent the labour force as a whole and do not reflect specific sectors (e.g., industry, academia, private sector), nor do they reflect individuals' positions (e.g., assistant, technical worker, manager). Another issue with having a critical mass of 30 per cent as one's goal is that, as Etzkowitz et al. (2000) noted, it is not sufficient for gender equity. If women remain isolated, if their affiliation with other women is stigmatized or if they are pressured to fit into stereotyped roles, then ' "critical mass" is meaningless' (p. 245). Just having a third of the professionals in a field be women does not create equity. The impact of a sense of isolation is reflected in Emma's experience, where value differences that were not apparent during post-secondary education became apparent in the business world.

> When Emma started her career in geology, everything seemed to be going per-
> fectly. She had worked hard throughout high school and, while not completely
> sure what she wanted to do, she knew that sciences were her strongest subject
> and that they fascinated her more than anything else. Her first year of university
> included a range of courses, one of which was introductory geology. This was
> her favorite class – and her highest grade, which didn't hurt!
>   The four years of undergraduate study proceeded smoothly. While there were
> hard courses (and boring courses), these only made her work harder to prove
> that she could succeed in anything she set her mind to. From the very first year
> she found summer positions in her field, first working as a field assistant and
> later in the oil industry. These positions gave Emma a range of experiences that
> affirmed her belief that geology was interesting and gave her the chance to put
> into practice all the things that she had learned from her textbooks. The indus-
> try position was particularly appealing, even glamorous, with relocation to a new
> city, good pay, and exciting social opportunities.
>   Emma finished her degree feeling confident of her success. Unlike some of her
> friends she had not encountered any negative gender experiences during her
> studies and was sure that if any did arise she would be able to handle them. She
> gained a position with a company where she had done a summer placement and
> began earning a good salary. Part of this new position, however, involved visit-
> ing oil drilling sites. At first, Emma was sure of herself, but the men she encoun-
> tered constantly questioned her. She was initially sure she could 'prove herself'
> to them, but after awhile this became very wearing. While some of the men
> thought she knew something, others were inclined to ignore her directions unless
> they checked with a male colleague.
>   Then there was life back in the office; the atmosphere that had seemed so
> inclusive was beginning to feel more questionable. The increasing politics, and
> the way that decisions were made, just didn't match her values. Were getting oil
> out of the ground and making a profit really the most important things? She
> knew she could complain about her treatment on-site and express her distaste
> for how things were done in the office, but she worried about the effect this would
> have on her career. Maybe she really wasn't cut out for this. Maybe she wasn't
> the right 'man for the job'.

Emma's belief that equality had been achieved, that everyone's career can be like Karen's if they work hard, was reflected by a substantial number of the young women we spoke with. Prior to having any work experience in their field, in particular, participants tended to believe that gender 'wouldn't be a problem unless you let it'. For example, one young woman in Study 2 stated:

> Even if there was just one [female student] it wouldn't make a difference, because you're not treated differently, and this whole idea really bothers me. I hate being singled out because I'm a girl [and they say] 'Oh, you're special because you're here.' Because I don't feel special. I feel anybody can come and do this too and it really bothers me when people put emphasis on 'Oh, there's girls here' . . . Yeah, we're here and we're going to continue coming!

After they had completed fieldwork, internships, or co-op terms the opinions of participants in Study 2 had often changed dramatically. When young women in our studies expected gender stereotypes to be a thing of the past they were surprised when they encountered instances of stereotyping, discrimination and harassment. By their final years of study, students were much more aware of the possible inequities of the workplace. Such early work-related experiences have a powerful impact on retention (Armour et al., 2000). Students in mechanical engineering and computing science described their experiences this way:

> You have to get tolerant of guys joking around . . . I have been witness to sexist comments, like, 'You might get good at making coffee.'

> It's difficult . . . I always feel I have to prove myself. Male co-workers get asked for help before I do and people assume I got into the company because of my looks; guys couldn't handle that . . . the attitude is that most women in computing science suck. Guys would stare at us.

To our participants, reliance on oneself appears unquestioned. Students and new graduates are particularly susceptible to the belief that they are individually responsible for coping with any inequities they face. The inadequacy of self-reliance, however, is reflected when one hits a difficult time, as one experienced professional expressed:

> I know how painful, how horribly painful the first experience with failure in my own eyes, in my family's eyes, in these people that had respected me and believed in me and made recommendations for me and found me funding – just that sense of failure was devastating. I see this in some of the students that work with me, the young women, so conscientious, so keenly aware of how others feel about them and their relationships. It's almost magnified beyond proportion. I think what would have helped me, and what I try and do with those girls when it shows up is just damp that down a bit. Say, 'Look, do you know how many things I've screwed up on the way? If you made a mistake, we'll figure out where, we'll fix it. Stop beating yourself up.'

Experienced women had often learned the importance of understanding the impact of the environment in which they work. These women frequently stressed learning to adapt to gender differences and having a back-up plan – strategies that would enable them to deal with barriers that they could not single-handedly break down or jump over. What is important to note, however, is that while the experienced professionals recognized the systemic nature of the issues they faced, the strategies they used to deal with these remained individualistic.

A frequently cited strategy was the need for support. Support/networks/ mentors were all seen as critical factors for success. Senior students, new graduates and experienced professionals cited talking with others as their most important strategy in career decision-making. In relating her experience one graduate student stated:

> You know what, I really did struggle my first year. I almost was no longer in the program. I didn't have a project any more, and things were not going well. The benefit – I did start talking to some people that I had contact with; to find out they were going through exactly – maybe their project wasn't falling apart, but in their mind, everything else was, academically. It really helped to find out that I wasn't the only grad student that was finding it difficult, and was finding some things pretentious, and other things really interesting and worth staying for. So it was nice to have a bit of a sounding board that actually made some of the same tones that I did.

Support could come from an array of different sources, but across the groups included mentors, family, peers/colleagues and networks. The following discussion from one focus group reflects many of these sources of support:

> *Student 1*: Family's definitely helpful, because they know you and they know what you're interested in, and sometimes they know things that you can't see in yourself. So I bring up, 'I want to do something in biology,' they say, 'That makes perfect sense; when you were little, your favourite book was *The Anatomy of the Cat*.' I don't remember that, but apparently, I have an interest there, and it's always been there.

> *Student 2*: I find that I talk to my roommate a lot, who is also fourth year in biological sciences. We very often bounce ideas off of each other, and experience the same things . . . Actually, talking to people in industry has kind of been helpful, and they have certainly some good points. I mean, they've been through this phase, they've graduated with their degrees. Most of the time, they've been men, but nonetheless, you're talking to someone in industry who knows that things don't work out exactly the way you planned, especially going into industry and not academia.

However, the support of family and friends is sometimes problematic. For example, one of the participants in Study 2 described how she dealt with her parents' expectations that she would forgo post-secondary education, help with the family business, and assist her mother with home/family responsibilities. When it became impossible for her to successfully complete the first year of her BSc. program in engineering she moved to another city where she began her first-year studies over again, but at a distance that was too great for her to be affected by her family's demands. She stated:

> If I stayed at [the first] school to study, I'd feel maybe I should be at home. So being here is better, although I have the guilt that they feel I'm abandoning them. But I figure if I can't help myself, I can't help you in 10 years. For me, leaving home was probably a good thing . . . I don't know if it's courage. It's being called stuck in a place you don't like very much, and thinking to yourself that you can't live like that for the rest of your life, so you have to change something. I don't know if I can, but I'd like to try.

Mentoring has been highlighted as a key strategy to aid women in mitigating the isolation that often leads to dropping out and helps reduce subjective barriers to entry (Etzkowitz et al., 2000). Many authors have noted that mentoring is needed throughout one's career, from undergraduate peer mentoring and study groups to graduate student mentors and workshops, to formal mentoring for women in university chair/dean positions (Byrne, 1993; Clark et al., 2000; Etzkowitz et al., 2000; Hyde and Gess-Newsome, 2000; Niemeier and Gonzalez, 2004). This continued desire for mentorship was reflected by our experienced professionals, 19 (of 21) of whom identified either having or wanting to have a mentor. This mentor was, importantly, not just someone to turn to for technical advice, but someone who could guide your career. One professional stated:

> So a good mentor is one that you can understand and that's going to be there for you, and that is as interested in your career as they are their own; that's really important . . . they'll help you, and they'll keep things in confidence. And that's really important; then you can go to them when you have a major issue, like a harassment issue or something like that.

The concern with mentors, however, is that finding someone to be your mentor, or realizing their importance, is often left up to the individual.

RECOMMENDATIONS AND CONCLUSIONS

During the last ten years, a considerable volume of research has been published on why there is still a low proportion of women in the sciences, especially at the decision-making level. Yet myths continue to exist that influence the career choice and progress of women in science. In this chapter, we have discussed many of these myths.

For example, our research has shown that career paths take unforeseen twists and turns and are much more heterogeneous than most young people expect. One of the ways of changing the expectation of linear career progress is through talking with women in STEM and hearing about their career paths. This often happens through mentorship and networking. All three of our groups of respondents were aware of the need for professional and social support in the form of mentors and networks. However, each group had a different way of accessing this support. The professionals were more likely to recommend hands-on experiences or learning from professionals in the workplace as the preferred sources of information. However, from the younger women's perspective, older professionals can be intimidating. The power differential and the professionals' apparent success in coping with the world of science and technology may detract from the message they are delivering. Because of this, and their greater comfort with the Internet, the senior students and new graduates preferred that source of information.

Drawing on this, our team, like others working in this area, has come to realize that a computer-mediated resource network may help to reduce the power differential and allow for a sharing of ideas, concerns and experiences in a manner that enables students and professionals to really 'hear' each other. Computer-based communication of the 'many-to-many' variety enables individuals to learn collaboratively and vicariously from the experiences and opinions of another regardless of her status. In addition, a computer-mediated resource network can link women who are isolated in a male-dominated environment.

Such a network not only provides links to information, but, more importantly, an opportunity for students, new graduates and professionals to discuss issues between and among themselves. Analysis of the discussions that occur could enable researchers to further understand how young women make the transition from school to work, how their career commitment is strengthened or weakened, and how mentors can most effectively share their knowledge with protégés. Cholmondeley (2005) worked with members of our research team when she pilot-tested the design of a resource network for women in STEM and evaluated its usability as the final project in her Master's of Communication and Technology program at the University of Alberta. (For further details see Cholmondeley, 2005; Armour et al., 2006.) While the resource network was only in operation for the duration of the pilot test, the feedback received and lessons learned will be critical for the development of future resources that are interactive and sustainable.

Participants in our focus groups and our interviews emphasized that practical hands-on experience, such as a science-related internship in a workplace or summer employment in a laboratory, had been crucial in determining their areas of career interest. We strongly recommend that such opportunities be available to as many young women as possible who express interest in scientific careers. Not only do these experiences allow them to make informed choices; we know from our research that they increase the commitment of women to their chosen field.

The discussion in this chapter indicates that many questions remain to be answered in our quest to find ways to enable women to fully participate in careers in the sciences, engineering and technology. These include how best to pass on to young women both the informal and the formal knowledge that can be critical to successful career choice and progress. For example:

- What are the most effective ways of sharing the knowledge that non-linear career paths are the norm so that flexibility is understood as essential in career planning?
- How can practical work experience be incorporated into the education of as many as possible of the young women who are interested in the sciences?
- Where and how do young women learn of the importance of communication and interpersonal skills, in addition to outstanding technical knowledge and ability?
- From whom do young women learn how to balance a career in STEM and a family, or to balance work life and personal life?
- What form of Internet resource would be the preferred source of helpful, satisfying advice and mentorship to women with questions about their career paths?

We will not find robust answers to these and similar questions if we continue to focus on recruitment and use the pipeline model as a point of reference. Our interventions should not be left only for moments of crisis; rather resources should be available to prepare individuals for the transitions that they will face.

Finally, we suggest the development of a 'scholarship of engagement' in which, rather than undertaking more cross-sectional studies, researchers build on existing knowledge with a view to testing and extending it through longitudinal studies. Such scholarship would be sensitive to the non-linearity of career paths, and would explore the influences on career choice and success over the span of a career. Thus would emerge a 'big picture' of the choices made by women in science, technology, engineering and mathematics, and a clearer understanding of how to address the low numbers of women in decision-making roles in these fields.

ACKNOWLEDGEMENT

Funding for the three studies reported in this chapter was provided by the Social Sciences and Humanities Research Council of Canada. The assistance of Grace Ennis, Coordinator of Women in Scholarship, Engineering, Science and Technology (WISEST) throughout these studies is gratefully acknowledged. The graphic design for Figure 10.1 was executed by Jaclyn Dobbe, Communications Assistant, Centre for Health Promotion Studies, School of Public Health, University of Alberta.

We regret that the untimely death of one of our co-investigators, Wendy L. Coffin, early in 2007 precluded her from seeing the final edition of this chapter.

Correspondence concerning this chapter should be addressed to Dr Helen M. Madill, Centre for Health Promotion Studies, School of Public Health, 5–10 University Extension Centre, University of Alberta, Edmonton, Alberta, Canada T6G 2T4.

NOTE

1. All names are pseudonyms; profiles are based on multiple individuals' experiences.

REFERENCES

Armour, M.A., Madill, H.M., Ciccocioppo, A.L., Stewin, L.L., Montgomerie, T.C. and Fitzsimmons, G.W. (2000), 'It's all about retention', In Conference Information and Proceedings National Conference for the Advancement of Women in Engineering, Science, and Technology. Canadian Coalition of Women in Engineering, Science, and Technology (CCWEST), St John's, Newfoundland, Canada, retrieved 11 July 2006, from www.mun.ca/cwse/Armour,Margaret.pdf.
Armour, M.A., Coffin, W., Cullen, D., Einsiedel, A.A., Madill, H.M., Montgomerie, T.C. et al. (2003), 'Women's views of their opportunities in the new economy: preliminary findings', *The Interim Report: Preliminary Research Findings 2002 WISEST*, University of Alberta, retrieved 11 July 2006, from www.uofaweb.ualberta.ca/wisest//pdfs/InterimReport.pdf.
Armour, M.A., Cholmondeley, P., Madill, H.M., Campbell, R., Einsiedel, A.A., Cullen, D. et al. (2006), 'Resources for retention: what did we learn by pilot testing the WISEST resource network?', In Conference Proceedings (CD-ROM), Canadian Coalition of Women in Engineering, Science, Technology and Trades (CCWESTT), Calgary, Alberta, Canada.

Berryman, S.E. (1983), *Who Will Do Science? Minorities and Female Attainment of Science and Mathematics Degrees: Trends and Causes*, New York: Rockfeller Foundation.

Brown, B.L. (2000), *Changing Career Patterns* (Document No. EDD-CE-00-219), ERIC Clearinghouse on Adult, Career, and Vocational Education.

Byrne, E.M. (1993), *Women and Science: The Snark Syndrome*, London: The Falmer Press.

CAUT (2006), 'CAUT Almanac of Post-Secondary Education in Canada', Ottawa ON: Canadian Association of University Teachers (Tables 3.11, 3.16, 3.17, 3.18).

CCWESTT (2006), 'Quickstats March 2006 – Canadian overview', retrieved 29 August 2006 from www.ccwestt.org/Stats.asp.

Cholmondely, P. (2005), 'Design and usability evaluation of a web-based network', unpublished course-based master's project, University of Alberta, Edmonton, Alberta, Canada.

Ciccocioppo, A.L. (1999), 'Themes in career decision-making of undergraduate women in science', unpublished master's thesis, University of Alberta, Edmonton, Alberta, Canada.

Ciccocioppo, A.L. (2005), 'Intervention strategies in the academic and career development of at-risk undergraduate students', unpublished doctoral dissertation, University of Alberta, Edmonton, Alberta, Canada.

Ciccocioppo, A.L., Stewin, L.L., Madill, H.M., Montgomerie, T.C., Tovell, D.R., Armour, M.A. et al. (2002), 'Transitional patterns of adolescent females in non-traditional career paths', *Canadian Journal of Counselling*, **1**, 25–37.

Clark, C., Howard, I., Lazare, S.E. and Weinberger, D.A. (2000), 'A peer mentoring program for underrepresented students in the sciences', in J. Bart (ed.), *Women Succeeding in the Sciences: Theories and Practices Across Disciplines*, West Lafayette, IN: Purdue University Press, pp. 149–68.

Cooper, C.L. and Lewis, S. (1999), 'Gender and the changing nature of work', in G.N. Powell (ed.), *Handbook of Gender and Work*, Thousand Oaks, CA: Sage Publications, pp. 37–46.

Crozier, S. (1999), 'Women's career development in a "relational context"', *International Journal for the Advancement of Couselling*, **21**, 231–47.

Dale, P.M. and Zych, T. (1996), 'A successful college retention program', *College Student Journal*, **30**, 354–61.

Etzkowitz, H., Kemelgor, C. and Uzzi, B. (2000), *Athena Unbound: The Advancement of Women in Science and Technology*, Cambridge, UK: Cambridge University Press.

Fels, A. (2004), 'Do women lack ambition?', *Harvard Business Review*, **82**(4), 50–60.

Glazer-Raymo, J. (1999), 'Taking stock: perspectives on women and leadership in higher education in the UK and the US', *Society for Research into Higher Education News*, **41**, 8–10.

Herr, E.L. and Cramer, S.H. (1979), *Career Guidance and Counseling through the Lifespan: Systematic Approaches*, 2nd edn, Boston, MA: Little, Brown & Company.

Hughes, K., Lowe, G.S. and Schellenberg, G. (2003), *Men's and Women's Quality of Work in the New Canadian Economy*, Research paper W/19, Work Network Ottawa, ON: Canadian Policy Research Networks.

Hyde, M.S. and Gess-Newsome, J. (2000), 'Factors that increase persistence of female undergraduate science students', in J. Bart (ed.), *Women Succeeding in the*

Sciences: Theories and Practices Across Disciplines, West Lafayette, IN: Purdue University Press, pp. 115–68.

Jacobs, J.A. (1999), 'The sex segregation of occupations: prospects for the 21st century', in G.N. Powell (ed.), *Handbook of Gender and Work*, Thousand Oaks, CA: Sage, pp. 125–41.

Lalande, V., Crozier, S. and Davey, H. (1998), 'Women's career development and relationships: a qualitative inquiry', paper presented at the annual conference of the National Consultation on Career Development, Ottawa, ON.

Li, S. (1996), 'University success: A comparison of two cohorts' first year transition', unpublished master's thesis, University of Calgary, Calgary, Alberta, Canada.

Madill, H.M., Montgomerie, T.C., Armour, M.A., Fitzsimmons, G.W. and Stewin, L. L. (1997), 'Attracting females to science careers: How well do special initiatives work?', Edmonton, AB: WISEST, retrieved 11 July 2006, from www.uofaweb. ualberta.ca/wisest//pdfs/brownreport.pdf.

Madill, H.M., Fitzsimmons, G.W., Montgomerie, T.C., Stewin, L.L. Armour, M.A. and Tovell, D.R. (2000a), 'I liked science, but now what do I do? Young women's perspectives following high school', Edmonton, AB: WISEST, retrieved 11 July 2006, from www.uofaweb.ualberta.ca/wisest//pdfs/greenreport.pdf.

Madill, H.M., Montgomerie, T.C., Stewin, L.L., Fitzsimmons, G.W., Tovell, D.R., Armour, M.A. et al. (2000b), 'Young women's work values and role salience in Grade 11: are there changes three years later?', *The Career Development Quarterly*, **49**(1), 16–28.

Madill, H.M., Cooley, J., Fairhurst, M.J., Armour, M.A. and Smith, J. (2003), 'Where do we stand: women in decision making positions in Canada's research intensive universities', in WISEST Preliminary research findings 2002, retrieved 11 July 2006, from www.uofaweb.ualberta.ca/wisest//pdfs/InterimReport.pdf.

Mainiero, L.A. and Sullivan, S.E. (2005), 'Kaleidoscope careers: an alternate explanation for the "opt-out" revolution', *Academy of Management Executive*, **19**, 106–23.

Miller, G.E. (2004), 'Frontier masculinity in the oil industry: the experience of women engineers', *Gender, Work and Organization*, **11**, 47–73.

Mitchell, K.E., Levin, A.S. and Krumboltz, J.D. (1999), 'Planned happenstance: constructing unexpected career opportunities', *Journal of Counseling and Development*, **77**, 115–24.

Meyer, J.P., Bobocel, R.D. and Allen, N.J. (1991), 'Development of organizational commitment during the first year of employment: a longitudinal study of pre- and post-entry influences', *Journal of Management*, **17**, 717–33.

Nash, L. and Stevenson, H. (2004), 'Success that lasts', *Harvard Business Review*, **82**(2), 102–8.

Niemeier, D.A. and Gonzalez, C. (2004), 'Breaking into the Guildmasters' Club: what we know about women science and engineering department chairs at AAU universities', *NWSA Journal*, **16**, 157–71.

O'Neil, D.A. and Bilimoria, D. (2005), 'Womens' career development phases: idealism, endurance, and reinvention', *Career Development International*, **10**, 168–89.

Orndorff, R.M. and Herr, E.L. (1996), 'A comparative study of declared and undeclared college students on career uncertainty and involvement in career development activities', *Journal of Counseling & Development*, **74**, 632–9.

Patton, W. and McMahon, M. (1999), *Career Development and Systems Theory: A New Relationship*, Pacific Grove, CA: Brooks/Cole.

Poggio, B. (2000), 'Between bytes and bricks: gender cultures in work contexts', *Economic and Industrial Democracy*, **21**, 381–402.

Seta, C.E., Paulus, P.B. and Baron, R.A. (2000), *Effective Human Relations: A Guide to People and Work*, 4th edn, Boston, MA: Allyn and Bacon.

Staples, B. (2006), 'Why American college students hate science', *New York Times*, 25 May, pp. 1870–71.

Super, D.E. (1980), 'Life-span, life-space approach to career development', *Journal of Vocational Behavior*, **16**, 282–98.

Super, D.E. (1990), 'A life-span, life-space approach to career development', in D. Brown, L. Brooks and Associates (eds), *Career Choice and Development: Applying Contemporary Theories to Practice*, 2nd edn, San Francisco, CA: Jossey-Bass, pp. 197–261.

Super, D.E. and Sverko, B. (eds) (1995), *Life Roles, Values and Careers: International Findings of the Work Importance Study*, San Francisco, CA: Jossey-Bass.

Tai, R.H., Liu, C.Q., Maltese, A.V. and Fan, X. (2006), 'Planning early careers in science', *Science*, **26**, 1143–44.

Taylor, A. (2005), 'It's for the rest of your life: the pragmatics of youth career decision-making', *Youth & Society*, **36**, 471–503.

Williams, F.M. and Emerson, C.J. (2001), 'Feedback loops and critical mass: the flow of women in science and engineering', www.mun.ca/cwese/GASAT_2001. pdf, retrieved 17 July 2003.

Xie, Y. and Shauman, K.A. (2003), *Women in Science: Career Processes and Outcomes*, Cambridge, MA: Harvard University Press.

PART IV

Enriching the educational experience

11. Achieving greater diversity through curricular change

Ilene J. Busch-Vishniac and Jeffrey P. Jarosz

INTRODUCTION

Although majority males are more likely to enroll in high school advanced placement science and math courses than are women and underrepresented minorities, it is at the undergraduate college level – when students are free to choose a school and a discipline – that the science, math and engineering classroom displays a distinct lack of diversity for the first time. Further, since a technical major in college is required for entry into science and engineering professions, this lack of diversity in college classrooms presages the lack of diversity seen in the technical professions. Without a change toward greater diversity at the college level, it is clear that we will not achieve significant diversity gains in the engineering and science professions.

In the USA, women are now 58 percent of all college students and 50 percent of those in science and engineering. However, within the technical fields there are big differences. Women are 51 percent of chemistry majors but only 22 percent of physics students and 20 percent of engineering students. Within engineering, women are only 14 percent of electrical engineering and mechanical engineering majors (Dedicated Engineers, 2006a). For underrepresented minorities, the problem is even more noticeable than for women. From 1993 to 1999 the African-American enrollment in engineering fell by 17 percent (Wulf, 2002, p. 20). The current African-American share of baccalaureates in science and engineering is 8.4 percent overall, but only 5.0 percent in engineering and 4.0 percent in physics. The current Hispanic share is 7.3 percent overall, 4.9 percent in math/statistics and 4.5 percent in physics (Dedicated Engineers, 2006b). Black women comprised only 2 percent of the 2001 recipients of bachelor's degrees in engineering (Society of Women Engineers, 2006, p. 62). The Hispanic share of microbiology baccalaureates is 10 percent, but only 2 percent of the baccalaureates in earth, atmospheric and ocean sciences (National Science Foundation, 2000, p. 21).

These statistics come at a time when the relative growth of women and minorities in college has been stunning. By the year 2010 it is anticipated that women will earn more degrees than men at every level of higher education, from associate's degrees to doctorates (Building Engineering and Science Talent, 2004, p. 1). The American Council on Education reports that the number of minority students attending US colleges jumped 51.7 percent in the 1990s, with all minorities posting double-digit gains in enrollment. From 1991 to 2001, Latino enrollment increased by 75.1 percent and African-American enrollment by 36.9 percent (Wills, 2005) – but not in science and engineering.

The grim statistics on student diversity in science and engineering at the undergraduate level are matched by equally gloomy statistics on the professoriate. Perhaps the most telling statistic is the following. In 1920, women comprised 26 percent of the full-time faculty in US colleges. In 1995, 75 years later and after many well-supported affirmative action programs, the figure had increased only five points to 31 percent of the professoriate being female! (Williams, 2000, p. 68). Although women are now earning proportionately more of the doctorates awarded in science and engineering (e.g. 44.7 percent of the biological science doctorates in 2002), they are not seeking faculty positions (Stewart et al., 2004, p. 362). For instance, women now comprise only 4 percent of the full professors and 6 percent of the associate professors in the nation's medical schools (American Association of Medical Colleges, 2005); they occupy only 12 percent of tenure-track positions in the top 50 US chemistry departments, despite 30 years of recruiting efforts (Fassinger et al., 2004, p. 298).

The number of African-American, Hispanic and Native-American professors is also quite low. While the three groups represent 23 percent of the US population (Congressional Commission on the Advancement of Women and Minorities in Science, Engineering and Technology Development, 2000, p. 10), they comprise just 4 percent of US engineering faculty. Of that 4 percent, a very high number teach at historically black colleges and Hispanic-serving institutions. Of the engineering faculty of majority-dominated schools, only 1 percent are black, Hispanic or Native (Slaughter, 2002).

Also, there is a heavier concentration of faculty from underrepresented groups at the junior ranks than for male majority counterparts. In 2000, among full-time doctoral scientists and engineers, 51 percent of the men were full professors compared to 24 percent of the women. Furthermore, the success rate for achieving tenure and remaining in the professoriate is much lower for underrepresented groups. In 1997, 63 percent of white male professors were tenured, compared to just 29 percent of black female professors (NSF, 2000, pp. 59–60). The large difference is partly due to women and minorities choosing to leave the fold and partly due to differences in the successful promotion rates in these populations. As a result, women and minorities are particularly underrepresented in the full professor and endowed chair ranks in science and engineering. As these positions are marks of distinction, it comes as no surprise that women and minorities are also significantly underrepresented in leadership positions associated with science and engineering such as department heads, deans, center directors, etc.

The engineering workforce reflects the lack of diversity seen in the student and faculty bodies. Although it has made strides in the last 25 years, the population of engineering professionals is still approximately 90.2 percent male and only 7.1 percent minority (CAWMSET, 2000, pp. 46–7; National Action Council on Minorities in Engineering, 2002, pp. 25–6; Chubin et al., 2005, p. 77). This lack of diversity persists despite unmet needs for technically trained personnel in the private and public sectors. Estimates of unfilled jobs in the USA requiring technology skills range from 500 000 to 900 000 (Margolis and Fisher, 2002, p. 2).

Taken together, these statistics portray a demographic with a very strong majority population and a minority population that is making only modest gains despite significant dedication of resources and programs. Given that the progress toward greater diversity has been so slow, it is reasonable to ask whether there is a compelling case to be made for seeking greater diversity in engineering and science. We believe the answer is a resounding yes! We present our version of the business case for diversity in science and engineering below; we also believe that women and minorities add a whole new perspective to science and engineering – a dimension that is positive and essential for progress.

Ironically, although diversity has stagnated in the science and engineering workforce, the community's understanding of its pressing need has become more sophisticated and has been more clearly articulated. No longer do we see diversity simply as a matter of social justice. Instead, diversity is now a business necessity driven by three primary factors:

1. the need for a large pool of potential employees – as noted above, there is an acute shortage of domestic workers with technical skills;
2. the globalization of business, triggered by technology itself, and the need to have an employee base that is flexible, competent, and accepted in a wide variety of cultures (Lucena, 2000; Swearengen et al., 2002; American Society of Mechanical Engineers, 2004); and
3. the desire to have a broad range of perspectives and experiences in order to enhance the function of design so critical to product development.

It is these three issues that provide the context and compelling need for improving the diversity in our pool of engineering and science students.

There is evidence that diversity has a direct impact on the bottom line of a business. Companies with high ratings for advancing women and minorities routinely outperform those with low ratings (Martin and Ferraro, 2000). Market research shows that Hispanics are increasingly the major driving force behind revenue growth in many consumer and service markets, responsible for 16 percent of the growth in aggregate consumer expenditures between 1998 and 2003. With the current buying power of the Hispanic market currently at $766 billion and projected to be $1.1 trillion by 2010 (Equal Opportunity Publications, 2006, p. 11), one can understand how a company that advances Hispanics would outperform a company without Hispanics.

Further, one can argue that scientific and engineering enterprises invest significant resources in training their technical staff. By not effectively utilizing and advancing their most talented women and minorities, a company loses its return on investment in human capital, often through attrition of talented women and minorities for more 'friendly' organizations. No company can long sustain a competitive edge while suffering such losses in trained personnel.

Aside from the business case, scientific discovery depends on the participation of all ethnic and gender groups, because the scientific method requires the minimization of bias. Scientific advancement requires that we consider *all* possibilities as explanations or solutions and our ability to conjure up alternatives depends on having a plethora of experiences. This was well stated by Rosser (1990, pp. 32–3):

> The standpoint determines the reality seen by the observer. Elimination of some bias can be achieved by attracting as many individuals from as diverse backgrounds as possible to become scientists. No one individual would have an unbiased view but diversity within the group of scientists might lead to a less biased world view.

Given, then, the compelling case for increased diversity in the student population studying science and engineering, and the large number of programs that have been aimed at promoting diversity, it is reasonable to wonder just what has prevented rapid progress in achieving diversity and equity. Indeed, in 2004 the entering class of medical students in the USA was majority female and quite diverse. The business and law school classes were also roughly half female and more diverse than at any other time in history. Why, then, is there little progress (and arguably some backsliding) on achieving diversity in science and engineering?

While the answers are undoubtedly many and varied, there is a simple truth that must form the framework for appropriate discussion, namely, that marginal approaches will always produce marginal gains at best. Here we define as marginal those approaches that either treat symptoms rather than root causes, or that focus on actions outside of the core problem. Our analysis of the work to enhance diversity in science and engineering schools finds much of it to be marginal on both counts. A large fraction focuses on enhancing numbers through symptomatic relief rather than making the profession more attractive. Further, there has been a strong tendency to use minor changes and additions rather than wholesale revamping to achieve diversity. For instance, many diversity initiatives have tried using 'add-ons' such as tutoring programs. While each add-on is meritorious as a *part* of a solution, we believe that this approach fails in the long term as a solitary approach because the curriculum is fundamentally flawed and because the rigors of the typical science or engineering program are not conducive to permitting 'add-ons' without increasing the pressure on students. Instead of tutoring students to meet the demands of a flawed curriculum, why not fix the curriculum?

Studies have proven that women and minorities are as capable of mastering science and engineering as majority males. They are certainly no less intelligent or industrious. Thus the low numbers of minorities and women in science and engineering are the result of factors other than intelligence. For instance, an exhaustive study called Women's Experiences in College Engineering indicates that most women who drop out of engineering do so with a solid B average. They drop out not because of poor academic preparation, but because of disillusionment. The curriculum seems abstract, narrow, rigid and unrelated to societal concerns and real-world problems (Dally, 1995, p. 85; Goodman et al., 2002, p. 10).

In this chapter, we focus on the core essence of the undergraduate experience for science and engineering students – the science, math and engineering courses taken. We consider these from two perspectives, both of which are important for efforts to enhance diversity: progress in how we teach (pedagogy), and progress for what we teach (curriculum).

PROGRESS IN HOW WE TEACH

In the past three decades there has been a growing emphasis on determining how students learn. The operational assumption is that an understanding of the learning process permits us to change how we teach in order to better match our pedagogy to the learning styles and processes used by students. A 2000 book entitled *How People Learn* contained a thorough discussion of the state of knowledge to that point and references to best-practice studies (Bransford et al., 2000). In this section we discuss the current state of pedagogy in science and engineering and briefly review some of the attempts to link learning and pedagogy.

The rigor of mastering fundamental scientific principles and the importance of accuracy in science and engineering have led to a 'boot-camp' atmosphere in many science and engineering programs (Tonso, 1996; Margolis and Fisher, 2002). Students compete with classmates for grades, because most courses are still graded on the curve and because many students aspire to enter graduate programs that are highly selective (such as medical school). Extensive lecturing is still the preferred method of instruction in most science and engineering classes; and faculty rely less on class discussion, more on graduate teaching assistants, and less on cooperative learning than college faculty in general (Astin, 1993, p. 30). In fact, many professors are proud of the rigor of study of engineering and science, and resist any change that might 'dilute' the curriculum. Engineering students are told in freshman year that a third will not survive until graduation and indeed the forecast comes true – even worse, *two*-thirds of the minority students will switch out (Walsh, 2003, p. 16). Introductory courses are unapologetically competitive, selective and intimidating, designed to winnow out all but the top tier. Scientists and engineers expect the next generation to rise, as they did, like cream to the top (Tobias, 1990, p. 10).

Add to this impersonal environment the demographic make-up of engineering and science programs and, as a result, women and minorities report feeling marginalized and facing a chilly environment (Etzkowitz et al., 2000, pp. 237, 245). The lack of hospitality undermines the academic performance of minority students (The College Board, 1999, p. 16). Women usually cite the climate as a reason for dropping out of science and engineering, not insufficient academic preparation (Goodman et al., 2002, pp. 10, 88). Women and minorities may feel that, despite their best efforts, they simply do not belong, as when an advertisement published in a respected education newspaper in 2006 read: 'We're Getting Technology to the People who Shape our Future' and pictured nine college students – all white males.

In contrast, learning research suggests that there are new ways to introduce students to science and that these new approaches make it possible for diverse individuals to develop a deeper understanding of the subject matter (Bransford et al., 2000, p. 6). An example of reversing the boot-camp, sink-or-swim environment of science education is the 'grand reform of introductory chemistry' at Harvard University. Professor Hirschberg, the instructor, applies the strategy of 'cover less and *un*cover more'. He begins the course with a philosophical lecture on the nature of science, stressing that persistence and curiosity are more important in science than academic brilliance. Students approach problems qualitatively, with reflection, and applications of principles are introduced at the outset. Hirschberg does not grade on the curve, so that each and every student can earn an A (Tobias, 1990, p. 59).

Traditional education in science and engineering focuses on the acquisition of calculating skills and memory. Students are expected to memorize, and tests assess their ability to remember facts and formulas. It was not the general rule in traditional science and engineering courses to train students to think and read critically or to solve complex problems (Bransford et al., 2000, p. 4). A better approach is that taken by Dr Neil Abraham of Bryn Mawr College, who designed a program to keep undergraduate women in science. In addition to designing introductory courses with a minimum of prerequisites so that young women who had not taken physics in high school could enroll, he also involved his students in talking and writing *about* physics, drawing on their verbal as well as quantitative skills (Kahle, 2002, p. 14). He thus took advantage of their verbal skills rather than limiting his approach to traditionally masculine hands-on tinkering and competition, or to memorizing.

Although some students learn well through writing, others learn better through experience. Native Americans, in particular, come from a culture in which nothing was written down, and a Lakota proverb says that 'We carry our learning on our backs'. The physics course 'Music and Sound' at the University of Toledo taps into this experiential learning style. Professor Bernard Bopp teaches wave motion, sound propagation, sound perception, physics of wind and string instruments, workings of the human voice and sound reproduction from LPs to MP3s, using many in-class demonstrations. For the final project, teams must design, build and play a new musical instrument (*Chronicle of Higher Education*, 2002, p. A20).

To illustrate that new knowledge is constructed from existing knowledge, faculty should draw students' attention to the incomplete understandings of earlier scientists and engineers, thus making them delve into the *process* of science and engineering. Students can read and discuss first papers by scientists who made discoveries, such as Fermi's 1934 paper on fission (Nair, 1997, p. 353). The scientists' own explanations of their work evoke the spirit of discovery in the student. Assigning first papers helps students see how science is done (Riley, 2003, p. 153). Including the student in the engineering process by reading essays such as Florman's 'Existential Pleasures of Engineering' or Petroski's 'To Engineer is Human' is also useful (Nair, 1995, p. 32). These approaches show that scientists are real people who are discovering – not just memorizing.

An extension of this view – that new knowledge is constructed from existing knowledge – is the need for faculty to pay attention to the knowledge and beliefs that students bring to a learning task, to use this knowledge as a starting point for new instruction, and to monitor students' changing conceptions as instruction proceeds (Bransford et al., 2000, p. 11). One excellent example is just-in-time teaching. JiTT is a learning strategy based on the interaction between web-based study assignments and an active learner classroom. Students respond electronically to carefully constructed web-based assignments which are due shortly before class, and the instructor reads the student submissions 'just in time' to adjust the classroom lesson to suit the students' needs. The heart of JiTT is the 'feedback loop' formed by the students' outside-of-class preparation which fundamentally affects what happens during the subsequent in-class time (Indiana University–Purdue University Indianapolis, Web Physics).

To transform how students learn science, Wieman's undergraduate class on 'The Physics of Everyday Life' at University of Colorado–Boulder uses technical innovations including clickers which instantly show how well students are understanding the material, online interactive simulations, and in-class experiments with data displayed to the students in real time. Each student uses an infrared transmitter, similar to a television remote control, to send votes to a computer, where they are tabulated and projected for the entire class on a screen. The system allows for active participation by all students and provides immediate feedback to the instructor and the students about misunderstanding of the material. 'Often, teachers who are experts in a subject misinterpret how students respond', Wieman said (University of Colorado, Physics Department, n.d.). 'The same words often mean something very different to students than they do to the faculty.' Clickers help avoid this problem by providing immediate feedback on how much the class as a whole or an individual student is understanding. Assigning students to sit in permanent groups of three or four throughout the semester and then using clickers to vote as a group on the predicted outcome of experiments has generated more student discussion and involvement. More students ask and respond to questions in class. Wieman also uses brief online surveys extensively to gauge students' backgrounds, interests and attitudes about learning physics.

The Accreditation Board for Engineering and Technology (ABET) outcome 3(d) requires engineering graduates to have the ability to function in multidisciplinary teams (ABET, 2006), and the importance of cooperative learning is widely recognized (Fulligrove and Treisman, 1990; Landis, 1994; Eastman, 1995; Courter et al., 1998; Feilchenfeld et al., 2002). When the University of Puerto Rico, for instance, compared students taking organic chemistry, pre-calculus and civil engineering, it found that students in the groups using collaborative learning received many more As and far fewer Ds, Fs and Ws (Morell et al., 2001, pp. 359–60). In addition, team experiences are excellent ways to teach product realization and marketing, and develop communication skills and leadership (Dally, 1995, p. 93).

Team experiences have the potential of reducing the isolation felt by women and minorities, but merely requiring students to work on teams is not the same as structuring cooperation among them or providing instruction in team dynamics (Smith et al., 2005, p. 95). A study at the University of Nebraska at Lincoln found that although team projects were assigned frequently, only half the students received any training in teamwork, and most did not know the purpose of teamwork or the characteristics of an effective team (Adams, 2001, p. 600). Only three out of nine institutions we surveyed require *teamwork* as a specific topic (Jarosz and Busch-Vishniac, 2006, p. 246).

Unfortunately, when students are left to group themselves, they tend to group in 'cliques'. Women and minorities, who are in the distinct minority in engineering classes, may even have trouble getting onto a team (Rosser, 1997, pp. 40–41). Once they are on a team, their mates may not take them seriously (Alexander et al., 1997, p. 3). Thus an understanding of team dynamics is a must for science and engineering faculty. Without it, team experiences can be more harmful than helpful to women and minorities (Tonso, 1996, p. 221; Rosser, 1997, pp. 40–41).

Research has produced a consensus that a supportive learning community is critically important for the success of minority students in math and science. Communities are built around intellectual interests, drive group interaction, and foster a supportive learning environment (Margolis and Fisher, 2002, p. 106).

CHANGING WHAT WE TEACH

While there has been a great deal of work on how people learn and its implications for how we should teach, there has been far less work on the curricular content, i.e. just what we ought to be teaching in science and engineering (McEneaney and Radeloff, 2000, p. 133). Most instructors are more willing to change their pedagogical methods than the curriculum, which they consider immutable and sacrosanct (Rosser, 1997, pp. 22, 36). This is unfortunate because there are many reasons why we need to change the curriculum in science and engineering degree programs significantly. In general the curriculum in science and engineering majors has changed little over the years (Torda, 1999, p. 7). Particularly in the physical sciences and those branches of engineering relying on the physical sciences, the result is that the standard curriculum is more or less the same it was in the 1950s, and as noted, the demographic composition of college faculty has not changed much since 1920!

Further, the required science and engineering courses in a degree program tend to have very little connection to one another or to applications for which the concepts might be employed. While this makes courses easier to teach independently of one another, it poses a challenge for students because it does not provide a glimpse of how topics interrelate. Because applications are either introduced late (as in the last two years of engineering) or not at all (as in many science majors), the social context for subject matter in science and engineering tends to be absent. This selectively disadvantages women and underrepresented minority students who are known to pursue degree programs because of their relevance to social and cultural issues of interest (Goodman et al., 2002, pp. 10, 167).

Additionally, the curriculum requirements have tended to bloat to the point that some programs (engineering in particular) cannot be finished in a standard four-year degree program (Kulacki and Vlachos, 1995, p. 225; NSF, 2002-160, p. 11), which presents a major problem for students with financial pressures on them. This group disproportionately includes the underrepresented minority students.

Science and engineering undergraduate programs also assume a high level of understanding of mathematics and science before students even enter college, and many students from our major metropolitan areas simply do not have access to this preparation. Thus we effectively require that students commit to a future in science or engineering before they even leave high school. There is no other set of degree programs that makes that same demand of students in the USA. A student can elect to major in Russian language without taking a single course in Russian in high school; in contrast, students wishing to major in engineering are *strongly* advised to take high school calculus and physics. This need for a very early commitment disadvantages African Americans and Hispanics, because fewer than 6 percent of them take calculus or physics in high school (Babco, 2003). It also disadvantages women, who are generally not taught about mechanical and electrical devices and are not exposed to technological career options in high school (Henderson et al., 1994, p. 337; Margolis and Fisher, 2002).

Creating Links, and Integration of Curricular Material

The traditional curriculum in science and engineering is fragmented, with fundamentals and prerequisites dominating the first two years and practical applications introduced in the last two – if at all (Dally, 1995, p. 86). Many computer science programs, for instance, devote early years to the technical aspects of programming, with applications and multidisciplinary projects at the end (Margolis and Fisher, 2002, p. 56).

However, the use of computers has expanded such that creative computing currently relies on language, visual design, problem definition and organizational skills as much as quantitative analysis, and it should be taught in an interdisciplinary setting. Examples of new holistic courses at Carnegie Mellon University (CMU) which integrate computing with other disciplines include:

- Software engineering – the entire class of 30–50 is integrated into a single software development team which works with an outside client, and technical writers and marketing students are incorporated into the group.
- Wearable computers – integrates industrial, mechanical and electronic engineering and software design with undergraduate and graduate students from different disciplines, and all work with an outside client.
- Building virtual worlds – interdisciplinary teams of three students work on virtual reality projects (Margolis and Fisher, 2002, pp. 57, 132).

A study conducted at Michigan State University (MSU) found an increased emphasis on applications, management, multimedia and simulations, and decreased emphasis on computer programming. Based on needs-assessment interviews, MSU now has an inductive, spiral curriculum in which students solve increasingly challenging problems using a variety of software packages. It assigns authentic, hands-on tasks requiring students to solve problems similar to those they will encounter in the workplace (Urban-Lurain and Weinshank, 2001, p. 537).

The University of Oklahoma uses an integration device called Sooner City. Freshmen are assigned a virtual plot of land on which to build a city by senior year. The chemistry, engineering, English and math departments tie their presentations together in Arc Explorer software. Sooner City incorporates graphics and design, surveying, strength of materials, soil mechanics, water resources, public policy and writing skill (Kolar et al., 2000).

The department of nuclear engineering at Oregon State University restructured a first-year nuclear engineering and health physics course in an effort to challenge students, make the curriculum more dynamic and relevant, and encourage teamwork. They learn nuclear forensics methods, radiation protection and radiation interaction by solving a fictitious murder (Higley and Marianno, 2001).

Introducing Social Relevance

Our current curricular structure tends to neglect the importance of social relevance, as shown in a survey of nine college algebra books with a 1992 copyright, in which there were 100 radioactivity exercises and only eight medical exercises (Campbell and Campbell-Wright, 1995, p. 143). Longitudinal research confirms that many students leave science and engineering so that they can do something to benefit society. Engineering and science need the efforts of the academic community to change their image by demonstrating technology's improvements in medicine, transportation, communication and the environment (Grandy, 1998, p. 615).

For example, the US Military Academy formed a partnership with Special People in the Northeast. Cadets majoring in mechanical engineering were assigned a senior year team project: to design and construct a ticket-tearing device for a man with cerebral palsy. The cadets' device enabled him to increase his working hours; and enabled the cadets to grow as engineers and as individuals (Catalano et al., 2000).

Pennsylvania State University's American Indian Housing Initiative conducts hands-on summer workshops in sustainable technologies and practices on the Northern Cheyenne Indian Reservation in Montana. Undergraduate students have constructed a daycare center featuring strawbale construction, natural lighting, and a highly efficient environmental control system. Though based in the Department of Architectural Engineering, it attracts students of various disciplines and both genders.

Mechanical engineering majors at Johns Hopkins University (JHU) worked with Volunteers for Medical Engineering in order to design and assemble a computer-guided pill-dispensing machine that is enabling a quadriplegic person to lead a more independent life. Students reported that the project integrated electronics, mechanics, ergonomics, computer programming and business administration in a real-world setting.

The University of Notre Dame has a Research Experience for Undergraduates on water resources in developing countries with practica in Benin, Haiti and Honduras. Nine out of ten participants the first summer were women, despite physical hardships and lifting requirements (similar ratio in subsequent years).

Colorado School of Mines has a program in Humanitarian Engineering, with projects in Africa, Asia and South America, funded by the Hewlett Foundation.

Addressing Diversity and Multiculturalism in the Curriculum

Work in social psychology, cognitive psychology and anthropology is making clear that all learning takes place in settings that have particular sets of cultural and social norms and expectations and that these settings influence learning and transfer in powerful ways (Bransford et al., 2000, p. 4). Women and minority students consider not only general social relevance, but the extent to which the curriculum is tied to values of their own gender and subcultures. Native-American college students, for instance, have demonstrated that they must be immersed in their culture, history and philosophy if they are to effectively understand their role in the Native communities. They learn best through local, culturally based and holistic methods. They then feel comfortable pursuing further science and math courses as they enter baccalaureate programs and the STEM workforce (NSF, 2002-072, p. 12).

Recognizing that botany, civic responsibility, economic development, environmental science, forestry, soil mapping and water study are relevant to Native Americans, the Oglala Lakota College developed an innovative engineering project for its 1300 students, who are spread out in ten centers across the reservation. The GeoProbe mobile soil/water lab is a track-mounted machine which can drill 130 feet and extract soil samples; it is installed in a trailer pulled by a van. The van is a clean room with generator, cabinet and tables. The van tows the unit to one of the ten college centers, where students conduct drilling and analyze the samples. The goals are research training for the students, but also economic development: to provide tribe members with drilling jobs (NSF, 2002-072, p. 13).

Noting that few African Americans select the physical sciences, Barbara Tewskbury of Hamilton College designed the Geology and Development of Modern Africa, a semester connecting the geology of Africa with evolution, history and politics. It connects the mineral resources of South Africa with the evolution of slavery, the Nile River with hydropolitics in North Africa, and the Sahara Desert with greenhouse warming. The rigorous hands-on course has no prerequisites and earns credit in the Geology Department as well as the Africana Department. It attracts many black students, many of whom subsequently student-teach the course and go on to take more geology courses (Tewksbury, 1995).

The PROMISE project at University of Nevada, Las Vegas, developed an undergraduate course to attract and retain women in earth science programs. 'Earth Systems: a Feminist Approach', is team-taught by a geologist and a sociologist. It seeks to situate science within its social and political context, and to strengthen women's confidence in science. The course stresses social action, field work, writing and synthesis (McEneaney and Radeloff, 2000).

A successful summer program for incoming science freshmen at the University of Maryland, Baltimore County consists of courses not only in calculus, chemistry and study skills, but also in African-American literature. The literature component reinforces necessary reading and writing skills, but also helps African-American students assert their identity and feel at home in science (Hrabowski and Pearson, 1993, p. 237).

In 1995, instructors of an introductory physics class at Utah State University presented brief biographical materials on women scientists and measured student attitudes. The survey indicated that even minimal inclusion of such material changed student perceptions of science as a strictly male endeavor (Marshall and Dorward, 1997, p. 284).

Innovative courses explore the intersection of science with race and gender. Virginia Polytechnic Institute has developed 'Engineering Cultures', and Massachusetts Institute of Technology has developed 'African Americans in Science, Technology and Medicine' and 'Science and Race, Sex and Gender in the US'.

Streamlining the Curriculum

The typical science or engineering curriculum adds new topics every year but fails to eliminate old ones. Unfortunately, the trend toward cramming more and more into the science and engineering curriculum 'runs in exactly the wrong direction. Few students will want to commit themselves to an educational track that is nearly all-consuming' (Williams, 2003, p. B13).

In 2000, the Mechanical Engineering Department at University of Michigan decided to run in the right direction. In order to accommodate diverse student backgrounds it removed as many barriers, such as strict boundaries between topics, as possible. There are now three integrated courses in design and manufacturing, two lab courses, and several redesigned courses in engineering sciences. Subjects required by all programs were reduced from 56 to 52 hours, related technical subject requirements were reduced from 17 to 8, and free electives went from 4 to 12. The curriculum is now flexible enough that dual degrees (ME + chemical, for example) can be obtained with the addition of one extra semester (Tryggvason et al., 2001, p. 442).

Starting Assumptions

> I assume that students in 103 are preprofessionals who have already decided on a career in science . . . I assume that the students have had some hands-on experience with how things work.　　　　　　　　　　　(Tobias, 1990, p. 30)

Liberal arts programs recognize that students enter college with different backgrounds, and the program must teach major subjects as though students have never seen the material before. In engineering and science, this is generally not the case. There is an expectation that students have certain levels of ability through earlier exposure to particular subjects, notably calculus and physics, whereas fewer than 6 percent of blacks and Hispanics take these subjects in high school. Hence, if one assumes that all entering freshmen are prepared in those two subjects, then 94 percent of blacks and Hispanics have been eliminated *de facto* from pursuing undergraduate degrees in science and engineering!

Mindful that students come to college with different backgrounds and with different goals, the Chemistry Department at the University of Arizona offers three different levels of introductory chemistry: honors chemistry; a standard chemistry for science, engineering and premed students; and a less quantitative chemistry for pre-nursing and non-science majors.

Other common, false assumptions include:

- All engineering students have good visualization skills.
- Computer science majors love video games, have learned a lot of computer codes, and have done a lot of programming.
- Engineering majors are skilled at using mechanical devices.
- These days, all freshmen are comfortable with computers.

Reducing Prerequisites and Shortening Critical Path Lengths

The goal of shortening critical path lengths is not to dilute the curriculum but to reconsider the actual needs of engineers and scientists and eliminate superfluous material. For example, the traditional physics lab in an engineering degree program could be replaced by a specific engineering physics lab integrating calculus and physics. A specific sophomore engineering math course combining vector algebra, vector calculus, and differential equations and integrated with engineering applications via team teaching would be more appropriate to an engineering major than the standard algebra-heavy math courses designed for math majors (Scheinerman, 2003).

Similarly, a program with many prerequisites across disciplines can condense them into a smaller number of specific prerequisites. When the University of Texas at Dallas developed a program in telecommunication engineering (TE), it combined electrical engineering (EE) and computer science, each of which has many prerequisites, but new courses were developed to replace some of them. For example, four EE prerequisites were condensed into two TE courses. The circuit sequence had 12 EE prerequisites, but the new program developed two TE courses to cover essential elements of circuits, signals and systems (Burnham et al., 2001).

Freshmen

Science and engineering faculty often assume that students who got into college must have excellent study habits and know how to conduct research. However, by throwing freshmen into the traditional 'sink-or-swim' environment, for which many are not in fact prepared, fully one-third of majority students and two-thirds of minority students sink, and of those who manage to swim, many fall short of reaching their maximum potential. The purpose of freshman orientation courses, therefore, is not to present science and engineering content, but to provide incoming students with the skills they need to succeed both academically and personally (Landis, 1994, p. 6). For example, Bonk designed a half-credit course for chemistry majors at Duke University on literature-search techniques (American Chemical Society, 2002, p. 31); and Landis led a consortium of 13 universities which designed and conducted required Introduction to Engineering Courses covering academic survival skills, engineering careers, group study, minority programs, and minority resources.

Gatekeepers

Gatekeeper courses are designed to weed out students who are less academically prepared or less sure they want to be scientists or engineers (Dally, 1995, p. 86). Women and minorities are typically less sure about their choice of a technical career. They need to know that faculty are 'pulling' for them, not trying to weed them out (Margolis and Fisher, 2002, p. 140).

Calculus is a typical gatekeeper course (Meade, 1993, p. 33). All engineering schools and most science programs require three or four semesters of calculus, and many calculus topics presented by mathematics departments are not necessary for scientists and engineers. Examples of calculus topics that are not necessary for mechanical engineers but are taught to them anyway include conics, Cramer's rule, Gauss's integral theorem, l'Hopital's rule, orthogonal functions, and transcendental functions (Jarosz and Busch-Vishniac, 2006, p. 244).

Admissions

Admissions offices may give unwarranted preference to students with certain backgrounds. In the mid-1990s, the Computer Science Department at CMU adjusted admission criteria to reduce the weight given to programming and code. The adjustment helped CMU to achieve gains in recruiting women (Blum, 2003).

The Twenty-first Century Liberal Art

In 1995, the NSF announced that engineering education should support diverse career aspirations. It should include:

- flexible degree options for those who wish to practice engineering;
- new paths for those who want a significant technical component to their education but who intend to pursue non-engineering degrees;
- engineering courses for non-engineering students (NSF, 1995, p. 9).

In order to support the different career aspirations, Lucena and Downey advocate the development of curricular tracks, for example: an engineering design track, an engineering management track, an engineering sciences track, and a public policy track.

Many schools now offer two separate degree programs: a BA in engineering science and a BS in a specific engineering discipline. In addition to its ABET-accredited engineering program, the University of Pennsylvania has a curriculum including technology as a liberal art, with an applied capstone societal project. It provides an interdisciplinary foundation with a strong technological component for students who pursue graduate work in fields other than engineering. Two separate degree programs are offered. The BSE is the traditional degree which prepares students to be professional engineers in ten realms such as electrical engineering. The BAS, Bachelor of Applied Science, is for careers in medicine, business and law, with concentration in one of five engineering realms such as biomedical engineering. A typical BSE requires 40 course units; the BAS requires a reasonable 36 course units. There are also many dual-degree options. For computer and cognitive science, for example, either of the following is possible:

1. BA in psychology from College of Arts & Science + BAS in computer science from the School of Engineering for 40 course units;
2. BA in philosophy from College of Arts & Science + BSE in computer engineering from the School of Engineering for 46 course units.

There is also a BAS with individualized major, requiring 36 course units, designed for careers in biotechnology, environmental control, healthcare, government, technical management, telecommunications or writing.

The development of tracks corresponds to ABET's requirement that all engineering programs offer the broad education necessary to understand the impact of engineering solutions in a global, economic, environmental and societal context, and a knowledge of contemporary issues (ABET, 2006). As stated succinctly by Williams (2003, p. B13): 'The convergence of technological and liberal-arts education is a deep, long-term, and irreversible trend. Students need to be prepared for life in a world where technological, scientific, humanistic, and social issues are all mixed together'. While the traditional role of engineering education was to train engineers for the workforce, the new engineering degree should be a basis on which to build in many directions. Engineering graduates will have a foundation that can be applied to most other professions. They will have knowledge in mathematics, physics, chemistry, software, humanities, English, speech, social studies, history and economics, as well as in engineering, giving them more breadth and depth than other undergraduate degrees. That diversity can help engineering graduates migrate to other professions, such as medicine, law and business management (Tryggvason et al., 2001, p. 443; Goodman et al., 2002, p. 167; Zobrist, 2003). As the optimum launching pad to challenging and rewarding professions, it will be more attractive to a diverse group of students (Carmi and Aung, 1993, p. 44).

REFORM OF THE UNDERGRADUATE MECHANICAL ENGINEERING CURRICULUM

These and related issues of curriculum content have been topics of research, but most of the work has been done on one or another single aspect of the problem. In contrast, we have undertaken a very broad curriculum reform program. We have chosen to focus our immediate attention on mechanical engineering. Mechanical is the largest of the engineering disciplines, ranking first in undergraduate enrollment and first in the number of baccalaureates awarded, and accounting for 19.4 percent of all engineering baccalaureates in 2004 (Gibbons, 2005). Mechanical engineers comprise 16.3 percent of the total engineering workforce, but unfortunately, mechanical is one of the least diverse of all the domains of science and engineering (Dedicated Engineers 2006a, 2006b).

In crafting a method for regenerating the mechanical engineering undergraduate curriculum, we have sought a process that removes the strong biases to keep that which already exists, while allowing for human judgments as opposed to automatic curriculum generation. What we have developed is a combination of engineering methods used for research in a technical discipline, and a series of workshops to bring in that critical human element. The engineering tools are of use primarily as they provide our committees with a basis for making decisions as the curriculum is dissected and reassembled. The work consists of the following tasks:

1. curriculum dissection – pulling the curriculum apart into individual topics based on course syllabuses;
2. topic evaluation – editing the topics list to eliminate topics no longer required while adding those necessary for the future;
3. topic association map generation – associating with each topic information on prerequisites for understanding, immediate successor topics, applications, potentially related non-technical material, and hours in class that should be dedicated to the topic;
4. solution of the optimization problem – using optimization techniques and the topic database to cluster topics in a logical manner; this permits us to assemble the topics into a totally new curriculum;
5. piloting – comparing new courses to existing ones and correlating with retention and recruitment data.

Curriculum Dissection and Topic Evaluation

Although curriculum reform projects typically examine course titles and assume that courses do not vary much from one institution to another, we chose to dissect the mechanical engineering curriculum at a level much more finely grained than courses. We compiled a list of the topics and subtopics required in the mechanical engineering curriculum of nine diverse schools, attempting to be as narrow and specific as possible. From the syllabuses for the technical courses required of all ME majors at those nine schools, we extracted 1392 individual topics.

Consideration of specific topics and subtopics, rather than whole courses, forms a more accurate baseline for assessment of the ME curriculum of the present and the future. It tells us what exactly we are teaching, i.e. what is the *de facto* body of knowledge (BOK) essential to students graduating with a baccalaureate in mechanical engineering. Listing the topics one by one reveals that some topics that are currently taught are no longer relevant or necessary, and examination of the list reveals that certain topics that *should* be taught are missing. Our analysis of the 1392 topics required at the nine schools in our survey revealed the following about the typical ME undergraduate curriculum.

The core knowledge required for a baccalaureate in ME can be mastered in four years or even fewer. Although each individual school in our survey required many unique topics, the number of topics required by all or most of the schools was comparatively small. Only 70 topics were common to all or most of the nine schools in our survey. Those 70 topics could be considered a core or BOK. Many of the topics required by only one school in nine could be eliminated if necessary. In fact, some of the topics, when isolated, were not even recognized by most ME faculty. Some of the many topics that might be dropped from the ME canon include: Abbe numbers, alpha prototypes, applets, arithmetic logic unit, classes and objects, conics, Cramer's rule, Fortran, gamma distributions, Gauss's integral theorem, Green's theorem, inheritance, l'Hopital's rule, mobile code, Nichols's plots, operators and friends, procedural abstraction, psychrometry, Routh Horowitz criteria, sweeps, transcendental functions, and waves. All of these topics, however, are currently required by one or more of the ME departments that we surveyed.

The baccalaureate engineering degree should be a launching pad for many professions, to include engineering practice, medicine, law and business (Carmi and Aung, 1993, p. 44). The current ME curriculum is heavily slanted toward practice. Of the topics required by the nine schools in our survey, 79 percent are judged necessary for engineering practice and 66 percent are necessary for engineering graduate school. Only 8 percent are seen as necessary for managing a business, and 6 percent for graduate school in medicine or law.

The current ME curriculum is stronger in technical skills than in professional skills (ability to function on multidisciplinary teams, understanding of ethical responsibility, ability to communicate effectively, understanding of the impact of engineering on society, knowledge of contemporary issues), but the importance of the professional skills is being emphasized more and more (Tryggvason et al., 2001, p. 440; ASME, 2004; Shuman et al., 2005). Improvement is particularly needed in knowledge of team dynamics, ability to communicate orally, and knowledge of contemporary issues.

The ME curriculum is very slanted toward classical mechanics and thermodynamics, and needs to be more interdisciplinary. Students need to be prepared for a society in which technological and scientific issues are mixed together (Williams, 2003, p. B13). The emerging fields are biotechnology, environmental study, information technology, nanotechnology and photonics (National Academy of Engineering, 2004, pp. 10–22), yet topics related to these fields are not common in the current ME curriculum.

The current curriculum provides an adequate basis in engineering science, mathematics, physics and chemistry, but not biology. None of the topics in the curriculum common to the nine schools in our survey were biology topics.

Topic Association Map Generation

Our curriculum reform team considered the list of 1392 ME topics and eliminated many which it found to be unnecessary or inappropriate for undergraduate study. It then added several new topics, such as non-Newtonian fluids. After this revision, the list consisted of 876 entries. The reform team then developed a database of the 876 remaining topics, associating with each topic information on prerequisites for understanding, immediate successor topics, applications, potentially related non-technical material, and hours in class that should be dedicated to the topic. The database will be a valuable teaching tool for presenting material to a more diverse group of students.

For instance, the database or topic association map supplies one or more technical applications to illustrate each topic. Traditionally, ME instructors rely heavily on automobile applications, but efforts were made to devise novel applications that would appeal to a diverse group of male and female students. Thus, instead of the classical auto applications, the topic association map suggests the listing shown in Table 11.1.

Table 11.1   Course topic and application

Topic	Application
Acids and bases	Fishing
Actuators and sensors	Insulin pumps
Analysis of displacement	Earthquakes
Bolts and rivets	Failure of the *HMS Titanic*
Boundary value problems	Organ pipes
Castigliano's first theorem	Diving boards
Central limit theorem	Risk statistics for diseases
Conservation of momentum	Ice skating
Creep	Salt water taffy
Data analysis	Setting house prices
Dimensional analysis	Why are we the size we are?
Eccentric impact	Sport accidents
Error analysis	Stock prices
Extrusion	Presses to make Silly Putty
Faraday's law of induction	Soda fountains
Flow measuring devices	New Orleans levees: gate size and shape
Fluid mechanics	Nature's design of sharks
Fluid surface tension	Why soap cleans
High-pass filters	Stethoscopes
Iron carbon systems	Kitchen knives
Kinetic molecular theory	Insulin pumps
Momentum equation	Avalanches
Plane Couette flow	Syringes
Pulleys	Elliptical exercise machines
Sampling errors	Newspaper polls

For example, in order to demonstrate the relationship among length, pressure loss and air velocity, a traditional method would be to describe a large municipal piping system. A more appealing application for a diverse group would be to compare the sounds of various musical instruments (trumpet versus tuba, etc.) with an in-class demonstration or at least an electronic sound byte (Guillaume, 2006).

An enduring problem, discussed by Blewett, is how to get a meaningful experience in the humanities and social sciences into the science and engineering curricula within the limited number of credit hours available in a four-year program (Blewett, 1993, p. 175). Emphasizing the links between technical and non-technical topics may alleviate the problem. Therefore, in addition to a technical application, the topic association map supplies related non-technical material for each ME topic. This will allow instructors to link science and engineering with arts, economics, history, literature and public policy. For example, lessons concerning a/d and d/a conversion can be accompanied by lessons on book scanning. Other linkages include those shown in Table 11.2.

The map lists the prerequisites for each topic. The most common prerequisite is the *first law of thermodynamics*. Other very common prerequisites include *force analysis* and *temperature*. These topics should obviously be presented very early in the curriculum.

Similarly, the map supplies post-requisites or 'successors', i.e. topics that naturally follow another topic. The most common successors are *design problems*, *design projects* and *ethics*. The frequent listing of these three topics does not imply that they must be saved until the senior year capstone project; it implies that they are pervasive and should be assigned throughout, from first semester through the last.

Finally, the map supplies estimates of the time required to cover each topic, ranging from 15 minutes for *matrix multiplication* to 45 hours for *kinematics and dynamics of machines*.

Solution of the Optimization Problem

The entire topic association map, with hours required, prerequisites, successors, technical applications and related non-technical material will be subjected to an applied mathematics optimization process, which will place topics in the most logical sequence. This approach, which relies on engineering and mathematical tools, will naturally cluster topics in a manner that should produce a radical, highly optimized curriculum for the entire mechanical engineering degree program. The precise grouping of topics into courses will depend on the goals of each institution expressed, in large measure, through their choice of criteria for optimization. These criteria

Table 11.2   Course topic and non-technical link

Topic	Non-technical link
Acceleration, measurement of	Roller-coasters
Acids and bases	The chemical basis for cooking
Binary representation	The impact on society of the computer
Biomaterials	Artificial joints, skin grafts
Buckling of columns	Greek and Roman architecture, Parthenon, Sampson
Control systems	The Crash of 1929
Coriolis acceleration	The literature of Isaac Asimov
Direct impact	Contact sports: boxing, football, punching bag
Feedback control	Obesity and human feedback control mechanisms
Forces and torques	Earthquakes, history of San Francisco
Gas compression	SCUBA gear
Geometrical optics	Eyeglasses and contact lenses
Gravity	Literature on space travel, amusement park rides
Infinite series	Religious concepts of the Infinite
Kinematics	Sports medicine, body mechanics
Manufacturing processes	Industrial Revolution
Maxima/minima	Stock markets
Measurement systems and techniques	Tracking a pandemic, Spanish Influenza 1918
Mixtures	Removing caffeine from coffee beans
Periodicity	Weather
Phase equilibrium	Icebergs floating in the sea, *HMS Titanic*
Pressure	Hypertension
Radiant heat transfer	Chernobyl, 3-Mile Island, Silkwood
Stefan Boltzmann law	Sunbathing and melanoma
Superposition	Music: Fourier components in music

might vary from shortening the critical path length (particularly at schools which accept large numbers of transfer students) to focusing on application clusters (which might be logical at schools in which the vast majority of students seek jobs immediately after obtaining their undergraduate degree).

Piloting

In autumn 2006, our team will pilot new applications in existing courses. In spring 2007 it will pilot one or two changes in existing courses. In autumn 2007 it will pilot completely new courses.

Plans call for piloting a freshman design course in graphics at California State University, Los Angeles (CSULA), JHU and the University of Washington; a solids course for sophomores at CSULA, MSU, Smith College and Stevens Institute of Technology; and a fluids course for juniors at CSULA and MSU.

THE ROLE OF COMMUNITY COLLEGES

Many students find community colleges an inexpensive way to complete half their college education. The average annual tuition at community colleges is $2191, a fraction of the cost at most four-year colleges (AACC, 2006).

The role of community colleges in educating scientists and engineers is not well known to the public, or even to the science and engineering community (Mattis and Sislin, 2005, pp. vii, 67). They are particularly important to the healthcare, registered nursing, licensed practical nursing, radiology, and computer technology workforces. Many would be surprised to hear that 45 percent of all undergraduate students in the USA – 11.6 million – are enrolled in the nation's 1186 community colleges. The percentage is even higher for two underrepresented minority groups: 55 percent of the nation's Hispanic students and 57 percent of the Native-American students attend them. Women are well represented also: 59 percent of community college students are female (AACC, 2006).

Of those who transfer to four-year engineering schools, a full 65.8 percent complete baccalaureates; unfortunately, only 19 percent of community college students transfer. Of African Americans who attend community colleges, only 8 percent transfer. Thus the community colleges are a source, as yet largely untapped, for producing scientists and engineers of the future, particularly women, Hispanic, and Native scientists and engineers (ASEE, 1995; Hendley, 1997, p. 22; Mattis and Sislin, 2005, pp. 8, 34, 59).

As is common throughout our education system, there is a lack of cooperation between two- and four-year colleges. Many four-year colleges do not accept academic credits earned at community colleges. Articulation agreements involve close examination of course content to see what can transfer for credit, a process which is time-consuming and labor-intensive (Hendley, 1997, p. 22; Mattis and Sislin, 2005, pp. 8–16).

To take advantage of the community college as a source of women and minority scientists and engineers, steps must be taken to improve transfer partnerships. Close collaboration between two specific schools, a two-year and a four-year, have been successful. Two schools can work out the course content for articulation. Prime examples of successful partnerships are Hudson Valley Community College and Rensselaer Polytechnic Institute,

Montgomery College and the University of Maryland, and Pima Community College and the University of Arizona. In addition to articulation agreements, outreach is necessary: visits from one campus to the next, job fairs or school fairs, special survival kits for transfer students, etc. Outreach helps the process. Statistics indicate that transfer students earn higher grades than the 'native population' (Mattis and Sislin, 2005, pp. 18–19, 85–6).

CONCLUSION

Science and engineering have made progress in diversity in some areas, but not in others. Women and minorities are still very underrepresented in certain areas, such as electrical engineering, mechanical engineering and physics; women are also very underrepresented in computer science. In some areas, such as the biological sciences and psychology, enrollment has become more diverse, but diversity of the faculty lags far behind.

Downey and Lucena hold that engineering is one dimension of personhood along with gender and ethnic identity. The sciences are mathematical worlds to which engineers resort for help, but they must always return to problem solving with people. The emphasis of the traditional curriculum on mathematical problem solving, drawing a boundary around a problem and not allowing sentiment or society or feeling or personality to intrude, causes students to choose between engineering and personhood (Downey and Lucena, 2003). Some students 'stick it out', but many choose to drop engineering in favor of personhood. If engineering is a predominantly white male environment, women and minorities are even more likely to drop out. While Downey and Lucena's work has focused on engineering, it likely can be applied equally well to science curricula. It suggests strongly that science and engineering curricula should be revised to provide greater opportunities for students to see the social and historical contexts of the field.

We believe that making the undergraduate science and engineering curriculum more attractive is the best solution to the lack of diversity in these fields, better than the marginal approaches and symptomatic relief we have seen to date. Some innovations have been implemented and praised, only to be discontinued as soon as their 'champion' left the campus (Torda, 1999, p. 9). While there have certainly been curriculum innovations, there has not been a comprehensive, systemic overhaul, such as the one which we are attempting for mechanical engineering. We believe that a careful topic-by-topic analysis of the curriculum provides a useful baseline for comprehensive reform.

We need the participation of women and minorities in our technical workforce, and we also need their perspectives. Scientific knowledge has been greatly enhanced by the unique contributions of women and minorities, though often they were not esteemed at the time. As Rosser (1990, p. 27) has stated, 'The scientific paradigms acceptable to the mainstream of the practicing scientists are convincing precisely because they reinforce or support the historical, economic, social, racial, political and gender policies of the majority of scientists at that particular time'. However, those who were once outside the scientific mainstream bring in new interests and new ways of knowing things. They often examined problems that were not considered worthy of scientific investigation by the mainstream (Rosser and Kelly, 1994, pp. 31–2).

For example, Ellen Richards Swallow was originally a home economist who wrote about the sanitation of the home and nutritious school lunches – topics that were of little concern to scientists. But her interest in clean homes led to study of sanitary water, sanitary soil and sanitary air. In 1887, she conducted an extensive survey of the quality of the inland bodies of water of Massachusetts, many of which were already polluted with industrial waste and municipal sewage. The scale of the survey was unprecedented and led to the first state water-quality standards in the nation and the first modern municipal sewage treatment plant, in Lowell, Massachusetts. Because of the prevailing scientific and gender norms, it is very unlikely that a male scientist would have developed methods to insure purity for the home and then extend them to the surrounding outdoor environment (Rosser, 1990, p. 38). Swallow thus brought a new perspective to science. Though she is now honored as a pioneer in environmental engineering and industrial ecology, she was dismissed from MIT. Her curriculum was regarded as too interdisciplinary, i.e. it did not fit neatly into the established scientific categories. She became known not for sanitary chemistry, but as the 'mother of home economics' (Hynes, 1995, p. 211).

Women and minority scientists and engineers such as Benjamin Carson, George Washington Carver, John Christian, Amelia Earhart, Jane Goodall, Marjorie Joyner, Lewis Latimer, Elijah McCoy, James West and Daniel Williams have advanced our understanding of pediatric neurosurgery, crop rotation, aircraft lubricants, transoceanic flight, primatology, cosmetology, electric incandescent lamps, steam engine lubrication, the electret microphone, and open heart surgery.

They have not only added to the existing categories of knowledge; they have actually added whole new categories of knowledge and brought new 'ways of knowing' (Rosser, 1990, p. 34). Diversity of perspective and ways of knowing enhance scientific discovery and engineering design greatly. One can only imagine how much science and engineering would be enhanced by the full, unfettered participation of men and women, majority and minorities.

REFERENCES

Accreditation Board for Engineering and Technology (ABET), Engineering Accreditation Commission (2006), 'Criteria for Accrediting Engineering Programs', retrieved from www.abet.org.

Adams, S. (2001), 'The effectiveness of the E-team approach to invention and innovation', *Journal of Engineering Education*, **90**(4), 597–600.

Alexander, B., Foertsch, J. and Gunter, R. (1997), 'Introduction to engineering EPD-160 all-women's section', Evaluation report, University of Wisconsin–Madison.

American Association of Community Colleges (AACC) (2006), retrieved from www.aacc.nche.edu.

American Association of Medical Colleges (AAMC) (2005), 'Women in US academic medicine', *Statistics and benchmarks 2005*, retrieved from www.aamc.org/members/wim/statistics/stats 05/start.htm.

American Chemical Society (2002), 'James Bonk: a hard act to follow', *Chemical and Engineering News*, 26 August, p. 31.

American Society of Mechanical Engineers (ASME), International Council on Education (2004, November), *A Vision of the Future of Mechanical Engineering Education*.

ASEE (1995), 'African Americans in higher education', *PRISM*, April, 10.

Astin, A. (1993), 'Engineering outcomes', *ASEE PRISM*, September, 27–30.

Babco, E. (2003), 'Trends in African American and Native American participation in STEM higher education', in Commission on Professionals in Science and Technology, May, retrieved from www.cpst.org/STEM.

Blewett, P. (1993), 'Introducing breadth and depth in the humanities and social sciences into an engineering student's general education curriculum', *Journal of Engineering Education*, **82**(3), 175–80.

Blum, L. (2003), Phone conversation with J. Jarosz, 24 June.

Bransford, J., Brown, A. and Cocking, R. (eds) (2000), *How People Learn: Brain, Mind, Experience, and School*, Washington, DC: National Academy Press.

Building Engineering and Science Talent (2004), 'Higher education, A Bridge for All', February, retrieved from www.bestworkforce.org.

Burnham, G. et al. (2001), 'The first telecommunications engineering program in the United States', *Journal of Engineering Education*, **90**(4), 653–7.

Campbell, M. and Campbell-Wright, R. (1995), 'Toward a feminist algebra', in S. Rosser (ed.), *Teaching the Majority*, New York: Teachers College Press, pp. 127–44.

Carmi, S. and Aung, W. (1993), 'Launching leaders', *ASEE PRISM*, March, 44.

Catalano, G., Wray, P. and Cornelio, S. (2000), 'Compassion practicum: a capstone design experience at the United States Military Academy', *Journal of Engineering Education*, **89**(4), 471–4.

Chronicle of Higher Education (2002), 'A physics class for nonmajors on the science of sound', 6 September, A20.

Chubin, D., May, G. and Babco, E. (2005), 'Diversifying the engineering workforce', *Journal of Engineering Education*, **94**(1), 73–86.

The College Board (1999), *Reaching the Top: a report of the National Task Force on Minority High Achievement*, New York: College Board Publications.

Congressional Commission on the Advancement of Women and Minorities in Science, Engineering and Technology Development (2000), *Land of Plenty: Diversity as America's Competitive Edge in Science, Engineering and Technology*, Arlington, VA: National Science Foundation.

Courter, S., Millar, S. and Lyons, L. (1998), 'From the students' point of view: experiences in a freshman engineering design course', *Journal of Engineering Education*, **87**(3), 283–8.

Dally, J. (1995), 'Anchored instruction and engineering education', in J. Bourne, A. Brodersen and M. Dawant (eds), *The Influence of Technology on Engineering Education*, Boca Raton: CRC Press, pp. 81–102.

Dedicated Engineers (2006a), 'Women in engineering and related fields', *D-E Communications*, June, retrieved from www.dedicatedengineers.org.

Dedicated Engineers (2006b), 'Minorities in engineering and related fields', *D-E Communications*, June, retrieved from www.dedicatedengineers.org.

Downey, G. and Lucena, J. (2003), 'When students resist: ethnography of a senior design experience in engineering', *International Journal of Engineering Education*, **19**(1), 168–76.

Eastman, C. (1995), 'Accommodating diversity in computer science education', in S. Rosser (ed.), *Teaching the Majority*, New York: Teachers College Press, pp. 160–68.

Equal Opportunity Publications (2006), 'Hispanic market', *Minority Engineer*, Winter, 10–11.

Etzkowitz, H., Kemelgor, C. and Uzzi, B. (2000), *Athena Unbound: The advancement of women in science and technology*, Cambridge: Cambridge University Press.

Fassinger, R., Scantlebury, K. and Richmond, G. (2004), 'Career, family, and institutional variables in the work lives of academic women in the chemical sciences', *Journal of Women and Minorities in Science and Engineering*, **10**(4), 297–316.

Feilchenfeld, N., Horn, T. and Mercuri, R. (moderators) (2002), 'Preparing women STEM majors to succeed', in *Women in Science: Opportunities in a Changing Landscape*, proceedings of a national symposium at Bryn Mawr College held on 26–27 October 2001, pp. 35–6.

Fulligrove, R. and Treisman, P. (1990), 'Mathematics achievement among African American undergraduates at the University of California, Berkeley: an evaluation of the Mathematics Workshop Program', *Journal of Negro Education*, **59**(3), 463–78.

Gibbons, M. (2005), 'The Year in Numbers', retrieved from www.asee.org/about/publications/profiles.

Goodman, I. et al. (2002), *Final Report of the Women's Experiences in College Engineering Project*, Cambridge: Goodman Research Group.

Grandy, J. (1998), 'Persistence in science of high-ability minority students: results of a longitudinal study', *Journal of Higher Education*, **69**(6), 589–620.

Guillaume, D. (2006), Email to J. Jarosz, 11 August.

Henderson, J., Desrochers, D., McDonald, K. and Bland, M. (1994), 'Building the confidence of women engineering students with a new course to increase understanding of physical devices', *Journal of Engineering Education*, **83**(4), 337–42.

Hendley, V. (1997), 'Recruiters hear a "Me, Too!" from community college students', *ASEE PRISM*, April, 21–6.

Higley, K. and Marianno, C. (2001), 'Making engineering education fun', *Journal of Engineering Education*, **90**(1), 105–7.

Hrabowski, F. and Pearson, W. (1993), 'Recruiting and retaining talented African-American males in college science and engineering', *Journal of College Science Teaching*, **22**(4), 234–8.

Hynes, H. (1995), 'No classroom is an island', in S. Rosser (ed.), *Teaching the Majority*, New York: Teachers College Press, pp. 211–19.

Indiana University–Purdue University Indianapolis, Physics Department, Web Physics, retrieved from webphysics.iupui.edu/jitt/what/html.

Jarosz, J. and Busch-Vishniac, I. (2006), 'A topical analysis of mechanical engineering curricula', *Journal of Engineering Education*, **95**(3), 241–8.

Kahle, J. (2002), 'Women in science – where are we now?', in *Women in Science: Opportunities in a Changing Landscape*, proceedings of a national symposium at Bryn Mawr College, 26–27 October 2001, pp. 13–16.

Kolar, R., Muraleetharan, K., Mooney, M. and Vieux, B. (2000), 'Sooner city – design across the curriculum', *Journal of Engineering Education*, **89**(1), 79–87.

Kulacki, F. and Vlachos, E. (1995), 'Downsizing the curriculum: a proposed baccalaureate program and contextual base', *Journal of Engineering Education*, **84**(3), 225–34.

Landis, R. (1994), 'Student development: an alternative to "sink or swim"', in *Proceedings of the 1994 ASEE Annual Conference in Edmonton*, Canada, June 1994.

Lucena, J. (2000), 'Making women and minorities in science and engineering for national purposes in the United States', *Journal of Women and Minorities in Science and Engineering*, **6**(1), 1–31.

Margolis, J. and Fisher, A. (2002), *Unlocking the Clubhouse: Women in Computing*, Cambridge, MA: The MIT Press.

Marshall, J. and Dorward, J. (1997), 'The effect of introducing biographical material on women', *Journal of Women and Minorities in Science and Engineering*, **6**(1), 279–94.

Martin, L. and Ferraro, G. (2000), 'Reaping the bottom line benefits of diversity', July, retrieved from www.centeronline.org/knowledge/article.cfm?=682.

Mattis, M. and Sislin, J. (eds) (2005), *Enhancing the Community College Pathway to Engineering Careers*, Washington, DC: The National Academies Press.

McEneaney, E. and Radeloff, C. (2000), 'Geoscience in social context: an assessment of course impact on attitudes of female undergraduates', *Journal of Women and Minorities in Science and Engineering*, **6**(2), 131–53.

Meade, J. (1993), 'Forging new alliances', *ASEE PRISM*, April, 26–33.

Morell, L., Buxeda, R., Orengo, M. and Sanchez, A. (2001), 'After so much effort: is faculty using cooperative learning in the classroom?', *Journal of Engineering Education*, **90**(3), 357–62.

Nair, I. and Majetich, S. (1995), 'Physics and engineering in the classroom', in S. Rosser (ed.), *Teaching the Majority*, New York: Teachers College Press, pp. 25–42.

Nair, I. (1997), 'Decision making in the classroom', *Journal of Engineering Education*, **86**(4), 349–56.

National Academy of Engineering (2004), *The Engineer of 2020: Visions of Engineering in the New Century*, Washington, DC: The National Academies Press.

National Action Council on Minorities in Engineering (2002), *The State of Minorities in Engineering and Technology*, New York: The NACME Journal.

National Science Foundation (1995), 'Restructuring engineering education: a focus on change', Arlington, VA, retrieved from www.nsf.gov/pubs/stis 1995/ nsf9565. nsf9565.txt.

National Science Foundation (2000), *Women, Minorities and Persons with Disabilities in Science and Engineering*, Arlington, VA: NSF.

National Science Foundation (2002-160), *Historically Black Colleges and Universities Undergraduate Program*, Arlington, VA: NSF.

National Science Foundation (2002-072), *NSF's Tribal Colleges and Universities Program*, Arlington, VA: NSF.

Riley, D. (2003), 'Employing liberative pedagogies in engineering education', *Journal of Women and Minorities in Science and Engineering*, 9(2), 137–58.

Rosser, S. (1990), *Female-friendly Science*, New York: Pergamon Press.

Rosser, S. (1997), *Re-engineering Female Friendly Science*, New York: Teachers College Press.

Rosser, S. and Kelly, B. (1994), 'From hostile exclusion to friendly inclusion', *Journal of Women and Minorities in Science and Engineering*, 1(1), 29–44.

Scheinerman, E. (2003), Email to J. Jarosz, 20 April.

Shuman, L., Besterfield-Sacre, M. and McGourty, J. (2005), 'The ABET "professional skills" – can they be taught? Can they be assessed?', *Journal of Engineering Education*, 94(1), 41–55.

Slaughter, J. (2002), 'Engineering education for the 21st century', Annual Conference of the American Society for Engineering Education in Montreal, Canada, 17 June 2002.

Smith, K., Sheppard, S., Johnson, D. and Johnson, R. (2005), 'Pedagogies of engagement: classroom-based practices', *Journal of Engineering Education*, 94(1), 87–101.

Society of Women Engineers (2006), 'What can we learn from international women in physics?', SWE, 52(1), Winter, 62.

Stewart, A., LaVaque-Manty, D. and Malley, J. (2004), 'Recruiting female faculty members in science and engineering: preliminary evaluation of one intervention model', *Journal of Women and Minorities in Science and Engineering*, 10(4), 361–75.

Swearengen, J., Barnes, S., Coe, S., Reinhardt, C. and Subramanian, K. (2002), 'Globalization and the undergraduate manufacturing engineering curriculum', *Journal of Engineering Education*, 91(2), 255–61.

Tewksbury, B. (1995), 'Connecting the geology of Africa with the prehistoric, historical, political, and economic evolution of the continent as a strategy for teaching introductory geology and attracting minority students to geology', *Journal of Geological Education*, 43(5), 492–6.

Tobias, S. (1990), *They're Not Dumb, They're Different*, Tucson, AZ: Research Corporation.

Tonso, K. (1996), 'The impact of cultural norms on women', *Journal of Engineering Education*, 85(3), 217–25.

Torda, P. (1999), 'An innovation that worked – a useful reminder', *Journal of Engineering Education*, 88(1), 7–9.

Tryggvason, G., Thouless, M., Dutta, D., Ceccio, S. and Tilbury, D. (2001), 'The new mechanical engineering curriculum at the University of Michigan', *Journal of Engineering Education*, 91(3), 437–44.

University of Colorado (n.d.), retrieved from www.colorado.edu/physics.phet.

Urban-Lurain, M. and Weinshank, D. (2001), 'Do non-computer science students need to program?', *Journal of Engineering Education*, 90(4), 535–41.

Walsh, K. (2003), 'The debate over diversity', *ASEE PRISM*, March, 16.
Williams, J. (2000), *Unbending Gender*, New York: Oxford University Press.
Williams, R. (2003), 'Education for the profession formerly known as engineering', *Chronicle of Higher Education*, 24 January, B12–13.
Wills, E. (2005), 'Minority students are making gains in higher education', *Chronicle of Higher Education*, 15 February, retrieved from http://chronicle.com/cgi-bin.
Wulf, W. (2002), 'Diversity in the engineering workforce', in *Women in Science: Opportunities in a Changing Landscape*, proceedings of a national symposium at Bryn Mawr College held on 26–27 October 2001, pp. 17–24.
Zobrist, G. (2003), 'Engineering degrees can be "steppingstones" to other professions', *Today's Engineer*, August, retrieved from www.todaysengineer.org.

12. Undergraduate student support programs

Bevlee A. Watford

INTRODUCTION

This chapter will discuss three different types of student support programs that have been implemented within the College of Engineering at Virginia Tech. Formally targeting women and other underrepresented minority populations, these programs were developed independently, but were based on existing programs at other institutions. It should be noted that specific program operational details may vary from one institution to the next, but the general intent of these types of programs remains consistent. The intent is to aid underrepresented students as they transition from high school to college, providing them with the information and skills they need to become successful students. The programs described in this chapter were developed for women, African-American and Latino students who are underrepresented populations in the College of Engineering.

Initially, this chapter will provide a discussion of why these types of programs are useful. The three primary areas of student development (academic, professional and personal) are presented. Then each support program is presented in enough detail to enable planning and implementation. It is not intended to present here an exhaustive description of all possible types of support programs. Instead, three programs will be discussed in detail: pre-college bridge or transition programs, mentoring programs and residential communities. Both the purpose and operational function of each program is provided. A separate discussion is provided on program advertising, as the activities are similar regardless of type of program. A short discussion of assessment and dissemination activities is also given. In conclusion, a bibliography is provided that includes documents on these and other types of student support programs.

STUDENT SUPPORT ISSUES

The transition for high school students entering college can be difficult. The students must adjust to being away from home, many for the first time. Even those students with parents who have attended an institution of higher education are dealing with a new environment very different than what they have been used to. As a result, many students may not have developed the skills necessary to make a successful transition. What students need is both the tools to be successful and the motivation to use those tools to their own advantage.

There are three primary areas of the students' development that these programs seek to address: personal, academic and professional development. Each of the programs presented in this chapter addresses each of these development areas, albeit in different ways. But the overall goal of each program is to support the student as they work towards earning their degree.

Personal development refers to helping the student to become comfortable within the new environment. Noting how difficult moving can be for anyone, it is particularly important to enable the student to feel 'at home' in this new campus environment. The goal is to enable the student to make the campus and surrounding community their new home, finding activities that they are accustomed to doing. For example, many students will find new hiking trails, or a dance studio to continue with specific activities they enjoy. They should be able to interact within the larger community, making a new place for themselves. It is important for students to learn how to find enjoyment and relaxation within the new environment. Equally important is knowledge of university offices and locations.

Professional development for the student entails making them think about their professional future. During high school, students tend to be focused on earning their entry into the institution of their choice. During college, they need to refocus their attention on their choice of major and career, determining the optimal path for them to get where they want to be. Therefore it is important to expose students to various majors of interest. In fact, many students may use this time to explore alternate majors, careers and pathways. Obtaining a position following commencement requires a set of skills that most students do not yet possess. This is the case for both professional employment and continued educational pursuits. In addition to determining a career path, the student must be given the skills to pursue it successfully.

Finally, many students are not prepared for the academic rigor of a higher education institution. Native intelligence will only take them so far – college can be much more challenging than high school. Students need to learn how to put more time into their academic study than they did previously. Compounding the problem is that, because of their prior academic success, they are either reluctant to, or simply do not know how to, ask for help. While they are knowledgeable regarding numerous technical and non-technical topics, they do not realize or understand that studying is a skill just like any other. There exist specific activities that the student can engage in that will promote their academic success.

For underrepresented students the isolation often experienced by being different can inhibit a student's ability to develop personally, academically and professionally. Therefore student support programs are designed to bring these student groups together, creating a community of students with similar characteristics who are pursuing a common goal (obtaining an STEM degree). Having this type of support group and associated activities has proven to be highly successful at increasing the retention of underrepresented students.

Finally, it should be noted that a student need not be part of an underrepresented group to obtain the benefits of participating in the programs described in this chapter. While these programs have historically been implemented and targeted at underrepresented students in engineering degree programs, they can most certainly be successfully applied to any type of student pursuing any type of degree program. In fact, as a result of the Michigan Supreme Court case, most of these types of programs initially developed for underrepresented students have been 'opened' to the larger group of students, often including financially disadvantaged and first-generation college students.

TRANSITION PROGRAMS

A transition or bridge program will bring the students to campus for a period of time, exposing them to life as a freshman student. It takes place the summer after high school graduation and prior to the students' initial fall enrollment. A bridge program, by definition, is designed to help students bridge the transition from high school to college. The bridge (or transition) program will allow the students to acclimatize to the university environment. The next sections describe the types of personal, professional and academic development activities that can be implemented during bridge (and many other) programs. This is followed by more specific information on the implementation of a bridge program. The program used as an example is the STEP program, a five-week summer bridge program implemented at Virginia Tech. Since its inception in 1995, the student participants in the summer bridge program have exhibited better academic performance and greater retention to degree than a similar group of non-participants.

The overall intent of the transition program is to have the participant experience life as an undergraduate student. They should live in the residence hall, learning how to share space and interact with a larger group of new students. They should have the opportunity to explore the campus and surrounding community, learning about (as examples) transportation systems, stores and recreational activities.

Personal development activities should be both structured and unstructured. For example, a scavenger hunt is a wonderful means of allowing students to explore both the campus and the surrounding environment. The requirement to attend classes and activities located in various campus facilities allows students to learn where these facilities are. It is also useful to bring in guest speakers from various campus offices to learn about available services. This would include such offices as Dean of Students, athletics, healthcare, residential and dining programs and other offices typically located organizationally within student affairs. Students should also learn about financial aid opportunities and regulations. In addition to departmental and college academic offices, the student should be made aware of the locations of various offices around campus. It is important for the student to be aware of the Financial Aid, University Registrar and other offices as they will have some need of them over the next several years. Some campuses provide tours on a regular schedule, and this task can often be facilitated by the admissions or alumni office.

It is worth noting at this point that early in the bridge program, students will need to be helped to make connections. For example, if a student wishes to meet a specific person, they should be provided assistance in setting up the meeting – as much as necessary. But the student must be weaned from having this type of accommodation. Perhaps the first stage would be to show the student how to find what they need through readily available information sources, such as a phone number, and assist them in making contact. But as time progresses, less and less facilitation should be provided. The key is that the students must learn to do for themselves. Higher education may well be the last safety net the student has – the next step is life on their own. It is a responsibility of the institution to provide the student the skills to be successful.

Professional development activities are equally important during this program. Developing a resumé is perhaps the most obvious skill needed. Career services offices, when they exist, provide a wide range of skill development workshops. Topics include dining etiquette, interviewing tips, instruction on how to work a career fair and more. Often there are 'canned' presentations that can be easily presented to the students by a trained professional. If there is no specific career services organization, then individuals should be found who can conduct such activities – using experts is definitely preferred. Students should be exposed to as many of these professional development activities as possible during the bridge program.

Professional development activities should also address investigating various majors and careers. Most faculty are delighted to interact with students and discuss both their own research and other departmental activities. Many departments have a specific person designated to speak with prospective students, and an undergraduate student advisor. Larger departments, colleges and centers often will have regularly scheduled career-oriented information sessions. Size of student group may be a consideration; for example, a facility tour may have a minimum or maximum number of students required. These experiences are best if optional for the student. A minimum number (three to four) may be required, but the students should be allowed to somewhat follow their own interests. Knowledge of special educational opportunities should be required information for all students. This would include cross-disciplinary activities that can enhance the students' undergraduate experience, for example, discussions of double majors or minors, study abroad opportunities, undergraduate research activities, cooperative education and more.

Academic development activities tend to focus on development of skills that will enhance a student's academic success. It is important to give the student instruction on the academic rules and regulations. The typical college or department level academic office will provide information regarding academic policies such as rules for dropping or adding a class, changing majors, important deadlines, grade changes and similar actions. The more information provided, the better. While it is not expected that the student will retain every detail, at least they will know where to go for information.

Often instruction in study skills is provided through the office of health or counseling services. Topics include note taking, test taking, reading comprehension, and general good study techniques including time management and organizational tips. A quick search of the Internet yielded numerous websites with downloadable information on academic skill development. The University of Michigan has an online training manual to provide study group facilitators and participants with practical resources to help strengthen students' academic skills. Academic advisors or related offices can also assist by providing access to services.

It is important to provide access to tutoring assistance during the bridge program. Recall the difficulty that these students often have in asking for academic assistance. The ready availability of tutors and help sessions can make the students more amenable to utilizing these services. They could be encouraged to do their work in the presence of the tutor – again to facilitate discussion and questions. A lounge in the residence hall is an excellent place to have tutors conveniently located with regular hours of availability.

Program Implementation Details

When possible, planning for a summer transition program should begin in the fall semester. There are numerous arrangements that need to fit within the existing institutional calendar, often requiring advance registration. This section is presented as a timeline of activities. While six to nine months for planning is best, this can be done in as little as three months, with an accompanying increase in stress level for the planners.

The dates and deadlines associated with the bridge program must be set in advance for advertising use. It is easiest to start with the desired dates for the camp, and then work backward to the start of planning. When setting the program dates, consideration should be given to both the start date of the fall semester and the general dates for high school graduation. Participants should be notified of acceptance at least two months prior to the start of the program. Allowing one month to apply following notification, and one month to select participants, the desired date to distribute advertising is approximately four months prior to program start.

A limiting factor is that bridge programs are typically restricted to incoming freshman, the Fastrac program at Tuskegee University being one noted exception. Admissions decisions may not be available until after a set date in the spring (typically April). Timely distribution of information requires close communication with the admissions department. They can provide the necessary names and contact information for the targeted pool of students. Another issue is that use of residential and dining facilities must be coordinated with the appropriate campus office. Not surprisingly, competition for summer residential space can be fierce due to other outreach programs (both academic and athletic), orientation, renovations and other general campus activities. Specific bridge program dates require confirmation with the residential programs office.

Preparing documents for printing and mailing also requires a substantial amount of time. Plan a month each for creating the brochure and website contents. Depending on the quantity required and their current workload, printing can take up to two weeks using a campus facility. A sample application is provided in Figure 12.1 (reprinted from www.ceed.vt.edu). Obviously, the application can be tailored to obtain specific desired information, but the general information indicated is very useful. Selection of applicants can be based on whatever criteria desired.

It should be noted that attending the summer bridge program may not be an option for all incoming freshman students. Many students need to

(Please type or print neatly. Incomplete, illegible, or handwritten forms will not be processed).

PERSONAL INFORMATION:

Name _____

Address _____ Street Apt #

City State Zip

Phone# ( ) Cell E-mail

SS# —OR—Student ID #

Date of Birth

Gender: □ Male □ Female

Did you submit a FAFSA form to Virginia Tech's Office of Scholarships and Financial Aid? □ YES □ NO

HIGH SCHOOL INFORMATION:

Name Graduation Date (month/year):

Address:

Class Size: Class Rank:

Current High School GPA

SAT Scores: Verbal Math OR ACT Scores

PARENT OR GUARDIAN INFORMATION:

MOTHER/GUARDIAN INFORMATION: FATHER/GUARDIAN INFORMATION:

Name _____ Name _____

Phone # _____ Phone # _____

Email _____ Email _____

Employment and Job Title _____ Employment and Job Title _____

Level of Education:
Less than High School
High School Diploma
Some College
Associates Degree
Bachelors Degree
Masters Degree or beyond

Level of Education:
□ Less than High School
□ High School Diploma
□ Some College
□ Associates Degree
□ Bachelors Degree
□ Masters Degree or beyond

LEVEL OF COMBINED PARENTAL/GUARDIAN INCOME:
☐ $0 – $40,000 ☐ $40,001 – $60,000 ☐ $60,001 – $80,000 ☐ $80,001 – $100,000 ☐ $100,000 +

SIBLING INFORMATION

Number of brothers or sisters: _____

Number of siblings currently enrolled in college: _____

LEADERSHIP/ACADEMIC ACHIEVEMENTS

On a separate sheet(s) of paper, please print or type answers to the following.

1) Please list any academic organizations, clubs, and awards. Also include other activities such as athletics, leadership positions, community service, church activities, etc. in which you have participated.

2) Everyone has strengths and weaknesses as a person. What are strong points about your character? What would you say are areas needing improvement? (no more than 300 words)

It is fully understood that in submitting this application to the Student Transition Engineering Program that I,

_____ , *hereby give the STEP program permission to use data from the program (surveys, photos, etc.) for*

funding, academic publications, and other such reports.

_____ , *agree to participate for the full duration of the five week program.*

Printed Applicant Name: _____

Applicant Signature: _____

Parent/Guardian Signature: _____

Date: _____

SEND APPLICATION TO:

STEP '06
215 Hancock Hall (0275)
Virginia Tech
Blacksburg, VA 24061

(DEADLINE FOR APPLICATIONS IS APRIL 17, 2006)

Virginia Tech does not discriminate against employees, students, or applicants on the basis of race, color, sex, sexual orientation, disability, age, veteran status, national origin, religion, or political affiliation. Anyone having questions concerning discrimination or accessibility should contact the Office of Equal Opportunity.

(540) 231-7500 (voice)

Figure 12.1   Application for summer bridge program

work to support their higher education enrollment. This being the 'last' summer with family, many students have vacation and other personal commitments. Therefore a waitlist of applicants is useful to ensure the full number of desired participants. The length and timing of the program can also impact the number of potential participants. It is strongly recommended that students attend the entire program – not arriving late or leaving early. There are often frequent requests for absence from this five-week bridge program. This includes everything from vacations to family reunions to weddings. It is the policy of this program not to allow attendance exceptions. This is not the only policy available, and this is mentioned only to emphasize that a policy is necessary.

Selected participants should be required to submit proof of medical coverage. A medical information form, such as shown in Figure 12.2, should be obtained and kept in a secure location. Copies of the medical form can be sent to the health center and given to program staff. Should a student require medical treatment, their form must be shown to the healthcare provider; hence the desire to have copies readily available. Students enrolled in for-credit courses typically have health coverage included as part of the school's fee structure.

Schedule of Activities

The length of the bridge program will determine the number of different activities that can be included. A program lasting less than one week would tend to focus on gaining campus familiarity, and learning the location of sources of academic and personal assistance. The emphasis would be on those things that the student will need to know with the start of the academic year. An introduction to campus resources, people and places is an efficient use of limited time. Obviously the program cost will decrease in direct correlation to the length of the program. A week or several days can be extremely beneficial to the student and can be implemented with a minimum room and board cost – which can be passed along to the student. All staff could be volunteer, including instructors, certainly not an ideal situation and potentially difficult to arrange.

A longer program can incorporate activities such as academic instruction, focusing on one or several subjects. As mentioned earlier, the students can be required to enroll as summer students, earning credits that may be used toward graduation. As time allows, additional activities may be scheduled. Care should be taken so as to not overwhelm the student, leaving plenty of time for personal needs and academic work.

Figure 12.3 depicts an example of a weekly schedule. There is a time set aside for weekly academic and professional development activities.

Additional activities may also be scheduled. Examples include etiquette dinners where students learn the basics of dining etiquette, leadership development workshops and recreational activities such as a visit to a local amusement park. Weekly advising meetings are part of this larger program. It was found that if not presented with an opportunity to discuss academic performance, the student would let things go until chances of recovery were minimal.

In this particular program, in order to keep the class size to a minimum, four different schedules were developed for the ~80 participants. The students were placed in groups of 20 and assigned a schedule. The decision as to what subjects to include in the bridge program should consider the subjects that the students have the most difficulty with during their first semester of enrollment. It should also take into account the varying level of academic preparedness that may be evident among the participants. As an example, initially students were randomly assigned to groups without any regard for their math preparedness. As a result, there were classes where some students were not challenged. To remedy this, it was decided to use a placement test to separate the students into similar cohorts.

Camp Implementation

Prior to their arrival, each student participant is sent a rule book detailing the various rules, regulations and things to know about the summer program. Due to its size (nine pages) it will not be reproduced here. Instead, the following list of topics shows what is included:

- Checking in and out: details about time and place
- Official meetings: letting the student know when and where they need to be
- Classes: locations, times, schedule of events
- Activities: special events, recreational activities
- Meals: when and where meals are provided
- Dormitory: rules about the residence halls, curfews, access
- Clothing: what to bring, particularly if special events are planned
- Transportation: use of student vehicles, local transportation around campus and town
- Telephones and mail: use and accessibility
- Medical facilities: access, location
- Miscellaneous information.

Initially developed many years ago, this document is being continually updated as new issues arise. A document of this type is very valuable as it

MEDICAL FORM

PLEASE PRINT: Complete all information where applicable and attach a copy of your insurance card.
Name of Special Event/Group Attending: STEP Summer Bridge Program

Participant's Name: _____
                        Last   First   Middle

Address: _____

Social Security # or Student ID # _____ Date of Birth _____ Male ☐ Female ☐

Full Name of Parent/Guardian: _____

Home Telephone: (_____) _____ Business Phone (_____) _____

If not available in an emergency, notify:
Name _____
Address _____
Telephone _____
Relationship to student _____

MEDICAL HISTORY

(To be completed by Parents or Yourself)

Is there a known history of: Yes   No

A.   Birth deformities (one eye, one kidney, etc.)   ____   ____
B.   Medical conditions currently under treatment   ____   ____
C.   Pre-existing injury currently under treatment   ____   ____
D.   Fractures or other disability type injuries   ____   ____
E.   Allergy (drugs, food, asthma, etc.)   ____   ____

F. Mental disorder or convulsions   ___
G. Known past illness of more than one week duration   ___
H. Contact lenses or glasses   ___
I. Date of last tetanus shot   ___ / ___ / ___

EXPLAIN ABOVE QUESTIONS ANSWERED 'YES'

I hereby state that the STEP program is not responsible for any pre-existing injury or recurrence of any pre-existing undisclosed injury or illness of the above participant prior to the first day the participant registers, and STEP will assume responsibility only for injuries or illness incurred while the above participant is participating in the program under supervision during enrolled program period. In signing this form, I understand that the insurance provided is a limited amount of coverage and is not meant to be comprehensive and that any expenses over the limit are my responsibility.

_____   _____
Signature of Parent/Guardian   Date

PARENTAL PERMISSION

The law requires that parental permission be obtained for operative procedures on minors. The parent should sign the following consent form so that such procedures may be promptly carried out and no unnecessary delays will occur with operative procedures. However, no operation will be performed, except emergency, without parents being contacted and fully informed.

I give my permission for such diagnostic, therapeutic, and operative procedures as may be deemed necessary for my son/daughter.

Signed _____   _____   _____
                          Date   Relationship

Figure 12.2 Medical coverage form for bridge program

Group A Schedule					
	Monday	Tuesday	Wednesday	Thursday	Friday
8:00 AM	Chem Lecture Davidson 3	Chem Lecture Davidson 3	Section 1 and 2 Chem Lab 213 and 217 ChemP	Chem Lecture Davidson 3	Chem Lecture Davidson 3
8:15 AM					
8:30 AM					
8:45 AM					
9:00 AM					
9:15 AM					
9:30 AM					
9:45 AM	Math Whit 277	Math Whit 277	Section 3 and 4 Chem Lab 213 and 217 ChemP	Math Whit 277	Math Whit 277
10:00 AM					
10:15 AM					
10:30 AM					
10:45 AM					
11:00 AM					
11:15 AM					
11:30 AM					
11:45 AM					
12:00 PM					
12:15 PM					
12:30 PM	lunch	lunch	lunch	lunch	lunch
12:45 PM					
1:00 PM					
1:15 PM					
1:30 PM					
1:45 PM					
2:00 PM	ENGE Randolph 212	Academic Analysis	ENGE Randolph 212	Academic Analysis	Seminar
2:15 PM					
2:30 PM					
2:45 PM					
3:00 PM					
3:15 PM					
3:30 PM					
3:45 PM					

Figure 12.3   Weekly schedule for summer bridge program

not only helps the student prepare for the experience; it also provides the ground rules for behavior. In addition to the rules and regulations, a release form should be used to allow future use of pictures and quotes from the participants.

Welcoming the families when they arrive is extremely important, for several reasons. For many students, this will be their first extended stay away from home, and both students and parents will have some natural concern. It is important that the first impression provided be one of competence, control and friendliness. Volunteer undergraduate students can be used to assist with the move in – this is something greatly appreciated as it provides both assistance with moving possessions and the opportunity to speak with current students about various issues. It is also useful to give an organized welcome for the parents. As arrivals will tend to be spread throughout the allowed arrival times, it is useful to provide multiple sessions. This way parents can take a break from unpacking, attend the short, 15-minute session and continue with their day. These sessions take the form of an introduction and question–answer session. Parents are extremely grateful for the interaction.

Some bridge programs (Georgia Tech being one example) have a more involved parent orientation, designed to give the parents a taste of what their student will be experiencing. This may require parents to stay overnight and attend guided sessions with program staff. Particularly for parents who have not attended a college or university, this can be a useful activity. Activities can include both students and parents and/or be conducted separately.

The first day of the bridge program is typically an orientation day for the students. A general meeting allowing for introduction of each participant and program staff is recommended. This is also the time to discuss rules, schedules and other pertinent information. A tour of the campus, with a focus on the locations of activities for the next day, is helpful to students. In general, having a specific activity that first evening ensures that students can become familiar and comfortable with each other and no one is sitting off to the side by themselves. Homesickness is always an issue and care should be taken to identify those students who are experiencing difficulty in adjusting to being away from home.

Likewise, a closing ceremony is recommended at the end of the transition program. Parents can be invited to attend and student academic achievement can be recognized. In one instance, the students created a slide show depicting activities that occurred throughout the program – this was then distributed to all students as a memento of the summer program. Group pictures can also be taken at this time. A lunchtime ceremony is particularly useful in that it requires the students to be checked out of the residence hall, gives parents time to arrive that morning and still allows for an early afternoon departure.

Financial Considerations

The key is determining the per student cost of the bridge program. Figure 12.4 lists costs associated with a five-week residential bridge

COSTS	Unit cost ($)	Total cost ($)
Room (per day, includes 4.5% tax)		
Participants (35 students)	19.00	22 610
Counselors	24.00	1 938
Board (per day, includes 4.5%tax)		
Participants (35 students)	20.65	24 574
Counselors	20.65	2 106
Telephones (1 per room)	81.00	1 701
Textbooks	300.00	10 500
Supplies	40.00	1 400
Insurance (per day)	0.47	16
Closing banquet	7.80	273
Personnel costs		
Program staff		15 000
Dorm counselors (3)		3 000
Instructional staff		23 000
Graduate assistants		7 540
Administrative support		5 000
Fringe benefits		
Faculty		1 379
Staff		1 150
General administration		
Materials/supplies		1 000
Printing/copying		1 500
Postage		500
Scholarships	150.00	5 250
T-shirts		450
TOTAL COST		129 887

Figure 12.4   Budget for summer bridge program

program for 35 students. Room and board are substantial costs. An institution may have different rates for summer usage, depending on the timing and type of the event. If the students are enrolled for credit they may have to pay tuition as well as a different room and board rate when compared to a summer outreach program. For situations when on-campus housing is not available, a contract can be negotiated with local apartment complexes or lodging establishments. This is not a preferred option. If possible, residential advisors should be housed as singles and the student participants in double rooms.

Some costs are optional. Telephones and Internet access may have a cost. Sometimes there is a charge for linens and cleaning services for common areas. General insurance is typically required for all students; this can be discussed with an office of risk assessment. Note the limitations in amount and cost of coverage as this information needs to be communicated with parents and guardians.

Textbooks and other academic supplies may be provided to the student at some cost. It can be beneficial to have the students purchase and utilize texts that are required for fall semester classes. If the students are enrolled in a course for credit, then there may be a required textbook. If supplies are not provided, then the student must be given a list of what they need to bring (somewhat like a pre-college class supply list). Any type of opening or closing activity should be included in the budget, but are obviously optional.

The class size is a consideration and should be kept within the limits of normal class sizes. Therefore, as the numbers of students grows, consideration must be given to use of multiple instructors for the same subject. Faculty are often the most expensive option for instructor positions. Graduate students can be recommended by their department and provide a high level of service at substantially less cost. The hope is to provide the students with an experience as close to the actual fall semester enrollment as possible. Exposure to actual faculty is the best option.

While other staff associated with this program are often on 12-month appointments, their costs should also be included in the budget. Real dollars are being paid for these positions and should be accounted for. Required fringe benefits should also be included. General administration costs include brochure development and printing, mailing costs, printing and copying costs, and other miscellaneous expenses.

A decision should be made as to whether or not to charge the student participants and how much. As these are incoming students, financial aid information is often available. Despite the benefits of attending the transition program, many students cannot afford the total cost. Charging a fee can make the program appear more meaningful to potential applicants, making them look at this opportunity more seriously. The availability of scholarships is a simple means of enabling those with less financial means to attend. Scholarships may also be provided for the fall semester based on performance during the bridge program.

MENTORING PROGRAMS

A mentoring program for first-year students can be invaluable in helping them become acclimatized to the university community. Mentoring occurs when a person who has successfully negotiated a particular area shares his or her knowledge and experience to assist others who are going through a similar process. Mentors help first-year students by serving as resources for academic issues, assisting in developing skills, and acting as a sounding board for new thoughts and ideas. Particularly for underrepresented students in STEM fields, it is important for them to be connected with other students who are like them, to help counteract potential feelings of isolation within the larger university community.

Choosing Mentors

The specific activities associated with the mentoring program will depend on the type of mentor provided. For freshman students, mentors can be upper-class students, graduate students, faculty, staff or industry representatives. There are certain advantages and disadvantages associated with use of each different type and level of mentor. Table 12.1 provides a sample list of topics that can be addressed between the freshman student and their mentor. It is obvious that certain topics are more easily addressed by a certain type of mentor. This does not preclude discussion of other topics – it is just intuitively clear that a current undergraduate student would be much more familiar with topics such as access to campus services, something an industry mentor would typically not have knowledge of. Similarly,

Table 12.1   List of mentoring topics

• Dropping and adding classes	• Interacting with instructors and advisors
• Class schedules	
• Opportunities	• Emergency services
– Study abroad	– Physical and mental health
– Undergraduate research	– Sexual assault awareness
• Student clubs and organizations	• Career advice
• Campus activities	• Graduate school opportunities
• Local activities	• Skills related to a job search
– Shopping	– Interviewing
– Transportation	– On-site visits
– Religious organizations	• Undergraduate student opportunities
• Study skills	– Study abroad
• Time management	– Research

a graduate student mentor could more readily discuss issues related to pursuit of a graduate degree. The following paragraphs discuss the benefits of each different type of mentor.

The positive influence of peer pressure can be harnessed through the use of upper-class student mentors. There is truth in the concept that students will listen to their peers more than to adults. The undergraduate student mentor has the advantage of having recently gone through what the student will be experiencing, giving the mentor enhanced credibility in the eyes of the student. The mentor can discuss experiences they had as a freshman, lessons learned and insights obtained.

Also of value is the fact that the mentor is currently a student. They have learned how to navigate and successfully progress through the university community, and can provide the necessary student perspective. One example would be student access to university systems. Typically the interaction between the student and the university is not the same as that afforded to faculty and staff. As an example, student access to a system to add and drop courses may not be the same as that given to advisors. The upper-class mentor is not only familiar with student systems, but is still using them. They can provide an insider perspective on how to be a successful student.

Use of graduate students as mentors can result in significant differences when compared to using an undergraduate student. While still operating within the university environment, the graduate student has moved beyond undergraduate student life. The advantage is that the student has a mentor who has successfully completed a baccalaureate degree, yet is not too far removed from life as an undergraduate. It is certainly an advantage if the graduate student earned their undergraduate degree at the current institution rather than from another school. Again, this lends greater credibility to the mentor. Another advantage is the fact that the mentor can address issues related to pursuing graduate education. They can discuss the decision process they used when considering graduate education, and general life as a graduate student. Again, the relationship is more peer-oriented, which will contribute to the success of the mentoring relationship. Another advantage that applies to both graduate and undergraduate mentors is the flexibility of their schedules, facilitating meetings between mentor and mentee.

Faculty and staff mentoring are distinctly different from peer-oriented mentoring. While faculty may be able to address many of the student life issues for the mentee, their position as an authority figure within the university requires additional consideration when developing a relationship with the student. The faculty mentor should remember that the student has an academic advisor; therefore that is not the role they should assume. In fact, for all mentoring relationships, effort must be made to utilize the existing structure and information sources within the university. A mentor's role should be to provide information and access to existing resources. This includes referrals to academic advisors, career and other university services.

Faculty mentors can be invaluable in helping the student to navigate through academic development issues. Establishing a relationship with a faculty member can assist the student in developing relationships with their instructional faculty, making it easier for them to communicate with their instructors about coursework. Faculty mentors can provide knowledge about academic opportunities such as undergraduate research and study abroad.

The use of industry mentors for students is an excellent means of providing the student access to professional development and career advice. Again, the key is that the student can talk to someone who is working as a professional in a STEM career. Students can obtain first-hand knowledge about the mentor's career path and goals. There are several organizations that specialize in providing industry mentors. MentorNet (www.mentornet.net/) has been providing industry (and faculty) mentors for students since 1997.

The decision as to what type of mentor to provide should consider several issues. Obviously the type of information or experience it is desired to provide to the student would be a primary concern. The availability of mentors and the ease of communication between the student and the mentor should also be investigated. Although electronic communication is generally available, the benefits of face-to-face meetings are real.

Program Implementation Details

The assumption is that a mentoring program will meet the needs of your students. A survey can always be utilized to elicit information about potential participation percentage, type of mentor desired, willingness to commit to participation, and more. Once the need for mentors is established, the first step is to solicit the mentors. The mentoring program described in the following paragraphs is a peer mentoring system, utilizing upper-class undergraduate students as mentors. Figure 12.5 is an example of an email sent to students advertising paid positions as mentors for incoming freshmen. All applicants are required to submit an application, shown in Figure 12.6. General information is requested and essays are required of both first-time and returning mentors.

For this mentoring program which begins in the fall semester, the hiring process takes place during the previous spring semester. Six months is prob-

> Are you interested in being a mentor for new freshmen in the College of Engineering?
>
> The College of Engineering, through a grant from the National Science Foundation, is seeking to expand our mentoring programs for entering freshman students. While AHORA, BEST and WEST have existed for several years, we now have added GUEST – the General Undergraduate Engineering Support Teams.
>
> If you are interested in a paid position as a mentor during the fall 2005 semester with any one of these programs, please see the attached job description and application. Completed applications are due March 1.

Figure 12.5   Email advertising mentoring positions

ably a good lead time, but when to start the mentoring program depends on the needs of the community of students served. This program uses the summer months to facilitate initial contact between the mentor and the incoming freshman or transfer student. As a result all mentors are interviewed and selected during a March–April timeframe.

Selection of mentors is not a task to be addressed without serious thought to the community needs. Generally, mentors should be knowledgeable about the local surroundings and life as a student. They should exhibit a strong desire to mentor and numerous other personality considerations. For this specific program, it is desired to ensure diversity of majors for the mentors, considering the academic degree program the mentor is pursuing. The freshmen are in a general engineering program, so the mentors often provide information on specific programs. Anecdotally, there were two sisters who both served as mentors over a four-year time-span, both of whom were pursuing degrees in mining engineering. As a result, the mining engineering department experienced a surge in the enrollment of female students, moving from 10 % to nearly 25 % female undergraduates.

Careful consideration should be given to conducting interviews, whether as a group or as individuals. The mentors can be very influential in the mentee's life. It is likely that suitable knowledge about interviewing processes can be found on most campuses. This particular program made use of procedures utilized by the university's Residential and Dining Programs staff to hire student resident advisors for the academic year, and conducted group interviews. This decision was made based on the need to hire approximately 80 undergraduate student mentors. With fewer mentors required, individual interviews are more feasible.

The key to spring selection is to be able to complete the hiring process prior to the end of the semester. Notification can be sent out two months prior to the end of the semester. That gives two weeks for applications, two weeks for determination of the interview schedule and a week to interview. Following this, those selected for a position require about one week to accept or decline, leaving about two weeks of the semester to finalize hiring details.

AHORA/BEST/WEST/GUEST TEAM LEADER
APPLICATION INFORMATION
FALL 2005
AHORA (Academic Hispanic Outreach Alliance)
BEST (Black Engineering Support Teams)
WEST (Women in Engineering Support Teams)
GUEST (General Undergraduate Engineering Support Teams)

REQUIREMENTS

- A minimum GPA of 2.5 is required.
- Students must be enrolled in a College of Engineering curriculum at Virginia Tech. Undergraduates must have completed their first year at Virginia Tech and be enrolled in an engineering curriculum by the start of the fall 2005 semester, i.e., GE students will not be considered.
- Students must be enrolled in classes at Virginia Tech during the fall 2005 semester. Undergraduates must be enrolled in a minimum of 12 credit hours.
- Team Leaders must be able to attend a training workshop on Friday, August 19, 2005. This should last approximately 6 hours.
- Team Leaders must be available for regular weekly meetings by registering for ENGR 1004: CEED Team Leader Seminar – Thursdays 2:00 to 2:50pm OR Fridays 9:05 to 9:55am. CRNs will be announced following the interview process.

GENERAL DESCRIPTION OF TEAM LEADER RESPONSIBILITIES

Team Leaders must contact their team members once a week during the fall semester and provide a written report of the contact. The method of contact can vary (i.e., phone or in person).
Team Leaders must contact their team members at least once during the summer, typically by regular mail. Contact information will be provided.

In general, Team Leaders will serve as resources for their teams (approximately 5 first-year engineering students) by providing information that will help them get acclimated to Virginia Tech. Team Leaders serve as sounding boards for various issues that confront first-year students, including what classes to take, how to interact with an advisor, joining professional societies, as well as other concerns that may arise. These students really need people with whom they can communicate and who understand the pressures they face as College of Engineering students. Problems may exist with teachers, roommates, boy/girlfriends, and parents, and they often need someone to talk to, sometimes just to express their thoughts. The Center for the Enhancement of Engineering Diversity will pay for each team to go out to dinner approximately once per month – a social get together for the purpose of relaxation. In addition, Team Leaders will be paid. (Currently, it is expected to be an hourly wage of $7 per hour for approximately 7 hours per week.)

To apply, please complete the enclosed form and attach an essay addressing one of the questions below:

If you have not previously worked as a mentor for this office, you must provide a one page (minimum), double spaced essay addressing the following question: *What personal characteristics do you have that would make you a good mentor?*

Returning mentors must provide a one page (minimum), double spaced essay addressing the following question: *Based on your previous experiences as a mentor and mentee (if applicable), what advice would you give to new mentors in this program?*

AHORA/BEST/WEST/GUEST TEAM LEADER
APPLICATION
FALL 2005
AHORA (Academic Hispanic Outreach Alliance)
BEST (Black Engineering Support Teams)
WEST (Women in Engineering Support Teams)
GUEST (General Undergraduate Engineering Support Teams)

I am applying for a Team Leader position for (please check one):

☐ AHORA   ☐ BEST   ☐ WEST   ☐ GUEST

Please print or type:

Name: _____   Student ID#: _____

Major: _____   GPA: _____

Current address information: Summer address information:

Figure 12.6   Application for a mentor position

Phone: _____ Phone: _____

Email: _____ Email: _____

As of August 22, 2005, my academic level will be (please check one):

☐ Sophomore ☐ Junior ☐ Senior ☐ Graduate Student

ESSAY

If you have not previously worked as a mentor for AHORA, BEST, WEST, or GUEST, you must provide a one page (minimum), double spaced essay addressing the following question:

What personal characteristics do you have that would make you a good mentor?

If you have previously worked as a mentor for AHORA, BEST, WEST, or GUEST, you must provide a one page (minimum), double spaced essay addressing the following question:

Based on your previous experiences as a mentor and mentee (if applicable), what advice would you give to new mentors in this program?

Graduate Students: Please provide the following details about your undergraduate degree*:

Degree and major
GPA
Year degree received

* Current graduate students must have received their undergraduate degree from Virginia Tech.

Please include a copy of your current resume with your application.

Applications are due Monday, March 1, 2005.

Candidates selected for interviews will be contacted via email on March 23, 2005. Initial interviews will be conducted weekdays March 25-31, 2005.

- complete the application
- print it out and sign below
- attach your essay
- attach your resumé
- submit to:

AHORA/BEST/WEST/GUEST
Center for the Enhancement of Engineering Diversity
215 Hancock Hall (0275)
Virginia Tech
Blacksburg, Virginia 24061

_____
Signature   *Date*

Figure 12.6 (continued)

This is a reminder to prepare adequately for the hiring process as specific documents are often required. A total of six weeks is desired from start to finish, not counting any pre-planning time. One disadvantage in this timeline is that plans for undergraduate students often change over the summer. They may obtain other opportunities, such as internships or research positions that conflict with the mentoring responsibilities. Additionally, given that the exact number of student participants or mentees will be determined after the hiring process is complete, the number of actual mentors required may increase or decrease. This latter issue is handled by explaining to the potential mentors that the position is contingent on the availability of students to be mentored. A waitlist of mentors can be created in case more are required.

Mentor training is another activity that requires a great deal of planning. It should be assumed that some training will be required, how much being up to the needs of those selected. Over the past years this program has developed a training manual, far too extensive to include here. Figure 12.7 is an example document used to describe the expectations of the mentors. Figure 12.8 is a typical training schedule suitable for a six-hour training session. The mentor training session is typically held on the Friday prior to the start of classes.

Incoming freshman students receive a brochure describing the mentoring program and inviting them to apply. While many applications are received during the late spring, the majority of the applications are submitted during freshman summer orientation as the program is heavily advertised during the college's orientation meeting. The deadline for applications is the end of July, coinciding with the end of orientation. At that time, the applicants are grouped into teams of four to six freshmen, and a mentor is assigned. The mentors are given contact information for the freshmen, and their first task is to contact them over the summer at home and introduce themselves. This sets the stage for a face-to-face meeting when the freshman arrives on campus. This is a team-based program, with one mentor assigned to several freshmen.

One-on-one mentoring is also an option; however, as this program services approximately 300 students, one-on-one mentoring is not feasible. There are additional benefits to team-based mentoring. It gives each freshman a group of students that they know and can interact with, and that they have much in common with. It helps the students broaden their own community of peers.

Operational Details

The actual structure of the mentoring program will vary depending on the needs and availability of the community. The program described here,

Center for the Enhancement of Engineering Diversity (CEED)
Mentor Training Workshop

MENTORING EXPECTATIONS

Preparing the Blue Print for a Strong First Year

It is very important for any new group that wants to build a solid foundation to share and discuss their mutual expectations. The following is an outline for you to follow for a 'Team Expectations' workshop. You may use this format or adapt it to meet with your needs.

Introduce the topic of Expectations.

It is important that all members of the team understand what the other members are expecting of them. This helps maintain a level of trust and cohesiveness necessary to work as a team for the semester.

It is important that expectations be discussed, written down, and re-examined throughout the semester. Expectations can and do change. It's okay to renegotiate them.

It is important that group members discuss what will happen if one or more members do not live up to the expectations agreed upon by the group.

II.   Ask team members to answer the following questions *individually* on a sheet of paper.

I expect the following things from the members of my team…

I expect the following things from my mentor…

If someone on the team is not meeting my expectations I will…

If I am not meeting the expectations of someone on the team, I expect they will…

Lead the team through a discussion of their expectations of each other and of you. Also share your expectations of them. Use a sheet of newsprint or a chalkboard to record the expectations that are shared so that everyone can see them. You can use the following questions to guide your discussion:

We expect the following things of each other…

We expect the following things from our mentor…

If someone on the team is not meeting our expectations, we agree to…

The mentor expects the following things from us…

At the close of the discussion, tell your team that you will write or type up all of the expectations that were discussed and hand them out at a later date so that everyone has a copy.

V.   If you run out of time, make sure to set aside time to finish it as soon as possible.

Figure 12.7   Expectations of student mentors

as a peer mentoring, team-based program, has several operational requirements. The mentors must contact each mentee weekly; this can be electronic or any other type of communication. The mentor must see each mentee every two weeks. The mentors submit weekly written reports on their team, commenting generally on how things are going. There are also required monthly reports on each individual team member. Each team is allowed to go off campus for dinner once per month (this is paid for by the mentoring program). This gives the teams an opportunity to meet in a relaxed environment away from the pressures of school. The program provides $6.00 per student to eat off campus. This increases to $7.00 per student if more than one mentoring team goes out together. Again, the intent is to broaden the students' knowledge of other, similar engineering students.

```
+-------------------------------------------------------------------+
|                      AHORA/BEST/WEST                              |
|                   Mentor Training Workshop                        |
|                                                                   |
|                   Saturday, August 25, 2001                       |
|                     10:00 am – 2:00 pm                            |
|                    Owens Banquet Room                             |
|                         AGENDA                                    |
|  • Introductions                                                  |
|  • Facts about first-year students                                |
|  • Mentoring                                                      |
|  • Employment expectations                                        |
|      Position description                                         |
|      Personnel guidelines                                         |
|  • Lunch                                                          |
|  • Peer helping                                                   |
|  • Your first team meeting                                        |
|      Expectations of group                                        |
|      Ideas from returning mentors                                 |
|          – picking a place to meet                                |
|          – activities                                             |
|          – possible questions from team members                   |
|  • Employee paperwork                                             |
+-------------------------------------------------------------------+
```

Figure 12.8   Mentor training workshop agenda

The mentors themselves are enrolled in a weekly seminar class. This permits the program director to meet weekly with all of the mentors to discuss issues and convey necessary information. This would include discussions about campus academic deadlines, activities of interest to the students, and any concerns they have. Two meeting times are scheduled, allowing the mentor to attend either. While this has caused some conflict with required classes, very few mentors have not been able to participate in one class or the other. As a result, in addition to being paid for this activity, the mentors also receive one credit of coursework.

One final component of this program is team course clustering. The mentoring team members are enrolled in the same sections of certain classes: calculus, engineering explorations, chemistry and lab. This increases the contact between team members and provides them with identical academic requirements. Furthermore, with underrepresented students, it ensures that they have someone that looks like them in each of these classes, reducing feelings of isolation.

It should be noted that clustering, also known as block scheduling, can be a difficult task, depending on the number of students involved and the scheduling process used by a specific institution. There is also some need for transparency where the student is concerned – they tend to worry when they see changes to their fall semester schedule. So it should be done at the same time that the scheduling process for all students is done. This task should be monitored closely to avoid undesirable class situations, such as a class of all women, or a class with none. Because of the widely differing numbers of women versus African-American and Latino students, this program clusters them differently.

The women are formed into teams based on where they live on campus. This way, they have other team members living close by, if not on the same floor. This is easily accomplished with the 150 or so women (this does not include those living in the residential community described in the next section). For course clustering, these women are simply batched in groups of ten and placed into classes without any formal grouping.

However, with fewer than 40 African-American freshmen in engineering (and similar numbers of Latino students), these students can be scattered all over campus. They are therefore batched into specific courses by mentoring team. With either method, the intent is to reduce the opportunity for any one of these students to be 'the only' in their class.

The mentoring program operates throughout the fall semester. Early on in the program's implementation, a full year of mentoring was provided, but this was discontinued for several reasons. Peer mentoring is designed to help the student become familiar with the institutional environment and learn to navigate their new location and activities. By the spring semester, many of the freshmen have found their niche, made friends and generally settled in. Previous mentees indicated that the mentoring program was no longer needed as they had found their way. While the teams and the mentors frequently got together and communicated informally, the formal structure of the fall semester program was considered intrusive. Financial considerations also influenced the decision to run the program during the fall semester only.

The program officially begins with welcoming receptions during the first week of classes. Many mentors have already met their mentees, visiting them as they moved into their residence hall, inviting them to dinner in the dining facility. However, the reception is the formal start to the program. It allows the teams to meet face to face and learn details about the program. Additionally, these receptions provide a means for the college to welcome the underrepresented students. It is truly wonderful to have a room filled with 150 freshman women engineering students or 100 African-American and Latino students, letting them see that there are actually a large number of students like them pursuing engineering degrees. The dean provides a welcome and the students get to interact with the faculty and staff in attendance. Typically the freshman advisors, the departmental academic advisors, and many department heads attend these receptions. This makes the students feel truly welcome.

Numerous other academic, professional and personal development activities are scheduled for the mentoring program participants. Because this is an activity involving approximately one-third of the freshman class, various engineering student organizations often schedule activities for these students. For example, the Student Engineers' Council schedules a Wing Night (as in buffalo wings) for the participants, a social event to take the pressure off of studying for exams. The teams get together to schedule classes for the next semester, attend seminars and student professional organization meetings. While events such as these enhance the program, it should be recognized that the emphasis of this program is providing a mentoring relationship for the student – someone they can talk to about various issues and concerns, and someone to help them learn how to become a successful and well-adjusted student.

Finally, a social event at the end of the semester brings the program to a close. Mentors often provide 'exam survival kits' and other goody bags to the mentees. Program assessment is achieved utilizing the tools developed and tested by the Assessing Women in Engineering Project, funded by the National Science Foundation (www.engr.psu.edu/awe/default.aspx). The information obtained helps to improve the program's next implementation.

To summarize, this is a list of things to be done.

1. Decide on time frame and other operational details for the mentoring program.
2. Develop advertising materials for mentors and mentees.
3. Advertise and interview mentors; provide mentor training.
4. Advertise the program to the potential student participants.
5. Assign mentors to mentees and provide contact information.

Financial Considerations

The availability of funding to support the mentoring program should also be considered. If mentors are to receive any form of compensation, then this must be arranged. The program described here pays each mentor about $700.00 for one semester. This reflects an average time commitment of approximately seven hours per week. The expectation is that, as a job requirement, there will be a degree of responsibility placed on the mentor that a volunteer activity would not create. Faculty and industry mentors often volunteer their time (which does not rule out compensation). Other costs include creation and distribution of advertising and application materials, and staff time to supervise the program.

RESIDENTIAL COMMUNITIES

One of the logistically easiest support programs to implement is a residential community. Also known as a living–learning community, this is a residential environment where similar students can live together. The simplicity comes from the fact that typically, freshmen are required to live in on-campus residence halls during their first year of school. Thus the primary logistical requirements for the students are handled by the campus housing offices. One caveat – this would seem an ideal support mechanism based on gender as residence halls have typically been male or female and as such do not appear to be exclusionary. It is believed that this would be a difficult program to implement without controversy if it were desired to have a program for African-American or Latino students. Therefore this section describes a female residential community. However, an important component of any student's education is exposure to diverse groups. Therefore every effort should be made to encourage students from underrepresented populations to participate in the residential community.

The mission of the learning communities is to bring together first-year students in a residential environment that provides encouragement and support during their pursuit of undergraduate degrees. This is accomplished by uniting participants' academic and residential lives with special programming throughout the year to teach strategies and skills for academic success, professionalism and personal development. Hypatia – a residential community for freshman women – was initially implemented in 2001. As with the other programs described in this chapter, Hypatia has been able to increase the retention of student participants through structured activities.

The initiation of this program began several years prior to its actual implementation. Surveys of incoming students were conducted to determine their interest in living within a residential community. Once sufficient interest was noted, discussions began with the Residential and Dining Programs office. Their participation and approval of this activity is essential to successful implementation.

Program Implementation Details

At this institution, there are several different residentially based programs (called Theme Housing), and the general advertising is handled by the Residential Programs offices. The applications are electronically submitted, then directed to the appropriate program director.

Basically, the students are invited to reside in one residence hall, in a communal environment. A two-credit course is required for all program participants during the fall semester, and they must continue to pursue an engineering degree in order to remain in the program. In the spring semester, there are various programming activities for the students. These are the only requirements. As this institution requires that all freshmen live on campus, this is an attractive option for many women. Given over 9000 rooms on campus, and perhaps 175 freshman women in engineering, the chances of having more than one female engineering student on any given residence hall floor are fairly small. This program guarantees that not only will their roommate be a female engineering student; they will be surrounded by rooms full of other students just like them.

Operational Details

The application simply requested student name and identification number and a response to an essay question. With few exceptions, most students are accepted. Applications are typically received in keeping with the existing university housing deadline, typically late spring. Selection of participants should be accomplished prior to the start of summer orientation, notifying the students as early as possible. This program has often had students decline the offer for various reasons, so a waitlist is essential. Once the participants have been identified, the housing assignments and fall semester schedules can be determined.

The residentially based program is a naturally self-supportive community. Study groups form but stay fluid, changing members as needs arise. There is always someone doing the same work. This is a relatively natural advantage that male freshman students, numbering approximately 1100, have always had. Clustering (or block scheduling), as described in the mentoring section of this chapter, is also utilized to enhance the feeling of community. A typical freshman schedule is developed for each group of ten residents. It is also important to reserve seats in more advanced classes, depending on the numbers of students who enter the program with advanced placement credits. Students should be informed of the clustering, and schedules should be closely monitored. The students have enough flexibility in selecting their other courses that they typically do not object to the clustering. In some cases, they are afforded benefits that other students do not have. For example, at this institution, many students must take a lab course in the spring as opposed to the fall semester due to limited seating. Participation in this program guarantees the student a seat in the fall lab. So there are additional perks for participation.

During the fall semester most student activities are done through the two-credit course. A syllabus for the course is shown in Figure 12.9. Again, the prominence of the three important developmental areas is evident in the activities. Academic-oriented activities include exposure to the various majors and academic opportunities available to students. The professional development activities begin with resumé writing and preparation for the career fair in late September. Personal development activities include discussions of issues facing women in STEM professions.

WEEK	DATE	AGENDA
		ENGR 1034–96621 Hypatia Fall 2005
		This schedule is tentative and subject to change. We hope during this class you will learn to appreciate the power of flexibility
1	8/22	Introductions and take pictures
	8/25	Academic integrity (Honors System Office) and icebreakers
2	8/29	Resumés
	9/1	Center for Academic Excellence and Enrichment (CAEE)
3	9/5	Study skills/time management/learning styles
	9/8	Service learning center
4	9/12	Engineering presentation with Olga Pierrakos
	9/15	Career services, *How to Prepare for Expo*
5	9/19	Issues in the workplace (gender-specific)
	9/22	Engineering clubs and student activities
6	9/26	Diversity
	9/29	Library information
7	10/3	Stress management/test-taking skills
	10/6	Career services, co-ops/extern and internships
8	10/13	Presentation skills with Professor Michael Alley
9	10/17	Alcohol and other drugs with Matt Stimpson
	10/20	Written communication
10	10/24	Women's health
	10/27	Aaron Barr's presentation and scholarships
11	10/31	Team building and project management
	11/3	Emerging engineers series
12	11/7	Group presentation work
	11/10	Emerging engineers series
13	11/14	MBTI
	11/17	Emerging engineers series
15	11/28	Group presentations
	12/1	Service learning/assessment/wrap-up
16	12/5	Group presentations

Figure 12.9   Syllabusses for residential first-year course

A second-year component was added to the program in fall 2004. Several first-year participants indicated a desire to remain associated with and living within the program. Utilizing an application process, students were permitted to return as second-year residents with specific leadership roles within the community. These second-year students take a one credit course associated with the community and its activities.

There are five standing committees as follows: assessment, recruitment, social, seminar, and academic support. Each second-year student must take a leadership role in one of these committees. Each first-year student is required to participate on at least one committee. The committees submit their annual plan early in the fall semester. For example, the academic support committee was charged with creating a student academic calendar and planning academic support activities each semester. The recruitment committee works to assist the college by participating in various recruiting activities. The seminar committee works with the course for the first-year residents. The social committee plans both social and community service activities. Finally, the assessment committee works with each committee to develop evaluation activities for each scheduled event.

Financial Considerations

The costs associated with implementing a residential program are few, but can be considerable. This program is directed by regular program staff, assisted by a graduate assistant who primarily deals with the second-year students. Additional costs are event-related. Each committee is provided with $250 in operating funds, more may be requested if necessary. Additional costs include advertising and development of the associated materials for both advertising and the courses. It should be noted, however, that this can be a fairly time-consuming program, and the person-hours and costs are not to be ignored.

Advertising

When considering program advertising, it is useful to consider all of the targeted audiences. The potential student participants (and their parents) are one group. These programs should be advertised at any event where potential students are present. Prospective financial supporters are another audience.

Advertising of the student support program may consist of a website, printed brochure and PowerPoint presentation for larger gatherings. Posters may also be useful for college fairs and other exposition-type events. Websites need not be elaborate. In fact consideration should be given to download time for those with slower connections. Digital pictures of students enhance the website, but also require more time to download. Clear links to important areas of information should be provided. Online applications are great for collecting and organizing information. Available survey tools can be utilized to create an acceptable and easy-to-use application. SurveyMonkey (surveymonkey.com) is one such tool. Website creation requires both design and technical skills which can be found in students, staff and faculty.

Printed documents require pictures with very high resolution. As discounts are frequently given for quantity, consider more uses for the printed brochure than just the mailing to prospective freshman applicants. These brochures can be utilized at all recruiting events throughout the year. They can also be given to prospective donors and organizations. A PowerPoint presentation for larger venues is useful. Fifteen minutes is an appropriate length but a five-minute presentation should also be readily available.

College fairs require more specific advertising items. Pictures can be matted and tacked to an appropriate surface, such as Velcro on felt. Posters can be created in PowerPoint and printed – this can be expensive. It is possible to find a departmental plotter that could be used for free or less cost than a commercial vendor. A banner, approximately six feet by three feet, was displayed by one university at a recent exposition. Made of cloth, these banners have vivid colors and are comparable in cost to a table-top display frame.

Finally, emailing contact with the targeted pool of potential applicants is very easy and quickly done. The increase in the numbers of students applying to college online plus the general availability of email makes this an efficient means of advertising to the students.

ASSESSMENT AND DISSEMINATION

It is important to comment on assessment of student support programs. Assessment is necessary to determine effectiveness of activities. It is also useful to have evidence of positive impact when advertising a program. Keep in mind that engineering students, if not all students, often fail to recognize the value and need of these programs, choosing not to participate. It is very useful to be able to show that those that participate experience greater success than those who do not. The sole reason for implementing these programs is to positively enhance the academic, professional and personal lives of the students.

Assessment and evaluation should be planned concurrently with the program planning. Attention should be given to both formative and summative assessment activities. Formative assessment refers to evaluation of the activities leading up to and including program implementation. It provides an opportunity to determine the effectiveness of the process being used to implement the program and the program implementation activities. Summative assessment focuses on the outcomes of the program and determines if the goals of the program have been accomplished. Expertise in assessment should be sought, and is easily found in a university environment.

Dissemination of information on the support program is equally important. Successful activities should be replicated to increase their impact. Being able to provide assessment information demonstrating program successes (and failures) helps other communities as they seek to benefit their students. Conference and journal publications, websites and other electronic documents are useful and helpful to many others.

OTHER SUPPORT PROGRAMS

There are numerous other activities that have been used to support students as they pursue a STEM degree. Undergraduate research activities and experiential learning or internships both serve to strengthen the connection a student has with their major and provide valuable professionally oriented experiences. Tutoring, supplemental instruction and other academic support activities are also useful. A bibliography is provided to show that there is a large amount of research on the effectiveness of various support programs. Anyone seeking to initiate a student support program would be well advised to examine the available literature.

CONCLUSION

This chapter has described the implementation of three different types of student support programs designed to support underrepresented students in a college of engineering, specifically the College of Engineering at Virginia Tech. It should be noted that these types of programs exist at most major engineering colleges, in varying forms and with varying operational details. It is important to design a program to fit within its own operational environment. The intent of these programs will be the same, regardless of the exact implementation details. Additional details regarding these and other Virginia Tech student support programs can be found at www.eng.vt.edu/academics/ceed.php.

Finally it should be noted that these programs are designed to support undergraduate students, and can be implemented for various populations. Historically, these types of activities were designed and implemented to address the isolation of underrepresented students within a majority environment. The intent is to create a community of students that support each other in pursuit of undergraduate degrees. It should be noted that any group of students, regardless of race or sex, can be involved in community building and mutual support.

ACKNOWLEDGEMENTS

The author would like to acknowledge the assistance of the staff of the Center for the Enhancement of Engineering Diversity at Virginia Tech for their assistance in assembling this material. The work of these individuals in implementing and continually improving the existing support programs is invaluable. Thanks go out to Cory Brozina, Sandra Griffith, Whitney

Edmister, Amanda Martin, Brad Matanin, Matt Stimpson and Tremayne Waller. Additionally, the author would like to acknowledge two professional organizations: the National Association of Multicultural Program Administrators (NAMEPA) and the Women in Engineering Programs and advocates Network (WEPAN). It was through initial involvement with these organizations and the knowledge gained that facilitated development of the programs described here.

BIBLIOGRAPHY

Bridge Programs

Anderson-Rowland, M.R., M.A. Reyes and M.A. McCartney (1997), 'Engineering recruitment and retention: a success', Frontiers in Education Conference.

Bottomley, L.J., S. Hajala and R. Porfer (1999), 'Women in engineering at North Carolina State University: an effort in recruitment, retention, and encouragement', ASEE/ISSS Frontiers in Education Conference, 10–13 November.

Boudria, T.J. (2002), 'Implementing a project-based technology program for high school women', *Community College Journal of Research and Practice*, **26**, 709–22.

Fletcher, S.L., D.C. Newell, M.R. Anderson-Rowland and L.D. Newton (2001), 'The women in applied science and engineering summer female engineering students bridge program: easing the transition for first-time', ASEE/IEEE Frontiers in Engineering Conference, 10–13 October 2001, Reno, NV.

Fletcher, S.L., D.C. Newell, M.R. Anderson-Rowland and L.D. Newton (2001), 'The WISE summer bridge program: assessing student attrition, retention and program effectiveness', ASEE Annual Conference and Exposition.

Kane, M.A., C. Beals, E.J. Valeau and M.J. Johnson (2004), 'Fostering success among traditionally underrepresented student groups: Hartnell college's approach to implementation of the math, engineering, and science achievement (MESA) program', *Community College Journal of Research and Practice*, **28**, 17–26.

Ohland, M.W. and E.R. Crockett (2002), 'Creating a catalog and meta-analysis of freshman programs for engineering students: Part 1: Summer bridge programs', proceedings of the ASEE Annual Conference and Exposition.

Zywno, M.S., K.A. Gilbride and N. Gudz (2000), 'Innovative outreach programmes to attract and retain women in undergraduate engineering programmes', *Global Journal of Engineering Education*, **4**(3), 293–302.

Internships

Callanan, G. and C. Benzing (2004), 'Assessing the role of internships in the career-oriented employment of graduating college students', *Education and Training*, **46**(2), 82–9.

Gault, J., J. Redington and T. Schlager (2000), 'Undergraduate business internships and career success: are they related?', *Journal of Marketing Education*, **22**(1), 45–53.

Johnston, S., E. Taylor and A. Chappel (2001), 'UTS engineering internships: a model for active work place learning', International Conference on Engineering Education, 6–10 August 2001.

Knemeyer, A.M. and P.R. Murphy (2002), 'Logistics internships: employer and student perspectives', *International Journal of Physical Distribution and Logistics Management*, **32**(2), 135–52.

Rompelman, O. and J. Devries (2002), 'Practical training in engineering education: educational goals and assessment', *European Journal of Engineering Education*, **27**(2), 173–80.

Mentoring

Gives, J.E., Y. Zepeda and J.K. Gwathmey (2005), 'Mentoring in a post-affirmative action world', *Journal of Special Issues*, **61**(3), 449–79.

Jacobi, M. (1991), 'Mentoring and undergraduate academic success: a literature review', *Review of Educational Research*, **61**(4), 505–32.

Kasprisin, C.A., P.B. Single, R.M. Single and C.B. Muller (2003), 'Building a better bridge: testing e-training to improve e-mentoring programmes in higher education', *Mentoring and Tutoring*, **11**(1), 67–78.

Kram, K.E. and L.A. Isabella (1985), 'Mentoring alternatives: the role of peer relationships in career development', *The Academy of Management Journal*, **28**(1), 110–32.

Tang, S.Y.F. and P.L. Choi (2005), 'Connecting theory and practice in mentor preparation: mentoring for the improvement of teaching and learning', *Mentoring and Tutoring*, **13**(3), 383–401.

Residential Programs

Anderson-Rowland, M. (1998), 'Using a roommate preference survey for students living on an engineering dorm floor', FIE Conference, pp. 500–504.

Heller, R.S. and C.D. Martin (1994), 'Attracting young minority women to engineering and science: necessary characteristics for exemplary programs', *IEEE transactions on Education*, **37**(1), 8–12.

Knapp, D. and G.M. Benton (2006), 'Episodic and semantic memories of a residential environmental education program', *Environmental Education Research*, **12**(2), 165–77.

Reyes, M.A., M.A. McCartney and M.R. Anderson-Rowland 'Transferring the knowledge in a bridge program: engineering students become coaches'.

Wilcox, P., S. Winn and M. Fyvie Gauld 'It was nothing to do with the university, it was just the people: the role of social support in the first-year experience of higher education', *Studies in Higher Education*, **30**(6), 707–22.

Undergraduate Research

Freeman, R.W. (2000), 'Undergraduate research as a retention tool', ASEE/IEEE Frontiers in Education Conference, 18–21 October 2000, Kansas City, MO.

Gates, A.Q., P.J. Teller, A. Bernat and N. Delgado (1998), 'Meeting the challenge of expanding participation in the undergraduate research experience', ASEE/IEEE Frontiers in Education Conference, 4–7 November 1998, Tempe, AZ.

Healey, M. (2005), 'Linking research and teaching to benefit student learning', *Journal of Geography in Higher Education*, **29**(2), 183–201.

Jimenez, M., R. Palomera and M. Toledo (2002), 'Undergraduate research and co-op education: a winning combination', ASEE/IEEE Frontiers in Education Conference, 6–9 November 2002, Boston, MA.

Lopatto, D. (2004), 'Survey of undergraduate research experiences (SURE): first findings', *Cell Biology Education*, (3), 270–77.

Miscellaneous

Chickering, A.W. and Z.F. Gamson (1999), 'Development and adaptations of the seven principles for good practice in undergraduate education', *New Directions for Teaching and Learning*, **80**, 75–82.

Madill, H.M., A.L. Ciccocioppo, L.L. Stewin, M.A. Armour and T.C. Montgomerie (2004), 'The potential to develop a career in science: young women's issues and their implications for careers guidance initiatives', *International Journal for the Advancement of Counseling*, **26**(1), 1–19.

Pascarella, E.T., P.T. Terenzini and L.M. Wolfle (1986), 'Orientation to college and freshman year persistence/withdrawal decisions', *The Journal of Higher Education*, **57**(2), 155–75.

Vera, C., J. Felez, J.A. Cobos, M.J. Sanchez-Naranjo and G. Pinto (2006), 'Experiences in education innovation: developing tools in support of active learning', *European Journal of Engineering Education*, **31**(2), 227–36.

Wintre, M.G. and M. Yaffe (2000), 'First-year students' adjustment to university life as a function of relationships with parents', *Journal of Adolescent Research*, **15**(1), 9–37.

PART V

Improving the professional experience

13. The representation and experience of women faculty in STEM fields

Xiangfen Liang and Diana Bilimoria

The overall proportion of women in science, technology, engineering and mathematics (STEM) occupations has grown over time, but has consistently remained low. Women constituted 12 percent of STEM occupations in 1980 and 25 percent in 2000, with a growth of only 3 percentage points between 1990 and 2000 (National Science Foundation, 2006a, chap. 3). In 2003, women earned 38 percent of science and engineering (S&E) degrees and 58 percent of non-S&E doctoral degrees, up from 8 percent and 18 percent respectively in 1966 (National Science Foundation, 2006b, Figure F-1). What are the implications of these overall numbers regarding the representation of women faculty in STEM fields in academic settings? What do we know about the everyday experiences of women faculty within STEM departments in universities? What concerted actions can be undertaken to address the issues of representation and experiences of women faculty, which would substantially transform academic institutions and enhance the recruitment, advancement and retention of women faculty in STEM disciplines? We address these and other related questions in this chapter, employing research findings drawn from multiple sources to illustrate women's representation and experiences in STEM fields.

In the following sections, we first provide an overview of the representation of women faculty in academic STEM. Next we discuss general findings about the everyday experiences reported by women faculty across STEM disciplines, particularly in research universities. Finally, we provide remedies and solutions to overcome the challenges and barriers faced by women faculty in STEM, drawn from activities and practices undertaken by the National Science Foundation's (NSF's) ADVANCE Institutional Transformation awardees across the USA.

THE REPRESENTATION OF WOMEN STUDENTS GRADUATING IN STEM FIELDS

The continuing dearth of women faculty can be traced in part to relatively small numbers of women students graduating in STEM fields and the great variations in major. According to Science and Engineering Indicators 2006 (National Science Foundation, 2006a, chap. 2), women earned more than half of all bachelor's degrees and S&E bachelor's degrees in 2002, with major variations among fields. Women earned more than half of the bachelor's degrees awarded in psychology (78 percent), biological/agricultural sciences (59 percent), and social sciences (55 percent), and almost half (47 percent) in mathematics. However, women received only 21 percent of bachelor's degrees awarded in engineering, 27 percent in computer sciences, and 43 percent in physical sciences.

While the number of women enrolling in S&E graduate programs has continued to increase over the past two decades except for a decline in computer sciences in 2003 (National Science Foundation, 2006a, chap. 2), in 2003 women received doctorate degrees ranging from 10.3 percent in mechanical engineering to 68.9 percent in the social science of area and ethnic studies (National Science Foundation, 2006b, Table F-2). In particular, the number of women receiving engineering degrees has remained flat at all degree levels, with just over 20 percent of bachelor's degrees, 21 percent of master's degrees, and slightly fewer than 18 percent of doctoral degrees. There has been little change in the percentage of women awarded doctoral degrees in engineering over the past five years (Gibbons, 2004), ranging from 17.9 percent in 1999, 15.9 percent in 2000, 16.9 percent in 2001, 17.4 percent in 2002, to 17.4 percent in 2003. Even within engineering, large variance is observable by field: the percentage of doctoral degrees awarded to women varies from 9.6 percent in computer engineering to 29.8 percent in biomedical engineering (Gibbons, 2004).

According to the 2004 annual report of Mathematical Sciences (Kirkman et al., 2005), while the total number of full-time graduate students in doctoral-granting departments was 10,707 in 2004, reaching its peak during the period 1995–2004, the number of female full-time graduate students in doctoral-granting departments was 3245 (about 30 percent). In a longitudinal analysis of graduate students in doctoral-granting departments in mathematics, the number of female full-time graduate students increased from 2691 in 1997 to 3245 in 2004, an increase of 21 percent, which is slightly above the total increase of 19 percent in number of full-time graduate students over the same period (i.e. from 9002 in 1997 to 10,707 in 2004). In a recent comparison, the number of female full-time graduate students in doctoral-granting departments or programs of statistics, biostatistics and biometrics decreased marginally from 2203 in 2003 to 2144 in 2004, a 3 percent decrease.

In brief, the number of female students and PhD recipients in STEM fields has been increasing in recent years. However, as the numbers presented in the next section show, these increases do not reflect corresponding increases in the number of female faculty in STEM areas, prompting many to refer to this phenomenon as a 'leaky pipeline' of faculty in these fields, which may result in even smaller proportions of female faculty members. Next, we take a close look at the representation of women faculty in STEM fields.

THE REPRESENTATION OF WOMEN FACULTY IN STEM FIELDS

The good news is that the number of women with S&E doctorates in academia increased more than sevenfold between 1973 and 2003, from 10,700 to an estimated 78,500, raising their share from 9 percent to 30 percent (National Science Foundation, 2006a, chap. 5), while the share of full-time faculty in S&E declined from 87 percent in the early 1970s to 75 percent in 2003 (National Science Foundation, 2006a, chap. 5, Figure 5–19). Other full-time positions in S&E rose to 14 percent of the total, and postdoctoral and part-time appointments stood at 6 percent and 5 percent, respectively (National Science Foundation, 2006a, chap. 5.

The proportion of women faculty in engineering has gradually increased from 8.9 percent to 10.4 percent of total tenured and tenure-track faculty from 2001 to 2004 (Gibbons, 2004). However, by rank, women faculty in tenured or in tenure-track engineering positions hold only 5.8 percent of full professorships, 12.4 percent of associate professorships, and 17.9 percent of assistant professorships (Gibbons, 2004). By field, the percentage of women faculty tenured or in tenure track varied from 3 percent in mining engineering to 23.1 percent in architectural engineering (Gibbons, 2004).

Academic chemistry exhibits very similar patterns of the underrepresentation of women faculty, even though relatively more women complete doctoral degrees in chemistry. In 2003–2004, women held only 12 percent of all tenure-track faculty positions and only 21 percent of assistant professor positions at the top 50 chemistry departments (Kuck et al., 2004). The American Chemical Society reported that the percentages of full-time, female, doctorate faculty members at PhD-granting universities, masters-granting institutions, baccalaureate institutions, and two-year colleges were 13, 20, 26 and 32 percent, respectively (Kuck et al., 2004, p. 356).

The estimated total number of full-time faculty in mathematical sciences for 2004–2005 was 20,224, of which 5302 (26 percent) were females (Kirkman et al., 2005). The number of females as a percentage of full-time faculty varied considerably among the groups in 2004, from 12 percent for doctoral-granting departments in private institutions to 32 percent for masters-granting departments. In fall 2004, the percentage of women in mathematical sciences was generally higher in statistics (26 percent) than in the doctoral mathematics groups (18 percent). Similarly, the percentage of tenured women faculty was highest in departments granting either a master or a baccalaureate degree only (21 percent), and lowest in doctoral-granting departments (9 percent). Women in mathematical sciences accounted for 52 percent of non-doctoral full-time faculty, and 4 percent of the part-time faculty in 2004. After reviewing data over the period 1998–2004, it is evident that the percentage of tenured/tenure-track women faculty in mathematical sciences has remained relatively stable over the seven years (see Table 1D in Kirkman et al., 2005).

Among S&E doctorate holders with academic faculty positions in four-year colleges and universities, females are less likely than males to be found in the full professor positions and are more likely to be assistant professors (National Science Foundation, 2001b, Table H-21). Taking a closer look at Table H-21 (National Science Foundation, 2001b), we found that women S&E faculty account for only 11 percent of full professor positions, 22 percent of associate professor positions, and 36 percent of assistant professor positions. This is consistent with findings from Nelson (2005), who examined the percentage of male and female tenured and tenure-track faculty in several disciplines, including S&E, at the top 50 US educational institutions, based on research expenditures: few female full professors in S&E with the percentage of women among full professors ranging from 3 percent to 15 percent. Nelson (2005) also noted that in all but computer science, the rank of assistant professor has the highest percentage of female faculty. In converse, the rank which has highest percentage of male faculty is typically that of full professor, and that is the rank held by the majority of male faculty as well. Fewer differences in rank exist between male and female faculty in early-career stages in S&E, but greater differences appear between 15 and 20 years after receipt of the doctorate (National Science Foundation, 2001a, Figure H-5).

Statistics also indicate that women are underrepresented in senior academic ranks and faculty leadership positions such as presidents, chancellors, provosts, deans and chairs (Hollenshead, 2003). This may be related to the difficulties women faculty in STEM face in academic career advancement (e.g. due to gender stereotyping and lack of mentoring), and the fact that they may not obtain the same levels of professional recognition for their scholarly work as do their male colleagues. In a comprehensive study of almost 60,000 faculty members at 403 academic institutions, Astin and Cress (2003) reported that male faculty attained tenure in a shorter amount of time than female faculty in all fields, with the exception of engineering. Other research has shown that women are less likely than men to receive tenure or promotion in STEM fields (National Science Foundation, 2001a; Rosser and Daniels, 2004). It has also been pointed out that the gender gap in compensation may be due in part to gender differences in rank, field (Astin and Cress, 2003), and promotions (National Science Foundation, 2003). As Astin and Cress (2003, p. 58) note, 'At research universities, 25% of men are in the more highly paid fields of physical science, mathematics/statistics, and engineering combined, compared to 6% of women. Likewise, more than twice as many women (33%) as men (16%) are in the less financially lucrative fields of education, health science and humanities combined.'

In summary, multiple sources and historical data reveal the long-standing and consistent underrepresentation of women in academic STEM fields. At each transition point in the academic career, a lower proportion of women advance to the next milestone than their male colleagues (National Science Foundation, 2000), compelling many to refer to the path from a bachelor's degree to a faculty position as a 'leaky pipeline' since it loses women at every step. Most problematic is the low proportion of women S&E faculty at the highest, full professor, level of the academic hierarchy. Even as the number of male university faculty increases in rank from assistant to full professor, the number of women faculty substantially declines (National Science Foundation, 1998). Furthermore, the percentage of women at full professor rank in S&E has not changed in the last two decades, despite consistent increases in the percentages of women getting PhDs in these fields.

THE EXPERIENCE OF WOMEN FACULTY IN STEM FIELDS

A variety of problems emerge from (a) the lack of a critical mass and (b) few women at the top of the academic hierarchy in STEM, particularly problems related to women's treatment as tokens at every level in the institution (see Kanter, 1977; Yoder, 1991). Rosser (2004) reports that low numbers of women S&E faculty result in women feeling isolated, having limited access to role models and mentors, and having to work harder to gain credibility and respect from their male colleagues. With constrained access to key academic networks, women junior faculty are left on their own to learn how to navigate the promotion and tenure process in a male-dominated environment. Many women opt out of S&E academic positions, choosing private sector positions because they become frustrated with the academic setting (Valian, 2004). Noting the clustering of most female professors at the assistant professor level, Nelson (2005) suggests that the number of female faculty who can safely take steps to change their departmental environments is much smaller than it might first appear.

While there are general myths of insufficient numbers of women graduate students available in the disciplinary recruitment pools for faculty, the data indicate that this is false (Trower and Chait, 2002). While the pipeline is scant for minorities, it is generally not true that the pipeline is insufficient for women in S&E. Rather, a number of factors cohere to create an environment that does not make academic S&E attractive to women early in their careers, and which derails large numbers of women from having successful long-term careers (Etzkowitz et al., 2000; Rosser, 2004). Individual psychological factors (gender schemas) culminating in subtle evaluation bias and the slow but steady accumulation of disadvantage to women (Valian, 1999) may explain some of women's proportional rarity at every level in academic S&E and why the academic glass ceiling exists. But other factors pertain to the systematic institutional structures and practices that place barriers on the recruitment, retention, advancement and leadership of women – practices of an exclusionary culture that result in inequitable distribution of workload and resources between the genders.

Using both qualitative and quantitative research and evaluation results conducted at several US universities funded through the NSF's ADVANCE program of institutional transformation (www.nsf.gov/advance), we illustrate below what women faculty in STEM disciplines experience, and their perceptions of their academic environments in comparison with their male colleagues. NSF's ADVANCE Institutional Transformation program awards significant funding to universities to increase the representation and advancement of women in academic S&E careers through university transformation, thereby contributing to the development of a more diverse national S&E workforce (National Science Foundation, 2002).

In two waves of focus groups and interviews about the career experiences of women faculty members at our own university between 2001 and 2004, we found several important themes (see Resource Equity Committee Report, 2003; 2004), including: (1) an overall chilly climate and unwelcoming community for women described by participants as exclusionary, unfriendly, marginalizing, tough, isolating, male-dominated and silencing; (2) a climate where 'everything is negotiable', manifested in perceptions of side deals and of unequal application of procedures; (3) lack of transparency in university rules, policies, procedures and practices; (4) a pervasive lack of mentoring; (5) disproportionate service and teaching pressures faced by women faculty; and (6) unfair or unequal access to/allocation of resources, including purchase of library materials, assistance from teaching assistants, access to services from support staff, travel money, and protected research time. Other research also addresses these multiple dimensions of gender-based resource inequity in academia (Long, 1990; Evetts, 1996; Preston, 2004; Valian, 2004). For example, women faculty receive less office and lab space, have less access to graduate student assistance, and get fewer services from support staff (Park, 1996).

The experiences of women faculty in STEM seem to derive from particular sets of beliefs held by (predominantly male) faculty and administrators. For example, participants in our own focus groups brought out the notion that at our university, leadership seems naturally male, and that masculinity appears to lead to power, manifested in conscious and unconscious ways. Other beliefs regarding academia voiced by participants included that the academic enterprise requires complete dedication at the expense of everything else, especially in early-career years, and that academia is essentially an individual profession, with individualized results and rewards. These mindsets contribute directly and indirectly to the treatment and advancement of women faculty.

We found evidence of other belief structures detrimental to women in academia, identified by research from other National Science Foundation (NSF) ADVANCE award institutions. For instance, Silver et al. (2006) mentioned several factors that impede the achievement of full professional equality at University of Rhode Island, which include:

> a belief that some male professors and administrators did not view female colleagues as equals but rather as second-class members of the faculty. Adding to the women's discomfort was their perception that individuals who raised complaints about disparate treatment were viewed as 'troublemakers,' a perception that discouraged the seeking of redress for mistreatment. (Silver et al., 2006, p. 4)

Other findings from a climate survey conducted at University of Rhode Island pointed out that 'men indicate stronger agreement with statement "a man should earn the income and a woman should care for her family"' (Harlow et al., 2005, slide 13). As a consequence, 'public treatment of women faculty in a less respectful manner than male faculty, such as addressing the women by the first names and the men by their title and last names' and 'Commenting to women faculty on the perceived appropriateness of their clothing' (Silver et al., 2006, p. 4) were commonplace occurrences. These belief structures also resulted in the lack of supportive supervision from upper-level academic leaders and inadequate performance reviews, described as ' "window dressing" efforts by the Dean to support women in Engineering programs rather than providing adequate funding for such efforts' and 'the failure to carry out annual performance reviews in the manner specified in the collective bargaining agreement' (Silver et al., 2006, p. 4).

Many of these qualitative research findings have been confirmed in climate surveys conducted in multiple institutions across the country. In a Faculty Worklife Survey conducted at University of Wisconsin–Madison in 2003 (response rate of 60 percent, final $n = 1338$), women faculty were less likely than men faculty to report that they are treated with respect by colleagues, students and department chairs, that colleagues value their research, and that they are included in decision making. In turn, women faculty members were more likely to report feeling excluded from informal networks and to agree that they had encountered unwritten rules more than men. Women were also less likely to agree that they 'fit' with their department and more likely to agree that they feel isolated in their department and on campus. As a consequence, women faculty were significantly less likely to report being satisfied with their jobs and the progression of their career at the University of Wisconsin–Madison, as compared to male faculty members (www.wiseli. engr.wisc.edu/initiatives/survey/results/facultypre/ contents.htm).

Interpersonal relations with other faculty have been perceived as particularly unpleasant by women faculty members across institutions, which results in lower satisfaction. In a climate survey conducted at the University of Rhode Island (response rate of 40 percent, $n = 700$), Harlow et al. (2005) reported that men experienced significantly more interpersonal support from colleagues and more career satisfaction than women, and women reported significantly more discrimination in the work environment than men. Similar results regarding interpersonal relations were found in another climate study conducted at University of Colorado in the fall of 2003 (www.advance.colorado.edu/surveyDRAFT.pdf, $n = 449$), even though a different survey instrument was used. In this latter survey, tenure-track men were found to have more favorable ratings of experienced interpersonal relations than tenure-track women; tenure-track women perceived their interpersonal relations to be more hostile, racist, homogeneous, disrespectful, non-collegial, sexist, individualistic, competitive, homophobic, non-supportive and uncivil compared to men. Work–family issues and institutional support were also addressed in the climate study conducted at University of Colorado in 2003. Tenure-track men were found to have higher evaluations than women on several measures of institutional support: accommodating family responsibilities, child care, health accommodations, career planning, teaching improvement, administrative opportunities, tenure clock adjustments and acquiring resources; tenure-track women scored higher on the remaining two items: family leave and partner/spousal hiring.

Job satisfaction, one of the frequently used indicators in the evaluation of institutional climate and the experience of male and female faculty members, has been addressed in multiple studies. As described in Figure 13.1, a climate survey undertaken at our own university, and emblematic of the prevailing situation at other institutions, indicated that women faculty report lower rates of satisfaction with their academic jobs than do male faculty. Specifically, the findings revealed that women faculty as compared with their male counterparts generally feel less supported and valued in their academic units, feel more pressure and restrictions, perceive that gender, race and family obligations make a difference in how faculty members are treated, rate their academic unit head's leadership lower, rate the resources and supports academic unit heads provide lower, perceive that compensation and non-research supports are less equitably distributed, perceive lower transparency in allocating compensation, office and lab space, teaching requirements and clerical support, and are less satisfied with their overall community and job experience (Report of the 2004 University Community and Climate Survey, 2004).

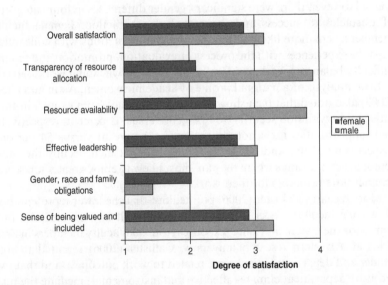

Except 'overall satisfaction', which was measured by degree of satisfaction (1 = Strongly dissatisfied, 4 = Strongly satisfied), all other items were measured by degree of agreement (1 = Strongly disagree, 4 = Strongly agree).

Source: Report of the 2004 University Community and Climate Survey (2004), available at www.case.edu/admin/aces/faculty_engagement_10_04.pdf

Figure 13.1 Perceptions of satisfaction by male and female faculty

From this survey, we examined how a sample of 248 non-medical school faculty members constructs their job satisfaction (Bilimoria et al., 2006). Our findings indicate that both women and men perceive that their job satisfaction is influenced by the institutional leadership and mentoring they receive, but this relationship is mediated by access to internal academic resources and internal relational supports from a collegial and inclusive immediate work environment. Women's job satisfaction derived more from their perceptions of the internal relational supports than the academic resources they received, whereas men's job satisfaction resulted equally from their perceptions of internal academic resources and internal relational supports received.

In measuring the campus climate for STEM women at Utah State University, Hult (2005) described that 42 women faculty members and a matched set of 40 male faculty members from the same SET colleges were interviewed. According to Hult (2005), there were no differences between men and women in sources of satisfaction. For example, both women and men felt satisfied with positive interactions with colleagues, access to campus resources, support of administrators, and positive teaching experiences. However, there were significant gender differences in four categories of obstacles to success and sources of dissatisfaction. Female faculty members were more likely to report negative interactions with colleagues; negative experiences with the process of evaluation, promotion and tenure; difficulty balancing work and family life; and overwhelming workloads.

In an analysis of a national profile of academic women, Astin and Cress (2003) also noted that men show a notable difference from women in their satisfaction with 'job security' (81 percent versus 62 percent, respectively) and 'opportunities for scholarly pursuits' (71 percent versus 54 percent, respectively). Astin and Cress (2003) argued that men occupy the more senior academic ranks where they are most likely to enjoy greater job security and more resources for their work.

More recently, Callister (2006) pointed out that the lower representation of women faculty in S&E departments may result in more negative outcomes for these women. Using responses from 308 faculty members in S&E fields at a western research university, Callister (2006) found that both gender and department climate are related to work outcomes, and that two facets of department climate (affective and instrumental) mediate the relationship between gender and both job satisfaction and the intention to quit. The mediating role of department climate indicates that female faculty members are not inherently unsatisfied or unhappy with their jobs, but rather that it is likely that they value department climate. Thus Callister (2006) concluded that universities can benefit from improving department climate, which then may improve the retention of both male and female faculty, but may have an even greater impact on improving job satisfaction and reducing intentions to quit of female faculty.

Rosser's (2004) study of almost 400 women who received NSF Power Awards during the period 1997–2000 found that the most significant issues/challenges/opportunities are (1) pressures women face in balancing career and family (e.g. dual career), (2) problems faced by women because of their low numbers and stereotypes held by others regarding gender (e.g. networking, negative social images), (3) issues faced by both men and women scientists and engineers in the current environment of tight resources, which may pose particular difficulties for women (e.g. time management, lack of funding), and (4) discrimination and harassment faced by women faculty. This study adds to extant knowledge about the experiences of women STEM faculty from the point of view of an elite group of researchers, the NSF Power Awardees; even these highly rewarded scholars see patterns of institutional challenges and issues that detrimentally affect the representation and treatment of women faculty on academic campuses.

Overall, the research conducted at multiple academic institutions suggests consistent findings that women faculty in STEM experience a chilly climate on campus, inadequate interpersonal relations, limited support from upper-level leaders, poor mentoring, lack of transparency in performance review, promotion and tenure evaluations, and overall lower satisfaction than their male colleagues. While these and other related experiences may appear small or even insignificant in isolation, they add up over time to result in a significant cumulative disadvantage (Valian, 1999), which if uncorrected result in perpetuation of the patterns of slow recruitment, advancement, retention and leadership of women faculty in academic STEM.

THE NSF-ADVANCE INSTITUTIONAL TRANSFORMATION PROGRAM

What can be done to improve the representation and experience of women faculty in STEM disciplines? How can the recruitment, advancement, retention and leadership of women STEM faculty be accelerated? What can be done to remedy the chilly climate in academic STEM? How can more women be moved into senior administrative and academic leadership positions? How can women's inclusion and participation in departmental decision making be enhanced? To address these questions at the level of institutional transformation, the NSF has created the ADVANCE program, with the goal 'to increase the participation of women in the scientific and engineering workforce through the increased representation and advancement of women in academic science and engineering careers' (www.nsf.gov/pubs/2005/nsf05584/nsf05584.htm). As of 2005, 19 universities have received NSF-ADVANCE Institutional Transformation Awards for proposing creative strategies and effective approaches to transform institutional climate, and a new set of institutional awardees is expected in 2006. These universities have focused on a variety of institutional transformation remedies at the following levels.

Institutional Level

Transformation at the institutional level addresses structural and policy changes that affect all university faculty, whether in STEM or other disciplines. Most of the ADVANCE institutions have focused on making institutional policies and structures more friendly toward families and work–life balance. Changes include child care assistance (building on-site structures or area referrals), automatic tenure-clock extension policies, dual-career hiring policies, parental leave policies, modified work duties and work release policies, and employee assistance plans. The implementation of these new structures and policies benefit both male and female faculty members. A concern often associated with the implementation of policies is inconsistent communication about available policies and services. There are great needs to communicate broadly about the availability of policies, tracking the use of policies, and developing methods to remind tenure review committees of policy details (Quinn et al., 2004).

In addition to review, change, and improved communication of key policies and structures, ADVANCE universities are also engaging in institutional transformation through improved accountability of administrators such as deans and chairs, improved data collection and dissemination about gender equity data, linking incentives to transformation (e.g. tying receipt of new faculty slots or endowed chairs to transformational activities and outcomes), improved leadership development of faculty leaders, and engagement of a wide circle of university faculty in the processes of transformation and re-institutionalization.

School/Department Level

ADVANCE institutions are devoting substantial attention to improving the micro-climates facing women faculty in their departments and schools/colleges. Bilimoria and Jordan (2005) undertook a case study of a department to identify the conditions under which the dual goals of inclusiveness and scientific productivity could be maintained; they determined that shared values and beliefs (e.g. regarding hiring of new faculty), constructive interactions (e.g. interactions that generate new resources and opportunities), participative departmental activities (e.g. team teaching across faculty ranks, department social events), integrative leadership (e.g. fair, equitable and supportive leadership), and inclusive departmental processes (e.g. transparent decision making) substantially improve the department culture. To warm up the academic micro-climate for women faculty, especially in STEM disciplines, universities are engaging in intensive leadership development of faculty supervisors such as deans and chairs (through workshops, individual executive coaching, training seminars), improved mentoring of junior faculty, and proactive department culture change (e.g. more transparency in how decisions are made, improved communication, and department-wide inclusive processes such as strategic planning).

Individual Faculty Level

Transformational changes at the individual faculty level include efforts to increase the awareness and skills of women faculty through career development coaching and assistance (e.g. enhanced access to resources and mentoring, goal and action planning), performance improvement skill building (e.g. improvements in teaching skills, lab supervision skills, grant writing skills, or interpersonal skills), and leadership development (e.g. increasing visibility in and contributions to the discipline or university). To enhance academic performance, networking and mentoring, many activities have been carried out across the 19 ADVANCE institutions, including distinguished scholar/lecture series, faculty mentoring workshops/ programs, and small grant funding (e.g. for travel to conferences or as bridge funding between grants) for women scientists.

Collecting and Disseminating Data about Gender Equity

A vital effort of the ADVANCE schools is to document and institutionalize the collection and dissemination of information relevant to the recruitment, advancement, retention and leadership of women faculty in STEM. ADVANCE institutions are documenting a variety of internal statistics and distributing them to key decision makers, including the number and proportion of women faculty by department, the number and proportion of women in tenure-line positions by rank and department, tenure and promotion outcomes by gender, years in rank by gender, time at institution by gender, the number and proportion of women who are in non-tenure-track positions (teaching and research), attrition of women faculty, the number and proportion of women faculty in administrative positions, the number and proportion of women faculty in endowed or named chairs, the number and proportion of women faculty on department and school/college promotion and tenure committees, salary of faculty by gender (controlling for department, rank, and years in rank), office and lab space allocation of faculty by gender (with controls such as field/department, rank, etc.), and start-up packages of newly hired faculty by gender (with controls such as field/department, rank, etc.).

Several gender equity indicators are required by NSF's cooperative agreement with the awardee universities to be collected annually at each ADVANCE institution, while other data are collected only periodically, sometimes dependent on the interests of the specific institution. Primarily NSF is interested in holding ADVANCE universities responsible for systematic data collection and dissemination associated with the following questions: What is the distribution of S&E faculty by gender, rank and department? What are the outcomes of institutional processes of recruitment and advancement for men and women? What is the gender distribution of S&E faculty in leadership positions in the institution? What is the allocation of resources for S&E faculty by gender at the institution? (Frehill et al., 2005). The measurement of these gender equity statistics and indicators helps inform the public about the internal university status of women faculty in STEM, focus administrative attention on key issues and inequities, and raise general awareness level among faculty members about issues pertinent to gender equity and inclusiveness.

CONCLUSIONS

In this chapter we have provided an overview of the current representation and experience of women faculty in STEM fields using extant data and research findings. Our review confirms that the representation of women faculty in academic STEM has increased steadily over the past decades, but still remains disturbingly low, particularly at the highest levels of the academic hierarchy. Drawing from recent research and evaluation findings, we conclude that women faculty members generally experience unfriendly environments within their STEM departments. They report low numbers of women faculty and administrators in their institutions, poor interpersonal relations with other faculty, staff and even students, limited support from upper-level leaders, poor mentoring, lack of transparency in performance review, promotion and tenure evaluations, and overall lower satisfaction than their male faculty colleagues. Recent efforts by the NSF to address these longstanding institutional patterns at the national level are most encouraging, and there is hope that comprehensive, multi-level interventions may provide potential remedies that result in institutional transformation and substantially improve the recruitment, advancement, retention and leadership of women faculty in STEM fields.

ACKNOWLEDGEMENT

This chapter was supported by an NSF ADVANCE Institutional Transformation Award, SBE-0245054, start date 9/1/2003, end date 8/31/2008.

REFERENCES

Astin, H.S. and Cress, C.M. (2003), 'A national profile of women in research universities', in L.S. Hornig (ed.), *Equal Rites, Unequal Outcomes: Women in American Research Universities*, New York: Kluwer Academic/Plenum Publishers, pp. 53–88.

Bilimoria, D. and Jordan, C.G. (2005), 'A good place to do science: an exploratory case study of an academic science department', available at www.case.edu/admin/aces/documents/science_department.doc

Bilimoria, D., Perry, S.R., Liang, X.F., Stoller, E.P., Higgins, P. and Taylor, C. (2006), 'How do female and male faculty members construct job satisfaction? The role of perceived institutional leadership and mentoring and their mediating processes', *Journal of Technology Transfer*, **31**, 355–65.

Callister, R.R. (2006), 'The impact of gender and department climate on job satisfaction and intentions to quit for faculty in science and engineering fields', *Journal of Technology Transfer*, **31**(3), 367–75.

Etzkowitz, H., Kemelgor, C. and Uzzi, B. (2000), *Athens Unbound: The Advancement of Women in Science and Technology*, Cambridge: Cambridge University Press.

Evetts, J. (1996), *Gender and Career in Science and Engineering*, London: Taylor and Francis.

Frehill, L., Jeser-Cannavale, C., Kehoe, P., Meader, E., Sheridan, J., Stewart, A. and Sviglin, H. (2005), *Proposed Toolkit for Reporting Progress Toward NSF ADVANCE: Institutional Transformation Goals*, prepared by ADVANCE Institutional Transformation Indicators Working Group.

Gibbons, M. (2004), 'The Year in Numbers', available at www.asee.org/publications/profiles/upload/2005ProfileEng.pdf

Harlow, L., Silver, B., Hedrick, M., Mederer, H., Woodard, A., Trubatch, J., Peckham, J., Wishner, K., Boudreaux-Bartels, F., Roheim, C., Swift, J., Pasquerella, L., Prochaska, J. and Mauriello, L. (2005), 'University of Rhode Island ADVANCE Project & Work Environment Survey Results: Preliminary findings', September, available at www2.wdg.uri.edu:81/testsite/index.php?id=1282.

Hollenshead, C. (2003), 'Women in the academy: confronting barriers to equality', in L.S. Hornig (ed.), *Equal Rites, Unequal Outcomes: Women in American*

Research Universities, New York: Kluwer Academic/Plenum Publishers, pp. 211–25.

Hult, C. (2005), 'How's the climate on your campus?', *Academic Leader: The Newsletter for Academic Deans and Department Chairs*, **21**(4).

Kanter, R.M. (1977), *Men and Women of the Corporation*, New York: Basic Books.

Kirkman, E.E., Maxwell, J.W. and Rose, C.A. (2005), '2004 Annual Survey of the Mathematical Sciences (3rd report), Notices of The AMS', available at www.ams. org/employment/surveyreports.html.

Kuck, V.J., Marzabadi, C.H., Nolan, S.A. and Buckner, J.P. (2004), 'Analysis by gender of the doctoral and postdoctoral institutions of faculty members at the top-fifty ranked Chemistry departments', *Journal of Chemical Education*, **81**(3), 356–63.

Long, J.S. (1990), 'The origins of sex differences in science', *Social Forces*, **68**(4), 1297–316.

National Science Foundation (1998), 'Science and engineering indicators 1998 (NSB-98-1), available at www.nsf.gov/statistics/seind98/.

National Science Foundation (2000), 'Women, minorities and persons with disabilities in science and engineering', available at www.nsf.gov/statistics/nsf 00327/.

National Science Foundation (2001a), 'Survey of doctorate recipients', available at www.nsf.gov/statistics/wmpd/figh-5.htm.

National Science Foundation (2001b), 'Survey of doctorate recipients 2001', available at www.nsf.gov/statistics/wmpd/employ.htm.

National Science Foundation (2002), 'General information: Program title – advance', available at www.nsf.gov/pubs/2002/nsf02121/nsf02121.htm.

National Science Foundation (2003), 'Gender differences in the careers of academic scientists and engineers: a literature review', available at www.nsf.gov/ statistics/nsf03322/.

National Science Foundation (2006a), 'Science and engineering indicators 2006 (NSB 06-01)', available at www.nsf.gov/statistics/seind06/.

National Science Foundation (2006b), 'Women, minorities, and personnel with disabilities in science and engineering', available at www.nsf.gov/statistics/wmpd/ graddeg.htm#doctoral.

Nelson, D.J. (2005), 'A national analysis of diversity in science and engineering faculties at research universities', revised 6 January 2005, available at http://cheminfo.chem.ou.edu/~djn/diversity/briefings/Diversity%20Report% 20Final.pdf.

Park, S.M. (1996), 'Research, teaching and service: why shouldn't women's work count?', *Journal of Higher Education*, **67**, 47–84.

Preston, A.E. (2004), *Leaving Science: Occupational Exit from Scientific Careers*, New York: Russell Sage Foundation.

Quinn, K., Lange, S.E. and Olswang, S.G. (2004), 'Family-friendly policies and the research university', *Academe: Balancing Faculty Careers and Family Work*, **90**(6), 32–4, available at www.aaup.org/publications/Academe/2004/04nd/ 04ndquin.htm.

Report of the 2004 University Community and Climate Survey (2004), available at www.case.edu/admin/aces/faculty_engagement_10_04.pdf.

Resource Equity Committee Report (2003), 'Resource equity at Case Western Reserve University: results of faculty focus groups', available at www.case.edu/ menu/president/resourcequity.doc.

Resource Equity Committee Report (2004), 'Resource equity at Case Western Reserve University: qualitative baseline data report', available at www.case.edu/admin/aces/images/NSF_ADVANCE_ACES_Year_1_Annual.pdf.

Rosser, S.V. (2004), *The Science Glass Ceiling: Academic Women Scientists and the Struggle to Succeed*, New York: Routledge.

Rosser, S.V. and Daniels, J. (2004), 'Widening paths to success, improving the environment, and moving toward balance: lessons learned from experiences of POWRE and CBL awardees', *Journal of Women and Minorities in Science and Engineering*, **10**(2), 131–48.

Silver, B., Boudreaux-Bartels, F., Mederer, H., Pasquerella, L., Peckham, J., Rivero-Hudec, M. and Wishner, K. (2006), 'A warmer climate for women in engineering at the University of Rhode Island', ASEE Annual 2006 Conference Proceedings Paper, available at ww2.wdg.uri.edu:81/testsite/index.php?id=1268.

Trower, C.A. and Chait, R.P. (2002), 'Faculty diversity: too little for too long', *Harvard Magazine*, **104**(4), 33–7, 98.

Valian, V. (1999), *Why So Slow? The Advancement of Women*, Cambridge, MA: The MIT Press.

Valian, V. (2004), 'Beyond gender schemas: improving the advancement of women in academia', *NWSA Journal*, **16**(1), 207–20.

Yoder, J. (1991), 'Rethinking tokenism: looking beyond numbers', *Gender & Society*, **5**, 178–92.

14. Upstream and downstream in the engineering pipeline: what's blocking US women from pursuing engineering careers?

Mary C. Mattis

BACKGROUND

Despite 30 years of efforts to increase women's (and minorities') represent-ation in the US engineering workforce, women's gains have actually eroded in the past decade. In 2002, women held just 11.6 percent of engineering jobs in business and industry. Between 1983 and 1999 women's representa-tion among practicing engineers increased by only 5 percentage points (US Department of Labor, 2002). More disturbing, there has been a marked decline in women's participation in college-level engineering study. In 2005, women accounted for 19.5 percent of recipients of bachelor's degree in engineering; however, they made up just 17.5 percent of freshmen engi-neering students, down from 19.6 percent in 1998–99 (ASEE, 2004). The recent declines in women's enrollment in undergraduate engineering pro-grams give cause for concern in that they have occurred during years of sub-stantial growth of total engineering degrees and enrollments (*Engineering Trends*, 2005). It is predicted that the maxima of students enrolled in US engineering programs will occur in AY2006–07 (possibly 2005–06), and the number of degrees will likely decline for at least five years thereafter (*Engineering Trends*, 2005). As the authors of a recent analysis of women in undergraduate engineering programs observe, 'If the fraction of women continues to decline during a period where the total number of degrees declines, the number of women awarded engineering degrees will suffer significantly' (*Engineering Trends*, 2005, p. 2).

This erosion in women's representation in academic engineering pro-grams and in the engineering workforce has occurred despite decades of effort and hundreds of millions of dollars expended to address engineer-ing's gender and racial/ethnic diversity gap. Research undertaken in con-junction with a 2003–05 study by the National Academy of Engineering identified over 400 initiatives targeting groups that are underrepresented in engineering, many of which target individual women students.

A bright spot in all of this is that in 2005, women accounted for almost one-half (45.5 percent) of graduates in the relatively new area of biomedical engineering and for just over 40 percent of environmental engineering graduates (Gibbons, 2005).

WHY DOES DIVERSITY IN ENGINEERING MATTER?

Better Engineering Solutions

In 1999, the US National Academy of Engineering (NAE) held a workshop on best practices for managing diversity in the engineering workforce. At the workshop the President of the NAE, William A. Wulf, made the following remarks about the importance of diversity in engineering:

> Many people talk about the need for diversity as an issue of equity, in terms of fairness, and that is a potent argument. Americans are very sensitive to issues of equity and fairness, so the argument resonates with many people. A second argument for diversity has to do with numbers, the fact that white males are becoming a minority in the population of the United States and that, unless we include more women and underrepresented minorities in the engineering workforce, we are simply not going to have enough engineers to continue to enjoy the lifestyle we have enjoyed for the last century or so. This, too, is a potent argument . . . My argument is essentially that the quality of engineering is affected by diversity or the lack thereof . . . As a consequence of a lack of diversity, we pay an opportunity cost, a cost in designs not thought of, in solutions not produced. Opportunity costs are very real but also very hard to measure (NAE, 2002).

Research shows that creativity increases and the range of potential solutions is expanded when teams of individuals from different personal, cultural and disciplinary perspectives work together (Basset-Jones, 2005; Cowan, 1995; McLeod et al., 1996; Paulus and Nijstad, 2003). As a consequence, the quality of engineering solutions, products and services is affected directly by the degree of diversity in engineering design teams.

Global Competitiveness

In 2005, 15 of the most prominent business organizations in the USA joined together to express deep concern about the USA's ability to sustain its scientific and technological superiority through the decade and beyond and to call for efforts to cultivate the skilled scientists and engineers needed to create tomorrow's innovations (Business Roundtable, 2005). They outlined these concerns in a report that was intended to be a call to action for the American academic and business communities:

- Increasing international competition:
    - By 2010, if current trends continue, more than 90 percent of all scientists and engineers in the world will be living in Asia.
    - South Korea, with one-sixth of our population, graduates as many engineers annually as the USA.
- Increasing reliance on and reduced availability of foreign talent to work in the USA:
    - More than 50 percent of all engineering doctoral degrees awarded by US engineering colleges are to foreign nationals.
    - Security concerns in the USA are reducing the number of foreign students, while competition for this talent from other countries and the opportunity to return to their home countries is increasing.
- Alarming domestic trends:
    - The number of engineering degrees awarded in the USA is down 20 percent from the peak year of 1985.
    - Although US fourth graders score well against international competition, they fall near the bottom or dead last by 12th grade in mathematics and science, respectively.

Pipeline versus Pathway

The analysis that follows examines findings of research on factors upstream and downstream that impact the representation of women in the engineering pipeline, along with the interdependence of these factors – the feedback loops from each end of the pipeline to the other. We have chosen to use the longstanding metaphor of the 'pipeline' to examine the barriers and opportunities upstream and downstream for increasing girls' interest in engineering, and women's representation in engineering careers. Recently, researchers have argued that 'pathway' is a more appropriate, if not more attractive, metaphor. Pathway connotes flexibility and freedom of movement, whereas pipeline brings to mind a mechanical and constrained course of action. We would argue that while pathway may be the ideal, pipeline continues to be the reality – attainment of an engineering degree in the USA requires lockstep conformity to a regimen of prescribed coursework beginning as early as elementary school. Success is correlated with staying that course, as opposed to deviating from it, even briefly.

The experiences of women at each juncture in the pipeline (elementary and secondary school educational institutions; undergraduate and graduate programs; and recruitment and participation in the engineering workforce) impact the 'flow' of women into engineering careers. There are important lessons to be learned from examining girls' and women's experiences at each juncture, lessons that, if heeded, would result in an increased flow of female talent into engineering careers. We have chosen to focus on the experiences of girls and young women 'upstream' and the experiences of employed women engineers 'downstream' in the pipeline.

WHAT'S HAPPENING UPSTREAM?

Gender Differences in Performance and Interest in Mathematics

Factors upstream have more of an impact on outcomes for women's participation in engineering than for their participation in other career fields such as teaching, or library science, or even business. Students who are interested in becoming engineers need to declare their major upon entering college and, to be accepted into an engineering program, they have to reach a threshold of math performance that requires math-intensive coursework in middle and high school. Adelman (1998) used evidence from the 11-year college transcript history (1982–93) of the High School and Beyond/ Sophomore Cohort Longitudinal Study, as well as the high school transcripts, test scores, and surveys of a nationally representative sample to examine the paths students planning to major in engineering take through higher education. Major findings of the study include:

- Curricular momentum begins in secondary school, and sets up both trajectories and boundaries. Secondary school mathematics study is the key booster to these trajectories, with performance in trigonometry the gate to potential science and engineering majors in college.
- Successful completion of advanced mathematics coursework in secondary school is critical to entering the engineering pipeline.
- Recipients of bachelor's degrees in engineering spent more time on calculus than any other course. For degree completers in engineering, one of every seven credits earned was in mathematics.
- Men and women who come to the engineering path look remarkably alike, yet very different from the women and men who never attempt to major in engineering. Women, however, have a higher academic performance profile (academic grade point average, class rank) than men, regardless of where they end up in college.
- Women who eventually complete engineering degrees had slightly higher SAT scores than male completers and were more uniform in test performance.

- About 4 percent of high school graduates with curricular momentum in mathematics and science and high-quality academic profiles were not interested in engineering; rather, for the most part, in preprofessional preparation in college and, for women, in health sciences/services. Women constitute 60 percent of this high talent group.

Given the importance of mathematics to pursuing a degree and a career in engineering, a considerable amount of research undertaken in the 1960s–1980s focused on gender differences in math performance to explain women's low representation in engineering (and science) careers. In early studies researchers disagreed about the specific age/grade when girls and boys' performance and interest in math diverges. Maccoby and Jacklin (1974) found few consistent gender differences in computational skills in the elementary school years. Hilton and Berglund (1974) found no gender differences in grade 5, with boys pulling ahead thereafter, leading to the inference that some critical change occurs at about grade 6. Several other early studies showed that at preschool and first grade, at least, there are no significant gender differences, but that at later elementary and higher levels, male advantage emerges in mathematical reasoning.

Recent research shows that gender differences in verbal, mathematical, and spatial abilities have declined over the decades since the earliest studies were conducted. Cross-country research shows few gender differences in the 8th grade with increasing gender differences in mathematics achievement developing by the 12th grade. However, gender differences in the USA are considerably smaller than the international differences at both grades 8 and 12 (American Institutes for Research, 2005).

Huang et al. (2000) found that, today, girls are taking high school science and math courses at approximately the same rate as boys: 94 percent of girls and 91 percent of boys take biology; 64 percent of girls and 57 percent of boys take chemistry; 26 percent of girls and 32 percent of boys take physics, and 64 percent of girls and 60 percent of boys take Algebra II. A meta-analysis by Hyde (2005) shows that in more than 100 studies involving more than three million subjects, the gap between women's and men's mathematics ability is nearly non-existent. The only consistent gender difference is in the area of three-dimensional spatial visualization: women consistently underperform on these tests compared to men. However, three-dimensional spatial skills can be improved and Hyde recommends that all engineering schools should have a first-year class that focuses on developing this aptitude.

The argument that lower performance of girls and young women in math prevents them from entering engineering programs does not account for the large increases in the representation of women in other math-based occupations; for example, in 2004–05, women earned 46 percent of bachelor's degrees in astronomy and 47 percent of medical degrees awarded by US colleges and universities; and the representation of women accepted to US medical schools in 2005 was 50.4 percent (AIR, 2005; AAMC, 2006).

Interest versus Ability

We know that ability in any field is shaped by a complicated mix of cognitive and attitudinal forces. A study conducted by researchers at the University of Michigan found that, contrary to widely held belief, girls are not underperforming in middle school and high school math; girls' and boys' achievement in math classes is virtually the same, but girls seem to have less interest in the subject, and this may be a contributing factor to the dearth of women in math-related occupations (Davis-Kean, 2002). When the researchers analyzed data for students by track (honors/college and regular/basic) and gender, they discovered that, overall, young women had slightly higher grades than young men within each group; grades for both girls and boys generally declined throughout high school. Interest in math generally declined for all groups through high school, but girls in the honors/college track started out with lower interest in 8th grade than boys in the same track, and their interest continued to decline even through the 12th grade while the boys' interest stabilized across high school.

The Extraordinary Women Engineers Project

No group is more aware of the challenge of changing girls' perceptions of and increasing their interest in engineering than women engineers themselves. The Extraordinary Women Engineers Project (EWEP) is a national initiative to encourage girls to consider pursuing a degree and subsequent career in engineering. The project is led by a coalition of women engineers who enlisted the support of US engineering associations and other partners. A key partner was the WGBH Educational Foundation, which conducted research for the project (EWEP, 2005).

Formed in spring 2004, the coalition began with a review of the question, 'Why are academically prepared girls not considering or enrolling in engineering degree programs?' As noted above, the issue is not one of ability or preparation. The group decided to focus on academically prepared girls and young women because the 'problem system' (and potential) solutions for this group are quite different than for girls who are not academically prepared. The group's working assumption was that the problem for academically prepared girls is perception. Girls do not understand what a career in engineering looks like and why they should consider it as a career option because the people who influence them – teachers, school counselors, parents, peers and the media – do not themselves have this understanding.

Methodology

To test this assumption, WGBH used qualitative consumer research methods to examine the views of target audiences: a national sample of girls ages 14–17 who were 'academically prepared' for college-level STEM courses; general high school girls; science and math teachers and school counselors; male and female engineering students; engineering professionals; and members of the Society of Women Engineers (SWE).[1] The research was conducted from June 2004 to June 2005. Research goals included:

- Ascertain high school girls' level of interest in and awareness of careers in the engineering field.
- Identify career motivators and barriers related to engineering.
- Analyze messages about engineering that high school girls are receiving from the engineering community.
- Explore messaging opportunities for increasing young women's participation in engineering.

Data were collected through a variety of qualitative methods: online focus groups and a follow-up online survey with high school girls who were taking competitive and challenging courses, including algebra, pre-calculus, chemistry and biology; online survey of high school girls taking challenging course loads with advanced placement (AP) English, US history, calculus, biology, physics and advanced courses in language arts; online survey and in-person focus group with teachers/school counselors working in public and private high schools; online survey of college engineering students; online survey of engineering professionals; and an online survey of SWE members.

Altogether, 4506 persons were interviewed or surveyed. Among the target audiences a substantial number had family members who were engineers: 55 percent of engineering students; 55 percent of engineers; 44 percent of SWE members. Among the high school girls taking challenging AP courses, 38 percent reported having a parent/guardian who works or has worked in a science-related field and 52 percent reported that a friend or family member was employed as an engineer, or who was majoring in engineering – larger percentages than among the girls in the online focus group. This is not surprising. If lack of awareness of what engineers do is a barrier to entering the field, then it stands to reason that individuals whose family members or friends are engineers are more likely to be enrolled in engineering programs, working as engineers, or on an academic trajectory geared toward majoring in engineering in college.

What do high school girls think about engineering?

The research found that high school girls believe engineering is for people who love *both* math and science. They do not have an understanding of what engineering is. They do not show an interest in the field. They do not think the field is 'for them'. When asked what are the first two words that come to mind when they hear 'engineer', girls provided the following list of words: math and science, smart, really smart, problem-solving, design, nerdy, building, hard, complex, men, cars, engines, don't know, trains, bridges, Dilbert (a US comic strip about a nerdy engineer), math, too difficult, science, machines, boring, boys.

When asked how interested they are in becoming an engineer, less than 10 percent of the high school girls reported such an interest; nearly 70 percent demurred. The perception that you had to be good both in math and science was a deterrent to some girls who were interested in one but not both subject areas. A fourth of the respondents in this group said they did not know enough about engineering to be interested.

Educators' views on what female students think about engineering

Teachers and school counselors reported that engineering is not a popular or well-understood profession, and may not be appropriate except for unique students. One-third of the respondents said that less than 5 percent of their students are interested in engineering as a profession. Many attributed this to a lack of awareness. Interestingly, almost half of this group reported that their schools offer classes related to engineering, such as robotics, but students don't think of robotics as engineering.

Perceptions about gender and engineering

In all the targeted groups, respondents reported that engineering is perceived to be a man's profession and that there is little encouragement for girls to consider it as a career option.

When high school girls were told by the researchers that national statistics show girls are not as interested in engineering, they were not surprised or upset. Many seemed to take it as a given that girls and boys have different interests. Reasons girls gave for this gender difference included: boys are more interested in technology; engineering is viewed as more masculine; building is a 'man's job'; when they think of machines they think of getting dirty. A number of girls pointed out that girls are not encouraged or exposed to engineering at an early age. As one girl observed, 'Engineering is something that is not introduced to girls as something we can do. Most girls think of it as a boy's job.'

Educators who were interviewed/surveyed reinforced the perception that girls and boys are interested in and motivated by different things. ('Males are

math- and science-oriented and females are more people/helping-oriented.')
They gave reasons such as: girls are interested in people, socialization and
family; there is little early exposure for girls (pre-high school); and there are
no role models.

Engineers and engineering students also agree that there is a gender disparity in perceptions about engineers. Reasons that they gave included:
strong stereotypes that support engineering as a male profession; a lack of
mentors and role models for women in the field of engineering; women do
not consider engineering mainstream or relevant; and most women have no
idea what an engineer actually is or the type of work he or she does. It is
their experience that engineers are stereotyped as geeks and that some girls
are discouraged from pursuing math and science, which results in an unfa-
vorable perception at a very young age. One respondent observed that girls
do not understand how engineering helps people.

When asked what the most discouraging thing about their jobs was, the
most common responses from women engineers were lack of support, lack
of respect, constant loneliness, and the glass ceiling they experience as
women in a man's world.

Career motivators for high school girls
The study found that professional interests for girls hinge upon relevance.
In the frame of reference of high school girls who were interviewed and surveyed, this means that a job is rewarding – and that the profession is for
someone 'like me'. They also want their future work to be enjoyable, with
a good working environment, make a difference, offer a good salary, and be
flexible; however, most said they do not personally know people who have
jobs with these ideal traits. The finding that girls are interested in a good
salary is particularly interesting since it is not part of the stereotype many
people have of what is relevant to girls in terms of career interests and is,
perhaps, a stereotype that they have internalized – as in the words of one
girl, 'As shallow as it sounds, money is the one thing I have to consider when
I'm choosing a job. I'm not going to do something that I know can't help
me pay bills.' The most popular fields/industries mentioned by the high
school respondents were medicine (particularly doctor, pediatrician and
veterinarian), business, entertainment and education. Only 3 out of 85 girls
mentioned engineering.

Key influencers of high school girls' career choices
Parents, peers, educators and the media were reported to be key influencers
and resources for information about career options. In order of importance
as an influence on their career choices, girls named parents, friends and
peers, teachers and siblings, and school counselors. Teachers and educators

who were surveyed agreed with the responses given by the girls. Parents are seen as the most important influencers, although three-fourths of the teachers and counselors felt they actively impacted students' choices about college and future careers.

What career influencers know about engineering

A key finding of the study was that career influencers, including educators, are not familiar with how to guide students toward engineering. As a result, the positive stories about engineering are not being told to high school girls and, we can assume, girls in lower grades. Educators admitted that they did not feel prepared to help their students explore the engineering profession: one-fourth of the group surveyed said they don't know enough about engineering to help students; instead, they suggested that students do research online or referred them to local university departments.

The research shows that among the key influencers of high school girls' educational and career choices, parents are not likely role models for engineering, unless they are working in a science field; peers largely hold negative perceptions of engineering; and educators do not feel prepared to guide students toward a career in engineering.

Messages from the engineering community

Another key finding of the research is that current engineering messages present the challenges and hard work involved in engineering but do not talk about the benefits and rewards. Engineers reported the following sources of enjoyment they derive from their jobs: involvement from start to finish provides satisfaction; the many interesting and diverse problems to solve which require creative thinking; and the financial benefits that provide a sense of success and comfort. However, when they were asked, 'If you were to give advice to a young person interested in engineering, what would you tell them?' the majority provided answers that emphasized the difficulties entailed in becoming an engineer. For example, many respondents said they would suggest trying it, *in spite of how difficult it may be*. Specific examples of what they would tell a high school student include:

Engineering is difficult and stressful, but you will realize that you're gaining that much more knowledge and experience.

Engineering is one of the toughest majors in college; you need to have confidence to get through it.

It's not easy – but if you're the type who when faced with a problem some would call impossible is even more driven to move mountains to find a solution, then you might have it in you to be an engineer.

A key finding of the study, then, was that current messaging about engineering – that it is difficult and challenging and requires strong performance in both math and science – is not aligned with key motivators of students – enjoying what I do, good working environment, making a difference, good income and flexibility. As an example, girls need to know that Engineers Without Borders provides needed technical assistance to people in developing countries, just as Doctors Without Borders provides medical assistance.

Messages about engineering that will align with high school girls' career interests

To explore messaging opportunities for increasing enrollment in engineering programs, messages were created that aligned with high school girls' top career motivators. These were tested with girls through an online survey. The study found that the messaging examples that resonated with high school girls fell into two categories:

- informational stories that told them more about what the engineering profession entails;
- positive personal stories that related engineering to the lifestyle that girls are hoping to attain.

Girls said they would like messages that showed what different types of engineers do, the salaries they make, and the colleges they attended. They would also like messages that focused on human-interest stories connecting an engineer's job with people and their surroundings. In the words of one respondent: 'How engineering is not just about drawing and cars. It can be about social issues, and third-world countries becoming better and their citizens happier.' In other words, messages need to tell high school girls how a career in engineering matches up to their top career motivators.

Recommendations

A fundamental shift in the way engineering is portrayed is required. To do this, the coalition recommended the following actions:

- Facilitate a dialogue within the engineering community on the need to redefine engineering as a desirable career option for academically prepared high school girls.
- Develop and test messages that illustrate engineering as a career that complements and supports community interests, family interests, and self-interests.
- Create materials using these tested messages to promote engineering to high school girls.

- Create training opportunities and resources engineers can use to promote engineering education and careers to girls, their parents and educators.
- Create training opportunities and resources school counselors and teachers can use to promote engineering education and careers to girls and their parents.

Adelman (2005) observed that 'Neither women nor men will choose engineering for the right reasons unless both the profession and engineering educators can reach out to a broad population with a full portrait of the richness of the culture and practice, with a well-defined map of its intersections with and divergences from bench science.' His recommendation: develop a traveling demonstration that puts clients and engineers together on high school stages to play out a project design that has cultural, economic and political dimensions, in addition to engineering tasks and calculations and scientific knowledge. This may do more to teach large populations of adolescents what engineering practice is about than summer camps for smaller populations. If presented creatively, these demonstrations of the 'object world' and 'social world' of engineering will show that women naturally belong in engineering practice – and as professors of engineering as well.

BEST PRACTICE: THE NATIONAL ACADEMY OF ENGINEERING'S ENGINEERGIRL! WEBSITE

EngineerGirl! (www.engineergirl.org) is the National Academy of Engineering website that targets middle school girls and adults who work with them in school and in out-of-school programs. Web surveys conducted by the NAE have shown that the website has been very successful in reaching girls (and boys) and women in a range of age groups, with the average number of visits to the site steadily increasing from 25 000 in 2003, to 37 000 in 2005. A number of major corporations in the USA have provided funding for the website because they recognize it as a vehicle for reaching out to girls at an age when it is important for them to be considering engineering as a career option.

Features of the EngineerGirl! website include 'Fun Facts' about engineering that would appeal to middle school girls; a section on 'Why Be an Engineer'; 'Great Achievements' of women engineers; and information on the academic coursework required to become an engineer. An essay contest on an engineering challenge (e.g. how to use engineering to save beached dolphins) is held annually. Cash prizes are given and winning entries posted on the site. The EngineerGirl! 'Gallery of Women Engineers' is designed to profile women who are diverse in terms of age, race and ethnicity, in a variety of engineering fields. The website is designed to portray a career in engineering as interesting and attainable, but also to let girls know that engineering is a helping profession, and that by becoming an engineer they can realize their goal of doing something meaningful with their lives and making a difference in the world.

WHAT'S HAPPENING UPSTREAM?

Adelman (2005) observed that the culture of engineering is a culture of industry, not universities, and that it is reasonable to assume the experiences of women in industry, where they are a distinct minority, seep down and are a disincentive for women in engineering programs. The workplace experiences of women engineers probably do not seep down to younger women and girls. However, these experiences do impact the retention of women in companies and firms, the decisions of some to work outside of engineering companies/firms, or to choose not to pursue a career as a practicing engineer. The small number of women in the engineering workforce that results, in part, from negative workplace experiences and environments, impacts younger women and girls in a more subtle way – by shaping their perceptions about what an engineer *looks like*, leading them to believe engineering is not 'for me'.

What does Research say about the Experiences of Women Engineers in Industry?

Scant research exists on the specific topic of women engineers in industry. Most studies have focused on women in the engineering workforce generally, examples of which are the benchmark studies carried out by Cooper Union, and SWE in 1989, and 1991, respectively. The majority of research since these benchmark studies has focused on women's experience in undergraduate and graduate engineering programs, whether as students or faculty.

Cooper Union's survey of women engineers and engineering students
In 1989, Eleanor Baum, Dean of Engineering at the Cooper Union for the Advancement of Science and Art, organized a survey of women engineers and engineering students who were members of SWE. Findings included:

- Over two-thirds of respondents had a family member who was an engineer.

- Women chose engineering because they wanted to do interesting work; they liked to solve problems; they wanted a career that offered opportunities to learn and to grow; they wanted a career that would offer a good salary; they wanted a career that was transferable around the world.
- Two-thirds of the women were under 35, reflecting the fact that few women went into engineering prior to 1970.
- The largest and most forceful complaint wasn't with their work. It was with the hurdles they confronted in getting their job. High school counselors, and math and science teachers discouraged them from going into engineering; they even discouraged them from taking advanced math and physics courses.
- As would be expected, respondents observed that they lacked role models in the workplace and that there were few women in upper management positions on a corporate level in engineering companies.
- Women engineers in industry reported high levels of career satisfaction, but at the same time, they pointed out a number of gender-related concerns: they felt they had to work harder than male engineers and that they were not being promoted at the same rate as male peers; socially they felt isolated; professionally, they felt their ideas, suggestions or complaints were not taken seriously; over half said they had experienced some sort of sexual harassment on the job; half believed they would be penalized if they took maternity leave; a third reported that they were excluded from decision making; only one company in seven where women engineers worked provided any child-care facilities (Baum, 1991).

SWE's Survey of Male and Female Engineers

The 1991, SWE conducted its own pilot survey which elaborated on the issues identified in the Cooper Union Study. In analyzing responses from male and female engineers in age-matched groups, the SWE study concluded that experienced women engineers were less positive about their work than experienced male engineers and that the women at higher levels were generally less satisfied with their employers. They reported lower levels of career satisfaction over a range of issues, covering job content, personal challenge, training and advancement opportunities, salary, support facilities and equitable treatment.

The SWE study also found differential salary patterns for male and female engineers surveyed. In 1990, the mean salary for female engineers of all ages was $45 000, compared to $52 000 for male engineers of all ages.

However, the SWE study showed that the youngest women were comparable or ahead of male counterparts in compensation, while the older women lagged behind. This cross-over in salaries occurred around age 30, and the compensation differential increased with career progression. The researchers observed that the cross-over appeared to occur at a time when a typical engineer would have six to eight years of work experience and would be poised to assume a management position; this is also the time when many women begin to leave the work force temporarily to have children (Catalyst, 1992).

Catalyst's Research and Advisory Services in US Corporations

In 1992, Catalyst[2] used qualitative methods – focus groups with male and female engineers and one-on-one interviews with male engineering supervisors – to examine the job experiences and career progression of women engineers in 14 US corporations, a study for which the author was the lead investigator. After the report of the study was published, Catalyst was asked to conduct proprietary research and provide advisory services to a number of companies employing women engineers, with which the author also was involved. Catalyst's study corroborated many of the issues detailed in the Cooper Union and SWE surveys; however; this study's qualitative research provided a more nuanced and richer perspective than the earlier surveys. The diversity of industry sectors included in the study allowed for the inclusion of engineers employed in a wide variety of settings – chemical and utility plants that are characterized by 24/7 operations; offshore oil rigs; high-tech research labs; and manufacturing units with production facilities in other countries.

Women engineers in the Catalyst study shared a number of work-related experiences with professional women in non-technical positions in companies that have been extensively documented in the research literature. They often found it difficult to break through the old boy network that is important for advancement in companies. Like women in other professions, women engineers in this study believed that by working hard and independently, they would be recognized and promoted. Like women in other professions, issues concerning work and family balance were found to be of paramount concern to women engineers. In addition to these problems, women engineers experience problems specific to the engineering environment, discussed below. Many of these problems also are common to women in scientific and technology positions.

The National Academy of Engineering's Initiatives to Increase the Representation of Women in the US Engineering Workforce

In 1999, the US National Academy of Engineering (NAE)[3] sought to revitalize interest in the status of women and other underrepresented groups in the US engineering workforce by bringing together stakeholders from industry, government, academia and non-profit organizations to share their knowledge and identify needs, and to discuss ways to address those needs. As first steps toward addressing this issue, the NAE convened the 'Summit of Women in Engineering'. Participants in the Summit developed the 'Celebration of Women in Engineering' website (www.nae.edu/ cwe), and convened a workshop to develop a business case for diversity in engineering in 1999. Also in 1999, the NAE established a Committee on Diversity in the Engineering Workforce, followed by a 'Forum on Diversity in the Engineering Workforce' in 2000. The NAE continued its efforts to communicate the urgency of addressing engineering's diversity gap with a workshop, 'Best Practices in Managing Diversity', in 2001. From 2003 to 2005, the NAE implemented an innovation initiative to identify and develop strategies for increasing the representation of women and other underrepresented groups in engineering.

The NAE's innovation initiative included an inventory of programmatic approaches to addressing this problem compiled by the author who was at that time the senior program officer for the NAE's Diversity in the Engineering Workforce initiative. Over 400 were identified. Focus groups were conducted with key stakeholder groups around the country and solicited testimony from thought leaders and influential people in engineering, business and the military, and researchers. Focus groups with industry representatives found that there was considerable concern about the impending retirements of a large number of engineers in their companies and the need for strategies to increase the talent pool. Industry representatives talked about programs that their companies fund to recruit and retain diversity in their engineering workforce, but many acknowledged that the shortage of women graduating from engineering programs in the USA represented a key challenge to increasing the representation of women in the ranks of their engineering workforce.

The NAE's research showed that the overwhelming majority of programmatic responses to this issue focus on individual, rather than institutional, change, including scholarships, summer camps, after-school programs, tutorial programs, robotics competitions, and support of college chapters of organizations such as SWE. In contrast, very few approaches for transforming the work environment and culture were identified. A handful of programs that companies/firms have developed specifically to address the culture and work environment for women engineers' participation have been identified by Catalyst and are described below. However, it is clear that more research is needed to update the information we have on the status of women engineers in industry and to identify corporate programs/practices that are effective in recruiting, retaining and advancing women in engineering careers. The fact that, today, women with engineering degrees are less likely than male peers to be working as engineers is an indicator that there is a continuing need to focus attention on this issue.

BARRIERS TO RETENTION AND ADVANCEMENT SPECIFIC TO THE ENGINEERING WORK ENVIRONMENT

Lack of a Critical Mass

First and foremost, women engineers lack a critical mass in companies and firms. In 2005, women were 11.6 percent of the engineering workforce. In comparison, women held half of all management, professional and related occupations in the US workforce (US Department of Labor, Women's Bureau, 2005). While most companies are focused on retaining and advancing women to their professional and managerial ranks, engineering companies are still focused on recruitment of women. Given the declining enrollment of women in freshman engineering programs, this situation is likely to worsen in the near future. Diversity matters to engineering firms for reasons outlined above. In addition, they need women to compete for government contracts. Additionally, many companies who outsource engineering expertise have diversity goals that require them to work with vendors who have a diverse workforce.

In contrast to other women professionals in industry, women engineers have fewer role models and mentors, and are more likely to feel isolated in the workplace. Lack of a critical mass also makes it more difficult to break down stereotypes and perceptions about women's ability and suitability for engineering work. Additionally, management may not perceive that the costs of providing flexible work arrangements or family-friendly policies to a relatively small group of women outweigh the benefits.

Conditions Unique to Field Locations

Manufacturing, power generation, oil and gas refining and many other engineering-based activities typically occur in plant and other field locations where the culture and work environment can be less than comfortable for women engineers. Creating a gender-inclusive work environment is more difficult in plant facilities than at corporate headquarters for several reasons. Field sites often include blue-collar and/or unionized workers who may not 'buy in' to the espoused corporate culture to the same extent as professional personnel. Harassment and intimidation also are more frequently encountered at these work sites than at corporate headquarters. Field sites are sometimes dirty and dangerous, and may require outdoor work. Thus the work environment in field locations may be perceived by women engineers as uninviting or, at the least, full of unknowns. Additionally, women engineers report that some male supervisors discourage them from taking jobs in field locations because they want to protect them from physically demanding or 'dirty' work, or they believe that women do not have the 'right stuff', or they are concerned that men will be uncomfortable working with women in those environments. The 24/7 schedules in many field locations also present barriers to women with children. 'Graveyard' shifts and call-outs in the middle of the night are not uncommon. Thus women engineers are relegated to staff work, which will not lead to significant advancement opportunities.

Career Advancement

In order for more women to advance to senior management positions in engineering companies, they will need to have greater access to meaningful developmental opportunities in manufacturing, sales, marketing, and supervisory positions in field or plant operations. Having overcome a number of obstacles to becoming engineers, women may be reluctant to switch to a management track in their companies. Also, leaving the technical track to take on a management role often is perceived as too risky. Women do not see other women in senior management roles and they fear they will not be able to return to the technical track if they fail in management. Women are more likely than male employees on the advancement track to be in two-career families. Since meaningful job rotations often involve relocations, women may find it more difficult to accept such assignments.

The Wage Gap

Data on pay differentials for male and female engineers indicate a continuing pattern of salary differentials for male and female engineers. In contrast to findings from the SWE member survey, 2004 starting salaries in Table 14.1 for female engineers do not appear to be competitive with those for male engineers. It is not clear whether the lower salaries for seasoned women engineers reflect time out of the workforce for raising children or lower access to high-level positions. Data on median salaries in 2003 for employed engineers with doctoral degrees, reported by the National

Table 14.1   Median annual salaries of engineers by years since degree – all degree levels, 2004

Years since degree	Male salary ($)	Female salary ($)
Less than 5	65 000	55 000
5–9	60 000	58 000
10–14	66 000	64 000
15–19	72 000	60 000
20–24	74 000	60 000
25–29	76 000	65 000

Source: National Science Board. Science and Engineering Indicators 2004, Appendix Table 3-26.

Science Foundation in 2002, provide a feel for how choice of engineering specialization might impact the gap in women's and men's overall earnings. Median salaries vary substantially, from $102 000 for electrical engineers, to $73 000 for industrial engineers; nonetheless, disparities in male and female salaries exist within all of these specializations (NSF, 2006).

CORPORATE STRATEGIES TO INCREASE THE PARTICIPATION AND RETENTION OF WOMEN IN INDUSTRIAL ENGINEERING

The following strategies are among those that have been developed by companies to address the unique challenges of managing and valuing employees in technology-based work environments.

Maintain a Dual Focus on Recruitment and Retention

Engineering companies will, no doubt, continue to focus on recruitment of women engineers, and may even have to increase their efforts in this area if the enrollment of women in engineering programs continues to decline. However, companies need to be equally, if not more, concerned about retaining the women currently in the ranks of their engineering workforce. This will require enforcement, or development, of policies and practices to address the aforementioned barriers to the participation and advancement of women engineers currently in their workforce. Seasoned women engineers can be positive role models and mentors to new female hires only if they are satisfied with their own career trajectory and potential for future advancement in the company.

Carry out Research to Identify Issues or Barriers for Women Engineers in Headquarters and Field Sites

Companies should implement a salary study that benchmarks salaries for male and female engineers, identifies systematic inequities, if any, and monitors salaries and other sources of compensation annually. Independent researchers should be engaged to conduct focus groups and interviews with both male and female engineers to examine perceived barriers to women engineers' advancement, along with opportunities to increase visibility and provide rewards for their contributions. Observations of field sites should be carried out to establish whether offensive materials and language or intimidating or harassing behavior toward women are tolerated. Women's perceptions and experiences related to access to developmental opportunities, mentors and coaching, family leave, flexibility, supervision should also be elicited and taken seriously.

Encourage the Formation of Women's Networks

Women's networks provide opportunities for increasing women's access to critical business information, identifying role models and mentors, and sharing personal and professional strategies for advancing in their careers. Support for women's networks is especially important in companies where women have not attained a critical mass and frequently feel isolated.

Create Greater Opportunities and Rewards for Employees on the Technical Track

Catalyst's research found that participants believed the only way to advance in their company was through management versus the technical track, and wanted more opportunities, in terms of rewards and recognition, to be created for engineers who did not want management positions. As organizations continue to reduce managerial levels and become flatter, the technical track will become increasingly important. Efforts should therefore be made to increase the visibility of positions and opportunities for achievement outside of management, thus tapping women's passion for engineering and their desire to be at the forefront of innovation.

Support Employees in Balancing Work and Family Responsibilities

Implementing policies and practices that are supportive of women's and men's desire to manage work–life commitments presents a greater challenge for employers with manufacturing facilities and other 24/7 operations; however, it is key to retaining women engineers. Management training in this area is also important, especially for persons supervising work at production facilities and other field locations – good policies and practices are ineffective if employees feel their continued employment or advancement will be jeopardized by using them.

Offer Rotation Opportunities for Women Engineers

Job rotation is critical for women engineers who are interested in advancement to senior ranks in their company. Offering rotations early in women's (and men's) careers provides exposure and visibility to different areas within the company, including production, research and technical areas, thereby helping new employees define their career interest, broaden their skill set, and developing a network of colleagues throughout the company. Rotations for seasoned women engineers should include exposure to sales, marketing and to international assignments. Mentoring programs offer additional support for employees as they move through rotations. Research should be undertaken to identify key development opportunities that have traditionally led to advancement in the organization, as well as new areas of business development that will be critical to future advancement. Rotation programs should be informed by this type of research. Rotation programs often are perceived as costly or burdensome to business units – issues such as headcount, salaries and benefits need to be addressed. Different approaches have been used by companies, including delegating a corporate division to serve as a cost center for employees in their rotation program or funding the program through the office of the chief executive.

Hold Managers Accountable

Accountability programs work by including effectiveness in developing and advancing women as a criterion in managers' performance reviews, and by basing a portion of their bonus on their results or 'good faith' efforts. Goals are typically established by division heads or a corporate team including the CEO and human resources executives, who assess their current and future business needs, identify high-potential female employees and work with managers to develop career plans that prepare women for senior positions. The rationale for accountability for diversity should include the business case, the company's commitment to the advancement of female engineers and underscore the vital role middle managers play in achieving company objectives. Sending this message 'down the pipeline' is extremely important.

Build Partnerships with Colleges and High Schools

Findings from research undertaken for the Extraordinary Women Engineers Project indicate that most girls have either little or no knowledge about careers in engineering. The profession has not taken seriously the issue of actively disseminating positive images of engineers and engineering challenges. Companies can impact middle and high school students' perceptions about engineering by sending women engineers into classrooms to work with students on projects that are exciting and linked to engineering skill sets, participating in career fairs, and offering internships and scholarships. By improving the work environment for their own women engineers and providing visibility for their accomplishments, companies can break down stereotypes of engineering as a male profession and provide role models for girls and young women.

BEST CORPORATE PRACTICES

Intel Corporation

Through the Volunteer Matching Grants Program, Intel encourages its employees to volunteer in local K-12 schools by matching volunteer hours with cash grants. Hours may be accumulated at school or away from school for a variety of activities, i.e. classroom presentations, chaperoning field trips, helping students with home work and a variety of other activities (Intel, 2006).

The Intel Computer Clubhouse is a creative and safe after-school learning environment where young people from underserved communities work with adult mentors to explore their own ideas, develop skills, and build confidence through the use of technology. The Clubhouse offers an environment that includes state-of-the-art computers and a variety of software and technological tools for use on projects in the visual arts, video, robotics, music and web and graphic design for its members, youth 10 to 18 years of age.

During National Engineers Week Intel introduced some new 'cool' science activities in the classrooms of schools in communities where the company operates. The 'cool' activities feature experiments with polymers, acids and bases, smells and more.

The Intel STRIVE Mentoring Program helps underperforming juniors and seniors at local high schools improve their academic performance, complete high school and continue to advance in their education either at a community college or a technical college. Each enrolled student has an individual mentor. Student/mentor teams meet once a month at an off-campus industrial or educational site to learn about career opportunities. Scholarships are provided to students demonstrating the most improvement.

BP plc Global Path to Diversity and Inclusion

BP launched its current diversity initiative in 2000 by creating a Diversity and Inclusion (D&I) function that is run by the Group Vice President of Executive Development and D&I. The Global Path to Diversity and Inclusion strategy includes three directives: (1) as a large global company, its leaders should reflect the local communities in which it operates; (2) its change effort will proceed in phases, first targeting its 600 most senior leaders, then the next 6000 middle managers, followed by the remaining 90 000 employees; and (3) diversity and inclusion is a business imperative, as well as a social responsibility. This strategy includes tracking demographics based on gender, nationality, and UK/US racial minorities (Catalyst, 2006a).

BP's D & I initiatives include:

- *Career advancement programs* that target all high-potential employees at corporate and various business/functional units. Programs include mentoring, by both senior leaders and peers; rotational assignments; targeted development programs; and secondments to organizations outside of BP. Participants are monitored by a team of group vice presidents representing business segments, functions and regions across BP.
- *Diverse selection panels*, implemented in 2002, determine who fills mid- to senior-level posts. This program was designed to enhance the selection process by addressing lack of diversity in selection panels that historically comprised entirely white men.
- *Tracking of diverse executive-level appointments* Various groups, including the central D&I team, are accountable for tracking executive-level diversity.
- *Recruiting for local hires* BP's recruiting efforts are designed to address local needs by hiring and developing local talent. In order to encourage local leadership, expatriates are limited to three-year stays at a particular site.
- *Mentoring portfolio* BP implements a range of mentoring programs that are utilized by diverse individuals across levels and functional areas. For example, the Mentor UP program, inspired by Proctor & Gamble's Catalyst-Award-winning program, pairs junior women and

men with senior executives of the opposite gender. The goal of the program is to give executives insight into the experiences of more junior staff.

- *Performance contracts* Each manager is bound by a performance contract used to assess goals related to managerial performance and business development twice per year. Performance on behavioral expectations including seven inclusion-related behaviors specified and measurable targets that include D&I metrics affect up to 25 percent of variable compensation (bonus); measurable targets, which include D&I metrics, impact 75 percent of variable compensation.

In 2006, BP received the Catalyst Award for these initiatives.

Georgia-Pacific Corporation

Georgia-Pacific's comprehensive diversity initiative is achieved through: (1) a diversity-of-thought concept, which maintains that different types of thinking stem from different dimensions of diversity and contribute to business innovation; (2) a consistently and frequently communicated business case for diversity; (3) a network of individuals and teams that provide vision, role modeling, and tactical solutions for the initiative; and (4) a set of programmatic components and accountability mechanisms that ensure that all employees receive developmental and promotional opportunities. These mechanisms are used to increase the representation of women in the pipeline and at senior levels. Among the various components of the company's diversity initiatives are (Catalyst, 2006b):

- *Champions/role models* Two of the CEO's 11-member executive management team serve as internal diversity champions. Their role is to communicate – throughout the organization – the importance of diversity to the business.
- *Field location diversity councils* In addition to core elements of the corporate diversity initiative, local entities can elect to develop field location diversity-related practices.
- *Entry-level engineering (ELE) program* The ELE program is designed to fill the Georgia-Pacific leadership pipeline by providing mills with a talent pool of engineers able to fill middle-level supervisory and technical positions. After being hired, each engineer completes a corporate training program that covers an array of technical, business knowledge, and professional development topics to provide ELEs with the skills and perspectives to conduct operations.

- *The alternative work schedule (AWS) program* allows employees to respond to the demands of personal life while continuing to support daily business requirements by offering flexible schedules, summer hours, and part-time work arrangements. Currently, 34 percent of corporate-based employees use some type of AWS. While most manufacturing companies have struggled to implement flexible work arrangements, certain Georgia-Pacific employees do work flexibly. A example of this is the flexibility offered to employees of the large Muskogee paper mill, where the mill manager commissioned an academic specializing in circadian rhythms to study his employees and their work flow, and proposed a variety of efficient work schedules (e.g. 8-, 10- and 12-hour shifts). Because of the emphasis the company places on best practices sharing, some other mills have adopted this program.

Georgia-Pacific received the Catalyst Award in 2006.

Corning Incorporated

Corning's Women in Manufacturing initiative was recognized with the Catalyst Award in 1988 (Catalyst, 1992). This initiative, recognized close to 20 years ago, was distinguished by its comprehensiveness and the fact that the process of assessing women's advancement grew out of the total quality program, designed to promote continuous improvement throughout the company. Corning's CEO recognized that the success of the program depended on tapping and developing Corning's female workforce. One result of this mandate was the quality improvement team – a task force designed to upgrade efforts in the recruitment, retention and upward mobility of women in management. The team had support from top management and input from both line and staff managers. It conducted research and, based on findings, recommended career development strategies to improve the upward mobility of women; new recruitment efforts; the implementation of a diversity education program; communication of policies and practices regarding women; the development of community initiatives to encourage women to work at Corning; and child care and part-time work initiatives. Corning's concept of 'total quality' fed into an integrated plan to promote women's career and leadership development.

An analysis of career paths of Corning senior executives identified feeder positions and key developmental experiences, key among which was plant manager. In order to encourage women to become plant managers, Corning had to address issues related to what were seen by women as unattractive conditions in plant facilities. The company also had to tackle women's perceptions that they would not be supported and were not willing to take the risk of failing in what was viewed as a male role. Steps that Corning took to address women's concerns included:

- mandating the inclusion of women in succession planning for key developmental assignments;
- developing a career ladder that encouraged movement between manufacturing and engineering;
- adopting a zero tolerance for sexual harassment policy;
- coaching and mentoring, including providing new women plant managers with a safety net of an experienced plant manager working with them in the background;
- linking diversity goals to supervisors' performance review and compensation

Outcomes of the initiative included an increase in women's representation in manufacturing from 22 percent to 28 percent; an increase in women's representation in 'A-level payroll' positions from 15 percent to 26 percent; and an increase in women plant managers from zero to five.

CONCLUSION

More research is needed to understand what would change the direction of trends in women's representation in engineering. We also need more current research on how women engineers in industry are faring – what has and hasn't changed since earlier studies and what new approaches companies have taken.

The messages about engineers and engineering careers that girls and young women receive tell them that engineering is not 'for them'. Messages about engineering still portray a largely unattractive career field populated by men. Television, in particular, but other media as well, have not done anything to change the 'face' of engineering presented to young people, whereas girls regularly see women physicians, scientists and lawyers on television. The power of media to reshape our perceptions and choices is reflected in the huge increase in interest in careers in forensic science – a particularly unappealing field for a variety of reasons – that has occurred in the USA. The engineering community must take an active role in creating and disseminating new messages about the profession.

Girls' perceptions that engineering is not for girls is not just a perception; it is a reality in terms of the low representation of women in the engineering workforce. The declining enrollment of young women in engineering programs will exacerbate the perception/reality. The feedback loop from downstream in the engineering pipeline to upstream in K-12 classrooms does not so much tell girls that women engineers have bad experiences in the workplace – something women engineering students are more likely to learn about – as it tells them women don't 'do engineering'.

Companies can reshape girls' perceptions by sending their women engineers into classrooms and increasing their visibility in other ways. But it will take an all-out effort that needs to be coordinated with schools. Companies also need to devise ways to increase the awareness and knowledge of key influences of girls' career choices, in particular, teachers and advisors/counselors. At the same time, companies need to continue to address features of the engineering work environment and culture that drive women employees out of the engineering workforce or stop them from entering in the first place.

Some companies are taking a leadership role in bringing about change upstream and downstream, but many more need to be involved. There have been a number of calls to action but little pick-up from other sectors, such as academia and government, aside from white papers and periodic calls to action. If increasing the representation of women and minorities in engineering is a national imperative for the USA, we will have to develop – as happened in reaction to Sputnik – the national will to do something about it.

ACKNOWLEDGEMENTS

The author gratefully acknowledges the WGBH Educational Foundation for its work developing and conducting research on behalf of the Extraordinary Women Engineers Project (EWEP). The author was a member of the Steering Committee for the research described in the 'Upstream' section of this chapter. Much of that material was derived from the EWEP research report. The author also acknowledges the ongoing importance and contributions of Catalyst's work with industry and the professions to advance female talent. The author held various research and executive positions at Catalyst between 1988 and 2002. Some of the material in the 'Downstream' section of this chapter was drawn from a 1992 report of Catalyst's research (and later its advisory work in corporations) related to women engineers in industry, for which the author was the lead investigator. Finally, descriptions of the BP plc and Georgia-Pacific Corporation initiatives were drawn from Catalyst's website.

NOTES

1. SWE, founded in 1950, is a not-for-profit educational and service organization that seeks to establish engineering as a highly desirable career aspiration for women and to empower women to succeed and advance in those aspirations.
2. Catalyst is a non-profit research and advisory membership organization working with businesses and the professions to build inclusive environments and expand opportunities for women at work.
3. Founded in 1964, the National Academy of Engineering (NAE) provides engineering leadership in service to the nation. The NAE operates under the same congressional act of incorporation that established the National Academy of Sciences, signed in 1863 by President Lincoln. Under this charter the NAE is directed 'whenever called upon by any department or agency of the government, to investigate, examine, experiment, and report upon any subject of science or art'. The NAE is a private, independent, non-profit institution. In addition to its role as advisor to the federal government, the NAE also conducts independent studies to examine important topics in engineering and technology.

REFERENCES

Adelman, Clifford (2005), 'Re: encouragement, not gender, key to success in science, Carnegie *Conversations*', The Carnegie Foundation for the Advancement of Teaching, available at http://carnegiefoundation.org/perspectives.

Adelman, Clifford (1998), *Women and Men of the Engineering Path: A Model for Analyses of Undergraduate Careers*, Washington, DC: U.S. Government Printing Office; National Center for Improving Science Education (NCISE).

American Institutes for Research (2005), *Reassessing U.S. International Mathematics Performance: New Findings from the 2003 TIMSS and PISA*, Washington, DC: American Institutes for Research.

American Society for Engineering Education (ASEE) (2004), *The Year in Numbers: American Society for Engineering Education Profiles of Engineering and Engineering Technology Colleges*, Washington, DC: ASEE, available at www.asee.org/colleges.

Association of American Medical Colleges (AAMC) (2006), 'Women in U.S. academic medicine statistics and medical school benchmarking 2004–2005', available at www.aamc.org/members/wim/statistics/stats05/start.htm.

Bassett-Jones, N. (2005), 'The paradox of diversity management, creativity and innovation', *Diversity Management: Creativity and Innovation*, **14**(2), 169–75.

Baum, Eleanor (1991), 'Women in engineering: creating a professional workforce for the 21st century', available at http://gos.sbc.edu/b/baum.html.

Business Roundtable (2005), *Tapping America's Potential: The Education for Innovation Initiative*, Washington, DC: Business Roundtable, available at www.businessroundtable.org.

Catalyst (2006a), 'Global path to diversity and inclusion, BP p.l.c. 2006 Catalyst Award Winner', available at www.catalyst.org.

Catalyst (2006b), 'Bridging cultures, leveraging differences. Georgia-Pacific Corporation, 2005 Catalyst Award Winner', available at www.catalyst.org.

Catalyst (1995), *The Catalyst Award: Setting the Standard for Women's Advancement*, NY: Catalyst.

Catalyst (1992), *Women in Engineering: An Untapped Resource*, NY: Catalyst.

Cowan, F. (1995), 'Exclusion of diversity and creativity impedes scientific innovation', *Science*, **9**(23); 11–17.

Davis-Kean, P., J. Eccles and M. Linver (2002), 'Influences of gender on academic achievement', paper presented at the biennial meeting of the Society for Research on Adolescence, 13 May, 2002.

Engineering Trends (2005), *Inside Engineering Education, April 2005. Women in Undergraduate Engineering Programs – Past, Present and Future*, 1–8, Washington, DC: Engineering Trends, available at www.engtrends.com.

Extraordinary Women Engineers Project (EWEP) (2005), *Extraordinary Women Engineers*, Final Report, Reston, VA: EWEP, available at www.engineeringwomen.org.

American Institute of Physics (AIP) (2005), *New Report on Women in Physics and Astronomy*, FYI: The AIP Bulletin of Science Policy News, **35**, 22 March, 2005, available at www/aip.org/fyi/2005/035.html.

Gibbons, M. (2005), *The Year in Numbers*, Washington, DC: ASEE, available at www.asee.org/colleges.

Hilton, T. and G. Berglund (1974), 'Sex differences in mathematics achievement: a longitudinal study', *Journal of Educational Research*, **67**, 3–46.

Huang, G.N. Taddese and E. Walter (2000), *Entry and Persistence of Women and Minorities in College Science and Engineering Education*, Jessup, MD: ED Publications.

Hyde, J. (2005), 'The gender similarities hypothesis', *American Psychologist*, **60**(6), 581–92.

Intel (2006), 'Intel in your community', available at www.inter.com/community/arizona/education.htm.

Maccoby, E. and C. Jacklin (1974), *The Psychology of Sex Differences*, Stanford, CA: Stanford University Press.

McLeod, P.L., S.A. Lobel and T.H. Cox Jr (1996), 'Ethnic diversity and creativity in small groups', *Small Group Research*, **27**, 246–64.

National Academy of Engineering (2002), *Diversity in Engineering: Managing the Workforce of the Future*, Washington, DC: National Academy Press.

National Science Board (2006), *Science and Engineering Indicators 2006*, Chapter 3: Science and Engineering Labor Force-Highlights, Arlington, VA: National Science Foundation, Division of Science Resources Statistics, available at www.nsf.gov/statistics/sein06/c3/c3h.htm.

National Science Foundation (2006), *Science and Engineering Indicators 2003, Volume 2*; Appendix Table 3-12, available at www.nsf.gov/statistics/seind06/pdf_v2,htm.

Paulus, P. and B. Nijstad (eds) (2003), *Group Creativity: Innovation Through Collaboration*, NY: Oxford University Press.

U.S. Department of Labor, Bureau of Labor Statistics (2002), *Current Population Survey*. Table 11. Employed Persons by detailed occupation and sex, 2002 annual averages.

U.S. Department of Labor Women's Bureau (2005), *News. Women in the Labor Force*, a databook updated and available on the internet, available at www.bls.gov/cps/.

Watson, W., E. Kumar and L. Michaelsen (1993), 'Cultural diversity's impact on interaction process and performance: comparing homogeneous and diversity task groups', *Academy of Management Journal*, **36**, 590–602.

Index

Tai, R.H. 218
Takaki, R. 129
Tang, J. 130
Tapia, A.H. 72, 75, 81
Task Force on Women, Minorities and
   the Handicapped in Science and
   Technology 30
Taylor, A. 222
teaching
   curricular content and 253–62
   learning style and 53, 54–5, 249–53
team-based mentoring 300, 301–4
Technion 102, 104–5, 109, 119, 125
technology
   high-tech sector (Israel) 101–25
   see also computer science; STEM
Tel-Aviv University 103
Tenenbaum, H.R. 160
tenure 19, 22, 33–4, 35
   -track positions 20, 118, 119, 160,
      246, 319, 320, 324–5
Teubal, M. 101, 112, 113
Tewksbury, B. 257
Thatchenkery, T.J. 132
Theme Housing 305
Thomas, K. 52, 55, 56
Thorn, M. 54
Tienda, M. 129
Tietjen, J.S. 160
time-in-study model 135, 136
TIME Magazine 201–2
Tisak, J. 135
Tobias, S. 250, 251, 258
Todd, K. 75, 80
Tolbert, P.S. 72
Tonso, K. 250, 253
topic association map generation 263,
   264–6, 267
topic evaluation 263–4
Torda, P. 253, 269
Toren, N. 118–19
'total quality' (at Corning) 358
trailblazers 93, 94–5
training 39
   human capital and (Israeli military)
      112
   management 354
   of mentors 300, 302
   workshop 300, 302
transition programs 17, 278–91

Trauth, E.M. 73, 80
Treisman, P. 252
Trix, F. 33
Trower, C.A. 322
Tryggvason, G. 258, 262, 264
Turkle, S. 83
Turner, J.C. 72
Tuskegee University 281

UA:WiSE Career Fair 220
'ugly' aspects of engineering education
   58, 62–7
Uhl-Bien, M. 77, 78
UK
   engineering industry 47–67
   government initiatives 22–3
universities
   African-American PhD candidates
      91–100
   curricular change 245–71
   experiences of women 8–9
   HE culture (UK) 52–7
   Israel 103–5, 118–19
   STEM programs 16–17
   see also faculty/faculty members;
         graduate education; graduates;
         students
University of Alberta 212, 236
University of Arizona 259, 269
University of Colorado 252, 324
University Community and Climate
   Survey 325
University of Maryland 97, 222, 258,
   269
University of Michigan 18–19, 21, 97,
   258, 280, 339
University of Nebraska 253
University of Nevada 257
University of Notre Dame 256
University of Oklahoma 255
University of Pennsylvania 261
University of Puerto Rico 252
University of Rhode Island 323, 324
University of Texas 259
University of Toledo 251
University of Washington 268
University of Wisconsin–Madison 324
upstream conditions (pipeline model)
   334–60
Urban-Lurain, M. 255